T0389786

Fou Lei

Fou Lei

An Insistence on Truth

By

Mingyuan Hu

BRILL

LEIDEN | BOSTON

The Library of Congress Cataloging-in-Publication Data is available online at http://catalog.loc.gov
LC record available at http://lccn.loc.gov/2017006126

Typeface for the Latin, Greek, and Cyrillic scripts: "Brill". See and download: brill.com/brill-typeface.

ISBN 978-90-04-34391-7 (hardback)
ISBN 978-90-04-34392-4 (e-book)

Contents

Foreword

Writing this book in 2013, I recalled Hannah Arendt's observation in 1959: 'No philosophy, no analysis, no aphorism, be it ever so profound, can compare in intensity and richness of meaning with a properly narrated story.'

We accompany Fou Lei from Shanghai to Paris and back. Contemplating his intellectual formation, we attend to his personality. We look upon a cosmopolite with a cosmopolitan attitude. Recreating the dialogues he held with his predecessors and contemporaries, we concomitantly create a dialogue with him. Working with sources not yet discussed, translated, or interpreted in juxtaposition, we make at once a piece of writing, translation, and research.

Our investigation is an experiment, one whose heart is Fou Lei's voice. This does two things: it counters a dehumanising tendency, more latent than manifest, in scholarship where a non-European may be concerned; it keeps a distance from metanarratives problematic to use, cumbersome to unpack.

As an historian, I see narratives big and small as illusory. I guard against entrustment of texts, even primary. Why, then, am I telling this story?

Thinking about Fou Lei and his writing for the past nineteen years, I believe he was one of those few who meant what they said, and who said what they meant. His words must be taken seriously. They were for him a matter of life and death.

M. H.
London
August 2016

Acknowledgements

I am beholden to Fou Ts'ong, Fou Min, Liu Thai-Ker, Jeannine Étiemble, Monique Werlen, and André-François Derivaz for sharing with me their memories. Marie-Odile Germain and Isabelle Mette at Bibliothèque nationale de France, Gregory Cingal at Fonds Jacques Doucet, and Robert Bonfils at Archives jésuites de la Province de France provided assistance during my repeated visits. Craig Clunas at the University of Oxford, Deborah Lewer at the University of Glasgow, and Eric Prenowitz at the University of Leeds kindly read this manuscript. I thank my students at the University of Leeds, in particular Alissia Dawood and Kit Skailes, for their responses. At the University of Glasgow, Nick Pearce, Clare Willsdon, and Debra Strickland backed me with their trust. Jean Levi at Centre national de la recherche scientifique and Romain Graziani at École normale supérieure de Lyon touched me with their grace.

What began as a research trip turned into an exile. My years in Paris were heartened by the belles amitiés of Maël Primet, Robert Terziev, Celia Levi, Abdelhamid Sadallah, Joëlle Moulin, Guy Vermeersch, Uli Sigg, and Chen Danqing.

I owe too much to the unflinching goodness of Mark Morgan, James Mudge, Barbara MacLaurin, Jean-Luce Huré, Linda Sandino, and Christine Guth.

Note on Transliteration

Pinyin is used in this book for the transliteration of Chinese terms, excepting established Wade-Giles names.

Fou Lei in both pinyin and Wade-Giles is Fu Lei; in French, he is Fou Lai. His courtesy name is Nu'an in pinyin; Nou-En in French.

In keeping with Fou's own romanisation of his surname, and following Claire Roberts, author of the first book-length academic publication on the subject, I retain the appellation Fou Lei.

Note on Translation

Fou Lei's writing in Chinese and French as well as the literature consulted for this study do not yet, for the most part, exist in English translation.

For the sake of linguistic transparency and for the convenience of future scholars, key texts are referenced in their original languages.

Unless otherwise indicated, all transcriptions from autograph documents and all translations from French and Chinese are the author's own.

Prologue

Michel de Montaigne believed that to judge a man, we must follow his traces long and carefully. This study of Fou Lei (1908–1966) traces, firstly, his footsteps as a cogent critic of art, literature, and politics, and as the most accomplished translator of French literature in China in the twentieth century, and secondly reveals a fraction of an intellectual labyrinth which meanders through the fragmented modern history of China – Oedipal, almost, in its disposition towards its past – and which winds about that history's love relations with the West, real or envisioned.

Fou Lei the translator and Fou Lei the art critic have been the subjects of recent publications by Nicolai Volland and Claire Roberts. The present work is an intellectual biography of Fou Lei and commences, by necessity, with a probing into his youth, which he himself scarcely mentioned, and the dissection of which is sorely missing in existing literature. Hitherto unpublished documents that I discovered in France and Switzerland contribute to this biography. A close examination of Fou Lei's early, and emotional, life is made with the purpose of contextualising his subsequent moral and existential choices. These choices in turn are historicised through his writing, translation, and correspondence. Archival findings in Paris make plain the agony in which he lived during his last years in China, where political predicaments were responsible for his death.

There are two dimensions to this investigation: intellectual and linguistic. A recurring theme is that of parallels, and a sustained concern that of how to reconstruct, then deconstruct, a lifelong process of resisting deracination through translation. Reluctant to frame my exploration within established discourses, I navigate in what I perceive to be Fou Lei's mental space. Allowing the material to dictate my treatment of it, I make my focus the internal life of an intellectual against external conditions. Fou Lei, who chose to live a strictly sedentary life in response to his circumstances, justifies and demands this treatment.

Other than situating Fou Lei, where pertinent, in his social milieu, I make apparent, and give accent to, a milieu of words, one with indistinct geographical and temporal boundaries, to glimpse the inner landscape of a multilingual literatus, the devotion of whose entire adult life was to the craft of language. For the same reason that a book on Joseph Conrad may not be expected to discuss Poland, I restrain, where possible, inclined elaboration on the elephantine subject that is China in my study of Fou Lei. I hope to illustrate the 'obsession with China' – as C.T. Hsia termed it – that he shared with his contemporaries without falling victim myself to that obsession.

And so I construct a history in the Greek sense of the word – enquiry (ἱστορία) – taking the form of an *histoire* – story. What I carry out is mere groundwork: the opposite of expansive; by no means definitive. The reader is invited to follow *un petit récit* of a fellow human, to scrutinise the biographer's analyses which, so far as is feasible, deal with the raw in the raw, and to debate, to expand, to refine. Scholars may find the material presented in constellation relevant to their own specialism, and make use of this study as they see fit.

For one thing illuminates another. This individualistically-driven narrative serves an historical purpose. It allows Fou Lei to take us from a post-revolutionary, post-May Fourth, post-White Terror Shanghai to an inter-war Europe during the Great Depression, and back to a China entering the Sino-Japanese War, then the Civil War, changing thereafter from a Republic to a People's Republic under increasingly totalitarian control and traversing endless upheavals into the Cultural Revolution. This voyage becomes thereupon a witness both to Fou Lei's desperate interactions with his time, and to his fierce defense of autonomy.

Notwithstanding our way of arguing being by and large linear, in no way should Fou Lei's journey be conceptualised as so. In a peculiarly three-dimensional manner, there was more a dislocation, or a continuous array of dislocations, that Fou Lei had to fathom in relation to his country, the political signification of which changed several times in the lifetime of that particular generation, than the easily supposed confrontation and integration between – and the very notions of – the so-called East and West.

Against decades of social destruction on a colossal scale, what did not change was Fou Lei's preoccupation with self-cultivation and with national salvation; inseparable, the latter was a generational presumption of civic duty and the former, a continuous act to which he adhered even as the latter led to him being betrayed. Fou Lei's chosen profession reconciled his twin projects; born together, they died estranged. The translator did not stop labouring on ruins. For this reason I dub his pursuit that of the untranslatable *Bildung*.

What this modern intellectual, decidedly archaic in his moral standing and profoundly romantic in a nineteenth-century sense, obliges, is multidisciplinary research from multiple angles. What this study of his youth, now positioned in relation to his life and work, reveals, are aspirations that were never fulfilled, seeds that never grew. What it portrays is a sensitivity determined to educate himself against all odds. To a certain extent, it is not so much an account of what he achieved – and achieve he did, formidably – as of how he was aborted, and why.

In times of war and turmoil, a man of letters turned time and again to art and literature as a refuge, and I raise, and leave open, questions about his conditions and reactions, still unresolved; questions of alienation and exile, imposed and chosen; questions of perceived roots, perceived universality; the question, as Simone Weil put it, of the relationship between destiny and the human soul.

PART 1

Shanghai in Revolution: An Unlived Youth

∴

Everywhere a Stranger

There is sometimes an ominous kinship between a person and their name. Our protagonist's family name Fou 傅 had little trouble finding a phonetically perfect transliteration in French, the language he spent his entire life translating. His given name Lei 雷 signifies thunder. The child cried an indignant cry as he came to this world, and with this annunciation was born a courtesy name: Nou-En 怒安, literally *fury peace*. His land-owning family from suburban Shanghai accorded the classical allusion, 'King Wen went into a fury, pacifying the people',[1] to their first-born.

Fou Lei was four years old when his father Fu Peng 傅鵬 (1888–1912), aged twenty-four, died. The high school teacher had been framed by local powers and imprisoned for three months. Released but not rehabilitated, he died of anguish.[2] Fou Lei's mother Li Yuzhen 李欲振 (1888–1933), widowed at twenty-four, was mortified by her husband's death. To seek his release, she had dogged the authorities with such tenacity that she overlooked her children's health. Fou Lei's two younger brothers and one younger sister all died before having to share either their brother's fate of fatherlessness, or his bleak childhood spent with a mother in mourning. An intolerance of injustice ran in the family and was ingrained in the heart of the young sufferer. Fou Lei later recalled that, as a boy, he saw only sorrow and heard no laughter (*Fig.* 1).[3]

To situate this grave-looking boy historically, his was a country undergoing gigantic transitions in the first decades of the twentieth century. The Qing dynasty was overthrown by the Xinhai Revolution in 1911, the year his father was sent to prison. A Republican government was set up in 1912, the year his father died. By then a few generations of Chinese élite had sought to transform the consciousness of themselves and of their people by studying the natural and social sciences from Western Europe and the United States. Under the threat of being divided as a nation by the very powers from which they wished to learn, they put forward proposals to reform the existing political, educational, and familial structures for the purpose of salvation. In a Republican China, semi-colonised Shanghai was vibrant with pluralistic cultures and charged with political undercurrents. Fou Lei received both private tutoring in classical

---

1　'文王一怒而安天下之民。' *Mencius* 孟子 梁惠王下; see also D.C. Lau (tr.), *Mencius* (Harmondsworth: Penguin, 1970), 63.

2　'出獄後以含冤未得昭雪，抑鬱而死。' 'Fou Lei on Himself' 傅雷自述 (1957) in *Complete Works of Fou Lei* 傅雷全集 (Shenyang: Liaoning jiaoyu, 2002), vol. 17, 5.

3　'故我童年只見愁容，不聞笑聲。' Ibid.

Chinese at home, with mathematics and English added to the programme, and school education in his teens in Shanghai, where he was immersed in avant-garde literary experimentation and engaged in political movements, anti-imperialist[4] and anti-authoritarian[5] alike.

FIGURE 1   *Fou Lei and his mother Li Yuzhen, 1912.*
THE FOU FAMILY TRUST.

4   Fou Lei participated in the May Thirtieth Movement of 1925, marching and making speeches on the street.
5   During the 1926 movement against scholar tyrants, Fou Lei was openly opposed to the authorities at his secondary school, which was affiliated with Datong University. Wu Zhihui

Rebellion marked Fou Lei from early on. His mother was domineering and he, disobedient. After the First World War and in the year of the May Fourth Movement, the eleven-year-old Fou Lei left home for his education. At thirteen he was expelled from elementary school for being unruly, and at sixteen from missionary school for voicing anti-superstitious and anti-religious opinions. Both times he enrolled in a different school of a higher standing by virtue of his academic excellence. Intelligence was never in question; his was prodigious. Studiousness he had in abundance, but only on his own terms. What repeatedly landed him in trouble was his vehement refusal to conform.

Between thirteen and sixteen, Fou Lei studied at Collège St. Ignace Zi-Ka-Wei, where French was in the curriculum. Issue 6 (September 1924–February 1925) of the Collège periodical *En Famille* includes a photograph from a theatre production in which the sixteen-year-old Fou Lei played what appeared to be a gangster. Fou Lei's heart was set on literature. At fifteen, he came under the influence of *The Students' Magazine* 學生雜誌. His collection of *Short Story Monthly* 小說月報 was confiscated by the priests at the Collège. With a few schoolmates Fou Lei circulated their own handwritten literary journal, its first issue being, almost surprisingly, in classical Chinese.[6] Riding a self-consciously iconoclastic tide, this generation, unlike the ones that followed, had not yet borne the eventual consequence of the New Culture Movement: that of a cultural deracination.

We turn now to the contemporary press for a picture of Fou Lei's intellectual milieu. Between c. 1910 and c. 1950, journals and newspapers were of paramount importance to the shifting dynamics of the cultural and political scene; indeed, they were where the scene largely took place. To speak of the activation of the New Culture Movement is to speak of the dazzling parade of words in *La Jeunesse* 新青年, a periodical of Peking University. In its opening manifesto of 1915, the Francophile editor Chen Duxiu 陳獨秀 (1879–1942) called for 'the youth of my country' to be 'autonomous rather than slavish, progressive rather than conservative, aggressive rather than laid-back, cosmopolitan rather than confined, utilitarian rather than transcendental, scientific rather than speculative'.[7] In his impassioned argument, Friedrich Nietzsche's

---

吳稚暉 (1865–1953) on the school board of trustees deemed Fou Lei a communist, which he was not, and ordered him arrested. See 'Fou Lei on Himself' in *Complete Works*, vol. 17, 5.

6   Ibid., 8.

7   '自主的而非奴隸的，進步的而非保守的，進取的而非隱退的，世界的而非鎖國的，實利的而非虛文的，科學的而非想象的。' Chen Duxiu, 'Letter to Youth' 敬告青年 in *La Jeunesse* 青年雜誌, vol. 1, no. 1 (9 September 1915).

master-slave morality was quoted, Henri Bergson's *L'évolution créatrice* mentioned, and Rabindranath Tagore, John Stuart Mill, Auguste Comte and Rudolf Eucken thrown in for good measure. In contrast to the six qualities Chen advocated, the six scorned had implicit connotations of being submissive, defensive, and worldly wise in a feudal-Confucian sense. Also appearing in the first issue of *La Jeunesse* was Chen's treatise 'French People and Modern Civilisation'. According to Chen, since Lafayette wrote *Déclaration des droits de l'homme et du citoyen*, Lamarck pioneered evolutionary theory, and Gracchus Babeuf proposed *la communauté des biens*, modern civilisation, of which the three dominant characteristics were in his view the theory of human rights, that of evolution, and socialism, owed its origins to the French.[8]

Other champions of the Movement were more attuned to Anglo-American schools of thought. Attesting an ongoing interest in nineteenth-century English philosophy, the third issue of *La Jeunesse* featured a translation of 'The Scientific Spirit in Modern Thought' of Thomas Henry Huxley,[9] whose *Evolution and Ethics* (1893) rendered in Chinese in 1897–98 by Yan Fu 嚴復 (1854–1921) had deeply impressed those concerned with their country's perilous condition.[10] Oddly, Huxley's caution against an unthinking analogy between biological evolution and societal change was all but neglected if not negated in its reception. Named the 'sick man of East Asia', first by an Englishman living in Shanghai towards the end of the nineteenth century, then translated as 東亞病夫 and quoted in self-warning contexts, the Chinese simultaneously found the humiliation unbearable and accepted that they were, as a race, the weaker animals in the world jungle, a condition which in turn 'explained' their military and diplomatic defeats vis-à-vis Britain, France and Japan since the mid-nineteenth century.

In 1917, whilst reading Philosophy under John Dewey at Columbia University, Hu Shih 胡適 (1891–1962), whose own chosen name Shih 適 took its cue from Yan Fu's summation of 'survival of the fittest' 適者生存, called for a literary reform to replace classical with vernacular Chinese.[11] Arguing that

---

8   Chen Duxiu, 'French People and Modern Civilisation' 法蘭西人與近代文明 in *La Jeunesse*, vol. 1, no. 1.

9   *La Jeunesse* 新青年, vol. 1, no. 3 (15 November 1915).

10   It can be argued, however, that some of the subtlety of Yan Fu's thinking and that of his immediate followers was lost on the New Culture generation.

11   Hu Shih, 'Initial Proposal of a Literary Reform' 文學改良芻議 in *La Jeunesse*, vol. 2, no. 5 (1 January 1917). Bertrand Russell observed of the educated in the China of 1920: 'As regards intellectual leadership, China is a country where writers have enormous influence, and a vigorous reformer possessed of literary skill could carry with him the great

classical Chinese was a dead language, he invoked the precedent of Dante writing in Italian instead of Latin, a 'Renaissance act' in his imagination. Having published in *La Jeunesse* Hu Shih's 'Initial Proposal of a Literary Reform' 文學改良芻議, Chen Duxiu, quick to turn reform into revolution, published 'On Literary Revolution' 文學革命論, in which he went so far as to assert: 'Where does the sublime and brilliant Europe of today come from? Through the Revolution.'[12] He was referring to the revolution of 1789, a supreme inspiration for his generation of radical thinkers, some of whom later became communists.[13]

Two revolutions, political and cultural, were effectuated within a decade. An engineered happening, the Literary Revolution and, by extension, the New Culture Movement (1915) – soon used interchangeably with the May Fourth Movement (1919), itself named after a political episode – was in every sense an historic event, and an endeavour mocked by older men of letters such as the Edinburgh- and Leipzig-educated Gu Hongming 辜鴻銘 (1857–1928) and Yan Fu himself.

Examining the diverse, high-spirited, at times well-researched and at times half-baked publications in the 1910s and 1920s, one realises that a self-critical regard for a lately formulated national heritage was routinely jumbled up with a craze for exemplary features extracted from the perceived West. Characteristic of the New Culture Movement, an ideological construct which propagated anti-Confucianism, individualism, liberty and progress, and which had Science and Democracy as its slogan, was the default position of approaching ethical, social, political, literary and artistic issues in a holistic manner, with a shared premise and all proposed solutions rolled into one. Underlying this less than methodic position was a Social-Darwinian anxiety,[14] an almost paralysing

---

majority of Young China. Men with the requisite gifts exist in China; I might mention, as an example personally known to me, Dr. Hu Suh [variant romanisation of Shih in Wade-Giles and Shi in pinyin]. He has great learning, wide culture, remarkable energy, and a fearless passion for reform; his writings in the vernacular inspire enthusiasm among progressive Chinese. He is in favour of assimilating all that is good in Western culture, but by no means a slavish admirer of our ways.' Bertrand Russell, *The Problem of China* (London: George Allen, 1922), 249.

12   '今日莊嚴燦爛之歐洲，何自而來乎？曰，革命之賜也。' Chen Duxiu, 'On Literary Revolution' 文學革命論 in *La Jeunesse*, vol. 2, no. 6 (1 February 1917).

13   Chen Duxiu himself was one of the founding members of the Chinese Communist Party in 1921; the founders took as their direct inspiration the Russian Revolution of 1917.

14   See Rudolf G. Wagner, 'The Canonization of May Fourth' in Milena Doleželová-Velingerová, Oldřich Král and Graham Sanders (eds.), *The Appropriation of Cultural*

postulate that China was disgracefully behind, from which it followed that a 'catching up' was urgently needed. Since it was concluded that China was socially backward, its morals were automatically blamed. Once the necessity of a political revolution was established, a cultural renaissance became imperative. After visiting China from 1919 to 1921, John Dewey observed: 'The movement is still for the most part a feeling rather than an idea'.[15] His critical view was to be echoed by Fou Lei a decade later.

If the Movement was epistemologically weak,[16] linguistically it flourished, albeit in a similarly hasty manner. The eager pursuit of ameliorating China's social, political, and cultural status quo and an opulence of translated literature had galvanised each other since the end of the nineteenth century. The 1920s witnessed, to quote Leo Ou-fan Lee, a whole century of European romanticism 'squeezed into one decade and swallowed up enthusiastically by one generation in China'.[17] The vernacular, now ideologically sided with the rhetoric of the Movement, knowingly transformed as a written language, its relations with classical Chinese in constant and individually differing flux. The word 'new' featured in the names of nearly half the journals circulated around that time. Nevertheless, it would be wrong to assume that they were new by turning their back on the past. It was rather an attitude. One of the most popular literary periodicals in the 1920s, the Shanghai-based *Short Story Monthly*, saw its editor-in-chief Zheng Zhenduo 鄭振鐸 (1898–1958) produce, between 1923 and 1927, long laborious series concurrently introducing foreign literature and researching classical Chinese writing. A dominant feature of such periodicals is miscellany: treatises, poems, fictions, essays, and translations of European, American, Russian, and Indian literature routinely shared space. Cosmopolitanism was another: for instance, Zheng Zhenduo's predecessor and colleague Mao Dun 茅盾 (1896–1981), likewise a proficient writer engaged in politics, reported in the same periodical pieces of current 'Literary News from Overseas'.

Capital: China's May Fourth Project (Cambridge, MA and London: Harvard University, 2001), 66–115.

15   Quoted in Vera Schwarcz, *The Chinese Enlightenment: Intellectuals and the Legacy of the May Fourth Movement of 1919* (Berkeley and London: University of California, 1986), 8.

16   For supporting arguments, see Edmund S.K. Fung, 'Were Chinese Liberals Liberal? Reflections on the Understanding of Liberalism in Modern China' in *Pacific Affairs*, vol. 81, no. 4 (Winter 2008/2009), 557–576.

17   Leo Ou-fan Lee, 'The Romantic Temper of May Fourth Writers' in Benjamin I. Schwartz (ed.), *Reflections on the May Fourth Movement: A Symposium* (Cambridge, MA: Harvard University, 1972), 78.

Conspicuous was the level of ardency and transparency in these publications. It was not uncommon for essays to perform as intimate letters openly addressing a friend or the editor himself. Authors responded to and criticised one another with an immediacy and directness unparalleled in Chinese history. The Imperial exam system having been abolished in 1905, scholar-officials 士大夫 as a state-serving bureaucratic class, an identity unchallenged for two millennia, disintegrated in form if not in spirit. Notwithstanding arguments for or against the New Culture Movement's being an Enlightenment of an historical as well as an intellectual nature, a generation of Chinese *lettrés* did make for themselves a near autonomous status, which in turn affirmed their metamorphosis from literati to modern intelligentsia. This print culture between c. 1910 and c. 1950 as an identity-making space and as a nation-forming agent was not something to be taken for granted. Consciously generated and tenaciously maintained, it was to be destroyed.

In 1926, Fou Lei began contributing to *The World of Fiction* 小说世界 and *New North Weekly* 北新週刊. Published alongside eminent figures such as Lu Xun 鲁迅 (1881–1936), the eighteen-year-old demonstrated a sophisticated command of language, seasoned and assured, conjoined with, and at times spoiled by, a juvenile exuberance of sentiments, unreserved and uncertain. In his literary debut, a short story entitled 'In Dreams' 夢中, Fou Lei spoke of romantic memories: 'She is indeed a lovely girl. She is my cousin. For reasons unknown, when I lay eyes on her I am drawn to her; she, too, appears attached to me.'[18] Fou Lei's mother had a particular liking for this girl. Since finding a suitable daughter-in-law was at the time customarily on mothers' minds as their sons entered adolescence, if not earlier, an espousal with this girl was a suggested option. 'And I,' wrote Fou Lei, 'although I do not wish for an early marriage, a heart who drifts and strays needs eventually to settle, to belong.'[19] After such musing, weariness set in, and he concluded: 'It is late at night, better go to dreams! Things of joy and sorrow are invariably to be sought in dreams!'[20] Fou Lei was conscious of his precocity, with which he was ill at ease. At eighteen, he lamented the loss of innocence. In an article recommending the novel *Heart* (*Cuore* by Edmondo De Amicis, 1886), he bewailed: 'We are but bordering between childhood and adulthood, yet already contaminated with all the sins of grown-ups. World peace is advocated daily, yet we do not even have peace in

---

18 '她，的確是一個活潑可愛的女孩子。她是我的表妹，不知道是何緣故，我一見她便覺戀戀，而她對於我，也時有依依的表現。' Fou Lei, 'In Dreams' 夢中 in *New North Weekly* 北新週刊, vols. 13–14 (January 1926).

19 '我呢，雖不希望早婚，但一顆漂浪無定的心，總須有個安頓，有個歸宿。' Ibid.

20 '夜深了，還是夢中去吧！悲歡的事，一總向夢中去尋覓吧！' Ibid.

school!'[21] In this reflection, adolescence, the mediating phase between childhood and adulthood, is curiously missing.

Fou Lei continued to speak of memories, in which the subject of his romantic love now became, surprisingly, a boy. What was surprising was not that he or anyone had such sentiments, but that he wrote about it, published it, discussed openly this type of 'anomalous love' in his narration, and declared it normal. More remarkable still was the matter-of-fact way he went about it. Recounting his and his schoolmates' infatuation with a boy in the same class, Fou Lei abruptly inserted the commentary that such a scenario was commonplace in any school. 'And to be thorough,' he said, 'till this day, we have still the same mentality and sentiments, only at times more ardent. And so, according to our past experiences, one may arbitrarily say that an unmarried young man, to rid himself of boredom, is indeed likely to amuse himself with the talk of such anomalous love, and there is nothing strange about it.'[22] In brief, he observed, he experienced, and he came to a conclusion, undisguised and unapologetic.

'A Scene from Memory' 回憶的一幕 appeared in *The World of Fiction*, but was it indeed fiction? As it was written in August 1926 and published in January 1927, one wonders if it had not been readily accepted by other journals, hence the delay. In any case, its publication tells us something about the liberal atmosphere in 1927 Shanghai. In this fictional world, the enamored protagonist bullied his object of affection out of jealousy and peer pressure. Seeing the boy cry, he wanted instantly to ask for forgiveness but was hesitant and 'cowardly, always too cowardly!'[23] He eventually wrote to him and received a gracious reply. He saw him once more, and found him no longer beautiful. Yet he longed for him still and, tormented by guilt and regret, confessed: 'Recollections, especially those of my first childhood love, indeed ripped open my tender heart. Repent! Repent!'[24] The theme of sin and atonement was to recur in Fou Lei's writing. If it were fiction that he was composing, Fou Lei appeared

---

21   '我們還都在童年與成年的交界上，而成年人的罪惡已全都染遍；口上天天提倡
      世界和平，學校里還不能和平呢！' Fou Lei, 'Recommendation of a Book that Will
      Make You Weep' 介紹一本使你下淚的書 in *New North Weekly*, vol. 16 (4 December
      1926).

22   '而且徹底的說：我們此時，對於這種心理，這種情緒，今還存着，有時竟會
      更熱切些。所以根據我們一些過去的經驗，可以武斷一句說：在一般未婚的
      青年，喜歡講這種變態的戀愛，來解除他的枯寂，實在是很可能的，毫不足異
      的。' Fou Lei, 'A Scene from Memory' 回憶的一幕 in *The World of Fiction* 小說世界，
      vol. 15, no. 4 (January 1927).

23   '怯弱，總是太怯弱了！' Ibid.

24   '往事的回憶，尤其是童年初戀的回憶，實在的撕傷了我嫩弱的心。懺悔吧！懺
      悔吧！' Ibid.

almost too direct to be a novelist. A commitment to reality, external and internal, exactly as it was perceived, no more and no less, clearly preoccupied him. Instead of bringing out the intricacy of a given story, his imperative to confess with exactitude overshadowed it.

There was more a natural critic in him. Reviewing a newly published collection of short stories applauded by Lu Xun, who had compared himself unfavourably with the novelist in depicting the psychology of youth, Fou Lei put his finger on each story concerned, gave snappy and pertinent judgements of what was good and what was left to be desired, and bluntly stated: 'I am indeed disappointed by what Mr. Lu Xun has to say this time!'[25] The young critic, unafraid to shock, was sure of his astuteness. The unambiguousness of his personality was altogether present on the page, possessing at once audacity, sensitivity, burning sympathy and raging indignation. A dog was harassed and killed by students and janitors at school; he wrote a furious piece avenging the dog.[26] Upon reading 'In Mourning of Yiren', an elegy by Wang Renshu 王任叔 (1901–1972) in the *New North Weekly*, he wrote his own 'In Mourning of Yiren' to be published in the same periodical. Wang Yiren 王以仁 (1902–1926) was a young writer who, desperately lovelorn, had been missing for months; search notices were put up by fellow writers in the newspaper and now came the confirmation: he had thrown himself into the sea. Fou Lei was deeply affected by this revelation. 'Yiren "took things too seriously", they say, but he is the sign that human hearts have not all died yet!'[27] Acknowledging an affinity with the dead poet, whose work he had read, Fou Lei reflected: 'I am an inexperienced youth; in theory I should have tasted little of society and seen little into the depths of the human heart. But in truth I have gulped the bitterest wine and burn scorchingly with outrage.'[28] The image of Yiren as an anarchist romantic outcast stirred Fou Lei into speculating on the three ways that youth of his day would turn out: those who drift along and surrender to the dictates of society, those who fight and win, and those who keep fighting, keep losing, and eventually give in. 'The first and the third are both losers, but one is weak, cowardly, despicable, a shameless laggard, and the other a real man unmovable by might

---

25   '但我覺得這一次魯迅先生的話，確使我失望了！' Fou Lei, '"Hometown" by Xu Qin-
      wen' 許欽文底《故鄉》in *New North Weekly*, vol. 29 (12 March 1927).

26   Fou Lei, 'Remembrance of a Dog' 關於狗的回憶 in *New North Weekly*, vol. 24 (5 February
      1927).

27   '以仁的"看得太認真了！"，正是人心還未盡死的表徵！' Fou Lei, 'In Mourning of
      Yiren' 懷以仁 in *New North Weekly*, vol. 30 (19 March 1927).

28   '我是未嘗問世的青年；論理對於社會的滋味也嘗得很少，對於人情的底蘊也窺
      探得不多。但事實上我已深深的喝過了酸辛之酒，炎炎的燃燒着憤恨之火。'
      Ibid.

or power, incorruptible by riches or honour, a defeated hero!'[29] He went on to imagine: 'In future I shall become the latter? Undoubtedly. My temperament fiery and willful and my heredity that of an unbendable nature, I will surely die a violent death on the battlefield, my corpse bare and covered with wounds!'[30] In an alarmingly fatalist tone, Fou Lei's self-image was as prophetic as was his portrait of the society: 'Where in China today is not filled with rot and stink? What is not monopolised by vile gentry? They are all tigers who eat men, fiends who kill without leaving a trace of blood. With their mouths and claws open, they are waiting for us to fall to our doom!'[31]

Looking at this pessimism that was almost passionate in its totality, and at this cynicism that did not sit comfortably with his age, one is compelled to ask a series of questions about Fou Lei and his time. After the mid-1920s, a dark sense of disillusionment crept in amongst the Chinese intelligentsia. The Republican experiments since the Xinhai Revolution had been futile, farcical even; threats from foreign imperial powers were as real as they were menacing, provoking social unrest; tensions within as well as between the Nationalist and the Communist parties were as intense as they were ugly, leading regularly to mass bloodshed.[32] News of Yiren's suicide came when Fou Lei had been vexed by 'the horror of the political situation and the agony of love'.[33] He had begun studying at Chizhi University, but it was not to his liking. A cousin of his,

---

29   '(一)(三)同是戰敗者,但(一)是懦弱卑劣的人,無恥的落伍者;(三)是威武不
      屈,富貴不移的大丈夫,戰敗的英雄!' Ibid. 'Unmovable by might or power, incor-
      ruptible by riches or honour' refers to Mencius' ideal.

30   '我將來一定要成為(三)種人吧!?這是無疑的,我執拗暴躁的脾氣,又秉有倔
      強不屈的遺傳性,我將來一定要遍體傷痕,暴屍沙場的!' Ibid.

31   '現在的中國哪一處不是陳腐的臭氣充滿着?哪一事不是惡劣的紳士把持着?他
      們都是吃人的老虎,殺人不見血的惡魔。他們張牙舞爪等着我們去送命呢!'
      Ibid.

32   Conflicts between the Communists and the Nationalists, between the leftists and the
      rightists within the Nationalist party, between warloards and both parties, and between
      the Chinese and the Japanese, led to killings and revolts from the mid-1920s onwards. Un-
      counted students died in the political protests in which Fou Lei participated. Three weeks
      after the publication of this article, on 12 April 1927, the Nationalist government activated
      in Shanghai a full-scale massacre of members of the Communist party; the Chinese Civil
      War broke out on 1 August 1927. For an account of the political upheavals between 1925
      and 1927, see Harold R. Isaacs, *The Tragedy of the Chinese Revolution* (London: Secker and
      Warburg, 1938).

33   '時局的恐怖,戀愛的痛苦。' Fou Lei, 'In Mourning of Yiren' in *New North Weekly*, vol.
      30 (19 March 1927).

Gu Lunbu 顧崙布, had just returned from France, where he had been on the Work-study Programme, majoring in engineering. Since the mid-nineteenth century, large numbers of Chinese students, funded by government or by family, had sojourned in the United States, Japan and Europe. Their purpose, in earnest or in pretense, was singularly simple: to learn in order to return and serve their country.

France was then far from alien to the young literates in Shanghai, 'Paris of the Orient'. From *New North Weekly* alone they would be amongst the first to learn about Monet's death in 1926; eager readers would encounter translations of Rousseau, Lamartine, Balzac and Maupassant on a daily basis; speaking of sculpture they would think of Rodin; Victor Hugo and Romain Rolland were their heroes. Already a keen cosmopolite and inspired by Gu Lunbu's example, in the autumn of 1927 Fou Lei decided to leave, with private resources, for France. His mother objected; Fou Lei was determined, and Gu Lunbu as well as Fou Lei's well-educated aunt Fu Yi 傅儀 succeeded in persuading his mother. The latter, fearing that her son would not return, insisted on him being engaged to Zhu Meifu 朱梅馥, the lovely girl from 'In Dreams'.

On 31 December 1927, Fou Lei boarded the André-Lebon sailing for Marseille. Within the nineteen-year-old's already impressive circle of friends was Sun Fuxi 孫福熙 (1898–1972), editor of *New North Weekly*, for which Fou Lei had become a regular contributor. Sun Fuxi had himself studied in France on the Work-study Programme between 1920 and 1925. His brother Sun Fuyuan 孫伏園 (1894–1966), pioneering editor of several influential journals since 1912, had at the time just launched the fortnightly *Contribution* 貢獻. It was agreed, before Fou Lei's departure, that during his voyage he would send letters to appear in *Contribution*.

FIGURES 2 AND 3   *Fou Lei (lower left) and friends, 1927; Zhu Meifu, 1931.*
THE FOU FAMILY TRUST.

We have thus firsthand documentation of Fou Lei's Journey to the West: sixteen letters in total, thirteen from the sea and three from France after his
arrival; some timidly relaxed, some riddled with anxiety. On 2 January 1928,
Fou Lei recalled the night of the tearful farewell: '... in the gigantic rumbling
noises of the crane, I had many dreams'.[34] Approaching Saigon on 5 January,
he intellectualised:

> Unequivocally I sense and remember the meaning, motivation and
> mission of my going abroad: they are supported and stimulated by the
> sympathy of my family and friends. Sometimes I am conceited indeed,
> anticipating riding the wind and waves to the other shore, getting my
> head down for years before stepping on the returning ship for the home-
> land... Oh! Aspiration! Oh! Ambition! And yet it is all but Dionysiac, all
> but Dionysiac! Instantaneously it breaks and dissolves into the scattered
> spindrift! Only wistfulness and distress remain after waking from the
> dream![35]

His mood swings frenetic, Fou Lei went on to rationalise:

> I have tried meticulously to analyse: what is the cause of my feeling of
> void and loneliness? I suspect: perhaps it is the bleakness of parting that
> frets at my heart; perhaps it is me being neurotic, conjecturing and mys-
> tifying everything; perhaps it is a reaction to the dull monotony of life at
> sea; perhaps it is the recrudescence of trauma; perhaps... what on earth
> it is, I cannot myself determine! A person caught in a situation is baffled;
> how much more baffled can I be?[36]

---

34 '那天晚上在起重機轆轆的巨聲中，做了許多的夢。' Fou Lei, 'Letters from a Voy-
    age to France, no. 1' 法行通信 (一), written on 2 January and published in *Contribution*
    貢獻, vol. 6 (January 1928).

35 '我明白地覺得，記得這次出國的意義、動機和使命；而這些意義使命之後，更
    有此次為我幫忙的諸親友的同情為後盾，為興奮劑。我有時確也很自負，覺得
    此次乘長風破萬里浪，到達彼岸，埋首數年，然後一棹歸舟，重來故土，……
    壯志啊！雄心啊！然而那是酒興，那是酒興！一霎時，跟著浪花四濺而破碎
    了！所剩余的只有夢醒後的恨惘與悲哀！' Fou Lei, 'Letters from a Voyage to France,
    no. 2' 法行通信 (二), written on 5 January and published in *Contribution*, vol. 7 (February
    1928).

36 '我嘗細細地分析：我的空虛寂寞，是起於甚麼？我疑惑：或者是離愁別意糾纏
    着我嫩弱的心苗；或者是神經質的我，常在疑神疑鬼，自弄玄虛；或者是海上
    生活的枯寂的反應；或者是舊創的覆發；或者是……到底是甚麼，，我自己總不
    能決定！當局者迷，我要迷到怎樣啊？' Ibid.

These psychological self-insights, fully conscious of unresolved issues and of germs of malady, are startling. Six days later, on 11 January, Fou Lei was writing his fifth letter, this time to his mother. After picturesque depictions of the Mekong and of Saigon, and after describing a fellow passenger and life on the ship, he ended the short letter with: 'Your only son'.[37] Two days later, on 13 January, in a long letter to his friends Moujun 牟均 and Xiejun 燮均, Fou Lei poured out his thoughts and emotions regarding his mother. Recalling how she expressed high expectations, over and over, often in tears, before his departure; how she recounted intermittently whilst sobbing the hope he represented for her miserable life; how he, deeply moved and crying also, promised her again and again to keep his personal integrity intact; how he, thinking about the sixteen years they had spent together, one depending on the other, worried about his mother being alone for the next five years in a convulsed country, 'Mother,' he exclaimed, 'you have gone so far as to cease to exist but for your son! In your world you have long ago cancelled at once yourself and my father! Now you live but for me, mother. Oh, your love! Your greatness! Your all-embracing love! Your sincere, complete, selfless love!'[38] Then followed guilt. Fou Lei reproached himself for all the tears his mother had shed in sixteen years over his stubbornness, tantrums, mischiefs and rebellions. Reminded once more of the self-assigned mission he must shoulder, he cried out that his heart was under insupportable pressure. He then reached resolution by juxtaposing his sins and his mother's love in eternity, freezing them as a stark pair of antitheses.

A prolonged bereavement had beyond doubt traumatised both mother and son. If Fou Lei demonstrated quintessential characteristics of a neurotic, we can understand why.[39] In a study of neurotic personalities, Karen Horney considered 'Educational theories, oversolicitude or the self-sacrificing attitude of an "ideal" mother' to be factors contributing to an atmosphere that 'more than

---

37   '你惟一的兒子'. Fou Lei, 'Letters from a Voyage to France, no. 5' 法行通信 (五), written on 11 January and published in *Contribution*, vol. 10 (March 1928).

38   '母親啊，你竟是沒有了你自己，只有你兒子一人了！你的世界里，你是早已把你自己和父親同時取消了！現在的你是只為我而生活着，母親啊，你的愛啊！你的偉大啊！你的無微不至的愛啊！你的真誠徹底，無目的的愛啊！' Fou Lei, 'Letters from a Voyage to France, no. 6' 法行通信 (六), written on 13 January and published in *Contribution*, vol. 11 (March 1928).

39   Fou Lei's mother Li Yuzhen, acting simultaneously as the culturally accepted stern father, was fixated on her son's excelling in his studies as revenge for the injustice that had brought the family tragedy and her misery. Fou Lei was habitually punished physically for not studying diligently or for not behaving compliantly. Psychological torment also contributed to Fou Lei's sense of guilt.

anything else lays the cornerstone for future feelings of immense insecurity'.[40] If on this journey Fou Lei's moods swung like a pendulum, we may easily hear the dark echoes of a repressed childhood and the perpetual tides of incurable frustration.

Fou Lei then expressed gratitude to Moujun for having criticised his world-weary outlook, and admitted he must be brave. 'Moujun,' he wrote, 'I tell you: the main reason for my going to France is of course to escape anguish, but for me the anguish [...] is predominantly that of learning, of the pursuit of life. I had long wished to put an end to the dispirited years and to fill up my empty brain.'[41] Promising Xiejun that he would bear in mind the latter's parting words, Fou Lei quoted these words from memory: 'I hope you will not forget that there is still a chunk of rotten meat in this world! That you must save those who suffer on it, that you must heal the wounds of this world!'[42] A heightened sense of obligation to save their nation, which they did not doubt for a moment needed saving, was shared by this distraught generation. And they were but nineteen years of age. When writing to Sun Fuxi about a friend he had made, a seventeen-year-old Russian who looked mature beyond his years, Fou Lei was full of envy. 'His worldly competence, courage and poise astonished me. I then considered their education and their nation in admiration. Their future will be great as their actuality is hopeful! Only a youth such as this can be deemed youth!'[43] The cult of youth, central to the activation of the New Culture Movement, aside, aspects of Fou Lei's early writing can be identified as emulations of his immediate predecessors. What is being recalled here is Zhu Ziqing's 朱自清 (1898–1948) essay 'White Man – God's Favourite', published in 1925.[44]

---

40 Karen Horney, *The Neurotic Personality of Our Time* (New York and London: Harper and Bros., 1937), 80.

41 '牟均，我告訴你：我此次的赴法，逃避煩悶固然是個大原因，但我之所謂煩悶者，其成分恐怕與福祺的有些不同。因為我的煩悶中，細細的分析起來，還是讀書的煩悶，追求人生的煩悶居多。' Fou Lei, 'Letters from a Voyage to France, no. 6' in *Contribution*, vol. 11 (March 1928).

42 '希望你不要忘掉世界上還有這樣的一塊爛肉！你應當救出在爛肉上受苦的人，你應當敷覆這世界的創痕！' Ibid.

43 '他老練的世故，勇敢和鎮靜，也使得我非常奇異。更進而嘆服他們的教育，他們的民族。啊，他們的將來，是如何偉大啊！他們的現象，如何可樂觀啊！像這樣的青年，才配稱青年呢！' Fou Lei, 'Letters from a Voyage to France, no. 4' 法行通信(四), written on 9 January and published in *Contribution*, vol. 9 (March 1928).

44 See Vera Schwarcz's translation of and comment on Zhu Ziqing's text in *The Chinese Enlightenment*, 169.

His early writing coloured by a vivid visual awareness, the alert observer in Fou Lei surfaced. Sympathising with two beggars, father and son, whilst looking at them from afar, he protested: 'How fate bullies men! How fate bullies men!'[45] When his companions, the Russian friend included, scorned an old English musician and his daughter, calling them impostors behind their back, Fou Lei found it difficult to comply: 'Shakespeare was once only a wandering actor! Now you all worship him!'[46] Realising that in his earlier sketch of the musician he had himself displayed implicit disregard, Fou Lei acknowledged self-contradiction. He clearly wrote as he thought. Instead of going back and smoothing out the inconsistencies, he left them bare, drew attention to them, and asked to be forgiven. 'Pardon me!' said he, 'After all, I am someone who thrives on contradictions and conflicts!'[47] An inner need to be frank overrode that of seeming coherence. Reciting in page after page the games that third-class passengers on the André-Lebon played, Fou Lei insisted on the imperative of adhering to set rules for any entertainment to make sense.[48] Perhaps the only time we catch a spontaneous youthfulness in Fou Lei is when he described a visit to the zoo: 'I finally became acquainted with tigers who "resemble cats and are large in size"; I had only known them from textbooks before.'[49] What followed was a priceless rendering of the physical movement of tigers. For once Fou Lei did not feel prompted to analyse, a force that dominated his appetite for descriptions.

On 3 February 1928, Fou Lei reached Marseilles. A disembarking German passenger heading for Budapest was short of money for the customs duty and too embarrassed to ask for help. Fou Lei lent him three hundred francs. Twenty-seven years later, saying to his son that sympathy itself meant little without solid action,[50] Fou Lei was not advocating anything he himself could not carry through. From Marseilles he went to Paris; there his first contact was

---

45 '運命的欺侮人啊！運命的欺侮人啊！' Fou Lei, 'Letters from a Voyage to France, no. 7' 法行通信(七), written on 18 January and published in *Contribution*, vol. 12 (April 1928).

46 '不禁令我想起莎士比亞當時也只是一個流浪的戲子呵，如今你們便五體投地的崇拜了！' Fou Lei, 'Letters from a Voyage to France, no. 8' 法行通信(八), written on 21 January and published in *Contribution*, vol. 13 (April 1928).

47 '但是，恕我吧！我本是在矛盾衝突中討生活的人！' Ibid.

48 Fou Lei, 'Letters from a Voyage to France, no. 9' 法行通信(九), written on 22 January and published in *Contribution*, vol. 14 (April 1928).

49 '從小在教科書上認識的 "似貓而形大" 的老虎，這次真的給我認識了。' Fou Lei, 'Letters from a Voyage to France, no. 7'.

50 '孩子，一個人空有愛同胞的熱情是沒有用的，必須用事實來使別人受到我的實質的幫助。這才是真正的道德實踐。' [My child, it is not enough to have only the enthusiasm to love one's countrymen. One must let others benefit from one's actual,

none other than the exiled Zheng Zhenduo, former editor of *Short Story Monthly*, Fou Lei's favourite periodical in his Collège days. Noting that the cost of living in Paris was half of that in Shanghai, he stayed a week at Hôtel Voltaire on Boulevard Saint-Germain before leaving for Poitiers, where he was to better his French before returning in the autumn to enroll at the Sorbonne.

The last of Fou Lei's 'Letters from a Voyage to France' was dated 22 February, when he had settled in a family house and taken up intensive studies. Long and placid reports of his life in the tranquil medieval town preceded vehement passages towards the end. He spoke, as a puritan and as a cynic, of the Chinese students he had seen in Paris: gambling and prostitutes appeared to be their main interests in life; Nationalist and Communist party members reportedly 'met with pistols ready'[51] every now and then. 'What heroes they make', Fou Lei mocked, 'sacrificing for the party and for the country!'[52] Knowing that what he said would hardly please anyone, he refused to be prudent: 'It is the truth I am speaking, not groundless allegation. The only way to offend no one is to say nothing! In this world, to say anything impartial is to incur public outrage. Ms. Chen Xuezhao asked if I belonged to either party; I said no. She said that was worse, as either party could then attribute me to the opposite camp at will. ... Ah, in that case, nothing at all can be said!'[53] This would have struck home to Fou Lei's readers the view of Chen Duxiu during heated debates in the mid-1920s over the fear of defying authority: 'China can never hope to advance unless there are some few who dare to publicly oppose public opinion.'[54] Publicly opposing public opinion, Fou Lei addressed his fellow students with didactic vigor: 'When all is said and done, each of you will have to return, and the result of your studies will be exposed to your countrymen! Your actual abilities will greatly affect China in future! Look, this is our future!'[55] His 'Letters' thus

---

material help. This is genuine moral practice.] Fou Lei's letter to Fou Ts'ong, 8 / 9 May 1955, in *Fou Lei's Family Letters* 傅雷家書 (Nanjing: Jiangsu wenyi, 2012), 119.

51   '聽說他們二黨(國民黨和共產黨)的中國學生，在法也常常手槍見面的。' Fou Lei, 'Letters from a Voyage to France, no. 16' 法行通信(十六), written on 22 February and published in *Contribution*, vol. 24 (September 1928).

52   '真算得英雄：為黨國犧牲！' Ibid.

53   '我說的是真話，又不是半句謠言。要不犯眾怒，那除非你不說話！在這世界上，你要說一句公平話時，就犯眾怒！她又問我有何黨派，我說沒有的，她說那更糟了！他們兩方可以任意說你是國民黨，或是共產黨。……啊，那簡直無話可說了！' Ibid.

54   See Vera Schwarcz, *The Chinese Enlightenment*, 141.

55   '可是無論你們怎麼樣包蔽隱瞞，你們不求上進，將來到底個個要回國的，你們數年來的成績，到底要宣示於國人的耳目之下的！你們實際的能力，也要大大

concluded, Fou Lei signed off hoping that, when he met his family and friends again, his own visage would be still the same.

Before leaving Paris, Fou Lei took a melancholy stroll in jardin du Luxembourg. The sight of rose-cheeked children agonised him: 'I have neither brothers nor sisters, I am a loner.'[56] His solitary promenade could have illustrated Baudelaire's *L'étranger*.[57] Unlike the Baudelairean stranger who had no homeland, at the end of the letter Fou Lei exclaimed: 'Think about our China!'[58] Thinking about his China was what he did throughout his stay in Europe. Prematurely conditioned to take responsibility for their troubled country, this generation had known anxiety better than perhaps any other psychic state. Meanwhile, the excess of romantic sentimentalism in Fou Lei was not to be reduced by *le spleen de Paris*. He knew that his was a youth not yet lived. As the André-Lebon approached the French shore he wrote: 'Life is but a big dream after all, and yet I find it still too big, too slow... Truly I fancy, truly I wish, that it be shortened, that the motion-picture projection be hastened!'[59]

影響於未來的中國的！看，這是我們的將來！' Fou Lei, 'Letters from a Voyage to France, no. 16' in *Contribution*, vol. 24 (September 1928).

56   '我是一個沒有兄弟，沒有姊妹的孤零人。' Fou Lei, 'Letters from a Voyage to France, no. 15' 法行通信(十五), written on 9 February and published in *Contribution*, vol. 23 (September 1928).

57   – Qui aimes-tu le mieux, homme énigmatique, dis? ton père, ta mère, ta sœur ou ton frère?
      – Je n'ai ni père, ni mère, ni sœur, ni frère.
      – Tes amis ?
      – Vous vous servez là d'une parole dont le sens m'est resté jusqu'à ce jour inconnu.
      Charles Baudelaire, 'L'étranger' in *Le spleen de Paris: petits poèmes en prose* (1869).

58   '想想我們的中國吧！' Fou Lei, 'Letters from a Voyage to France, no. 15' in *Contribution*, vol. 23 (September 1928).

59   '人生原不過是一場大夢，但我終還嫌其太大，太慢……我真幻想，我真希望，人生快縮短些吧！映演得加快些吧！' Fou Lei, 'Letters from a Voyage to France, no. 13' 法行通信(十三), written on 2 February and published in *Contribution*, vol. 18 (June 1928).

PART 2

The Spleen of Paris: A Bildungsroman

∴

Crisis: What Bruges Did Not Appease

A sketchy account of Fou Lei's Parisian years (1928–31) has long been settled in existing literature:[1] that in autumn 1928 he commenced studies at the Sorbonne – true; that around the same time he made the acquaintance of several Chinese artists, with whom he lived in suburban Paris – untrue. These artists he did not meet until later, and at the suburban address he stayed but for the last year. As for the Sorbonne, he was enrolled for only two years.[2] Neither the education he would have received, nor his known circle of friends, suffices to explain the singular sophistication that asserted itself as soon as the young man returned to his country. So decisive a transformation deserves more than a sketch, and mere speculation would not do. Documents unearthed in Europe now make possible a narrative. Intimate, often poignant, these discoveries suggest the depth and nuance of Fou Lei's intellectual growth.

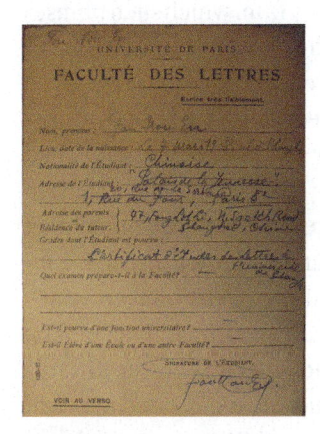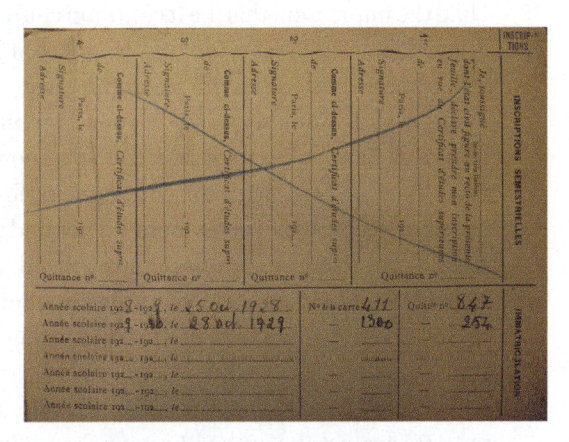

FIGURES 4 AND 5   *Fou Lei's registration card at the Sorbonne (front and back).*
ARCHIVES NATIONALES DE FRANCE (PHOTOGRAPHS BY AUTHOR, 2011).

On 5 February 1929, a letter marked confidential from Abbaye de Saint-André in Bruges was sent to Paris. The only, and hitherto unknown, description of

---

1   Published biographical accounts of Fou Lei derive largely from the periodically updated official 'Fou Lei Chronology' 傅雷年譜 edited by Fou Min and Luo Xinzhang. For a recent version, see *Complete Works of Fou Lei*, vol. 20, 331–344.
2   See Fou Lei's Sorbonne registration card (*Fig.* 5).

Fou Lei that we have from this period, it merits full quotation. 'Cher Monsieur Daniélou', wrote Père Dom Édouard Neut:

> Monsieur Fou Nou-en will have given you his impressions of Saint-André; I hope they leave him with pleasant recollections and that contact with the monks will have been useful and beneficial to him. He arrived Monday evening. I received him. He appeared extremely reserved, and even more so the following day after a brief visit. On Wednesday I refrained from meeting him. On Thursday morning, he asked to see me in order to take his leave. I expressed my regret at such a hasty departure which had not allowed us to get to know each other. He believed in my sincerity and opened up about the crisis from which he was suffering. We then had a long conversation. He took my advice to stay another day or two. On the same day, after dinner, second conversation. Then it never dried up. He became very amiable, very talkative, and raised a thousand questions concerning Catholicism. He said the Benedictine monastery had made a good impression on him and thanked me for understanding him so well. I had the impression that, be it common courtesy from which such phrases arise, there was a real sympathy. He asked if he could return with one or more friends; I said that he would be most welcome any time. He asked what kind of Chinese people I knew. I replied that I knew both Christians and pagans. He then said, 'Do you know any communists?' – 'I had tried to be in touch with the communists, for I love Chinese people very much; but my frock keeps them at bay and, each time I was in contact with them, I sensed a movement of recoil, and I did not insist.' He insisted: 'Would you have me bring the communists to you?' – But certainly; all these rapprochements are useful, as they allow us to appreciate and love one another. I spoke of a certain publication that was hostile towards China, by an atheist moreover, and told him that I had defended his compatriots against the author. Leaving, he said to me: 'You are not only my friend, you are our friend.' – In terms of advice, I suggested that he be not nervous in the course of the crisis from which he suffers, that he be patient and know to wait, and be good to his fellow man, whoever he may be. I told him that, inasmuch as he is good to others, he would find peace.[3]

---

3 'M. Fou Nou En vous aura donné ses impressions de St. André; j'espère qu'elles lui laissent un souvenir agréable et que ce contact avec des moines lui aura été utile et bienfaisant. Il nous arriva le lundi soir. Je le reçus. Il se montra extrêmement réservé. Le lendemain, lui ayant fait une brève visite, il le fut encore davantage. Le mercredi, je m'abstins de le rencontrer. Le jeudi matin, il me fit demander afin de prendre congé de moi. Je lui exprimai tout le regret que me causait ce départ un peu précipité et qui ne nous avait pas permis de faire connaissance.

This is at odds with the existing picture we have of Fou Lei, one which is devoid of Catholic contacts.[4] From the detailed nature of this report, one may conjecture that both correspondents had in mind the possibility of Fou Lei following in the footsteps of Lou Tseng-Tsiang 陸徵祥 (Pierre-Célestin Lou, 1871–1949), diplomat and twice Prime Minister of the Republic of China, who headed the Chinese delegation at the Paris Peace Conference of 1919 and subsequently refused, along with Wellington Koo 顧維均 (1887–1985), to sign the treaty of Versailles. After the death of his Belgian wife in 1926, and after decades of disillusionment with successive Chinese governments[5] that he had served, Lou converted to the Benedictine order in 1927. He was, in 1929, at Abbaye de Saint-André itself. Seeing Fou Lei's insistent exchange of communist

---

Il crut à ma sincérité et s'ouvrit sur la crise dont il souffrit. Nous eûmes alors une longue conversation. Il suivit mon conseil de rester encore un ou deux jours. Ce même jour, après le dîner, seconde conversation. Puis, ça n'a plus tari. Il est devenu très aimable, très causant. Il m'a demandé des renseignements sur mille choses touchant le catholicisme. Il m'a dit la bonne impression que lui faisait le monastère bénédictin et m'a remercié de le comprendre lui aussi bien. J'ai eu l'impression que, quelle que soit la part de politesse que pareilles phrases impliquent nécessairement, il y avait ici une vraie sympathie. Il m'a demandé de pouvoir revenir avec un ou plusieurs amis; je lui ai dit qu'il était ici tout à fait le bienvenu, n'importe quand. Il m'a demandé quel genre de chinois je connaissais. Je lui ai répondu que je connaissais des chrétiens et des païens. Il m'a dit alors: « Connaissez-vous des communistes? » – « J'ai cherché à entrer en relation avec des communistes, parce que j'aime beaucoup les chinois; mais ma robe les a retenus de s'approcher de moi et, chaque fois que j'aillais entrer en contact avec eux, j'ai senti un mouvement de recul et je n'ai pas insisté ». Il a insisté: « Permettriez-vous que je vous amène des communistes? » – Mais certainement; tous ces rapprochements sont utiles, car ils nous permettent de nous apprécier et de nous aimer les uns les autres. Lui ayant parlé de certain ouvrage hostile à la Chine, écrit d'ailleurs par un athée et lui ayant dit que j'avais pris la défense de ses compatriotes contre cet auteur, il m'a dit en partant: « vous n'êtes pas seulement mon ami, vous êtes notre ami. » – En fait de conseil, je lui ai donné le conseil de ne pas s'énerver au cours de la crise dont il souffre, d'être patient de savoir attendre, et d'être très bon pour son prochain quel qu'il soit. Je lui ai dit que, dans la mesure où il serait bon pour autrui, il trouverait la paix.' Dom Edouard Neut's letter to Jean Daniélou, 5 February 1929; conserved at Archives jésuites de la Province de France.

4 Neither Fou Lei's own account nor the secondary literature, including the official 'Fou Lei Chronology', mentions any Catholic connection. That said, in a 1934 letter to Romain Rolland, Fou Lei referred to a stay at Abbaye de Saint-André, a topological name not translated into Chinese in Fou Lei publications, and a biographical detail so far overlooked in Fou Lei literature.

5 Lou Tseng-Tsiang's mentor, the diplomat Xu Jingcheng 許景澄 (1845–1900), was betrayed and beheaded by the Qing government during the Boxer Rebellion in 1900. The deliberately confusing orders Lou received from the Beiyang government in 1919 during the Paris Peace Conference regarding Europe's decision to grant Shandong to Japan were partly responsible for provoking the May Fourth demonstration.

information with Père Dom Édouard Neut, one might imagine that politics were touched upon in their conversation. Indeed it would be unimaginable to have left them out – after thirteen years of chaotic warlordism in China, Chiang Kai-shek's 蔣介石 (1887–1975) Northern Expedition (1926–28), armed by the Soviet Union, had eventually succeeded in dissolving the Beiyang armies backed by Japan. On 29 December 1928, the Northern warlord Zhang Xueliang 張學良 (1901–2001) pledged allegiance to Chiang's Nationalist government, signifying a nominal reunification in the country. Setting the capital in Nanjing, Chiang was to dismiss his Russian advisors and begin killing his Chinese communist allies as well as opponents within his own party almost immediately.[6] All of this did not resolve – only escalated – domestic and international tensions, now pregnant with upheavals all the more violent, and doomed.

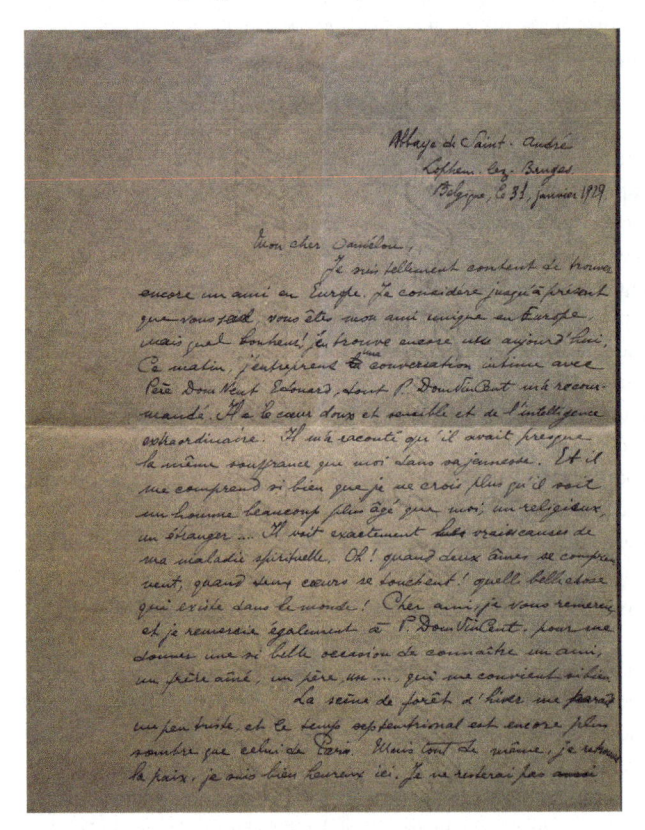

FIGURE 6   *Fou Lei's letter to Daniélou from Abbaye de Saint-André, 31 January 1929 (first page).*
ARCHIVES JÉSUITES DE LA PROVINCE DE FRANCE (PHOTOGRAPH BY AUTHOR, 2011).

6 For an account of these immensely complex and turbulent years, see Donald A. Jordan, *Northern Expedition: China's National Revolution of 1926–28* (Honolulu: University of Hawaii, 1976).

The nature of Fou Lei's crisis is yet to be determined. His impressions of Saint-André had reached Paris five days before Père Dom Édouard Neut's report. 'Mon cher Daniélou', he wrote:

> I am so happy to have found yet another friend in Europe. Until now I have considered you, you alone, to be my only friend in Europe, but what happiness! Today I find still another. This morning I had an intimate conversation with Père Dom Édouard Neut, whom Père Vincent had recommended to me. His heart is gentle and sensitive, and his intelligence extraordinary. He told me that, in his youth, he had gone through almost the same suffering. And he understands me so well that I no longer believe him to be someone older, religious, and foreign... He sees exactly the true causes of my spiritual malady. Oh! When two souls understand each other, when two hearts are touched by each other! What a beautiful thing that exists in the world! Dear friend, I thank you, and I thank also Père Vincent for giving me such a beautiful opportunity to know a friend, an elder brother, a father, a ... who suits me so well.[7]

Fou Lei then announced his intention to return imminently to 'la Maison', for he had 'trop abandonné mon travail' [abandoned my work too much], and ended the letter saying: 'Truly, my dear friend, it is you that I miss a little during my bucolic stay.'[8]

This 'only friend in Europe' has not been anywhere discussed in relation to Fou Lei. Fou Lei himself did not mention his European friends by name in his published writing. During the Anti-Rightist Campaign of 1957, forced to give an account of his life, Fou Lei wrote a terse autobiography of a dozen or

---

7   'Mon cher Daniélou: Je suis tellement content de trouver encore un ami en Europe. Je considère jusqu'à présent que vous seul, vous êtes mon ami unique en Europe, mais quel bonheur! J'en trouve encore un aujourd'hui. Ce matin, j'entreprends une conversation intime avec Père Dom Neut Edouard, dont P. Dom VinCent m'a recommandé. Il a le cœur doux et sensible et de l'intelligence extraordinaire. Il m'a raconté qu'il avait presque la même souffrance que moi dans sa jeunesse. Et il me comprend si bien que je ne crois plus qu'il soit un homme beaucoup plus âgé que moi, un religieux, un étranger... Il voit exactement les vraies causes de ma maladie spirituelle. Oh! quand deux âmes se comprennent, quand deux cœurs se touchent! quelle belle chose qui existe dans le monde! Cher ami, je vous remercie et je remercie également à P. Dom VinCent pour me donner une si belle occasion de connaître un ami, un frère aîné, un père, un... qui me convient si bien.' Fou Lei's letter to Jean Daniélou, 31 January 1929; conserved at Archives jésuites de la Province de France (see *Fig*. 6).

8   'Vraiment, mon cher ami, c'est vous qui me manquez un peu dans mon séjour champêtre.' Ibid.

so pages.[9] His years in Europe took up one short paragraph, in which we read: 'In France I was more often in contact with foreigners, such as university professors, critics, sinologists, musicians, the director of École des beaux-arts and other old painters; I was less in touch with students from our own country.'[10] He made no allusion to Catholics; the communists would not have appreciated it in any case. That Fou Lei did not convert to Catholicism is certain, not least because his openly anti-religious stance which had had him expelled from missionary school coincided with general anti-imperialist sentiments in China in the mid-1920s, now and again directed towards missionaries; it was concomitant also with his anti-superstitious opposition against ritualistic practices at home, which had created explosive conflicts with his mother. Fou Lei's atheism, or indeed agnosticism, appeared to be of an intellectual nature. Asked by the English musician on the André-Lebon if he believed in any god, Christian *or* Chinese, Fou Lei replied in simple English: 'I cannot accept any theory or doctrine without having studied it. I have studied neither philosophy nor theology, hence cannot blindly have any faith'.[11]

When later responding to Daniélou's query as to why he did not believe in God, Fou Lei wrote: 'You were born sane and normal, and raised in an environment full of kindness, tenderness and compassion. Naturally you can always find yourself on a normal path. Whereas I, my heart was wounded, too young, by tragic events in my family; I keep, in my childhood, the saddest notion of life that I can never erase. Brought up by a suffering, sentimental, capricious, stubborn mother, I imperceptibly received the complete heritage of her character, good and bad. Having had human vileness unveiled too early to me, I become fatally sceptical. Since the awakening of my intelligence, I have always had hatred and horror for what one calls justice and goodness, which exist only in

---

9   The first five of the eight sections have been posthumously published. See 'Fou Lei on Himself' in *Complete Works*, vol. 17, 5–12.

10 '留法期間與外人來往較多，其中有大學教授，有批評家，有漢學家，有音樂家，有巴黎美專的校長及其他老年畫家；與本國留學生接觸較少。' Ibid., 6.

11 Fou Lei, 'Letters from a Voyage to France, no. 8'. That Fou Lei did not fail to recount this in the letter published in Sun Fuyuan's *Contribution* might not have been a coincidence. Shortly before his departure for France in December 1927, *New North Weekly* (vol. 2, no. 3) published a translation of Bertrand Russell's 1924 book *Icarus, or the Future of Science* which Fou Lei, the periodical's regular reader and contributor, could not have missed. Russell had visited and lectured in China seven years previously. Amongst the Chinese élite with whom he came in contact was the editor Sun Fuyuan, whose brother was Sun Fuxi, editor of *New North Weekly*. Fou Lei's response to the musician here echoes the central message in Russell's 'Why I Am Not a Christian'. Published in 1927, the essay might not have escaped the attention of Russell's admirers in China.

my conscience.'[12] Fou Lei knew his friend's family well,[13] and there is truth in the contrast he drew. A remarkable Catholic intellectual, Madeleine Daniélou (née Clamorgan, 1880–1956) profoundly impressed her favourite son, in spiritual aspiration as in literary orientation. In his *Mémoires* (1974), Jean Daniélou (1905–1974) dedicated many pages to the recounting of her influence. Thanks to her, 'the picture that I had of Christianity was one that was always incontestable for me, and I have never gone through a true religious crisis.'[14]

Vital as it was, upbringing was not the only determining factor. Daniélou's brother Alain, whom Fou Lei also knew, was a Hinduist and perceived eccentric.[15] Fou Lei came now to his main argument: 'Moreover, the notion

---

12   'Vous êtes né sain, normal, élevé dans un milieu plein de bonté, de tendresse et de pitié, naturellement, vous pouvez toujours vous trouver dans la voie normale. Tandis que moi, mon âme fut trop jeune blessée par des tragiques événements de ma famille, je garde dans mon enfance la plus triste notion de la vie que je ne peux jamais effacer. Elevé par une mère souffrante, sentimentale, capricieuse, entêtée, j'ai reçu insensiblement l'héritage complet de son caractère bon et mauvais. Dévoilé trop tôt pour moi, la laideur humaine, je deviens fatalement sceptique. Depuis mon intelligence éveillée, j'ai toujours de la haine et de l'horreur pour ce qu'on appelle la justice, la bonté qui n'existe pour moi que dans ma conscience.' Fou Lei's letter to Daniélou, 7 June 1930; conserved at Archives jésuites de la Province de France.

13   On 31 December 1928, whilst away in Italy, Daniélou received a letter from his mother, who mentioned: 'Fou est venu dîner' [Fou came for dinner]. (Letters from Madeleine to Jean Daniélou are conserved at Archives jésuites de la Province de France.) That Fou Lei and Daniélou became immediately close in winter 1928 is thus indicated. Half a year later, in a letter Fou Lei sent to Daniélou, he passed on his best wishes to the latter's mother Madeleine, brother Alain and sister Catherine. Throughout 1930, Fou Lei paid visits to Madeleine Daniélou as well as to Catherine and her husband, Georges Izard.

14   '[…] l'image que j'ai eue du christianisme est une image qui a toujours été pour moi incontestable et je n'ai jamais traversé de véritable crise religieuse.' Jean Daniélou, *Et qui est mon prochain?: Mémoires* (Paris: Stock, 1974), 34.

15   The diversity within the Daniélou family fascinated François Mauriac, who famously wrote: 'Voici Alain Daniélou, auteur du *Polythéisme hindou*, frère du père Jean Daniélou, fils de Madame Daniélou qui fut presque une fondatrice d'ordre et peut-être une sainte. Je finis par retrouver sur cette figure curieusement « asiatisée » quelques traits qui rappellent ses origines. Il traite de la religion hindoue en savant, du ton le plus objectif, sans aucune ferveur apparente. Quel mystère qu'une famille!' [Here is Alain Daniélou, author of *Polythéisme hindou*, brother of Father Jean Daniélou, and son of Madame Daniélou who was just about the founder of an order and possibly a saint. I end up finding in this curiously 'Asianised' figure some traits which recall his origins. He deals with the Hindu religion as does a scholar, in the most objective tone and with no apparent fervour. What a family mystery!] (*L'Express*, 14 July 1960.)

of science and the development of reason do not allow us to believe in an invisible Being. I often say: "Reality seems already so uncertain to me, how can I believe in a surreality that is even more vague and mysterious?"[16] With his rationalism – or indeed, his certitude of the uncertain – resolutely expressed, although Fou Lei had 'raised a thousand questions concerning Catholicism', his spiritual crisis in January 1929 was not a religious one. The trip to Bruges did not bring him close to any faith. That Fou Lei found 'a friend, an elder brother, a father' in the sympathetic Père Dom Édouard Neut would have us consider that, at the time, a deep sense of existential isolation was pushing him over the edge. In a foreign land, one has yet to confront one's past.

 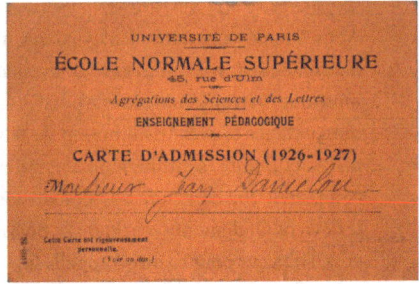

FIGURES 7 AND 8   *Jean Daniélou's matriculation card at the Sorbonne; his card of admission to*
                    the agrégation at École normale supérieure.
                    ARCHIVES JÉSUITES DE LA PROVINCE DE FRANCE (PHOTOGRAPHS BY
                    AUTHOR, 2011).

They met in winter 1928. Fou Lei was twenty and Jean Daniélou twenty-three. A gifted Parisian intellectual, Daniélou, whose father was a government minister and whose mother an educator, had studied literature and philosophy at the Sorbonne and passed his *agrégation* in grammar in 1927 (see *Figs.* 7 and 8). Amongst his friends were Jacques Maritain, Charles Du Bos, Robert Garric, and Gabriel Marcel.[17] Within his circle were Jean-Paul Sartre, Raymond Aron, Paul

---

16   'D'ailleurs, la notion des sciences et le développement de la raison ne nous permettent
       pas de croire à un Être invisible. Souvent je dis : « la réalité me semble déjà si incertaine,
       comment puis-je croire à la surréalité qui est encore plus vague et plus mystérieuse. »' Fou
       Lei's letter to Daniélou, 7 June 1930.
17   Jean Daniélou, *Et qui est mon prochain?*, 62–72.

Nizan, all of whom his own age, and Marxist intelligentsia too.[18] Daniélou's passion was for literature. Jean Cocteau asked him to translate his libretto for Igor Stravinsky's *Oedipus Rex* into Latin.[19] François Mauriac was his favourite novelist, with whom he became close.[20] Daniélou's father had hopes of a political career for his son, and was disappointed when Jean's vocation was revealed to be a religious one. After a year's military service, in 1928 Daniélou joined the Rome-based Compagnie de Saint-Paul as a layperson. Being the only French member, he was asked to found and direct a foyer in Paris to provide foreign students with lodging, food and cultural activities. A hotel was purchased on the corner of rue du Four and Boulevard Saint-Germain; named la Maison de la Jeunesse, it was envisaged as a cultural centre at the heart of the Latin Quarter.[21] Before its inauguration in December 1928, Daniélou sent out invitations to eminent university professors and government officials.[22] Decades later, a cardinal, Daniélou spoke of this year 'absolument passionnante' spent as the director of la Maison, and noted: there was 'un chinois'.[23]

This was Fou Lei. How he came to live there, we do not know. But a Jesuit named Frédéric Vincent Lebbe (1877–1940), who might have been the P. Dom VinCent who recommended Père Dom Edouard Neut in Bruges to Fou Lei,[24] was likely to have been involved in arranging it.[25] Jacques Maritain's

---

18   Ibid., 55.

19   Ibid., 62.

20   Ibid., 67–68.

21   Ibid., 75.

22   Invitations and responses of the invited are conserved at Archives jésuites de la Province de France.

23   'Il y avait là des Marocains que Lyautey avait envoyés comme étudiants, dont Mohammed el-Fassi qui a été ministre des Affaires étrangères du Maroc et avec lequel je suis resté très lié, un Chinois, un Ethiopien...' [There were Moroccans whom Lyautey had sent over to study – one of them was Mohammed el-Fassi, who was (later) Minister of Foreign Affairs of Morocco and to whom I remained close – a Chinese, an Ethiopian...] (Jean Daniélou, *Et qui est mon prochain?*, 75.) Although Fou Lei and Daniélou stayed in touch well into the 1960s, Daniélou did not mention Fou Lei in his *Mémoires* by name. In a letter to Daniélou on 20 June 1929, Fou Lei sent his best to friends at la Maison; the first he mentioned was Fassi.

24   Fou Lei's letter to Daniélou, 31 January 1929. See note 7 in this chapter.

25   Vincent Lebbe, himself Belgian, went to China as a missionary in 1901, and returned to Europe in 1920 to help Chinese students with accommodation and registration, organising them into associations. In 1925, he co-founded le Foyer des étudiants d'Extrême-Orient in Paris. It was probably there, or through other Chinese students or officials in Paris, that Fou Lei was led to Lebbe and to la Maison de la Jeunesse.

(1882–1973) wife, the poet Raïssa Maritain (1883–1960), recorded a meeting with Lebbe in 1924 in her journal. In this 'admirable missionary, to whom one attributes miracles', she saw 'a soul clean as steel'.[26] To Lebbe Jacques Maritain expressed his wish to enter into contact with the Chinese in order to later establish apostolate with the élite of this people; Lebbe said that this had been his own wish for twenty years.[27] Maritain's desire to get to know the Chinese élite came true after four years, if not earlier. Not only did he and his wife hold well-known salons, where Daniélou was a regular guest, he sometimes went to la Maison to take part in the talks and debates organised by Daniélou, whose *invités* were writers, scholars, politicians, and students alike.[28] Fou Lei knew Maritain personally and perhaps even well, for a year and a half later, when Daniélou was training to be a Jesuit in Laval, Fou Lei wrote and informed him: 'Monsieur Maritain left awhile for Switzerland to give lectures. Upon his return he fell ill and has not quite recovered.'[29]

Daniélou, who had 'vivacious eyes in a happy face and spoke precisely and rapidly in a high voice', had 'an occasionally explosive personality, which gave away an electrical temperament always ready to short-circuit that which he could not concede.'[30] 'This was not a man of half measures,' judged Louis-Henri Parias in his portrait of Daniélou as 'un divin impatient', 'and the force provoked by his spoken words won him adherence'.[31] Under Daniélou's direction, la Maison de la Jeunesse was a veritable intellectual hub, drawing in brilliant minds from his existing and expanding circles. The young

26 See Raïssa Maritain, *Journal de Raïssa* (Paris: Desclée de Brouwer, 1964), 157–158.

27 In 1928, Vincent Lebbe returned to China and adopted Chinese nationality under the name Lei Mingyuan 雷鳴遠. He helped establish, amongst other things, two Chinese orders within the Roman Catholic Church. Caught in the Nationalist/Communist conflict and imprisoned by the communists in 1940, Lebbe died shortly after his release.

28 Simone de Beauvoir, having studied at the Catholic girls' school founded by Daniélou's mother, was also once present at a debate. See Jean Daniélou, *Et qui est mon prochain?*, 75.

29 'Monsieur Maritain était parti pendant quelques temps pour faire des conférences en Suisse. Au retour, il est tombé malade et il ne s'est pas encore tout à fait remis.' Fou Lei's letter to Jean Daniélou, 7 June 1930.

30 'Homme de taille moyenne, au regard vif et mobile, au visage heureux, à l'élocution précise et rapide, à la voix aiguë'; 'Sa personnalité parfois explosive, révélait un tempérament électrique toujours prêt à court-circuiter ce qu'il ne pouvait admettre.' Louis-Henri Parias, 'Portrait: un divin impatient', 13; conserved at Archives jésuites de la Province de France.

31 'Ce n'était pas l'homme des demi-mesures, et l'entraînement que provoquait sa parole emportait l'adhésion...' Ibid.

philosopher Emmanuel Mounier (1905–1950), before one morning moving in to la Maison on a whim, wrote to his elder sister: 'On Sunday I went to an inter-denominational orthodox-catholic-protestant gathering at Maritain's. There were the greatest Russian theologian (Serge Boulgakov), the pastor Monod, leading figure of Protestantism, Pierre Péguy (one of Charles Péguy's sons), and Jean Daniélou... It was beautiful to see all these men of perfect rectitude, brothers who are slightly enemies, deep down moved by the same emotions, speak with such rawness and at the same time hold such respect for one another.'[32]

The general ambiance at la Maison as experienced by Fou Lei echoes Mounier's description of that at Maritain's. In summer 1929, upon receiving news from Daniélou that la Maison was to close down, Fou Lei wrote: 'I cry because I lose all the charming youths that once filled la Maison, and the con-versations between *camarades* full of gaiety and sympathy; even the quarrels and disputes have their charm and are of extreme innocence! I remember the evenings we spent with young people from around the world. How sincere and joyful we were, tranquil and happy.'[33] Daniélou's grand-niece affirmed: 'Jean passionately loves debates, even stormy ones.'[34] Made cardinal in 1969, Danié-lou once described himself as 'by nature a pagan. It is only with considerable effort that I am a Christian.' Fou Lei was captivated by this erudite, liberal, char-ismatic Daniélou. In June 1929 he wrote: 'I am truly consoled by your sympathy and, indeed, I always have vivid impressions recalling your faith and your zeal for truth, your magnanimity of spirit and charm of soul, your courage and tal-ent for work...'[35] A year later, in July 1930 he wrote: 'From the very beginning of our acquaintance, that is to say winter 1928, I immediately took you for a

32   Cited in Emmanuelle de Boysson, *Le cardinal et l'hindouiste: le mystère des frères Daniélou* (Paris: Petite Renaissance, 2008), 85–86.

33   'Je pleure parce que d'abord je perds toutes les charmantes jeunesses dont elles sont remplies dans la Maison, ces conversations entre les camarades pleines de gaietés et de sympathies, même des querelles, des disputations, ont un charme et d'une innocence ex-trême! Je me souviens des soirées que nous avons passées ensemble, avec les jeunes âmes venant de tous les côtés du monde. Comme nous étions sincères et joyeux, tranquilles et heureux.' Fou Lei's letter to Daniélou, 20 June 1929; conserved at Archives jésuites de la Province de France.

34   Emmanuelle de Boysson, *Le cardinal et l'hindouiste*, 193.

35   'Je suis vraiment consolé par votre sympathie, et d'ailleurs, j'ai toujours de vives impres-sions en me rappelant de votre foi et votre zèle pour la vérité, votre grandeur et charme d'âme, votre courage et talent pour le travail...' Fou Lei's letter to Daniélou, 20 June 1929.

great friend in my life. I have always had an admiration for your knowledge, your noble heart and elevated soul.'[36] That Daniélou was a brother figure for Fou Lei, one that he so needed, is clear. To what extent Daniélou fulfilled this role for him is more questionable. Of the years he passed as a young man in Paris, Daniélou wrote: 'Well I am absolutely loyal, but to few things and to few people. Since I have plenty of spontaneity, a great faculty for sympathy, I can give the impression that I am more committed than I actually am to the causes that affect me, but which are not essential for me. In my youth, I built contacts and friendly terms without engaging wholly. The real commitments were to come later.'[37] Amongst the mountains of personal notes and documents that survived Daniélou is one of the thousands of letters to his mother, where he gave news of Fou Lei and added, 'If he would be converted!'[38]

What might have the conversations, 'quarrels and disputes' that so delighted Fou Lei been about? From Daniélou's jottings as the director, now conserved at Archives jésuites de la Province de France, we may attempt to draw a picture of the literary life at la Maison. In Daniélou's calm, rounded handwriting, authors listed to be read and discussed were Henri Bergson, Julien Benda, Paul Claudel, Charles Péguy, Jacques Maritain, François Mauriac, Plato, René Descartes, Ernest Renan, Hippolyte Taine, André Gide, Albert Thibaudet, Victor Hugo, Comte de Lautréamont, François-René de Chateaubriand et al. Particular works discussed were Benda's *Trahison des clercs*, Plato's *Apologie de Socrate*, Péguy's *Notre jeunesse, Jeanne d'Arc, Eve* and *L'Argent*, Maritain's *Primauté du spirituel* and *Art et scolastique*, Renan's *L'Avenir de la science*, Chateaubriand's *Génie du Christianisme*, Shakespeare's *Hamlet* and more. Invited speakers included Jacques Maritain, Louis Laloy, Charles du Bos, Jean Guehenno, Louis Massignon, Robert Garric, Pierre Péguy, Georges Izard, and Emmanuel Mounier.

A neat parallel can be discerned between the readings at la Maison and Fou Lei's publications shortly after his return to Shanghai. In a long essay entitled

---

36   'Dès les premiers temps de notre connaissance, c'est-à-dire en hiver de 1928, je vous ai
      tout de suite pris comme un grand ami de ma vie. J'ai toujours une admiration pour votre
      savoir, votre cœur noble et votre âme élevée.' Fou Lei's letter to Jean Daniélou, 7 June 1930.
37   'Alors je suis absolument fidèle, mais à peu de choses et à peu d'êtres. Comme j'ai beau-
      coup de spontanéité, une grande faculté de sympathie, je peux donner l'impression que
      je m'engage plus que je ne le fais dans des causes qui me touchent, mais qui ne sont pas
      pour moi primordiales. Pendant ma jeunesse, j'ai noué des contacts, des liens d'amitié
      sans m'engager totalement. Les vrais engagements viendront plus tard.' Jean Daniélou, *Et
      qui est mon prochain?*, 65.
38   Letter from Jean to Madeleine Daniélou, 6 April 1931; conserved at Archives jésuites de la
      Province de France.

'Literary and Artistic Currents in Contemporary France',[39] Valéry, Bergson, Proust, Claudel, Benda, Gide and Taine were comprehensively cited. Fou Lei's mention of Benda's position against Bergson, for instance, echoed one of the topics that Daniélou had set down on paper. That the literary life at la Maison had a direct impact on Fou Lei's grasp of the subject is evident; it is equally noticeable that writers of the Catholic Renaissance such as Maritain, Péguy and Mauriac, with the exception of Claudel, were decidedly left out. 'Decidedly', because the most talked-about author at la Maison, according to Daniélou's reading plans and preparatory notes, was without doubt Charles Péguy (1873–1914). In 1929, Daniélou, Mounier and Izard founded the *Cercle Péguy*, which contributed to a revived interest in this *intellectuel engagé*.[40] Fou Lei's name was listed (see *Fig.* 12).[41]

What we witness in the activities of la Maison is two generations of French intellectuals at play. Writers, philosophers, critics, politicians, their literary tastes were as wide as their ideologies were diverse. To say nothing of the subtle divergence in even profound philosophical rapprochements,[42] bubbling around 1928–29 at la Maison, and indeed in Paris at large, were these already-or-future big names, some left, some right, some Catholic, some protestant, some atheist, some atheist-turned-Catholic, some conservative, some revolutionary, some atheist existentialist, some Catholic existentialist, some socialist, some communist, some with surrealist inclination, some anarchist, and some who had or were to change or merge their positions more than once later on.

---

39 See Fou Lei, 'Literary and Artistic Currents in Contemporary France' 現代法國文藝 思潮 in *New Review of Current Affairs* 時事新報 星期學燈 (30 October, 6 November and 13 November 1932). The article was written on 18 October 1931.

40 After the First World War, writers of the politically disengaged *la Nouvelle Revue Française* dominated the scene. At odds with them, Péguy was out of fashion between 1920 and 1928; it was not until after 1929 that he was appreciated again. Péguy was also Madeleine Daniélou's favourite author, and his *Eve* her favourite book. The *Cercle Péguy* facilitated the publication of *La pensée de Péguy*, which led directly to a return of interest in the thinker. See Jean Daniélou, *Et qui est mon prochain?*, 58–59, 76.

41 A few names on the left, including Fou, can be identified as *camarades* at la Maison. The names on the bottom right – Ramon Fernandez, Julien Benda, Romain Rolland, Jérôme and/or Jean Tharaud, Daniel Halévy, Hervé de Peslouan, André Suarès, Robert Garric – are all established writers who had known, worked with and admired Péguy.

42 For example, as much as Daniélou admired Maritain's erudition and spirituality, his lineage was Bergsonian and Péguyist whilst Maritain's Bergsonism was firmly married with Thomism, something Daniélou instinctively loathed. See Jean Daniélou, *Et qui est mon prochain?*, 64.

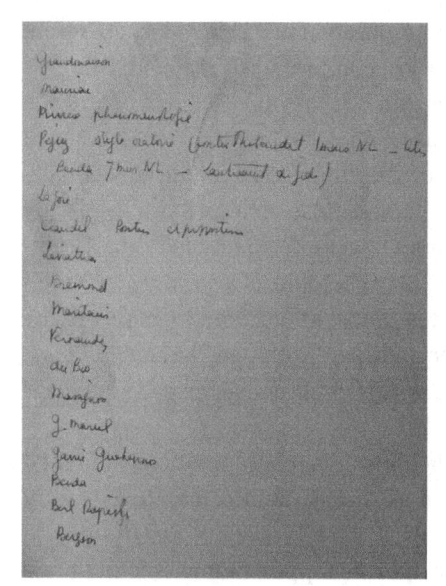
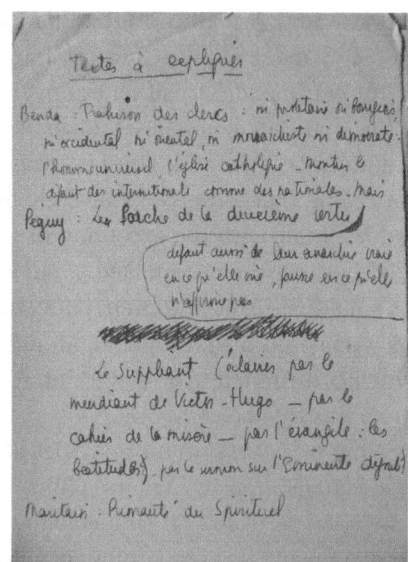

FIGURES 9 AND 10   *List of authors discussed at la Maison de la Jeunesse; 'Texts to be explained'*
(Jean Daniélou).
ARCHIVES JÉSUITES DE LA PROVINCE DE FRANCE (PHOTOGRAPHS BY
AUTHOR, 2011).

FIGURES 11 AND 12   *Topics related to Péguy; list of names of the Cercle Péguy (Jean Daniélou).*
ARCHIVES JÉSUITES DE LA PROVINCE DE FRANCE (PHOTOGRAPHS BY
AUTHOR, 2011).

The sheer complexity of France's intellectual and political landscape between the end of the First World War and the Great Depression would have impressed Fou Lei. Contrary to what some of his countrymen might have presumed, for Fou Lei the 'West' was far from being a source of straightforward solutions. It was itself in a *tourbillon*. Outside the Daniélou circle, a dissemblance of convictions at the time as seen between two Simones – Simone Weil and Simone de Beauvoir[43] – is somewhat indicative.[44] In early 1929 precisely, de Beauvoir and Sartre took their long walks and had their long talks, from which their existentialism is thought to have taken shape. Thirty years later, de Beauvoir reflected in *La force de l'âge*: 'What appears most important to me now in those conversations is not so much what we said as what we took for granted: it was not so; we were wrong, more or less about everything. To define ourselves we had to exhaust all these misconceptions, for they expressed one reality: that of our situation.'[45]

Precisely in 1929, a crisis was perceived by Daniélou's intellectual circle: 'I felt, we all felt, the necessity of a mobilisation of the minds facing the dramatic events – the Wall Street Crash, Fascism, and the emergence of Nazism.'[46] With this accord, Gabriel Marcel, Charles Du Bos and François Mauriac launched the journal *Vigile*; Daniélou was involved in its preparation. At the same time Emmanuel Mounier became acutely aware of the crisis inherent in the capitalist society; the result was the journal *Esprit* that he founded with Georges Izard – poet, lawyer, future politician and Daniélou's brother-in-law;

---

43   Both Fou Lei's age, they graduated from the Sorbonne in 1928, taking the first and second places in philosophy.

44   In *Mémoires d'une jeune fille rangée*, de Beauvoir recounted: 'A famine had devastated China. I was told that upon hearing the news, Weil wept. Those tears, more than her philosophical gifts, reinforced my respect for her.' See Simone de Beauvoir, *Mémoires d'une jeune fille rangée* (Paris: Gallimard, 1958), 312. Their only encounter was however less accordant. 'One day I managed to approach her. I no longer remember how the conversation evolved: in a sharp tone she declared that only one thing counted today on earth, namely the revolution that would end starvation for everyone. I retorted, in a manner no less peremptory, that the problem was not to give men happiness, but to make sense of their existence. She looked scornfully at me: "One can see that you have never been hungry." Our relation ended there.' Ibid.

45   'Aujourd'hui ce qui me semble le plus important dans ces conversations, ce sont moins les choses que nous disions que celles que nous prenions pour accordées: elles ne l'étaient pas; nous nous trompions, à peu près en tout. Pour nous définir il faut faire le tour de ces erreurs car elles exprimaient une réalité: celle de notre situation.' Simone de Beauvoir, *La force de l'âge* (Paris: Gallimard, 1960), 21.

46   'Je sentais, nous sentions tous la nécessité d'une mobilisation des esprits face aux événements dramatiques – le krach de Wall Street, le fascisme, l'apparition du nazisme.' Jean Daniélou, *Et qui est mon prochain?*, 76.

Daniélou was also involved in its preparatory stage. Decades later, commenting on the split between Mounier and Izard, neither of whose eventual political activities he appreciated, Daniélou said: 'What characterised the beginnings of *Esprit* was much more a reflection on politics than a political engagement.'[47] Here we see yet another divergence, this time amongst the Catholic revivalist thinkers, between the active and contemplative modes of reaction against the perceived materialistic and collective crisis.

Daniélou's clear-cut liberal scepticism and his 'talent for work'[48] were conceivably a point of reference when Fou Lei told his friend, two years later, that amongst the many projects that he envisaged to soon realise in China was founding a journal.[49] He ended up co-founding three in total.[50] In *L'Art* 藝術旬刊, the first of the three, Fou Lei published an article in 1932 entitled 'Our Work' 我們的工作, where he made use of the French Revolution to attest his views on the current situation:

> Freethinking and scepticism, these two spirits have been harshly criticised by the so-called 'left-leaners' or by supporters of a dictatorship of a certain class for being 'nonrevolutionary' and 'reactionary', just as the same dispositions were seen as 'revolutionary' and 'rebellious' in eighteenth-century Europe. They were to them – the left and the right alike – tantamount to dissidence in religion, the *hérésie* that all the Popes in history punished. Of course, revolutions are so called because they are absolute and certain and allow for no hesitation whatsoever. Perchance, in a country where historical preparation is sufficient and where the society has evolved to an appropriate degree, this absolute certitude is the very psychological condition needed. Revolutionary theorists argue that, in the case where the historical preparation is insufficient and where the society has not evolved to an appropriate degree, certitude and resolution are all the more in need; this could be true, provided that the general premise – research, understanding, and judgement – be free of error.

---

47   'Ce qui a caractérisé les débuts d'*Esprit*, c'est beaucoup plus une réflexion sur la politique qu'un engagement politique.' Ibid., 77.

48   '[V]otre […] talent pour le travail' was one of the qualities Fou Lei admired in Daniélou. Fou Lei's letter to Daniélou, 20 June 1929.

49   See Fou Lei's letter to Jean Daniélou, 17 September 1931. This journal became *L'Art* 藝術旬刊, founded in September 1932 and co-edited by Fou Lei and Ni Yide 倪貽德 (1901–1970), a Tokyo-trained artist and art historian.

50   The other two were *Current Affairs* 時事匯報 and *New Account* 新語, founded in the autumns of 1934 and 1945.

Nevertheless, when a country and a nation[51] come to a big turning point in history, there is bound to be an intricate, complex, variegated myriad of chaos and contradiction. To strike a way out of this chaotic and contradictory actuality, superficial understanding and investigation simply would not do as a proper preparation. What profound studies to which thinkers like Voltaire and those of the *Encyclopédie* such as Diderot had committed themselves before the outbreak of the French Revolution; yet they did not instantly bring forward a proposition, nor force it upon others as the final solution to everything.[52]

This emphasis on learned preparation for political action was to recur. It is in this light that we see a metamorphosis in Fou Lei – from a cynical rebel, somewhat confused and dangerously vehement, before 1928 to the sceptical, still indignant, *libre penseur* that he projected in his published writing in the early 1930s – and argue that the incisive observer in 1930s and 1940s Shanghai received his critical political education in 1929 Paris. One needs to take into account the studies he made at Faculté des Lettres at the Sorbonne, which would have exposed him to academic approaches to sundry schools of thought, led him to other *milieux* and introduced him to other *personnages* than we have so far noted, but it is one thing to learn about an author in the lecture theatre, quite another to discuss with connoisseurs who care passionately about or even know the author personally, or who are themselves reflective carriers

---

51 Derived from 國 (state) and 民 (people) respectively in classical Chinese, 國家 (country) and 民族 (nation) in vernacular Chinese are ideas both interchangeable and separate, given the sustained sovereign ambiguity of China in early twentieth century. See also Prasenjit Duara, 'De-Constructing the Chinese Nation' in *The Australian Journal of Chinese Affairs*, no. 30 (July 1993), 1–26.

52 '自由思想與懷疑這兩種精神，在所謂"左傾"或某個階級獨裁的擁護者目中，自然已被嚴厲地指斥，謂為"不革命"與"反動"，正如這類思想在十八世紀的歐羅巴被視為"革命"，為"叛逆"一樣。這對於他們——不論左右——無異是宗教上的異端邪說，為歷代教皇所判罰的"hérésie"。固然，所謂革命是絕對地肯定的，決不能有絲毫躊躇。在歷史已經準備得很充分，社會已經演化到很恰當程度的國家，這種絕對肯定的精神，也許正是最需要的心理條件。革命理論家要說，在歷史未曾準備得充分，社會沒有演化到恰當程度的場合，更需要肯定和果斷；這也許是對的，如果他的大前提——研究，認識，判斷，沒有錯誤的話。然而一個國家，一個民族，到了歷史上大轉扭的時間，必定是錯綜萬狀的一片混亂和矛盾；要從這混亂、矛盾的現象中去打出一條生路，決非是淺薄的認識與研究，可以成為適當的準備的。法國大革命爆發之前，服爾德，狄德羅一般百科全書派的思想家，對於一切政治，哲學上的進程和學說，曾用了何等深刻的研究功夫，然而他們並沒立刻拿出一種主張來，強迫人家承認是解決一切的總結論。' Fou Lei, 'Our Work' 我們的工作 in *L'Art*, vol. 1, no. 8 (November 1932).

of different trends of thinking, day in and day out, in the same place where one eats and sleeps.[53] Equally formative would have been the direct involvement with spontaneous discourses on current affairs and self-generated topics. In spring 1929, Izard wrote to Daniélou that he was impressed with the intellectual profile of la Maison, and proposed a precise study of the relationship between Catholicism and Socialism.[54] Situating this proposition in the wider socio-historical context of Communists' and Catholics' interrelated efforts in mobilising youth in 1920s and 1930s France,[55] one wonders if the very name of la Maison de la Jeunesse may not have recalled that of contemporary youth associations such as Jeunesse Ouvrière Chrétienne and Jeunesse Communiste. At any rate, French Catholics' serious apprehension of a communist revolution around this time was unlikely to be absent from la Maison. By being at la Maison de la Jeunesse, a short-lived spot barely remembered in history, Fou Lei was amidst, possibly without awareness of its historical signification, a fraction of the forefront of early twentieth-century intellectual élite in France, predominantly Catholic but by all means varied, vibrant, and open. If, at that time, the understanding of young Chinese students, however informed or cosmopolitan, of the so-called West before they actually went abroad, generally resembled that of 'peeping through a tube at a leopard',[56] Fou Lei had indeed rubbed shoulders with the leopard, however partially or briefly.[57]

His name having appeared on Daniélou's preliminary list for the Cercle Péguy and not mentioned thereafter, Fou Lei was likely not to have been involved with this particular Catholic revival on a conscious or active level. Judging from his writing, the exposure at la Maison left visible marks, but they were of a nature more linguistic and temperamental than theoretical or devotional. In 'Cézanne' (1930), Fou Lei's first published piece of art criticism, we read: 'A true artist must be a harbinger of his time. He has a sharp vision which penetrates

---

53   For example, Georges Izard knew Benda; Daniélou knew Claudel.

54   Georges Izard's letter to Daniélou, 29 April 1929. Letters from Izard to Daniélou during this period, now conserved at Archives jésuites de la Province de France, touch upon a wide range of topics.

55   See Susan B. Whitney, *Mobilizing Youth: Communists and Catholics in Interwar France* (Durham and London: Duke University, 2009).

56   The idiom 管中窺豹 [peeping through a tube at a leopard] suggests lacking firsthand knowledge of a subject or missing the big picture.

57   Fou Lei's friendship with these Catholic intellectuals, only now revealed, decidedly lacked the self-advertising aspect of, say, Xu Zhimo 徐志摩 (1897–1931)'s interactions with the Bloomsbury Group. In his 1947 novel *Fortress Besieged* 圍城, Qian Zhongshu 錢鍾書 (1910–1998) mockingly let one of his characters brag 'Bertie wanted to know how much sugar I took in my tea', Bertie being Bertrand Russell.

the future, an acuminous sensitivity which entails constant discontent with reality, and resolute courage which enables him to wear the thorn crown and to go on the crucifix, so long as that satisfies his artistic desire to create.'[58] Here the Christian reference becomes a figure of speech. What resonates is Renan's mid-nineteenth-century vision of Jesus as a suffering mortal.[59] Overtly religious vocabulary crept into Fou Lei's writing; it so did, arguably, as a metaphorical device.

In autumn 1931, Fou Lei published, in the Parisian journal *L'Art Vivant*, an article entitled 'La crise de l'art chinois moderne'. Resounding contemporary concerns in France, 'la crise' was used by Fou Lei to address China as he opened the discourse: 'L'état de crise domine toutes les activités de la Chine moderne: crise politique, crise économique, crise artistique. Il serait d'ailleurs étonnant qu'à la rencontre du courant occidental, la Chine restât paisible dans son cadre antique.'[60] [The state of crisis dominates all activities in modern China: political crisis, economic crisis, artistic crisis. It would moreover be astonishing if, meeting with Western currents, China stayed tranquil within its antique framework.] A year later, Fou Lei translated this article into Chinese for his own journal *L'Art*.[61] Worth noting is that 'la crise' became 恐慌, literally 'panic', in the Chinese version.[62] It might not have been a hypothetical equivalent unconsciously chosen, for while 'la crise' populated contemporary French vocabulary, 恐慌, if not an exact linguistic equivalent, was its exact counterpart in the contemporary Chinese press, used particularly frequently to describe outbreaks of economic turbulence. Fou Lei's natural interest could already be seen as in what one may call 'cultural translation'; when it came

---

58 '真正的藝術家，一定是時代的先驅者，他有敏慧的目光，使他⋯直遙矚著未來，有銳利的感覺，使他對於現實時時感到不滿，有堅強的勇氣，使他能負荊冠，能上十字架，只要是能滿足他藝術的創造慾。' Fou Lei, 'Cézanne' 塞尚, first published in *Eastern Miscellany* 東方雜誌, vol. 27, no. 19 (10 October 1930).

59 See Ernest Renan, *Vie de Jésus* (Paris: Michel Lévy Frères, 1863). For Oscar Wilde, Jesus was an artist.

60 Fou Nou-En, 'La crise de l'art chinois moderne' in *L'Art Vivant* (September 1931), 467–468.

61 It is of interest to consult Claire Roberts' English translation, made directly from the Chinese, of this article in *Friendship in Art: Fou Lei and Huang Binhong* (Hong Kong: Hong Kong University, 2010), 40. Chapters 1 and 2 of Roberts' book contribute to a biographical and contextual understanding of Fou Lei's early critical writing.

62 The equivalent of 'crisis' would be 危機, literally 'dangerous crucial point'. 恐慌, which Fou Lei used in lieu of 'crisis', means 'panic', or literally 'fear and flurry'. Noting his article's original French title and source of publication – *L'Art Vivant* (September 1931) – Fou Lei was legitimately liberal in translating his own text.

to communicating with a specific audience, be it French or Chinese, he concerned himself with employing apt connotations.

In this substantial article, characterised by a desire to say it all and to say it all thoroughly, Fou Lei explores 'the cause of the current crises' which 'do not appear evident to foreign countries'.[63] His was one of several articles in an issue dedicated to China and Chinese art. The editor Florent Fels (1891–1977) knew Fou Lei and asked for his collaboration.[64] Altogether the issue is an intriguing ensemble, not only for its diversity of topics and prominence of contributors, but because one senses a dialogue between the authors. Fels himself opened 'Chinoiseries' with a compressed historical account of Orientalism: when Marco Polo came back from the great Mongolian country, he gave us the most important description of Asia in the Middle Ages, and 'Tout ce qui parvenait d'Extrême-Orient semblait hors de la logique, étrange, biscornu' [all that went as far as to the Far East seemed out of logic, strange, quirky]. Speaking about how 'once more, an Asian art came to influence the arts of the West', about Watteau's 'naturalisation' of Chinese fashion into French art, about Voltaire's and Diderot's interest in China's hitherto ignored philosophy, and about Chinese opera's lacking in the creation of types,[65] Fels moved, with hardly any transition, onto cooking: 'The Chinese cuisine – the best in the world after the French – appears still to many a gourmet as a stack of weird recipes where the most unspeakable products like dog, boiled cat, disgusting fried and adorned insects compete. The success of Chinese restaurants in Paris proves that we now abandon such prejudices as we begin to realise that there exists, over

---

63   'Pourtant cet état n'apparaît pas nettement à l'étranger; en tout cas, il faut aller au delà de
       l'apparence pour trouver dans la politique aussi bien que dans les arts, la cause des crises
       actuelles.' Fou Nou-En, 'La crise de l'art chinois moderne' in *L'Art Vivant* (September 1931),
       467.

64   See Fou Lei's note in 'The Crisis in Modern Chinese Art' 現代中國藝術之恐慌 (*L'Art*,
       vol. 1, no. 4, October 1932). '去夏回國前二月，巴黎 L'Art Vivant 雜誌編輯Fels君，囑
       撰關於中國現代藝術之論文，為九月份 (一九三一) 該雜誌發刊《中國美術專
       號》之用，因草此篇以應。茲複根據法文稿譯出，以就正於本刊讀者。原題為
       La Crise de l'Art Chinois Moderne.' [Two weeks before returning to China last summer,
       Mr Fels, editor of the Paris magazine L'Art Vivant, urged me to write an essay about
       Chinese modern art for a special issue on Chinese art scheduled for September (1931).
       I agreed and drafted the following. I now offer the readers of this magazine a translated
       version for their comment. The original title was 'La Crise de L'Art Chinois Moderne' and
       I have retained the notes that accompanied the French version. (Translation by Claire
       Roberts in *Friendship in Art*, 40.)]

65   See Florent Fels, 'Chinoiseries' in *L'Art Vivant* (September 1931), 475–476.

there, a country of new men, holders of unknown and formidable forces.'[66] Fels' analogy with cookery was reprised by Ta-Tchou-Tse, who in his article was happy to confirm that Chinese cuisine corresponded 'perfectly with Chinese art and literature' before giving a whole page and a half of recipes.[67]

Politics and gastronomy shared space comfortably. In the issue's opening piece 'La Chine' by Doctor Scié-Ton-Fa, veteran diplomat and author of *La situation actuelle de la Chine* (1925), Parisians were thus told: 'Being a strong civilisation, China will not Europeanise, which for her would be impossible and undesirable.' Sounding as an over-optimistic patriot and a spokesperson of the early republican ideal, Doctor Scié presented Sun Yat-sen 孫逸仙 (1866–1925) as 'father of the Chinese Revolution, founder of the Chinese Republic', introduced Sun's 'Three Principles of the People', advocated 'La Jeune Chine' [the Young China], and ended by declaring: 'That in which Sun Yat-sen succeeded was the awakening of China's national consciousness! He created the religion of the Chinese Motherland! Nothing will be able to stop the formidable Chinese community that has departed for the relay race of human civilisation, and China will progress and modernise like all the great human forces!'[68] One is reminded that, thirty years previously, the scholar and journalist Liang Qichao 梁啟超 (1873–1929) had published 'On the Young China' 少年中國說 (1900) in his own newspaper, drawing a wholesale contrast between a young and an old man to propagate a young as opposed to an old nation-state.[69]

Scié's was not the only politician's voice in the issue. George Soulié de Morant (1878–1955) – former French consul in China, sinologist, translator of Chinese literature, and prolific author on Chinese art, music, theatre and medicine – also wrote, albeit on a less political subject: 'Le costume en Chine'.

---

66   Ibid., 476.

67   Ta-Tchou-Tse, 'La cuisine chinoise' in *L'Art Vivant* (September 1931), 481. More than fifty articles on gastronomy appear in *L'Art Vivant* between 1925 and 1939.

68   'Ce qu'a obtenu Sun-Yat-Sen, c'est le réveil de la conscience nationale de la Chine! Il a créé la religion de la Patrie chinoise! Rien ne saura plus arrêter le formidable corps chinois qui a pris le départ dans la course de relais de la civilisation humaine, et la Chine progressera, se modernisera comme toutes les grandes forces humaines!' Scié-Ton-Fa, 'La Chine' in *L'Art Vivant* (September 1931), 440.

69   The young for Liang Qichao represented all values positive and hopeful: 'The old China of today is the work of the old Chinese; the young China of tomorrow is the responsibility of the young Chinese.' In 1918, after the Beiyang government signed an unequal treaty with Japan, the Young China Association, taking its cue from Liang and in imitation of the Young Italy (1831) founded by Giuseppe Mazzini, was established. Overtly political and nationalistic, one of the branches of the Association later developed into the Chinese Communist Party.

Abel Bonnard (1883–1968), poet, novelist and politician, who had studied at École du Louvre and who later became a notorious collaborator of Fascist Germany, wrote orientalistically indeed about Chinese painting. As was the norm, China was Asia, and Chinese painting Asia itself: 'We love Asia for the escape she offers us'; 'What characterises them [Chinese paintings] first of all is the sentiment of a universal life'; 'from this attention to detail is a leap to the sentiment of the infinite'; 'Western works of art make noises to attract us, they come out to meet us. Those from the Far East do not seek us, they wait for us'; 'The painters who made them were not only sophisticated artists, but philosophers and poets. They are separated from us only by the insignificant distance of centuries. Effectively, they are our friends.'[70] Effectively, Chinese painting was being safely confined to those bygone ages, for how else would it offer an infinite escape?

Attesting to an estimable tradition of sinological study, two German scholars contributed: 'Les édifices chinois' by Ernst Fuhrmann (1886–1956), who had researched architecture in China in the early 1900s and authored two books on the subject, and 'Les bronzes anciens de la Chine' by Alfred Salmony (1890–1958). This interest in bronze was reinforced by 'Les bronzes à figures animales et humaines' of H. d'Ardenne de Tizac (1877–1932), director of musée Cernuschi and translator of Stephen Bushell's *Chinese Art* (1904–1906) into French (1910). A learned essay 'La calligraphie chinoise' was supplied by Georges Margouliès, linguist, student of the sinologist Paul Pelliot, and professor of Chinese literature at the Sorbonne; he had in 1930 visited China as chargé de mission for the French government. As a rule, Chinese civilisation was presented as a homogeneous entity; the discussion of each of its arts was presumed to reveal something ultimate about that civilisation itself, and vice versa. Under this premise, commonplace observations such as that calligraphy 'correlates with the whole of the Chinese civilisation'[71] gave comforting reassurance.

The concentration on a classical, idealised China reached its climax in 'La vieille Chine' by René Schwob (1895–1946). A Jewish-turned-Catholic disciple

---

70   '[N]ous aimons l'Asie pour l'évasion qu'elle nous offre'; 'Ce qui les caractérise d'abord, c'est le sentiment de la vie universelle'; 'mais de ce souci du détail, il passe d'un bond au sentiment de l'infini'; 'Les oeuvres de l'art occidental font du bruit pour nous attirer, elles viennent au devant de nous. Celles de l'art d'Extrême-Orient ne nous recherchent pas, elles nous attendent'; 'Les peintres qui les firent n'étaient pas seulement des artistes raffinés, mais des philosophes et des poètes. Ils ne sont séparés de nous que par l'insignifiante distance des siècles. En réalité, ce sont nos amis.' Abel Bonnard, 'Peintures chinoises' in *L'Art Vivant* (September 1931), 446.

71   '[...] liée à l'ensemble de la civilisation chinoise'. Georges Margouliès, 'La calligraphie chinoise' in *L'Art Vivant* (September 1931), 461.

of Maritain and critic of art and literature, Schwob was writing about journeying in China. What one encountered was of course none other than 'the old China'. At the seashore surged his contemplation: 'European civilisation multiplies. Chinese civilisation took its course in the depths. Here the two human directions are brought face to face.'[72] Brought face to face with Europe, China was yet consistently the Other, consistently ancient; its civilisation *took* – and not takes – its course. It is in this context that we reconsider Fou Lei's initiative to explore 'the cause of the current crises' which 'do not appear evident to foreign countries', and his account, at the outset of the article, firstly of the perceived decline of artistic genius since the end of the Ming dynasty in the seventeenth century, and secondly of 'la renaissance moderne' of classical Chinese painting at the end of the nineteenth century, as an attempt to bridge 'la vieille Chine' and the China of his day for his Francophone readers.

Following Fou Lei's was a short provocative piece directly addressing contemporary China and its art. In 'Évolution' by André Duboscq – author of *Sous le ciel de Pékin* (1919), *L'Évolution de la Chine: politique et tendances (1911–1921)* (1921) and *La constitution chinoise* (1924) – we first hear that the evolution of China is more a question of adoption and assimilation than one of progress in the Western sense: 'notre "progrès"' [our progress], in Duboscq's words. He saw, nonetheless, Chinese art as evolving in the same direction: 'dans le sens du nôtre' [in our direction].[73] That some Chinese painters now painted in the 'Western' manner was not a fact to be ignored – 'To understand that Chinese artists have only set about painting in oil in our Western manner for a short while, despite having long had a knowledge of our art, we need to think about the rapid rhythm of China's evolution since little more than twenty years ago, that is to say, since the fall of the empire.'[74] And the fall was due, it would seem in his implicit causal account, to the West as a matter of course: 'In the middle of the last century, the age of treaties began; contacts were intensified and European

72   'La civilisation européenne multiplie. La civilisation chinoise agissait dans les profondeurs. Les deux directions humaines se confrontent ici.' René Schwob, 'La vieille Chine' in *L'Art Vivant* (September 1931), 467.

73   'Tout au plus me permettrai-je cette simple remarque que l'évolution de la Chine se faisant dans le sens d'une adoption, d'une assimilation plus ou moins profonde de notre « progrès », il serait étrange, incompréhensible même que l'art chinois n'évoluât pas lui aussi, et dans le sens du nôtre.' André Duboscq, 'Évolution' in *L'Art Vivant* (September 1931), 476.

74   'Pour s'expliquer que, depuis peu seulement, les artistes chinois se mettent à peindre à l'huile et selon nos méthodes occidentales, en dépit de la connaissance déjà ancienne qu'ils ont de notre art, il faut penser à la rapidité du rythme de l'évolution chinoise depuis une vingtaine d'années au plus, autrement dit, depuis la chute de l'empire.' Ibid.

ideas made their way to China. In 1911, the revolution broke out' and 'a whole new world transported by the "Young Chinese," I dare not say penetrates, but from that moment on juxtaposes itself with the Chinese world and begins at any rate to influence the educated youth, so much so that they express themselves and act as if their racial core had transformed too – this obliges us Europeans to act on our side, like it or not, as if it were really so. But that is another story…'[75]

One could hardly find a more Eurocentric articulation. Not that what Duboscq said was not true – on the contrary. Fou Lei himself went straight to the point: Western civilisation penetrated 'chez nous à la manière d'une invasion'[76] [us in the manner of an invasion]. The sheer linguistic separation of identity in Duboscq's 'notre "progrès"', 'dans le sens du nôtre', 'nos méthodes occidentales', 'notre art', and in Fou Lei's 'chez nous' is indicative of a notional one. Observing that the world transported by the 'Young Chinese' now 'juxtaposes itself with the Chinese world', Duboscq effectively denied the 'Young China' its legitimate place; what he meant by 'Chinese' was necessarily old. In other words, to him the 'Young China' was not authentically Chinese; neither were its educated youth, largely Europhile. This attitude cannot but make it psychologically difficult, not to mention conceptually confusing, for the patriotic Chinese who embraced the idea of Western culture with genuine passion and who had hoped precisely to appropriate this culture to rejuvenate their own.[77]

Some of these authors are likely to have been the 'university professors, critics, sinologists' that Fou Lei recorded he was in contact with. In 1927, Institut des hautes études chinoises de Paris was founded; In March 1929 it became part of the Sorbonne. A good number of Chinese students and scholars gave as well as attended lectures. André Duboscq from the Law Department, along with others, gave a series of conferences on China. Fou Lei, then studying at the Sorbonne and in touch with major Chinese cultural figures in Paris, would

75 'Au milieu du siècle dernier, l'époque des traités s'ouvre; les contacts s'accentuent, les idées européennes prennent le chemin de la Chine. En 1911, la révolution éclate. Tout un monde nouveau transporté par les « Jeunes Chinois », je n'ose pas dire pénètre, mais se juxtapose dès ce moment au monde chinois et commence en tout cas à influencer la jeunesse instruite, à tel point que celle-ci s'exprime et agit comme si son fond racial s'était aussi transformé – ce qui nous oblige, nous Européens, à agir de notre côté, bon gré mal gré, comme s'il en était vraiment ainsi. Mais cela est une autre histoire…' Ibid.

76 'Il fallut donc attendre les événements qui se précipitèrent vers la fin du XIXᵉ siècle, pour que la civilisation occidentale pénétra chez nous à la manière d'une invasion.' Fou Nou-En, 'La crise de l'art chinois moderne' in L'Art Vivant (September 1931), 467.

77 For a thought-provoking cross-examination of Chinese artists' endeavours in mid-1920s France and the French reception of them, see Craig Clunas, 'Chinese Art and Chinese Artists in France (1924–1925)' in Arts asiatiques, vol. 44 (1989), 100–106. Judging from this 1931 issue of L'Art Vivant, things had changed little.

not have missed them. And yet, the presence of China in France – even for the China specialists – seemed not to have been an entirely comfortable one. 'In recent years', wrote Duboscq in 1931, 'young Chinese painters flocked to Europe. What should we think about it?'[78] Why there was a question of thinking anything about it at all is another story, but here is what Duboscq thought: 'So far, nothing very remarkable to report, but there are promises. One senses quite often in these Chinese artists a clear-cut commitment to break with the art of their country, and I confess that I regret it a little.'[79]

In 1932 Fou Lei wrote: '"Your moral doctrines of thousands of years, your system which is superior to our Western ones, are they henceforth abolished?" "Your aesthetics, which is full of philosophy and poetry, why do you abandon it all?" "You have such a beautiful national tradition, why do you come to study our oil painting?" Western friends often thus ask us, but we, have we considered these questions ourselves?'[80] These questions were no doubt *sympathiques* and the regrets genuine; the warning against iconoclasm was particularly judicious. Yet, with an abundance of racial emphasis, implicit was a question of power. And the tension we perceive here is a mostly unself-conscious contradiction: for the educated Chinese, it was the need both to learn from the 'West' and to preserve their assumed cultural identity; for the Europeans, it was as attractive for the Orientals to be scrutable as it was for them to remain an exotic Other. At bottom there was, for both, at once an appetite for communication and an insistence on difference.

In 1931 Fou Lei ended his French article, which read as proudly as it was apologetic: 'In the meantime, it is sad but inevitable to see this country, after having shone in the past through a subtle art, tormenting itself in full crisis and wishing for the materialism that the West is about to reject!'[81] One hears echoes of Tagore's and many others' 'spiritual East / material West' divide. A year later, Fou Lei considered again this crisis and turned an ever-critical eye

---

78 'Enfin, au cours de ces dernières années, les jeunes peintres chinois affluèrent en Europe. Qu'en faut-il penser?' André Duboscq, 'Évolution' in *L'Art Vivant* (September 1931), 476.

79 'Jusqu'à présent, rien de très remarquable n'est à signaler, mais il y a des promesses. On sent assez souvent chez les artistes chinois un parti pris très net de rompre avec l'art de leur pays, et j'avoue que je le regrette un peu.' Ibid.

80 "你們數千年的倫理，道德，比我們西方更優越的制度就此廢棄嗎？" "你們滿含着哲理和詩意的美學為何把它一概丟了？" "你們是有那麼美麗的傳統的國民何必來學我們的油畫？"西方的朋友時常這樣的問我們，而我們自己，有沒有想到這些問題？' Fou Lei, 'Our Work' in *L'Art*, vol. 1, no. 8 (November 1932).

81 'En attendant il est triste, mais fatal, de voir ce pays, après avoir brillé dans le passé par un art subtil, se tourmenter en pleine crise, désirant ce materialisme que l'Occident, lui, est déjà sur le point de rejeter!' Fou Nou-En, 'La crise de l'art chinois moderne' in *L'Art Vivant* (September 1931), 468.

towards China's general, indeed psychological, condition: 'As one enters old age, one's thinking and doing take one of these two routes: first, die-hard conservatism; second, childlike naïveté. A senile nation acts likewise.' Arguing that adamantly adhering to tradition had more of a chance of rejuvenation than did thoughtlessly following others, Fou Lei proposed: a dignified old nation, whilst rejecting change for the sake of preserving its antiquity, was after all using its brain to evaluate the new culture; out of this quiet combat would then be born a crisis in its inner life, whereupon would grow its future. A wide-eyed old nation, he declared, having lost its rational bearing, rushing after this today and that tomorrow, would never walk its own path – 'and yet this is precisely the situation in China today.'[82]

Continuing Liang Qichao's nation/person analogy, Fou Lei here subverts Liang's radical proposition for ultimately the same purpose, namely an eventual renaissance of some description. Fou Lei's argument, abounding in dichotomies resembling those of Liang, is that of a self-designated young carrier of a self-designated old civilisation, an identification that his Western friends contributed to making it impossible to brush off. It is worth asking, in this context, how European Orientalism in turn shaped Chinese self-perception, and whether this can be considered a second invasion in the sense that ideological concerns came to interfere with or even override artistic ones. For better or for worse, how to synthesise Chinese and Western art was to varying extents a fixation of countless Chinese artists in the first decades of the twentieth century. Alluding to a certain artist he knew who did 'excellent Chinese works' but who started afresh with oil painting instead of seeking to take advantage of it, Duboscq's final question was indicative: 'I am certainly more curious to know

---

82 '一個人到了老年，他的思想和行為總不出兩途：(一)是極端的頑固守舊；(二)是像小孩般的天真與幼稚。一個衰老的民族亦是這樣，或者是固執傳統與成見而嚴拒新思想，或者是不問是非，毫無理智地跟着人家亂跑。顯然前者比後者更有再生——或者說返老還童——的希望。因為前者雖然固執，但究竟還在運用他的頭腦。一個古老的民族，在表面上雖然要維持它古文化的尊嚴而努力摒拒新文化，但良心上已經在暗暗地估量這新文化的價值，把它與固有文化的價值評衡。於是在民族的內生命上，發生一種新和舊的交戰，一種crise。於是它的前途在潛滋暗長中萌蘖起來。至於天真而幼稚的老民族，根本已失掉了自我意識，失掉了理智的主宰，它只有人云亦云地今天往東，明天往西的亂奔亂竄：怎麼能走出一條自己的路來？然而這正是現代中國的情形。' Fou Lei, 'I Will Say It Again: Where Are We Headed? ... To the Depths!' 我再說一遍：往何處去？……往深處去！ in *L'Art*, vol. 2, no. 1 (January 1933). For a translation of this text in its entirety, see Claire Roberts, *Friendship in Art*, 45–47.

at what Sino-European compromise he could arrive, than I am only to know to what degree his talent will atain in our art.'[83]

Its pertinence aside, we encounter in Duboscq's vocabulary the banner of 'notre art' once more. Medium appeared, to him and to many, to be the equivalent of an art's nationality – does art have a nationality? – and in this case it happened to be oil. In the Sino-European context, the significance of medium was as symbolic as it was technical. Fou Lei confessed that he 'fell in love with Chinese painting' – the 'notre art' proper to *him* – when 'studying Western painting in the Louvre'.[84] Might it have been a reaction somewhat nationalistic, or a quest for roots somewhat instinctual?[85]

All the same, Duboscq's misgivings were not uniquely Orientalist; some of his contemporary French critics appeared to have perceived crises in post-war painting practice en masse. This issue of *L'Art Vivant* ended with 'La peinture est morte? Vive la peinture!', which had ostensibly nothing to do with China, but which provided subtle points of comparison. Jacques Guenne, who had interviewed Matisse in 1925, here took a stance against the famed and influential 'docteur Elie Faure' who 'had just diagnosed that pictorial art was in its death throes'.[86] Amusingly taking Doctor Faure apart, Guenne fired away: 'Moreover, does not art proceed essentially through exchange? Is it not most often the influence of a foreign art that managed to create the quintessential national art? Is Greco not the painter most characteristic of the genius of Spain, though he was not born there? [...] All values after the War have been subject to disorderly speculation; it is no surprise that painting has also provoked contemptible and ridiculous bids.'[87]

---

83 'Je suis certes plus curieux de savoir à quel compromis sino-européen il pourrait arriver, que je ne le suis de connaître le degré qu'atteindra son talent dans notre art.' André Duboscq, 'Évolution' in *L'Art Vivant* (September 1931), 476.

84 '我最早愛上中國畫，也是在二十一二歲在巴黎盧浮宮鑽研西洋畫的時候開始的。' [It was when I studied Western painting in the Louvre at the age of twenty-one or twenty-two that I fell in love with Chinese painting.] Fou Lei's letter to Fou Ts'ong, 27 May 1965, in *Fou Lei's Family Letters*, 456.

85 *Guohua* 國畫 [national painting] was coined around the turn of the twentieth century in China to describe the centuries-old tradition of ink painting on paper. Used to distinguish the genre from oil painting, it carried nationalistic connotations. See Aida-Yuen Wong, 'A New Life for Literati Painting in the Early Twentieth Century: Eastern Art and Modernity, a Transcultural Narrative?' in *Artibus Asiae*, vol. 60, no. 2 (2000), 297–326.

86 '[...] venait de diagnostiquer que l'art pictural était à l'agonie.' Jacques Guenne, 'La peinture est morte? Vive la peinture!' in *L'Art Vivant* (September 1931), 493.

87 'Par ailleurs, l'art ne procède-t-il pas essentiellement par échanges? N'est-ce pas le plus souvent l'influence d'un art étranger qui parvint à susciter l'art le plus essentiellement

Fou Lei's formerly unidentified Parisian circle sheds light on his literary and intellectual formation between 1928 and 1931.[88] His presence in the spiritual and worldly pursuits of some of his friends is equally traceable.[89] At Archives jésuites de la Province de France, buried in boxes are Daniélou's handwritten notes, undisclosed and unpublished, revealing his wish to go to China as a missionary. Analysing his reasons for going, he observed: 'China is at a critical point in her history. The hearts and spirits are distraught and in search – the students in particular; if the Church does not assert its influence on them, they will go to the Protestants and rationalists.'[90] Contemplating that his desire to engage in public life might lead to missions that nearly guaranteed 'deprivation, deception, and danger – perhaps death, perhaps martyrdom', he confessed fear. Almost certainly dated 1930/1931,[91] these thoughts were informed by his conversations with Fou Lei at the time.[92] Christian faith never penetrated Fou Lei's

---

national? Greco n'est-t-il pas le peintre le plus caractéristique du génie de l'Espagne, bien qu'il n'y soit pas né? [...] Toutes les valeurs, après la guerre, ont fait l'objet de spéculations désordonnées, et il n'est pas surprenant que la peinture ait suscité aussi de méprisables et ridicules enchères.' Ibid.

88 Between years and decades, some of Fou Lei's contacts in France remained those from his la Maison days. In a newly discovered letter of 1931 addressed to the scholar Wu Mi 吳宓 (1894–1978), who carried out research at Oxford University and the Sorbonne between 1930 and 1931, Fou Lei enquired about rhyming in classical Chinese poetry on behalf of an Italian poet Sales. Sales can now be identified as one of Fou Lei's *camarades* at la Maison. In a letter to Daniélou on 20 June 1929, Fou Lei extended his greetings to a few friends, Sales included.

89 The musicologist and sinologist Louis Laloy, friends with Maritain, was listed as a speaker at la Maison. Laloy helped Fou Lei organise an exhibition of Liu Haisu 劉海粟 (1896–1994) in Paris in June 1931 and, two months later, joined them on their return journey to Shanghai. Les Amis du peuple chinois, which supported Mao Zedong 毛澤東 (1893–1976), was founded in Paris in 1934 by Laloy, André Malraux, Paul Vaillant-Couturier and Étiemble who, thirty years later, became un grand ami to Fou Lei.

90 '[...] la Chine est à un moment critique de son histoire; les esprits et les âmes sont désemparés et cherchent, les étudiants en particulier; si ce n'est pas l'Église qui prend de l'influence sur eux, ils iront aux protestants, aux rationalistes.' Jean Daniélou, 'Election sur la Chine', conserved at Archives jésuites de la Province de France. Continuing the pros and cons, Daniélou made a point of noting his ability to 'faire Chinois avec les Chinois' [be Chinese with the Chinese], but recognised that he had no natural disposition to speak foreign languages.

91 The notes were made when Daniélou was 'dans la compagnie'; neighbouring documents in the same file are dated 8 December 1930 and 23 August 1931 respectively.

92 Claudel, French consul in China between 1895 and 1905 and an acquaintance of Daniélou, could have been an inspiration also.

intellectual makeup.[93] Neither did China become the preoccupation of Daniélou. Each had his own crisis to face. Chacun sa chimère.[94] Chacun sa crise.

---

93   In a letter to Daniélou (7 June 1930), Fou Lei wrote: 'Vous avez votre foi et votre salut
      dans Dieu, moi aussi, j'ai ma foi, mais dans la fatalité même; j'ai mon salut, mais dans les
      misères humaines!' [You have your faith and your salvation in God. I too have my faith,
      but in fatality itself. I have my salvation, but in human misery!]
94   Title of Baudelaire's poem, 'Chacun sa chimère' [To every man his chimera] in *Le spleen
      de Paris*.

CHAPTER 3

Malady: Child of the Century by Lac Léman

Fou Lei's health was never robust. Between studying French in Poitiers and enrolling at the Sorbonne, he worked himself into a state of nervous exhaustion. This episode recurred. At la Maison, he was for a time taken ill.[1] On 1 June 1929, he travelled to Haute Savoie, where he stayed in a chalet on the Swiss side of a Franco-Swiss village.[2] Of this vacation we had known little. That his first published translations were made that summer, when his immersion in art history and music was also confirmed, marks the importance of the location. Field research in 2011 has made possible a reconstruction of the circumstances under which these activities took place.

Parting appeared to repeatedly trigger in Fou Lei an intense need to write. Shortly after arriving in Saint-Gingolph, he sent letter after letter to Daniélou. A testimony to the lyrical style of his French writing at the time, his first letter reads:

> The solitary life on vacation thrusts me at once into joy and into melancholy. You would not imagine what sad impressions you would have, listening to the simple and melodic sounds of piano floating on water and in the profound silence of the woods; or during the night, when the black veil stretches out entirely over the lake, you see only the faint glimmer shivering in the fishermen's little boats... no noises, the world sleeps, the living beings intoxicated in their sweet dreams; even the waves flow more silently, for fear of awakening the tranquilly resting souls. And I, all alone, I believe myself dead. Or I live in another world where there are only solitary voyagers wandering in the infinite darkness and bemoaning

---

1 In a letter to Daniélou (20 June 1929), Fou Lei recalled his room (no. 168) 'pendant mon malade' [during my illness]. In another (7 June 1930) he thanked Daniélou for having arranged, back in January 1929, his visit to Abbaye de Saint-André; upon his return, Daniélou had found him to have 'meilleure mine' [looked much healthier].

2 We have a photograph of the chalet and Fou Lei's recollection in family letters in 1962 of the region's natural beauty. The published chronology of Fou Lei (*Complete Works of Fou Lei*, vol. 20, 332) notes that he spent months in Geneva in 1929 before going to Saint-Gingolph with friends for a few weeks. Letters from him to Daniélou show this to be inaccurate. In Saint-Gingolph he passed the entire summer, the first half alone. In July he was joined by the Sun brothers; in August they were joined by the family of Liu Haisu. Liu recounted this summer in *Essays from Travels in Europe* 歐遊隨筆 (1983), though he is not to be read for factual accuracy.

© KONINKLIJKE BRILL NV, LEIDEN, 2017 | DOI 10.1163/9789004343924_005

their unfortunate destiny, and young tormented souls pouring forth tears in front of stirring natural scenes. The views inspired by Rousseau and Lamartine relive themselves in my heart, and propel me still deeper into melancholic ecstasy. There was a storm over the lake yesterday. This violent change of scene in the water disturbed me. I wanted to weep in a desperate voice, seeing that nature is too powerful and man too frail. Here I feel perpetually isolated, alone, abandoned. I have so much jealousy of your joyful life filled with faith and peace. You are valiant; you work for a precise goal that is your true happiness. Whereas I, alas! Once the real face of life is unveiled in front of me, I cannot cover it again with its mask: its ugliness is imprinted in my heart and impossible to erase. I am well aware: I am too ambitious; I want to embrace the whole world, and touch the secret of life at one stroke. But deep down I was wrong! Strength is lacking in me, I am spoiled by sensitivity, and finally God does not allow me. I thus understand that a Werther, a Faust or a René is a miracle which one should not hope to have every century![3]

---

3   'La vie solitaire de la villégiature me plonge profondément à la fois dans la joie et dans la mélancolie. Vous ne sauriez imaginer quelle impression triste vous auriez en écoutant des sons simples et mélodieux du piano, flottant sur l'eau, dans le profond silence du bois; ou bien encore, dans la nuit, au moment où le voile noir s'étend complètement sur le lac, vous ne voyez que des lueurs faibles s'éclatant dans les petites barques de pêcheurs... pas de bruit, le monde s'endort, les êtres vivants s'enivrent dans leurs beaux rêves, les ondes même, s'écoulent plus silencieusement, de peur de réveiller les âmes reposantes tranquillement. Et moi, se trouvant tout seul, je me crois mort, ou au moins je vis dans un autre monde où il n'y a que des voyageurs solitaires, errant dans les ténèbres infinies, se plaignant leur destin infortuné; et de jeunes âmes tourmentées, versant leurs larmes devant l'émouvante scène naturelle. Les spectacles dont inspiraient par Rousseau, par Lamartine revivent dans mon cœur, et m'enfoncent encore plus profondément dans les extases mélancoliques. Il y a eu un orage hier sur le lac, ce changement violent de la scène de l'eau me troublait. J'ai envie de pleurer d'une voix désespérante en trouvant que la nature est trop puissante et l'homme trop faible. Je me sens toujours isolé, solitaire, abandonné ici. J'ai vraiment beaucoup de jalousie pour votre vie si joyeuse, pleine de foi et de paix. Vous êtes vaillant, vous travaillez pour un but précis qui est le véritable bonheur pour vous. Tandis que moi, hélas! une fois la vraie figure de la vie dévoilée devant moi je ne peux plus jamais la recouvrir avec son masque: sa laideur imprime dans mon âme et impossible de l'effacer. Je sais bien: je suis trop ambitieux, je voudrais embrasser le monde entier, toucher le secret de la vie d'un seul coup, mais au fond, je me suis trompé! la force me manque, la sensibilité me gâte, et enfin Dieu ne me permet pas. Je comprends ainsi qu'un Werther, qu'un Faust, qu'un René est un miracle dont on ne doit pas espérer de l'avoir tous les siècles.' Fou Lei's letter to Daniélou, 5 June 1929; conserved at Archives jésuites de la Province de France (see *Figs*. 13 and 14).

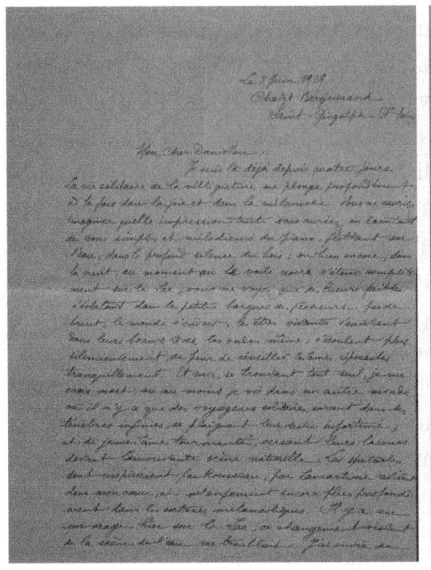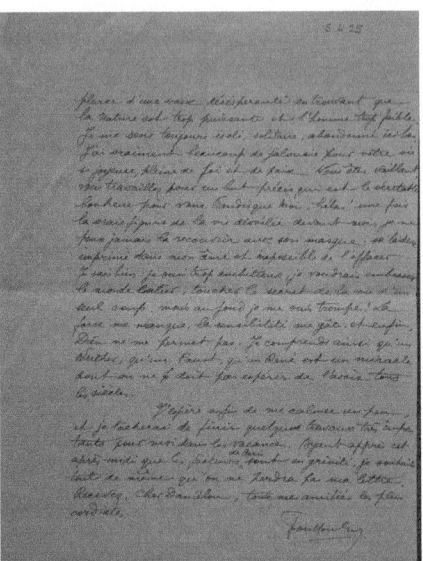

FIGURES 13 AND 14   *Fou Lei's letter to Daniélou, 5 June 1929.*
                     ARCHIVES JÉSUITES DE LA PROVINCE DE FRANCE (PHOTOGRAPHS
                     BY AUTHOR, 2011).

The 'lac', the 'voyageur solitaire', the 'âme tourmentée'… its vocabulary bearing unmistakable marks of Lamartine and Rousseau, Fou Lei's French was *aisé*. His conscious mirroring of these writers could not have found a better setting than the otherworldly Saint-Gingolph, where he continued to Byronise, five days later: 'For reading, I take always *René* with me. I do not know in what manner he enchants me so! It is there that I find the portraits resembling me, the same melancholy from which one had suffered as does a young man of today.'[4] The paralleling continued as he quoted a few phrases from *René* (1802) and said: 'Isn't it so, that this sadness of life, this despair of the world, this vague ennui, often found their way in me? And the solitary promenades, the long hours of meditation in front of a tombstone whilst hearing the bell ring, or by a little stream savouring its murmur… aren't they the exact accounts of my life?'[5] Meditating 'devant un tombeau' exactly as René had done more than

---

4   'Comme lecture, je prends toujours « René » avec moi. Je ne sais de quelle manière qu'il m'enchante tant! C'est dans lequel où je trouve de portraits semblables à moi, la même mélancolie dont on avait souffert autant qu'un jeune homme d'aujourd'hui.' Fou Lei's letter to Daniélou, 10 June 1929; conserved at Archives jésuites de la Province de France.

5   'N'est-ce pas, cette tristesse de la vie, ce désespoir du monde, cet ennui vague, se trouvaient souvent chez moi? Et des promenades solitaires, des longues heures de méditation devant

a century ago, Fou Lei's identification with the hero reached its conflicting climax: 'René said: "A great heart must contain more grief than a small one"; I have it in abundance, grief, and yet I am so small!!'[6] Chateaubriand's shadow René was reincarnated in the pages of Fou Lei. Daniélou, in an oblique sense, had become for him the priest figure in *René* who would diagnose his malady. Moreover, he may well have been Fou Lei's imagined Amélie, whose sympathy and assurance of affection gave consolation,[7] and whose devotion to religion was found by Fou Lei to draw a gulf between them. René's Amélie eventually became a nun. Though Fou Lei knew nothing about it, Daniélou, for entirely different reasons, was at this time considering becoming a Jesuit. A year later, answering Daniélou's question about faith, Fou Lei wrote: 'But do you not feel a barrier raised always between our two intimate souls. I feel it, and I am greatly saddened ever since its discovery was revealed in me more than a year ago.'[8]

Filled with 'this sadness of life, this despair of the world, this vague ennui', Fou Lei, wandering along lac Léman, knew himself to be a young romantic par excellence. What is here meant by 'romantic' calls for examination. Writing about the romantic temper of May Fourth writers, Leo Ou-fan Lee likened a traditional Chinese man of letters, a *wenren* 文人, to an *artiste* in nineteenth-century France, for he 'feels himself different and therefore, in a sense, superior, because he is more "capable of heightened emotional responses than are ordinary men". His hypersensitivity, which dooms him to suffering for life, can also be a blessing, a gift of feeling that average mortals do not possess. His narcissistic pose of a genius misunderstood or unreceived (huai-ts'ai pu-yü) is, in fact, a gesture of self-deception in order to ease away his anxieties over his political impotence.'[9] With *wenren* being taken for granted as the cultural and political élite, not only were political unrest and ills of the time an

---

6 'René a dit: « Une grande âme doit contenir plus de douleur qu'une petite »; j'en ai d'une abondance, la douleur, et cependant, je suis si petit!!' Ibid.

7 In his letter to Daniélou on 20 June 1929, Fou Lei wrote: 'Je vous remercie infiniment de votre intime amitié que vous m'avez assurée. Je suis vraiment consolé par votre sympathie.' [I thank you infinitely for your intimate friendship of which you have assured me. I am truly consoled by your sympathy.]

8 'Mais ne sentez-vous pas une barrière qui s'élève toujours entre nos deux âmes intimes. Moi, je la sens, et je suis bien peiné dès que cette découverte fut révélée dans moi il y a plus d'un an.' Fou Lei's letter to Daniélou, 7 June 1930; conserved at Archives jésuites de la Province de France.

9 Leo Ou-fan Lee, 'The Romantic Temper of May Fourth Writers' in Benjamin I. Schwartz (ed.), *Reflections on the May Fourth Movement*, 81.

honoured theme in literati literature, they inspired some of the most profound and poignant creations going back at least to Qu Yuan 屈原 (343–278 B.C.). In the first decades of the twentieth century, this theme was uttered, with urgency and with personal disturbance, in renewed languages and on unprecedented subjects, and the voice of the *wenren* was transformed, now with an added Faustian thrust. In perhaps the most romantic of May Fourth poets, Xu Zhimo 徐志摩 (1896–1931), Leo Ou-fan Lee observed: 'Hsü [Xu] as well as most of his contemporaries tended to view their favorite Western authors as a pantheon of romantic heroes: Rousseau, Byron, [...] Shelley, Keats, Goethe, Tolstoy, Nietzsche, [...] Hugo, Romain Rolland, [...] Gorky, Tagore, Lamartine, Maupassant.'[10] Since canonisations say something about the canonising party, it may be asked whether these all-embracing yet selective romantic identifications reveal latent correlation, or whether they are in effect forms of projection or compensation. Looking at individual cases, we need to ask what was happening, linguistically and conceptually, in this phenomenal course of zealously appropriating European writers – mostly *through* Chinese translations – into their own vernacular Chinese; why it is that a change of temperament can be detected in this process; if there was an inner need for change to begin with, and whether the translation itself was not part of a larger cultural transformation in process.

To answer these questions we come once again to the denotation of 'romantic'. Already for Goethe, romanticism was disease. A manifold phenomenon encompassing distinct stages in time and diverse flavours in places, with historical hindsight romanticism has been described as 'une crise de la conscience européenne'[11] by the French scholar Paul Van Tieghem, and the English scholar F.L. Lucas facetiously referred to 11,396 of its theorisations.[12] Literature of and on romanticism is immense; this is not the place to spill more ink on it. For the reason that Isaiah Berlin's appraisal highlights the fantastically elusive nature of the notion, his three-page attempt at describing the so-called romantic characteristics deserves space:

> [...] it is youth, the exuberant sense of life of the natural man, but it is also pallor, fever, disease, decadence, the *maladie du siècle*, [...] It is nostalgia,

---

10   Ibid., 78.

11   Paul Van Tieghem, *Le romantisme dans la littérature européenne* (Paris: Albin Michel, 1948), 247.

12   'And so I am daring to add yet another to those 11,396 discussions of Romanticism. But I shall deal only briefly with older theories; and I shall not feel all is lost, if my readers harden their heads against the new theory that I offer now.' F.L. Lucas, *The Decline and Fall of the Romantic Ideal* (Cambridge: Cambridge University, 1948), 4.

it is reverie, it is intoxicating dreams, it is sweet melancholy and bitter melancholy, solitude, the sufferings of exile, the sense of alienation, roaming in remote places, [...] It is energy, force, will, life, *étalage du moi*; it is also self-torture, self-annihilation, suicide, [...] It is the convulsion of great empires, wars, slaughter and the crashing of worlds. It is the romantic hero – the rebel, *l'homme fatal*, the damned soul, [...] It is art for art's sake, and art as an instrument of social salvation. It is strength and weakness, individualism and collectivism, purity and corruption, revolution and reaction, peace and war, love of life and love of death.[13]

With these varied and contradictory connotations as separately exact as they are conjointly interdependent, one wonders if 'romantic' can be used with any semantic precision at all. Yet it does register something oddly identifiable, either as a state of mind unbound by time and place, or as a specific occurrence subject to specific causes. Analysing the roots of romanticism as an historical movement and not as a permanent state of mind, Berlin reiterated the link, though unclear, between the two revolutions, namely the so-called romantic revolution and the French Revolution. 'As we read history, there is a general sense that something catastrophic occurred towards the end of the eighteenth century.'[14] We know that many things catastrophic occurred in China at the beginning of the twentieth century, and that the New Culture Movement (1915), of which the Literary Revolution (1917) was part, was launched with no less drama after the Xinhai Revolution (1911). Historical relativism aside, from a psychological point of view, to what extent can parallels be drawn between the two sets of political happenings in France and China and between the resembling consequences, as it were, of romantically inclined consciousness? Alfred de Musset spoke, in *La confession d'un enfant du siècle* (1836), of the spirit of his time as that of 'fils de l'Empire et petits-fils de la Révolution'[15] [sons of the Empire and grandsons of the Revolution]. The absence of a national father figure, namely Napoleon I, was on Musset's mind. In a post-Qing, or might one say post-Ming, China, the question is whether there was ever such a figure. The reign of the Qing was a foreign one. Its emperors, though uniformly 'sons of heaven' 天子, were Manchurian.[16] Founder of the Republican government (1912) and briefly Father of the Nation 國父, Sun Yat-sen died when the nation had long been a headless animal, one whose body

---

13   Isaiah Berlin, *The Roots of Romanticism* (London: Pimlico, 1999), 16–18.
14   Ibid., 6–7.
15   Alfred de Musset, *La confession d'un enfant du siècle* (Paris: Charpentier, 1859), 8.
16   One may indeed argue that the Han race had by then been psychologically insecure for centuries.

remained all the while horrifically alive, plagued by the very feudalism that the Revolution was supposed to have overthrown but apparently in vain. Between 1916 and 1928, the warlords who quickly seized and ruthlessly competed for absolute power cared little for democracy; neither did they respect Sun Yat-sen's Republican ideal. Fou Lei's generation – grandsons of an Empire and sons of a Revolution, to appropriate Musset's formulation – knew from birth chaos, collapse, conflicts, confusion, humiliation, danger, horror, incertitude, fear, bitterness, and despair. If, immediately after the Revolution, despite the social and political turmoil that ensued, culturally China enjoyed a veritable new era, naively optimistic and rousseauesque in its assertion of the self and in its pursuit of a renaissance, the political violence between 1925 and 1927 brought disillusionment as devastating as it was complete.[17] A generational gloom can be observed in the younger Chinese men and women of letters, many of whom now idealists-turned-cynics. A profound letdown grieved the older champions of the New Culture Movement who had once shared Lu Xun's appeal: 'Save the children...'[18] Not only were the very children that the Movement was meant to save orphaned after the Revolution, they were now betrayed and beheaded in the massacres of 1925–27. Corpses stacked on the streets of Shanghai; Fou Lei could have been one of them. At one point he was so recklessly involved in the student movement that his mother hauled him back to their suburban home. It was precisely in 1927, the year of the White Terror, that Fou Lei, aged nineteen and already an *enfant du siècle*, published bleak, anxious articles in Shanghai.

He was soon to pinpoint a parallel between the aftermath of an unsuccessful revolution at home and post-revolutionary France in the nineteenth century. Failure to settle on an agreed-upon form of government characterised both. Since 1800, France had witnessed six political regimes – the Consulate, the Empire, the Restoration, the July Monarchy, the Second Republic and the Second Empire – before establishing the Third Republic. Since 1898, China had

---

17   Vera Schwarcz observed of the Chinese intellectuals: 'Before 1919, the language of their iconoclasm had been marked by violence of an abstract kind. It reflected the confident rage of young men at war with old ways of thinking. By 1927, the writings of May Fourth veterans had become filled with the blood and gloom of actual historical experience.' (Schwarcz, *The Chinese Enlightenment*, 149.) On the other hand, the whole notion of 'May Fourth', a self-serving May Fourth construction, has been questioned by scholars such as Michel Hockx. See, for example, his 'Is There a May Fourth Literature? A Reply to Wang Xiaoming' in *Modern Chinese Literature and Culture*, vol. 11, no. 2 (Fall 1999), 40–52.

18   '救救孩子...' [Save the children...] was the last sentence of Lu Xun's *A Madman's Diary* 狂人日記 (1918), widely considered China's first modern story and a cornerstone of the New Culture Movement.

seen consecutive attempts at constitutional monarchy, Republicanism, revival of the monarchy, federalism, anarchism and Bolshevism, none of which functioned.[19] Writing in *L'Art* in 1932, Fou Lei said:

> [...] despite the preparations made by their thinkers, after the outbreak of the [French] Revolution, upheavals still dragged on for a century [...]. But if we compare their internal conflicts with those of China, ours appear to be a thousand times more complex still. They only had four or five centuries' history to overthrow, and we have twenty to cut off altogether. Is this possible, especially within a short space of time? Most revolutionaries would of course respond positively. Because they consider being nonrevolutionary a disgrace, they do not realise that revolution is the last resort.[20]

Here Fou Lei was onto psychological analysis, and the French Revolution continued to provide him with a point of comparison: 'On the surface of it, the Revolution at the end of the eighteenth century was a triple jump in history, an acute sudden change. And yet, was not the entire nineteenth century recompensing for the previous journey that had been rushed and jumped over?'[21]

The validity of such historical analogies is not the subject of discussion here; what is of interest is not whether we determine there to be a parallel, but that Fou Lei perceived there to be one. From there we may allow such a juxtaposition to illuminate the specificity and fluidity of each of the juxtaposed historical experiences. Neither nineteenth-century France nor early twentieth-century China constitutes a static entity. Fou Lei was quick to diagnose his own

---

19 In France there were Jacobins, monarchists, Bonapartists, republicans, and so on. In China there were radical liberals, progressive liberals, conservative liberals, conservative traditionalists, monarchists, anarchists with socialist or individualist inclinations, republicans, left- or right-leaning nationalists, communists, and so forth.

20 '因此法國的大革命，雖然先有了那般思想家的準備，一待大革命爆發之後，還是擾攘了一世紀 [...]。然而把這些衝突和現代中國的衝突一比，又顯得我們的比他們的要複雜萬倍了。他們只是推翻四五世紀的歷史，而我們則要把二十個世紀的傳統一並斬斷。這是不是可能的事，尤其是不是在短時間內可能的事？一般革命者當然要以肯定的語氣回答。因為他們以為不革命是一種羞恥，他們並沒有想革命是不得已的行為。' Fou Lei, 'Our Work' in *L'Art*, vol. 1, no. 8 (November 1932).

21 '十八世紀末期的大革命，在表面上彷彿是歷史上的一個三級跳遠，是一個劇烈的突變，但整個的十九世紀，不是在補走前世紀所連奔帶跳越過的途程麼？' (Ibid.) Fou Lei's scepticism of the French Revolution echoed that of Hippolyte Taine, whose *Les Origines de la France contemporaine* (published between 1875 and 1893) he might have been reading, and who from historical research drew the conclusion that they – Taine's generation – had had to pay for the radicalism of their fathers and grandfathers.

malady and name it 世紀病, a literal translation of *le mal du siècle*, a term little used by his contemporary writers in China. It so happened that *le mal du siècle*, or the consciousness of it, lingered far beyond a siècle in France. Addressing an *état d'âme*, one implicitly troubled by the times, variants of *le mal*'s romanticism played out in literature after the Franco-Prussian War (1870–71) and even through la Belle Époque, resonating anew after the First World War. Marcel Arland's 1924 article 'Un nouveau mal du siècle' in the *NRF* is an example; Georges Lecomte's 1931 'Mal du siècle' in *Le Matin*, which Fou Lei happened to read, is another. Lecomte juxtaposed the *mal* of around 1930 in France with that of around 1830, drawing parallels between youth after the War and youth after the Revolution. With a hundred years in between, both generations, according to Lecomte, were somewhat lost at not having participated in the immediately past historic events, in whose consequences they yet lived. Three years after his melancholic summer in Switzerland, Fou Lei translated, back in Shanghai, Lecomte's 'Mal du siècle' for publication in the *Morning Paper* 晨報. In the translator's afternote he reflected: 'This article speaks of the mental state of contemporary French youth. His [Lecomte's] analysis of their disquietude and sadness is detailed and thorough; moreover, what he describes bears more than a slight resemblance to today's youth in China. After reading it, does the reader think the same?'[22]

Fou Lei's concern with a contemporary *mal du siècle* in his country, arising from his personal experience and from his analogical understanding of France's modern history, stubbornly informed some of his choices, literary and social. In 1933 he published, as a sequel to his translation of Lecomte's 'Mal du siècle' (28 October 1932), an article entitled 'The Anguish of Modern Youth' 現代青年的煩悶 in the same *Morning Paper* (1 January 1933). 'This is not to give rise to the anguish of youth in modern China', wrote Fou Lei, '– this anguish which they may have already felt without my evoking it – but because anguish is the fountainhead of artistic creation. [...] And only at the awakening of the heart and soul do human beings feel this anguish. It would not be unhelpful to give this stimulus to the Chinese who have been receiving the doctrine of *sagesse* for thousands of years to the point of numbness.'[23] And yet, two years

---

22   '本文系針對現代法國青年的精神狀態而言。他分析他們的煩悶與悲哀，至為詳盡；且
      其所述，與現代中國青年界不無相似之處，不知讀者閱後，亦有若何感奮否？' Fou Lei,
      translation of 'Mal du Siècle' 世紀病 by George Lecomte in *Morning Paper* 晨報 (28 October 1932).

23   '這並非要引起現代中國青年們的煩躁——這煩躁，不待我引起，也許他們已經感到
      ——而是因為煩悶是文藝創造的源泉[...]。而且煩悶惟有在人類心魂覺醒的時候才能
      感到，在這數千年來為智(sagesse)的教訓磨練到近於痲痹的中國人精神上給他一個
      刺激，亦非無益之事。' Fou Lei, 'The Anguish of Modern Youth' 現代青年的煩悶 in

later, in 1935, a married man and father, in mourning for his mother, Fou Lei translated André Maurois' *Sentiments et coutumes: le mariage – parents & enfants – l'amitié – le métier & la cité – le bonheur* (1934), with 'le bonheur' as the concluding state. The translator elucidated, 'The whole book centres around *sagesse*, [... it is] the moral doctrine of the twentieth century',[24] and confessed that he translated the work 'to augment a little courage for fighting heroes' at a time 'when politics are changing and the whole country is panicking'.[25]

Anguish, a presumed stimulant when *sagesse* led to paralysis, now assumed the form of an affliction for which *sagesse* was the cure. This tension between romantic disgruntlement and a search for sagacity was to recur. Seven years later, in 1942, during the Sino-Japanese War Fou Lei translated Bertrand Russell's *The Conquest of Happiness* (1930).[26] In the preface he wrote: 'The shackles of reality fetter each of us. We are all submerged in the abyss of distress. Since we can neither encourage everyone to become a revolutionary, nor suppress one's instinct of seeking life and happiness, is not the question of struggling for a free and sound mind under the existing burden – in order to taste the fruit of life – the most pressing one?'[27]

Consistent in Fou Lei's undertakings was the conviction that literature could exert a power tantamount to that of politics in transforming people's states of mind; the conviction, one may add, of a *wenren*. Typically, the politically frustrated *wenren* took their spiritual escape in art and literature. Fou Lei exercised this escape with self-consciousness. In summer 1929, down and alone, no revolutionary and in search of happiness, he concluded the first Saint-Gingolph

---

    Morning Paper (1 January 1933). In 'Letters from a Voyage to France, no. 6' (1928), Fou Lei
    had used 煩悶 (anguish) to describe his state of mind before leaving China; see chapter 1,
    note 41.

24   '全書要以明智之說(sagesse)為立論中心，[...] 亦二十世紀之道德論也。' Fou Lei, 'Translator's Preface to Maurois' *Five Questions in Life*' 莫羅阿《人生五大問題》譯者弁言 in *Fou Lei Discusses Literature* 傅雷談文學 (Nanjing: Jiangsu wenyi, 2010), 231.

25   '於此風雲變幻，舉國惶惶之秋，若本書能使頹喪之士萌蘗若干希望，能為戰鬥英雄添加些少勇氣，則譯者所費之心力，豈止販賣智識而已哉？' Ibid.

26   This was immediately followed by Fou Lei's re-translation of Romain Rolland's *Vie de Beethoven* (completed in March 1942; published in 1946).

27   '現實的枷鎖加在每個人身上，大家都沉在苦惱的深淵里無以自拔；我們既不能鼓勵每個人都成為革命家，也不能壓抑每個人求生和求幸福的本能，那末如何在現存的重負之下掙扎出一顆自由與健全的心靈，去一嘗人生的果實，豈非當前最迫切的問題？' Fou Lei, 'Translator's preface to Russell's *The Conquest of Happiness*' 羅素《幸福之路》譯者弁言 (completed in January 1942; published in 1947) in *Fou Lei Discusses Literature*, 235–236. Read this in juxtaposition with Fou Lei's 'Translator's Preface to Rolland's *Vie de Beethoven*' 羅曼羅蘭《貝多芬傳》譯者序 (*Complete Works*, vol. 11, 5; see chapter 5, note 36), and one senses a yearning for heroism as intense as the need for Russellian *sagesse*.

letter to Daniélou: 'I hope to finally calm down somewhat and will try to finish, during the vacation, a few pieces of work that are very important to me.'[28] The work can now be identified as literary translation. In his last Saint-Gingolph letter, Fou Lei resolved: 'From now on I will busy myself further with fine arts and with music: this will distract me a little.'[29]

Monique Werlen, the granddaughter of Fou Lei's hosts, Raymond and Elisabeth Berguerand (née Chaperon), conjectured that her family, who also owned a local hotel, might have let the first floor of their chalet in the summer.[30] Yet Werlen's grandmother spoke only of 'les chinois' when Werlen was young.[31] In Daniélou's personal file, where a small selection of photographs of his family is set aside, there is one of Fou Lei and local boys by the lake in Saint-Gingolph, dated June 1929 (see *Fig.* 15). From his letter to Daniélou on 26 July 1929, we learn that Fou Lei had been joined by the Sun brothers – Sun Fuxi who had studied at École des beaux-arts in Lyon between 1920 and 1925, and Sun Fuyuan who had temporarily abandoned journal-editing in China; they had come to Europe in 1929 to audit classes at the Sorbonne in the autumn.[32] Liu Haisu 劉海粟 (1896–1994) and his family were to join them in August. 'There will be a small gathering of artists from the Far East',[33] Fou Lei anticipated. Founder of the Shanghai Art Academy at the age of eighteen, Liu Haisu had come to Paris via Japan in March 1929 on a government mission to 'investigate European art and to promote Chinese art in Europe'. Upon Liu's arrival, Fou Lei was introduced to him as his French teacher and interpreter. It can be

---

28   'J'espère enfin de me calmer un peu et je tacherai de finir quelques travaux très importants pour moi dans les vacances.' Fou Lei's letter to Daniélou, 5 June 1929.

29   'Je m'occuperai désormais davantage des beaux-arts et de la musique: cela me distraira un peu.' Fou Lei's letter to Daniélou, 24 August 1929; conserved at Archives jésuites de la Province de France.

30   The author's interview with Monique Werlen, 10 August 2011, Saint-Gingolph.

31   It might not have been a solely business arrangement, as documents found in the chalet today suggest that Sun Fuxi was a friend of the family, and that this friendship continued in correspondence well into 1937. In his 1925 book *Reminiscences from the Wild* 山野綴 拾, Sun Fuxi recounted painting trips from Lyon to villages in Savoie in summer 1922. He might have made the acquaintance of the Berguerands on similar trips during his first sojourn in Europe.

32   'Nous sommes souvent à la pêche, nous faisons aussi le canotage et la natation. Ils sont des gens connaissant bien vivre, ils ont des goûts exquis et de l'esprit artistique. C'est très agréable pour moi.' [We often go fishing, and do canoeing and swimming too. They [the Sun brothers] know how to live well; they have exquisite tastes and artistic spirit. It is very pleasant for me.] Fou Lei's letter to Daniélou, 26 July 1929; conserved at Archives jésuites de la Province de France.

33   'Il y aura une petite réunion des artistes extrême-orientaux.' Ibid.

observed that in summer 1929, Liu, twelve years Fou Lei's senior, began to re-place Daniélou as the guiding figure in his life. By virtue of being near, he ful-filled the brother/father role that Fou Lei needed.[34]

FIGURE 15   *Fou Lei and local friends in Saint-Gingolph, summer 1929.*
ARCHIVES JÉSUITES DE LA PROVINCE DE FRANCE.

FIGURE 16   *Chalet Berguerand, 1929.*   FIGURE 17   *Chalet Berguerand, 2011.*
PHOTOGRAPH BY FOU LEI.   PHOTOGRAPH BY AUTHOR.

---

34   Fou Lei told Daniélou about Liu Haisu: 'Il travaille énormément sa peinture et nous faisons souvent de très intéressantes conversations sur l'art. Il m'encourage beaucoup.' [He works very hard on his painting and we often have very interesting conversations about art. He encourages me a great deal.] Fou Lei's letter to Daniélou, 24 August 1929.

FIGURE 18   *Fou Lei, Sun Fuyuan, Elisabeth Berguerand, Frédérique (Mimi) Berguerand,*
             Raymond Berguerand and Sun Fuxi in front of the chalet, summer 1929.
             THE BERGUERAND FAMILY ARCHIVE.

They became friends with their hosts (see *Fig.* 18).[35] In his first Saint-Gingolph
letter to Daniélou, Fou Lei had evoked the sounds of the piano – Madame
Berguerand was an ardent player and teacher.[36] Despite his astute appreciation
of music, Fou Lei later admitted that he had tried his hand at the piano but had
no talent for it. In a letter to Madame Berguerand in 1934, he wrote: 'I do music
criticism from time to time. I bought a phonograph in France and an entire collection of classical records, but I can no longer become a musician, not even amateur.'[37] In 2013 Monique Werlen discovered, amongst her grandmother's piano
sheet music, a collection of fifty Chinese songs signed by Fou Lei as a present.[38]

---

35   In the years that followed, Fou Lei and Sun Fuxi continued to send letters, postcards, and
      photographs to the Berguerands from Paris and China. In 1934, when Liu Haisu was again
      in Europe, a letter under his dictation arrived from Geneva to arrange a stay at the chalet.
36   When we discovered, in the chalet attic, a 1931 letter from Fou Lei to Madame Berguerand,
      and read aloud the last sentence '… mes meilleurs souvenirs à Monsieur Berguerand et à
      Mimi, ma petite chère amie qui doit bien avancer au piano' [My best memories to Mon-
      sieur Berguerand and to Mimi, my dear little friend who must progress well in piano],
      both Monique Werlen and her brother burst into laughter. Their mother, Mimi, hated the
      piano, despite their grandmother's keen attempts to teach everyone in the house to play.
37   'Moi, je fais des critiques musicales de temps en temps. J'avais acheté en France un
      phonographe et toute une collection de disques classiques, mais je ne peux plus devenir
      musicien, même amateur.' Fou Lei's letter to Madame Berguerand, 6 September 1934; the
      Berguerand family archive.
38   In 'Letters from a Voyage to France', we read that the old English musician on the André-
      Lebon showed great interest in the sheet music that Fou Lei had with him, and asked
      kindly for another copy to be acquired and sent to his Singapore address; see Fou Lei,

Madame Berguerand, who came from the noble Chaperon family, was a devoted amateur painter.[39] Liu Haisu, twice exhibited at the Salon d'Automne (1929, 1930), could not write in French; Fou Lei sent photographs of Liu's paintings and leaflets of Liu's exhibition to Saint-Gingolgh.

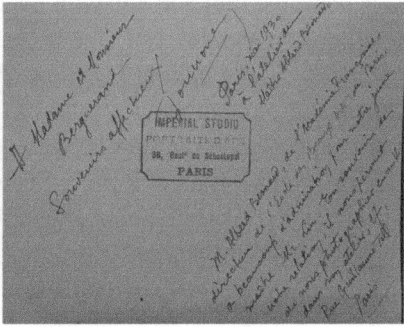

FIGURES 19 AND 20   *Zhang Xian, Zhang Yunshi, Liu Haisu, Paul-Albert Besnard and Fou Lei in the studio of Besnard, 1930; Fou Lei's inscription on the reverse.*
THE BERGUERAND FAMILY ARCHIVE.

In one of the photographs Fou Lei sent to the Berguerand family in May 1930, we see him, Liu Haisu, Liu's wife Zhang Yunshi 張韻士 (1899–1970) and the painter Zhang Xian 張弦 (1901–1936) in the studio of Paul-Albert Besnard (1849–1934), director of École des beaux-arts (*Figs.* 19 and 20).[40] Fou Lei's interest in art history was initiated around the time he met Liu Haisu, if not earlier.[41] Whilst studying at the Sorbonne, he audited classes at École du Louvre.[42] Apart from

'Letters from a Voyage to France, no. 7'. Fou Lei must have offered his own copy to Madame Berguerand. The sheet music is probably *Fifty Songs in Chinese* 中文名歌五十首 (Shanghai: Kaiming, 1927), co-edited by Feng Zikai 豐子愷 (1898–1975).

39   Monique Werlen remembers that her grandmother was always writing letters and playing the piano, and that the day before she died, she was still painting (interview with author, 10 August 2011, Saint-Gingolph). Historian André-François Derivaz, who knew Madame Berguerand personally, remembers her as 'une dame très digne' [a very dignified lady] (interview with author, 12 August 2011, Monthey).

40   This photograph, of which Liu Haisu kept a copy, has been well published.

41   Fou Lei may have read, for instance, Maritain's *Art et scolastique* at la Maison. Amongst Daniélou's study notes from this period, now conserved at Archives jésuites de la Province de France, are pages he transcribed from the works of Maritain and Ruskin. Daniélou had contacts at École du Louvre.

42   '在法四年：一方面在巴黎大學文科聽課、一方面在巴黎盧佛美術史學校聽課。' 'Fou Lei on Himself' in *Complete Works,* vol. 17, 5. In Fou Lei's own account, no exact years of attendance at either the Sorbonne or École du Louvre were given. Since records of auditors from this period have not been kept at École du Louvre, we have no way of knowing the years in which Fou Lei was enrolled.

having 'very interesting conversations about art',[43] he and Liu Haisu also visited Edmond François Aman-Jean (1858–1936), the symbolist painter, and Maurice Denis (1870–1943), co-founder of Les Nabis.[44] An anti-academic position shared by all three – Besnard, Aman-Jean and Denis – was reiterated in Fou Lei's critical writing on contemporary art in China two years later. It is perceivable that Fou Lei, with his pedantic knowledge and the penetrating manner in which he went about his subjects, exerted considerable influence on Liu Haisu: throughout Liu's long life, his work from these years was arguably the most grounded. It so happens that some of Liu's iconic oeuvres from this European sojourn can now be set in context in Saint-Gingolph. The houses in the 1929 composition of *Express Train* still stand today, down the road from the chalet, by the lake and behind 'le rapide' – the train's name back in those days (*Figs.* 21–26). The geometric series of houses featured in another painting, exactly as Liu saw it in 1929, is poised not far from the railway (*Figs.* 27 and 28).[45]

 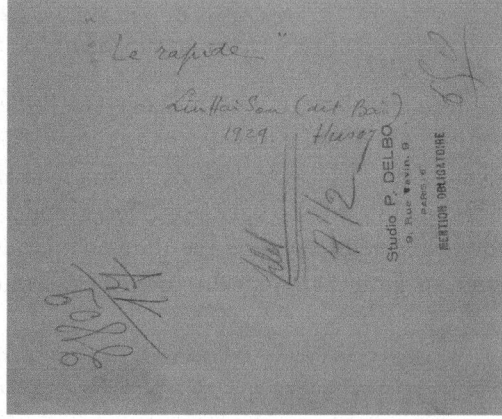

FIGURES 21 AND 22   *Photograph of Liu Haisu's painting sent to the Berguerands; 'Le Rapide' written on the reverse.*
THE BERGUERAND FAMILY ARCHIVE.

---

43   See note 34 in this chapter.

44   In his letter of 7 June 1930 to Daniélou, Fou Lei wrote: 'I am making good progress in my studies of art history. I had the opportunity to frequent the studios of great contemporary French masters Albert Besnard and Aman Jean. We will see Maurice Denis later on.' Their meeting with Matisse in October 1929 has been recorded. See 'Fou Lei Chronology' in *Complete Works*, vol. 20, 333; Claire Roberts, *Friendship in Art*, 20–21.

45   The author has not located Liu Haisu's *Express Train*; its publication can be found in, for example, Michael Sullivan's *Art and Artists of Twentieth-century China* (Berkley and London: University of California, 1996).

FIGURE 23 *Liu Haisu,* Express Train. *1929, oil on canvas, location unknown.*

FIGURE 24 *View from the chalet.* PHOTOGRAPH BY AUTHOR, 2011.

FIGURE 25 *Detail of Liu Haisu's painting.* THE BERGUERAND FAMILY ARCHIVE.

FIGURE 26 *'Le Rapide,' Saint-Gingolph.* PHOTOGRAPH BY AUTHOR, 2011.

FIGURE 27 *Photograph of Liu Haisu's paint-*   FIGURE 28 *View of local houses in*
ing sent to the Berguerands.   *Saint-Gingolph.*
THE BERGUERAND FAMILY   PHOTOGRAPH BY AUTHOR,
ARCHIVE.   2011.

Fou Lei's earliest translations, of *Carmen* by Prosper Mérimée and of two
short story collections by Alphonse Daudet, were made for the purpose of
learning French when he was twenty, and he lost the manuscripts not knowing when or where.[46] In the same second-floor chamber of the chalet Berguerand where some postcards from Fou Lei recently resurfaced, Monique
Werlen chanced upon an old copy of Daudet's *Les contes de mon moulin.* Fou
Lei's first known translation, again made without the intention to publish, was
likewise from the chalet: *Légende de Saint Gingolph.*[47] Translating a language
into one's own as solely a way of learning the former whilst studying the latter – the exclusivity of this motivation should not be overlooked. One recalls
that Goethe translated Pierre Corneille's *Le Menteur* at the age of sixteen,
and that Stefan Zweig, after seeing in print his first volume of poetry at the
age of nineteen, spent years translating Baudelaire, Verlaine, Keats, William

46   'Fou Lei on Himself' in *Complete Works*, vol. 17, 8.

47   Appearing in *Huaxu Press Anthology of Essays on Art and Literature* 華胥社文藝論集
      (Shanghai: Zhonghua shuju, 1931), this translation of *Légende de Saint Gingolph* 聖楊喬
      而夫的傳說, finished in the middle of the night on 13 September 1929, was followed by a
      translator's note, where Fou Lei explained that the story was from an old book in his hosts'
      house in the legendary village, and that he had forgotten to jot down the Swiss author's
      name; for this he apologised to his readers.

Morris, Charles Van Lerberghe, Camille Lemonnier, and Emile Verhaeren.[48] A voluntary urge, in practice it is an extended process of identifying as well as inventing equivalents,[49] all the while exploring the creative potential of one's mother tongue. The method, or rather result, of this cognitive process is to an extent empathetic.[50] Particularly affecting in Fou Lei's debut translation of *Légende de Saint Gingolph*, where one detects precision and elegance, qualities for which the translator was to become renowned, is its lyrical descriptions, for which classical Chinese has an indulgent facility. Plunging into a foreign tongue heightens one's linguistic sensitivity. French was to be acquired; Chinese was no longer taken for granted. Fou Lei's lucid, at times florid French of this time retained some of the constructions of his early Chinese. His vernacular Chinese, meanwhile, was becoming noticeably structured. Translating, in this sense, is inhabiting one space without leaving another. Eventually it reshapes one's relation to both.

Towards the end of this summer, Fou Lei demonstrated a state of mind more focused;[51] the work he assigned to himself had everything to do with it. From Abbaye de Saint-André to the chalet Berguerand, Fou Lei's acute suffering from *mal du siècle* in 1929 was of paramount importance to our understanding of his youth. I would go so far as to suggest that his activities in the years to come were a continued reaction against it, it being believed to be an individual as well as collective ill, and a conscious effort to overcome it. For he could have remained a would-be René; he did not.

---

48   See Stefan Zweig, *The World of Yesterday* (London: Pushkin, 2009), 140–147.

49   For case analyses of the complexities of equivalent-forming practices amongst authors in Republican China, see Lydia Liu, *Translingual Practice: Literature, National Culture, and Translated Modernity – China, 1900–1937* (Stanford: Stanford University, 1995).

50   *Légende de Saint Gingolph* recounts the return of the baron to his native village. Rumoured to have died years ago in a faraway battlefield, he was heartbroken to discover the re-marriage of his wife. Not wanting to jeopardise her happiness, he lived anonymous and saintly in the same village until his death. Fou Lei deemed this 'a work of absolute success in literature', not least for its moral message. See Fou Lei, Translator's note after 'The Legend of Saint Gingolph' in *Complete Works*, vol. 15, 347.

51   See Fou Lei's letter to Daniélou, 24 August 1929.

Remedy: The Promise of Tainean Scientism

The vocation of the translator is a mysterious one. In October 1929, shortly after his return to Paris, Fou Lei published a preface with only the beginning of Hippolyte Taine's (1828–1893) *Philosophie de l'art* (1865–82) translated. To say it betrayed an urgent need to communicate is an understatement. In this preface, which proceeds seamlessly from introduction to cultural commentary, we hear for the first time the voice that is unmistakably Fou Lei's – that of single-minded clarity, transparency, and intensity.

Taine, wrote Fou Lei, 'cultivated a thorough kind of scientific spirit when very young. Convinced that the spiritual life of mankind was dominated and influenced by the material, he said that social sciences (including philosophy, literature, art and religion) could be analysed in the same way that natural sciences were. The criteria of his judgement were *race, milieu, moment*. This is the system that his critic-predecessor Sainte-Beuve had advocated but that was pushed to an extreme by Taine.'[1] Describing Taine's method, Fou Lei said: 'He situates history, literature, philosophy and the fine arts all in the time and place where they emerged and developed, and collects contemporary documents that recorded social actuality, intending thereby to arrive at the *loi* which generated such civilisations through purely scientific, purely rational dissections.'[2] Moving on to *Philosophie de l'art*, Fou Lei wrote with admiration: 'This *Philosophie de l'art* is the application of his method to the fine arts. You can see him making a clear opening declaration of his *système* and *méthode* in Part I, thus deriving "the definition of art"; in Parts II, III, and IX, he continues to speak of the great schools of art in Italy, Flanders and ancient Greece, ending with his "ideal in art". This is his – Taine's aesthetics!'[3]

---

1 '他從極年輕的時候，就孕育了一種徹底的科學精神，以為人類的精神活動是受物質的支配與影響，故他說精神科學 （包括哲學，文學，美術，宗教等） 可與自然科學同樣的分析。他所依據的條件便是種族，環境，時代三者。這是他的前輩批評家聖伯夫 (Sainte-Beuve) 所倡導而由他推之於極端的學說。' Fou Lei, 'Translator's Preface to Taine's *Philosophie de l'art*' 泰納《藝術論》譯者弁言 (1929) in *Huaxu Press Anthology of Essays on Art and Literature* (1931); see *Fou Lei Discusses Art* 傅雷談藝術 (Nanjing: Jiangsu wenyi, 2010), 147.

2 '他把歷史，文學，哲學，美術都放到它們的生長的地域和時代中去，搜集當時的記載社會狀況的文件，想由這些純粹科學，純粹理智的解剖，來得到產生這些文明的定律。' Ibid.

3 '這本《藝術論》便是他這種方法之應用於藝術方面的。你們可以看到他在第一章里，開宗明義的宣布他的"學說"和"方法"，繼即應用於推求"藝術之定義"；在第

At this point came the translator's brisk interrogation: 'But then follows the question: the epoch of La Fontaine no doubt produced La Fontaine, the Flanders in the epoch of Rubens no doubt produced Rubens, and Italy in the epoch of Michelangelo and Raphael no doubt produced Michelangelo and Raphael, and yet why is it that people of the same *race, milieu* and *moment* as theirs were not all La Fontaine, Rubens, Michelangelo and Raphael?'[4] After questioning Taine's historical determinism, Fou Lei continued to probe as well as to speculate: 'Admittedly, "Geniuses do not appear in every generation", and the mass is always vulgar, but how can the psychological dissection of the artist's creative process be entirely ignored? Are the causes of human civilisation limited to purely material conditions of *race, milieu, moment*? What exactly is the so-called "genius"? Is it what he [Taine] claims to be "acute sensitivity"? Why is this "acute sensitivity" not possessed by ordinary people, and how do those who do possess it develop their sensitivity to a mature extent?'[5]

That 'geniuses do not appear in every generation' was a thought Fou Lei had expressed in a letter to Daniélou four months previously.[6] It is as far as historiographical traditions in China had gone to explain the presence, or the lack thereof, of geniuses at any given time. In the same letter Fou Lei spoke, albeit vaguely, of his own literary ambitions. The questions he raised on 'the creative process of the artist' and on the nature of the 'acute sensitivity' are enquiries as scholarly as they are personal. Analysing the spiritual dimension of the creative individual almost exclusively against his or her social environment was, elaborate as it was as a method, not convincing enough for Fou Lei who, like Taine himself, was deeply interested in the rôle of the artist. It has been said that Taine, with his formula of *race, milieu, moment*, forged handcuffs for his own analysis. His psychological determinism, continuing the Lockean tradition of empirical psychology, 'undermines the conception of the soul

---

二、三、四編里，他接着講意大利，佛蘭德斯及古希臘等幾個藝術史的大宗派，最後再講他的"藝術之理想"，這便是他，——泰納的美學了！'Ibid.

4 '然而問題來了：拉封丹的時代固然產生了拉封丹了，魯本斯時代的佛蘭德斯固然產生了魯本斯了，米開朗琪羅，拉斐爾時代的意大利也固然產生了米開朗琪羅，拉斐爾了；然而與他們同種族，同環境，同時代的人物，為何不盡是拉封丹，魯本斯，米開朗琪羅，拉斐爾呢？'Ibid., 148.

5 '固然"天才是不世出的"，群眾永遠是庸俗的；然而藝者創造過程的心裡解剖為何可以全部忽略了呢？人類文明的成因是否只限於"種族，環境，時代"的純物質的條件？所謂"天才"究竟是甚麼東西？是否即他之所謂"銳敏的感覺"呢？這"銳敏的感覺"為甚麼又非常人所不能有，而具有這感覺的人又如何的把這感覺發展到成熟的地步？'Ibid.

6 Fou Lei's letter to Daniélou, 5 June 1929. See chapter 3, note 3.

as containing innately certain timeless maxims of virtue',[7] and was reacted against in his own day by thinkers engaged in 'wrapping the soul once more in the old veils of mystery'.[8] Sainte-Beuve, for instance, did not think any scientific approach would be able to explain completely a work of art.[9] The ultimate criticism of Taine's *méthode* was thus voiced by Fou Lei, well informed behind his lucid, almost simple articulation: 'To answer all these questions would require psychological dissection, but with Taine psychology is subordinated to biology.[10] Therefore, at best he explains only half the art work, and the other, more mysterious half is still unknown to us. This is the weakness of Taine's entire doctrine, and the great defect of positivism.'[11]

The year of Fou Lei's arrival in France, 1928, saw the country celebrating Taine's centenary. Newspaper, journal and book publications were generous in their attention to the towering intellectual of two generations ago who had since drifted somewhat into oblivion. Given the near simultaneity of the 1920s Chinese press with its counterparts in Europe, it is hardly surprising that on 15 June 1929, appearing in *Contribution* alongside Fou Lei's 'Letters from a Voyage to France, no. 12' (entitled '一路平安抵法！' [Safely arrived in France!]) was an article on Taine by Zeng Zhongming 曾仲鳴 (1896–1939), a scholar and politician then studying in France. If Fou Lei received copies of *Contribution* posted from Shanghai, he would have seen Taine's name printed next to his own. Even excluding this possibility, after his arrival in 1928 he could have read about Taine in newspapers such as *Le Figaro*.[12] Taine's centenary was officially celebrated at the Sorbonne in the presence of the President of the Republic.[13]

---

7   Martha Wolfenstein, 'The Social Background of Taine's Philosophy of Art' in *Journal of the History of Ideas*, vol. 5, no. 3 (June 1944), 354.

8   Ibid.

9   Thomas H. Goetz, *Taine and the Fine Arts* (Madrid: Playor, 1973), 26.

10   This is pertinent in the context of *Philosophie de l'art*. Taine's methods vary according to the subject he treats, reflecting different preoccupations. For example, in *Origines de la France contemporaine*, prompted by his country's defeat in 1871 and unfinished by the time of his death, Taine incessantly explores human nature.

11   '這些問題都有賴於心裡學的解剖，而泰納卻把心理學完全隸屬於生理學之下，於是充其量，他只能解釋藝術品之半面，還有其他更深奧的半面我們全然沒有認識。這是泰納全部學術的弱點，也就是實證主義的大缺陷。' Fou Lei, 'Translator's Preface to Taine's *Philosophie de l'art*' in *Fou Lei Discusses Art*, 148. Fou Lei's criticism echoed Zola's observation: 'M. Taine évite de parler de la personnalité; [...] On sent que la personnalité le gêne terriblement.' Émile Zola, 'M.H. Taine, Artiste' in *Mes Haines* (Paris: Flammarion, 2012), 236.

12   See 'Le Centenaire de Taine' in *Le Figaro*, no. 472 (21 April 1928).

13   Horatio Smith, 'The Taine Centennial: Comment and Bibliography' in *Modern Language Notes*, vol. 44, no. 7 (November 1929), 438.

His name was amongst those listed in the reading programme of la Maison de la Jeunesse. Fou Lei's encounter with him by early 1929 was guaranteed. When the Sun brothers visited Saint-Gingolph in 1929, they might have spoken, amongst other things, of Taine, the introduction of whom their friend Zeng Zhongming had written and they had published.

In the same summer, one author that was likely not to have been missed out in the conversations in the chalet Berguerand would have been Bertrand Russell, whom Sun Fuyuan knew personally and whose rational scepticism manifested itself in Fou Lei's writing from this time on. For Russell as for many Chinese thinkers, a fundamental difference between China and the West lay in the development of science: 'It is science that makes the difference between our intellectual outlook and that of the Chinese intelligentsia. [...] The real problem for the Chinese intellectuals is to acquire Western knowledge without acquiring the mechanistic outlook.'[14] This preoccupation with science was evidenced in Fou Lei's publication, a decade after Russell spent a year in China and made his observation. In the greater early twentieth-century context of the propagation of 'science' in China, Fou Lei's choice of Taine was not a random interest, nor an isolated phenomenon. In the translator's preface he wrote: 'We know that the crucial key to modern civilisation is the breakdown of the dream of all-powerful science. Around 1870, when Darwin's *Theory of Evolution* had been published, Marcellin Berthelot's *Chimie organique fondée sur la synthèse* had been proclaimed, and Zénobe Gramme's first engine had been built, the whole of Europe fanatically hoped to use this new tool – science – to open a new path, for the universe and life to reach a complete, new resolution. Unfortunately, in 1914, the cannons by the Rhine brought this wonderful dream down to pieces.'[15] This judgement echoed Russell's observation seven years previously: that the War made some Chinese intellectuals rethink the promises of learning from the West.[16] And Fou Lei asked: 'Now who dare say that science is the truth and the absolute?'[17]

---

14 Bertrand Russell, *The Problem of China*, 81.

15 '我們知道，現代文明的大關鍵，是在於科學萬能之夢的打破。一八七〇年左右，達爾文的進化論發表了，貝特洛的化學綜合論宣布了，格喇姆的第一個引擎造好了的時候，全個歐洲都熱狂的希望能用了新發明的利器——科學——來打出一條新路，宇宙，人生都可得一個新的總解決。不幸，事實上一九一四年萊茵湖畔的一聲大炮，就把這美妙的幻夢打得粉碎。' Fou Lei, 'Translator's Preface to Taine's *Philosophie de l'art*' in *Fou Lei Discusses Art*, 148.

16 Bertrand Russell, *The Problem of China*, 193–194. Thinkers such as Liang Qichao expressed similar views.

17 '科學即是真理，即是絕對的話，在現在誰還敢說呢？' Fou Lei, 'Translator's Preface to Taine's *Philosophie de l'art*' in *Fou Lei Discusses Art*, 148.

A general disenchantment with scientism would have been something Fou Lei came across in a scholarly context at la Maison de la Jeunesse, as its reading programme drafted by Daniélou suggests.[18] Speaking of realism and naturalism in literature as having the same fate of meeting a 'dead end' as positivism, Fou Lei wrote: 'Isn't Taine's *Philosophie de l'art*, then, art criticism of the past, and isn't it incomplete "aesthetics" by today's standard? The reason for my introducing this book lies precisely in its shortcoming, for this extreme scientific spirit is precisely the scholarly method our modern China most needs.'[19] The two uses of 'isn't' in his question and the two of 'precisely' in his own answer lay bare the writer's temperament. The conviction of his own reason and the assertive manner of his reasoning demonstrate a force of will matched by that of Taine, the author he translated. 'Especially within Chinese academia', Fou Lei argued, 'where general knowledge of art is extremely impoverished, to have a clear understanding of art, then, one cannot but begin with the fundamentals of this genre of positivism. Human civilisation takes its course from the external towards the internal; getting straight to the core of the matter without having apprehended the outward causes is something that absolutely does not exist.'[20] Taine, indeed, abandons deduction in an abstract vacuum, and begins, in an empirical vein, with external facts to arrive at the internal core. Not that Fou Lei dismisses the core, the presumed objective of historical writing in China, but his stress on 'causes' here has specific overtones. Pronounced causal deduction, like systematic contextualisation, was not consciously present in

---

18   It was Bergson, whose name repeatedly appeared in Daniélou's preparatory notes (conserved at Archives jésuites de la Province de France), and whom Fou Lei quoted in his essays in the early 1930s, who said 'We must rid ourselves of all forms of the metaphysical illusion (including the scientific form).' Quoted in Irving Babbitt, *The Masters of Modern French Criticism* (Boston and New York: Houghton Mifflin, 1913), viii. In a post-war context, positivism held a debatable, even equivocal, place amongst critical thinkers. See, for example, André Lalande's 'Philosophy in France, 1919' in *The Philosophical Review*, vol. 29, no. 5 (September 1920).

19   '這樣說來，泰納的這部《藝術論》不是早已成為過去的藝術批評，且在今日的眼光中，不是成了不完全的"美學"了麼？然而我之介紹此書，正着眼在其缺點上面，因這種極端的科學精神，正是我們現代的中國最需要的治學方法。' Fou Lei, 'Translator's Preface to Taine's *Philosophie de l'art*' in *Fou Lei Discusses Art*, 148–149.

20   '尤其是藝術常識極端貧乏的中國學術界，如果要對於藝術有一個明確的認識，那麼，非從這種實證主義的根本著手不可。人類文明的進程都是自外而內的，斷沒有外表的原因尚未明了而能直探事物之核心的事。' Ibid., 149.

China's historiographical canon, of which thinkers such as Liang Qichao had been avid critics.[21]

Then came Fou Lei's forthright critique: 'Scholarship in China is backward and chaotic because our ancestors knew only to chant its arcane verve and flavour without knowing where this verve and flavour came from. Therefore all we see in the "national studies" is sparseness, chaos, and arcaneness!'[22] 'Verve and flavour' 神韻氣味 being a clichéd expression in classical art criticism, the point here made on the latter's lack of system and method is trenchant. Shortly before this preface was published, Fou Lei had met Teng Gu 滕固 (1901–1941) in Paris. The Japan-trained theorist was on his way to the University of Berlin, where he was to begin a doctorate in art history.[23] Celebrated author of *A Concise History of Chinese Art* 中國美術小史 (1926), Teng Gu was noted for incorporating causal analysis of stylistic evolutions in Chinese painting and for proposing new periodisations on this basis. Fou Lei's initiative to translate *Philosophie de l'art* and his impatient preface were likely prompted by his conversations with Teng Gu.[24]

---

21   For in-depth discussions on a grander scale, see Benjamin Elman, *A Cultural History of Modern Science in China: New Histories of Science, Technology, and Medicine* (Cambridge, MA and London: Harvard University, 2006), David Kwok, *Scientism in Chinese Thought, 1900–1950* (New Haven and London: Yale University, 1965) and Susanne Weigelin-Schwiedrzik, 'On the Compatibility of Chinese and European History: A Marxist Approach' in Prasenjit Duara, Viren Murthy and Andrew Sartori (eds.), *A Companion to Global Historical Thought* (Chichester: Wiley Blackwell, 2014), 243–256. See also Alfred Bloom, *The Linguistic Shaping of Thought: A Study in the Impact of Language on Thinking in China and the West* (Hillsdale, NJ: Lawrence Erlbaum, 1981); Marwa Elshakry, 'When Science Became Western: Historiographical Reflections' in *Isis*, vol. 101, no. 1 (March 2010), 98–109; Fa-ti Fan, 'Redrawing the Map: Science in Twentieth-Century China' in *Isis*, vol. 98, no. 3 (September 2007), 524–538; Axel Schneider, 'Between Dao and History: Two Chinese Historians in Search of a Modern Identity for China' in *History and Theory*, vol. 35, no. 4, Theme Issue 35: Chinese Historiography in Comparative Perspective (December 1996), 54–73.

22   '中國學術之所以落後，之所以紊亂，也就因為我們一般祖先只知高唱其玄妙的神韻氣味，而不知此神韻氣味之由來。於是我們眼里所見的"國學"只有空疏，只有紊亂，只有玄妙！' Fou Lei, 'Translator's Preface to Taine's *Philosophie de l'art*' in *Fou Lei Discusses Art*, 149.

23   For wider contexts of Japan's influence on Republican Chinese authors' approach to art historical writing, see Julia F. Andrews and Kuiyi Shen, 'The Japanese Impact on the Republican Art World: the Construction of Chinese Art as a Modern Field' in *Twentieth-Century China*, vol. 32, no. 1 (November 2006), 4–35.

24   We can be sure of a kinship established between Fou Lei and Teng Gu at their first Parisian meeting. After his return to China in the early 1930s, Teng Gu recruited Fou Lei on

Taking the state of art historical scholarship as a direct reflection of the academic status quo in China, Fou Lei affirmed a cultural importance attributed to art that was in part a legacy of Cai Yuanpei 蔡元培 (1868–1940). The liberal thinker, educator, chancellor of Peking University and patron of the arts had effectively advocated replacing religion with aesthetic education in China after his studies in Germany and France at the beginning of the century.[25] Teng Gu was under Cai's influence from early on. With Cai's help Liu Haisu came to Paris on a government mission. The much younger Fou Lei, immediately *camarades* with Teng Gu and involved in Liu Haisu's enterprise, shared Cai Yuanpei's vision. In effect, overlooked in existing literature is Fou Lei's intellectual relationship with older, pre-May Fourth generations. Taking up as he did, with great confidence, the rôle of the translator as cultural commentator and as initiator of spiritual transformation, he was self-consciously in the footsteps of illustrious predecessors such as Yan Fu. It cannot be stressed enough, in late Qing and particularly early Republican China, how proud and noble a profession that of translator was, and how pivotal its cultural and political impact on the changing society, hungry for thought and inspiration.

In his formidable study of Yan Fu, Benjamin Schwartz pointed out that the translator of Thomas Huxley, Herbert Spencer, Adam Smith, and John Stuart Mill was the first Chinese to realise the conflict between the Christian tradition and the infidel thought of eighteenth- and nineteenth-century Europe, and that before him, only Wang Tao 王韜 (1828–1897) had vaguely heard of positivism.[26] From the Collège St. Ignace Zi-Ka-Wei in Shanghai to la Maison de la Jeunesse in Paris, it was the Christian tradition that Fou Lei was conveniently and abundantly exposed to, and yet it was the 'infidel thought of eighteenth- and nineteenth-century Europe' in general and positivism in particular that he was attracted to. As a matter of fact, throughout his career Fou Lei stayed clear of translating Catholic writers. Voltaire he eventually translated, and his choice of Taine, who had been named 'a son of Voltaire',[27] was not in the least incidental.

---

more than one occasion, either to document archaeological excavations or to teach at the university. For Teng Gu's pursuits after returning from Germany, see ibid., 32.

25   See an English translation by Julia Andrews of Cai Yuanpei's essay on art replacing religion in Kirk Denton (ed.), *Modern Chinese Literary Thought: Writings on Literature, 1893–1945* (Stanford: Stanford University, 1995), 182–189.

26   Benjamin I. Schwartz, *In Search of Wealth and Power: Yen Fu and the West* (Cambridge, MA: Harvard University, 1964), 37.

27   Hilda Laura Norman, 'The Personality of Hippolyte Taine' in *PMLA*, vol. 36, no. 4 (December 1921), 531. Norman is not alone in likening Taine to Voltaire.

Both Taine's and Fou Lei's own *race, milieu, moment* are vastly complex subjects of study, requiring historical efforts that this current analysis does not pretend to make. Speaking in purely abstract terms, the religious tension in Taine's France is not entirely dissimilar to the Confucian structure being shaken in Fou Lei's China, in so far as a conscious but far from clear-cut mental emancipation was involved. For Fou Lei in 1929, however, there appeared to be more a contrast than an analogue. In the preface he wrote: 'The Occidentals have walked from the world of God to the world of man (the Renaissance) and returned to the real present life from the vague afterlife; they have thus expanded the "self" in the "real world" and, rebuffed at the highest point of material culture, are now looking for a new path. We Orientals are still left behind, having not moved one step.'[28]

Implicit in this statement are dichotomies between the religious and the secular, the material and the spiritual, and the Occident and the Orient. Speaking in stark binary terms was commonplace amongst May Fourth authors. In his self-perception as an immobile entity – self-orientalist in effect – Fou Lei was curiously Hegelian. Assuming a certain historical linearity – 'Material culture is not ideal culture, and yet without this step, how can other new paths be found?'[29] – he elaborated it as such: 'Who dare say that the measures of human evolution are not unanimous? Who dare say that the chaos in modern China is not due to a lack of preparation in the revolution of thought? We need to catch up, by night and day, with the battalion of humanity, and bear the same mission as they in finding the truth. At present, we more than anyone are in need of food and tonic for thought. I dare say that the most powerful tonic is scientific spirit; it is positivism!'[30]

These are problematic claims. The rationale is: (1) China is behind the West; (2) this distance is characterised by: (a) retarded material development; (b) a lack of thought preparation, (b) being a cause for (a); (3) humanity is marching as one, and China needs to catch up by following the same course as the West; 4) science is needed to boost (b) in order to amend (a). Underlying it all is a Darwinian anxiety and, indeed, the premises of parallel evolutionism.

---

28 '西洋人從神的世界走到人的世界(文藝復興)，由渺茫的來世回到真實的現世；
     更由此把"自我"在"現世"中極度擴大起來，在物質文明的最高點上，碰了壁又
     在找新路了。我們東方人還是落在後面，一步也沒有移動過。' Fou Lei, 'Translator's Preface to Taine's *Philosophie de l'art*' in *Fou Lei Discusses Art*, 149.

29 '物質文明不是理想的文明，然而不經過這步，又哪能發見其他的新路？' Ibid.

30 '誰敢說人類進化的步驟是不一致的？誰敢說現代中國的紊亂不是由於缺少思想
     革命的準備？我們需要日夜兼程的趕上人類l'humanité的大隊，再和他們負了
     同一的使命去探求真理。在這時候，我們比所有的人更需要思想上的糧食和補
     品，我敢說，這補品中的最有力的一劑便是科學精神，便是實證主義！' Ibid.

It is assumed that China and the West are on the same track with the same final destination. It follows that what is 'missing' in China is a phase resembling the Enlightenment in Europe, and that flawed as it may be, it cannot be bypassed. This leads to Fou Lei's last sentence in the preface: 'Therefore, I still introduce this *Philosophie de l'art* of Taine, hoping that after understanding and knowing how to use this scientific spirit, we will try to remedy its shortcoming!'[31]

Throughout his life, Fou Lei never managed to reconcile cultural relativism and universalism; the constant revision of the two made for the greater part of his endeavour as a translator and as a critic. The assumptions of universality here witnessed in his 1929 writing were to wane from the 1930s onwards. Almost by intuition, and likely not to have been consciously registered as such, Fou Lei's conviction in parallel evolutionism was to quietly give way to historic particularism. As it happens, the systematic and the intuitive are sometimes at odds within him, and a certain intricacy can be detected in his attitude towards science. In keeping with the May Fourth obsession with science and democracy as supreme remedies for China's existential crisis, Fou Lei's advocacy of scientism at this point was not remotely free from being militant. 'Truth' and 'science' were after all watchwords of his time; with vocabularies such as 'revolution', 'battalion' and 'mission', and with repeated formulations such as 'Who dare say' and 'I dare say', his rhetoric assumed an intellectual and even moral hauteur. It is as clear to see how much he had assimilated in a year in Paris, as it is to see how much his pre-occupations were those informed and formed during his years in Shanghai.

When something is taken as a remedy, it is important to ask what the remedy is for. Taine, in 1849, considered science the sole remedy for the general poisoned condition of the nineteenth century, 'the only road along which one can advance without becoming spattered with mud'.[32] Despite expressing scepticism in 1854, he 'clings to science, insisting that there can be found in it a new art, morality, politics and religion and that these should be sought'.[33] In other words, science is a counterpoison and a means to an end. Such a disposition, though in a very different context, bears resemblance to that of Fou Lei. Taine believed his France to have been ill for a century. That China was ill was for Fou Lei's generation, and several generations before him, a given. Keenly aware of the depression of his generation, Taine explained: 'The democracy excited

---

31 　'因此，我還是介紹泰納的這本《藝術論》，我願大家先懂得了，會用了這科學 精神，再來設法補救它的缺陷！' Ibid.

32 　Hilda Laura Norman, 'The Personality of Hippolyte Taine' in *PMLA*, vol. 36, no. 4 (December 1921), 548.

33 　Ibid.

our ambitions without satisfying them; the proclaimed philosophy lighted our curiosity without contenting it.'[34] Every word could have been written to describe Fou Lei's disillusioned contemporaries in early Republican China, and yet 'finding the truth' was what he envisioned the mission of the battalion of humanity to be. Believing 'We will find truth but not calm. All that we can cure at present is our intelligence; we have no hold on our feelings',[35] Taine resigned himself to 'years of rejecting and detesting all parties', and turned to 'science and honour' as a refuge, living in philosophy.[36]

Having no hold on his feelings – one would not have normally associated this with the poised scholar that was Taine.[37] In a speech written for his uncle's centenary, Taine's nephew, André Chevrillon (1864–1957), reflected: 'You recognise, in this young man, a vague and undefined aspiration, purposeless, the *Sehnsucht* of romantic poets and musicians, what Musset named *la maladie du siècle*.'[38] In a penetrating study of Taine's personality, Hilda Norman diagnosed: 'Taine was permeated with the ills of all three stages of the *mal du siècle*. He bears traces of Byronism, of the disillusionment of the Second Empire, and of the despair of the decadents.'[39] Juxtapose words in Taine's early correspondence with those of Fou Lei as a young man, and we find in the translator a kindred spirit of the translated. 'I yawn, I wertherize, I byronize', wrote Taine to his most intimate friend Prévost-Paradol, 'I wish I were at the bottom of the Red Sea.'[40] To Daniélou Fou Lei wrote: 'My true deliverance will be my death. I await it with impatience.'[41] The attraction of Taine for Fou Lei ran infinitely deeper than what we have so far unravelled.

---

34 Ibid., 542.

35 Ibid., 541.

36 Taine's letter to Prévost-Parodol: 'Je me résigne pour de longues années à n'être d'aucun parti, à les détester tous, à souhaiter ardemment l'avènement du seul qu'on puisse suivre, celui de la science et de l'honneur. En attendant je vis dans la philosophie.' Quoted in Jean-Paul Cointet, *Hippolyte Taine: un regard sur la France* (Paris: Perrin, 2012), 40.

37 See descriptions of Taine in Edmond and Jules de Goncourt, *Journal: mémoires de la vie littéraire* (Paris: Fasquelle Flammarion, 1956), vol. 1, 1247 and 1254 (entries of 1 March and 14 March 1863).

38 André Chevrillon, 'Discours pour le centenaire d'Hippolyte Taine' (first version, conserved at Fonds Jacques Doucet).

39 Hilda Laura Norman, 'The Personality of Hippolyte Taine' in *PMLA*, vol. 36, no. 4 (December 1921), 541.

40 Quoted in ibid.

41 'Ma véritable délivrance sera ma mort! Je l'attends avec impatience.' Fou Lei's letter to Daniélou, 8 January 1931; conserved at Archives jésuites de la Province de France.

Many a Taine scholar has detected in this restrained *savant* 'un poète logicien', 'un artiste refoulé' and 'un romantique tourmenté'. Taine himself once said of the historian Michelet: 'M. Michelet est poète, c'est pourquoi il est philosophe.' [Michelet is a poet; that is why he is a philosopher.] Victor Giraud asserts that Taine's poetry dictated his philosophy, and that he invented his doctrines to legitimise his way of seeing the world and his manner of painting it.[42] Giraud may be right. It is with no less poetry that Fou Lei rendered Taine's poetic passages in *Philosophie de l'art*. To write is to see; to think is to see also. How much of our thinking – thinking as realised in writing – is guided by our intuition of the aesthetics of language – of its sound and imagery? To Taine, 'en vérité la tête la plus solide de la France d'aujourd'hui'[43] [in truth the most solid head in France today], Nietzsche, another poet-philosopher, dedicated his *Beyond Good and Evil*.[44]

Chevrillon thus discussed Taine's writing: 'From there one learns above all to write with exactitude, that is to say to think exactly.'[45] This Tainean attribute was in part responsible for a change in Fou Lei's writing around 1930, for the writer he had been translating could not but exert impact on his language, albeit a different one. The most striking aspect of Fou Lei's translator's preface is its style. Each clause develops a clear idea; each idea builds upon the previous one and leads to the next. Inner logic appears to organically structure his sentences, balanced and coherent. There is substance; there is force. It is then and there that, metaphorically speaking, his writing began to resemble his *physique*. Prominent is the bone structure, angular and lean. Fou Lei's vernacular Chinese now appears perfectly classical in the French sense of the word.

There is sometimes danger in writing too well. Taine, with 'his gift for seeing the causes and their association', was interested in 'the truths that concern collectivities'.[46] To his own dismay he enjoyed what Horatio Smith called 'the disastrous success of his generalisations'.[47] Arguably it was the poet-logician's

---

42   Victor Giraud, *Essai sur Taine, son oeuvre et son influence* (Paris: Hachette et Cie., 1902), 162.

43   Emmanuel Le Roy Ladurie, 'Ouverture du colloque' in Michèle Le Pavec et el., *Taine au carrefour des cultures du XIXᵉ siècle* (Paris: Bibliothèque nationale de France, 1996), 17.

44   Jean-Paul Cointet, *Hippolyte Taine*, 8.

45   'On y apprenait surtout à écrire avec exactitudes, c'est-à-dire à penser exactement.' André Chevrillon, 'Discours pour le centenaire d'Hippolyte Taine' (first version, conserved at Fonds Jacques Doucet).

46   '[...] son aptitude à voir les causes et leur liaison'; 'les vérités qui concernent les ensembles'. Ibid.

47   Horatio Smith, 'The Taine Centennial: Comment and Bibliography' in *Modern Language Notes*, vol. 44, no. 7 (November 1929), 437.

generalisations that satisfied Fou Lei's desire to 'embrasser le monde entier, toucher le secret de la vie d'un seul coup'[48] [embrace the whole world, and touch the secret of life at one stroke]. Bearing in mind Victor Giraud's impression that it is Taine's 'tour d'imagination' that explains his 'vues sur l'ensemble et sur le fond des choses',[49] we recall Thomas Goetz's judgement that 'Scientism, the desire for systematic and exact knowledge in all fields of human activity, ran parallel to the Romanticism of mid-nineteenth-century France'[50] and a similar argument from Alan Pitt: 'far from representing a stale scientism, the outlook of French positivism in the 1840s, 1850s and 1860s was deeply coloured by Romanticism.'[51] Amongst Taine's methods there are as many borrowed from the natural sciences, mirrored notably in his superimposition of analogies, often botanical, as there are romantic premises such as seeing art as indigenous to a tradition.[52] As did Ruskin, Taine utilised art criticism as a social critique.

With recurring episodes of cerebral exhaustion in their lives, pessimistic romantics they both were at the age of twenty. At twenty Taine wrote: 'I felt violent and passionate admirations in front of beautiful things and above all in the countryside. I suffered, thinking that I did not know how to use this force and this ardour.'[53] Eight years later, Edouard de Suckau, Taine's friend from École normale supérieure, responded to his dilemma: 'Will you tell me that you are a scholar and not a poet? But you say you want to be one and the other, and you can be if you so wish – like nature, which is at the same time science and poetry, unity and diversity, abstraction and reality. You know Pascal's saying, that to be truly great one must not be only at one or the other extreme, but at both and fill the space in between.'[54] Another six years, and Taine came

---

48   Fou Lei's letter to Daniélou, 5 June 1929.

49   Victor Giraud, *Essai sur Taine, son oeuvre et son influence*, 162.

50   Thomas H. Goetz, *Taine and the Fine Arts*, 35.

51   Alan Pitt, 'The Cultural Impact of Science in France: Ernest Renan and the Vie de Jesus' in *The Historical Journal*, vol. 43, no. 1 (March 2000), 81.

52   Martha Wolfenstein, 'The Social Background of Taine's Philosophy of Art' in *Journal of the History of Ideas*, vol. 5, no. 3 (June 1944), 339–340.

53   'J'éprouvais des admirations violentes et passionnées en face des belles choses et surtout en face de la campagne et je souffrais en songeant que je ne savais comment employer cette force et cette ardeur.' Quoted in Jean-Paul Cointet, *Hippolyte Taine*, 25.

54   Edouard de Suckau's letter to Taine, 6 July 1856: 'Me diras-tu que tu es savant et que tu n'es pas poète? Mais tu dis vouloir être l'un et l'autre, et tu peux l'être si tu le veux – à l'exemple de la nature qui est à la fois science et poésie, unité et diversité, abstraction et réalité. Tu sais le mot de Pascal, que pour être vraiment grand il ne faut pas être seulement à l'une ou l'autre extrémité mais aux deux et remplir l'intervalle.'

to the point: 'I probably wanted to unite two irreconcilable faculties. I must choose: to be an artist or an orator.'[55] Unable, or deciding that he was unable, to realise his artistic force,[56] Taine designated himself an orator.

Fou Lei's writings and correspondence between 1927 and 1931 manifest similarly agitated passions and a thirst for order. We continue to observe, in his early twenties, a tumultuous journey struggling likewise to reconcile the extremes and to choose. Translating Taine at this time, he was little aware of the dialogue he was to continue with the dead Frenchman for more than three decades to come. In uncannily corresponding veins, both Taine and Fou Lei wrestled with an excess of melancholia and applied themselves, with single-minded will, to overcoming this malady. Science for them was more than a remedy. Personal as could be, it was a metaphor, and scholarship a way of life. And if we discern austerity and rigidity in both Taine's and Fou Lei's personalities, we know that lying underneath were forces as vehement as they were demonic.

---

55   Taine's personal notes, 10 October 1862: 'Probablement j'ai voulu allier deux facultés inconciliables. Il faut choisir, être artiste ou orateur.'

56   Taine aborted his only attempt at a novel, titled *Etienne Mayran*. In a letter to Daniélou in autumn 1930, Fou Lei told of his attempt at an autobiographical novel, otherwise unrecorded and which came to no fruition.

CHAPTER 5

Fever: From Werther to Beethoven

When someone young is infected with romantic fervour, a self-prescribed remedy of a metaphysical kind – cold science in this case – is unlikely to be an immediate cure. Neither is enlightenment always followed by *sagesse*. 'I tell you: one must have chaos in one, to give birth to a dancing star. I tell you: you still have chaos in you.'[1] Thus spoke Zarathustra. In his late twenties Taine underwent a prolonged depression. His continued scientism was arguably an intellectual and emotional necessity. At twenty-one Fou Lei translated the first chapter of *Philosophie de l'art*, published it, and abandoned it. He did not go back to translating it in full until twenty-nine years later.

In October 1929, Fou Lei stayed at 20 rue de la Sorbonne, just opposite the main entrance of the University. It was probably a temporary student accommodation, since la Maison de la Jeunesse had closed down. On 29 October, Fou Lei and Daniélou lunched in a Chinese restaurant in the Latin Quarter.[2] When Daniélou headed for Laval on 20 November to join the Jesuits, his *grandes vacances* ended.[3] For Fou Lei they had just begun. Eight months later, in June 1930, from 75 rue de Gergovie he wrote to Daniélou, apologising for the long silence and elucidating at length, in response to his friend's question, why he did not believe in God. He then recounted:

> In this past year, several big events took place in my life. First of all, I am deeply attached to my friend Liu, who is very blasé in his artistic and social life in China. He teaches me, little by little, a kind of *sagesse* through which I finally acquire definitive peace. Then for a while I fell into debauchery, which brought me much material trouble and a nasty disease that I still cannot shake off today. I was worn out physically and morally during the first two months of this year; well, I was relieved thinking: 'This is an adventure that has broadened my experiences and which will serve me in future.' Finally, for two months now I have been consoled by love. I met a young girl who has borne extraordinary suffering for her age (she is only seventeen). But our two hearts harmonise marvellously, and

---

1 Friedrich Nietzsche, *Thus Spoke Zarathustra* (London: Penguin, 2003), 46.
2 A note dated 22 October 1929 from Fou Lei to Daniélou with the invitation to lunch is now conserved at Archives jésuites de la Province de France.
3 'Mes grandes vacances sont terminées.' Jean Daniélou, *Et qui est mon prochain?*, 79.

we fell in love shortly afterwards. There again, my friend Liu intervened to teach me prudence in love. Truth be told, I am at present very happy and heartened. I hope the fevers of my anxious youth[4] cool down more and more and that a laborious period will come so that I can cultivate my mind further.[5]

Fou Lei's frankness surprises. 'Une sale maladie' [a nasty disease] as a result of debauchery – towards the end of 1929 no doubt – is the last thing one would expect of him, and yet it makes sense. He was highly strung. After a summer trying to calm himself down with work, upon returning to Paris he translated the first chapter of *Philosophie de l'art* and prefaced it in a matter of days.[6] Jean-Paul Cointet observes the youth of Taine as one which 'does not live, does not have fun, does not enjoy. For this youth of Taine and of his generation had no youth; it lived in a kind of maceration and of monastic cell, with work, science, analysis, and exuberant reading, thinking of nothing but preparing oneself for the conquest of the society.'[7] Fou Lei's 1928 'Letters from a Voyage to France' attested all these traits. Social, political, and cultural anxieties dominated his

---

4   'Les fièvres de ma jeunesse' [the fevers of my youth] is possibly an evocation of 'la fièvre de Werther' [the Werther fever] which, after the publication of Goethe's *The Sorrows of Young Werther* (1774), swept Germany and Europe more widely.

5   'Depuis un an, plusieurs grands évènements se passent dans ma vie. D'abord, je suis intime-ment lié avec mon ami Liu qui est bien blasé dans sa vie artistique et mondaine en Chine. Il m'enseigne peu à peu une sorte de sagesse par laquelle j'acquis enfin une paix définitive. Ensuite, je suis tombé pendant quelques temps en débauche, ce qui m'apporte beaucoup d'ennuis matériels et une sale maladie que je ne peux pas encore me débarrasser aujourd'hui. J'étais abattu physiquement et moralement durant les deux premiers mois de cette année, enfin je me suis soulagé en me disant : « Voilà une aventure qui enrichit mes expériences et qui me servira dans mon avenir. » Enfin, depuis deux mois je suis encouragé par l'amour. Je fais la connaissance d'une jeune fille qui a supporté des souffrances extraordinaires pour son âge (elle n'a que 17 ans). Mais nos deux âmes s'harmonisent merveilleusement et nous nous éprenons peu de temps après. Ici encore, mon ami Liu intervient pour m'apprendre la prudence dans l'amour. A vrai dire, je suis maintenant très heureux et très encouragé. J'espère que les fièvres de ma jeunesse inquiète s'apaisent de plus en plus et une période laborieuse viendra pour me permettre de me cultiver davantage.' Fou Lei's letter to Daniélou, 7 June 1930; conserved at Archives jésuites de la Province de France.

6   Fou Lei returned from Switzerland to Paris on 20 September 1929. The translation and pref-ace were finished on 11 October 1929.

7   '[…] une jeunesse qui ne vit pas, qui ne s'amuse pas, qui ne jouit pas. Car cette jeunesse de Taine et de sa génération n'a point eu de jeunesse; elle a vécu dans une espèce de macération et de cellule, avec le travail, avec la science, avec l'analyse, avec des débauches de lectures, ne pensant qu'à s'armer pour la conquête de la société.' Jean-Paul Cointet, *Hippolyte Taine*, 48.

discourses with his compatriots. Even with Daniélou he talked most of all 'about my country, our actual state and past glory'.[8]

Romantic longing was the subject of Fou Lei's earliest publication. Now twenty-two years of age, this ardent young man was capable of violent passion. He fell in love. Madeleine was her name.[9] She adored Fou Lei, and called him 'mon petit fou' [my little nutcase]. Liu Haisu later told their story, which now circulates in popular biographies of the painter. Intending to marry Madeleine, Fou Lei wrote a letter to his mother announcing this and declaring that one was free to choose one's own spouse; therefore, he said, his engagement to his cousin Zhu Meifu, arranged by his mother, should be called off. After showing this letter to Liu Haisu and asking him to post it, he rushed out. Some time later, he saw Madeleine being intimate with another man. Furious, and mortified at having broken the hearts of his mother and fiancée, Fou Lei went home and took out a pistol, ready to kill himself. Madeleine ran to Liu Haisu for help. The latter arrived in time to reveal that he had in fact never posted the letter, whilst taking it out of his pocket – this was the intervention to which Fou Lei alluded in his letter to Daniélou. Given Liu Haisu's known tendency for exaggeration, all this could have been deemed semi-fictional if not for the fact that Fou Lei was indeed this intense, this dramatic, this extreme. His suicide attempt à la Werther probably did not see an immediate rupture of this volatile affair. Seven months later, in January 1931, he wrote to Daniélou:

> My situation has become worse and worse. Adding to it again the disillusionment of love: I am totally demoralised. Not only am I embarrassed for want of money, but what is sadder, is that I find myself in an Orient-Occident crisis. I am too Chinese to completely adapt to be European. But on the other hand, I am too Europeanised to live in the old tradition of our nation. At the end of the three years that I have spent in France, I am increasingly aware of this moral conflict. I endure its consequences every day. I lost the love on which I have lived for seven years without too much despair. Now, all is finished. I can neither work nor have fun. I know

---

8 In his letter to Daniélou on 7 June 1930, Fou Lei reminisced on the time they spent together in the old days of la Maison de la Jeunesse.

9 A recent publication of Fou Lei's letters to his friends and family has left untouched previously omitted references and details, including an allusion to Madeleine. In a letter on 6 December 1936, to Liu Kang 劉抗 (1911–2004), a painter and close friend during their shared Parisian years, Fou Lei, already married, confessed a crush he had on a woman, but assured his friend that he loved his wife too much for there to be any danger, adding that he was through with the exigency of his youth, 'thanks to my Madeleine'. See *Fou Lei's Letters to His Friends* 傅雷致友人書信 (Nanjing: Jiangsu wenyi, 2010), 22.

that what I have just told you will cause you anguish, but what can you do about it? I was born a victim of this age.[10]

How it eventually ended with Madeleine, we do not know. Neither do we know why Fou Lei lost his love of seven years, an allusion to his betrothal with Zhu Meifu. In spring 1931, shortly after he wrote this letter, Fou Lei began translating Romain Rolland's (1866–1944) *Vie de Beethoven*.[11] In it, we find the following words:

'My life is much sweeter than before', he wrote to Wegeler, '[...] She loves me, and I love her. These are the first happy moments I have had in two years.' For these moments he paid dearly. In the first place, this love made him more aware of the misery of his infirmity, and of the precarious conditions of his life that made it impossible for him to marry the one he loved. Also, Giulietta was coquettish, childish, selfish; she made Beethoven suffer, and in November 1803 married Count Gallenberg. – Such passions devastate the heart; and when the heart is already weakened by disease, as was Beethoven's, passions are likely to ruin it. It was the only time in his life when he seemed to have been on the brink of succumbing. He went through a desperate crisis, as we know from one of his letters: the Heiligenstadt Testament to his brothers Carl and Johann, with the instruction: 'to be read and executed after my death'. It is a cry of revolt and of harrowing pain. We cannot hear it without being penetrated

---

10   'Ma situation va de pire en pire. S'ajoutant encore la déception de l'amour: je suis complètement abattu. Non seulement je suis gêné à cause de l'argent, mais ce qui est plus triste, c'est que je me trouve dans une crise d'orient-occident. Je suis trop chinois pour m'adapter entièrement en européen. Mais par contre, je suis trop européanisé pour vivre dans la vieil tradition nationale. A la fin de ces 3 ans où je passe en France, je m'aperçois de plus en plus de ce conflit moral. Je subis tout les jours ses conséquences. J'ai perdu l'amour duquel je vis pendant 7 ans sans trop de désespoir. Maintenant, tout est fini. Je ne peux ni travailler ni m'amuser. Je sais que tout ce que je viens de vous dire vous ferait beaucoup de peine, mais que voulez-vous? Je suis né victime de cette époque.' Fou Lei's letter to Daniélou, 8 January 1931; conserved at Archives jésuites de la Province de France.

11   Fou Lei's translation of *Vie de Beethoven* could not find a publisher in 1932, since a Chinese translation already existed. He had a shortened version of it adapted for *International Translation* 國際譯報, a Nanjing-based newspaper where it appeared as an article. Fou Lei's 1942 re-translation of the book was published in 1946, when the rival translation had long been out of print.

with pity. He was very close to ending his life. His inflexible sense of morality alone stopped him.[12]

It might not be too far-fetched to recognise a similar intensity of pathos between the two passions and, indeed, between the two crises. In the same letter to Daniélou, Fou Lei, too, spoke of death. Such desperation was accumulative, and the *chagrins d'amour* were the last straw. He had, in effect, been deprived and torn for over a year. Since 1930, the exchange rate had become excessively expensive for the Chinese. Fou Lei's mother had had to send an allowance twice as much as at the beginning of his sojourn; she wrote and begged him to come home.[13] In autumn 1930, Fou Lei wrote to Daniélou, now from a suburban address: 'Monsieur Liu will return to China in spring 1931. He advises me to leave with him. But I cannot think about the return without shivering. Firstly, what have I learnt during these two and a half years in France? Then, in a country where one knows only massacres and misery, what is the point in going there to torment oneself over them still more?'[14] It is in this light that we recall Daniélou's undisclosed contemplation of a missionary vocation in China sometime between December 1930 and August 1931.[15] His understanding of Fou Lei was possibly the reason for both motivation and caution.

---

12 ' « Je vis d'une façon plus douce, écrit-il à Wegeler, [...] elle m'aime, et je l'aime. Ce sont les premiers moments heureux que j'aie depuis deux ans. » Il les paya durement. D'abord, cet amour lui fit sentir davantage la misère de son infirmité, et les conditions précaires de sa vie, qui lui rendaient impossible d'épouser celle qu'il aimait. Puis, Giulietta était coquette, enfantine, égoïste; elle fit souffrir Beethoven, et en novembre 1803 elle épousa le comte Gallenberg. – De telles passions dévastent l'âme; et quand l'âme est déjà affaiblie par la maladie, comme l'était celle de Beethoven, elles risquent de la ruiner. Ce fut le seul moment de sa vie, où il semble avoir été sur le point de succomber. Il traversa une crise désespérée, qu'une lettre nous fait connaître: le Testament d'Heiligenstadt, à ses frères, Carl et Johann, avec cette indication : « pour lire et exécuter après ma mort ». C'est un cri de révolte et de douleur déchirante. On ne peut l'entendre sans être pénétré de pitié. Il fut tout près de mettre fin à sa vie. Seul son inflexible sentiment moral l'arrêta.' Romain Rolland, *Vie de Beethoven* (Paris: Hachette, 1927), 23–25.

13 Fou Lei's letter to Daniélou, autumn 1930; undated and conserved at Archives jésuites de la Province de France.

14 'Monsieur Liu va rentrer en Chine au printemps 1931. Il me conseille de partir avec lui. Mais je ne peux pas penser à mon retour sans frissonner. D'abord, qu'est-ce que j'ai appris pendant ces deux ans et demi en France? Ensuite, dans ce pays où l'on ne connaît que de massacres et de misère, à quoi bon d'y aller pour s'en tourmenter encore davantage?' Ibid.

15 Coolly he anticipated 'peut-être la mort, peut-être le martyre' [perhaps death, perhaps martyrdom]. Jean Daniélou, 'Election sur la Chine'; conserved at Archives jésuites de la Province de France. See end of chapter 2.

In 1930, Daniélou's brother-in-law Georges Izard had his first book *A la source de la pensée religieuse de Péguy* in print. He encouraged Fou Lei to write a book in French.[16] Despite sober misgivings about his own abilities – 'only I am so young, my art is not cultivated enough, my spirit only in a pell-mell state, and my tools, my French, are too lame...'[17]– Fou Lei started working on an autobiographical novel. 'I do not know if I will succeed. I am so very unsure of myself.'[18] With his own uncertainty he went on to find fault: 'What is terrible in me, is that not only do I lack faith in religion, humanity, and all that other people believe to be true and certain, but I doubt my own personality, my existence itself.'[19] Fou Lei's scepticism was consistent, and his self-deprecation as pronounced as his pride. By 1931, Izard had been trying to find him jobs that would keep him in France, but nothing seemed to have materialised.[20] Disheartened, Fou Lei pondered, now in January 1931, his imminent return to China. 'And what life must I lead there?!' he cried out, 'It will be a relentless fight, a permanent struggle. And I am too hard to even slightly bow to the absurdity of society, above all in a society like ours!'[21] Total pessimism. 'Life disgusts me,' said he, 'but I cannot leave it, this is the tragedy. [...] My true deliverance will be my death! I await it with impatience.'[22]

Claustrophobia devours these words. Dread verges on hysteria. Fou Lei's morale reached its bottom. The very difference one observes between the letters in 1929 and those in 1930 and early 1931 to Daniélou is that his profound

---

16   Fou Lei's letter to Daniélou, 7 June 1930: 'Izard me dit que si je pouvais écrire un livre en français, un roman, par exemple, il m'aiderait à publier.' [Izard says if I could write a book in French, a novel for example, he would help me publish it.]

17   '[...] seulement je suis si jeune, mon art n'est pas encore assez cultivé, mon esprit n'est que dans un état pêle-mêle, et mes outils, mon français, sont trop impuissants...' Ibid.

18   'Je ne sais pas si je réussirai. Je suis tellement peu sûr de moi-même.' Ibid.

19   'Ce qu'il y a de terrible chez moi, c'est que non seulement je manque de foi en religion, en humanité, en tout ce que les autres croient vrai et sûr, je doute de ma propre personnalité, de mon existence même.' Ibid.

20   Fou Lei's letter to Daniélou, 8 January 1931: 'Izard tâche toujours de me trouver quelques choses, mais c'est très difficile.' [Izard is trying to find me something, but it is very difficult.] At the bottom of this letter he wrote: 'Excusez-moi si cette lettre vous parviendra bien tard, parce que je l'ai écrite, mais j'attends qu'on me passe un timbre pour l'envoyer.' [Forgive me if this letter reaches you very late, for I have written it, but am waiting for someone to give me a stamp.]

21   'Et quelle vie je dois mener là-bas?! Ce sera un combat acharné, une lutte permanente. Et, je suis trop dur pour me soumettre un peu à l'absurdité de la société, surtout dans une société comme la nôtre!' Ibid.

22   'La vie me dégoûte, mais je ne peux pas la quitter, voilà la tragédie. [...] Ma véritable délivrance sera ma mort! Je l'attends avec impatience.' Ibid.; see chapter 4, note 41.

but nameless ennui had transformed into concrete misery. 1930 for Fou Lei as opposed to 1929 for Fou Lei was essentially a question of pitiless inexorable suffering as opposed to that induced largely by acute hypersensitivity.[23] He had read Romain Rolland's *Vie de Beethoven* before; but at no point had it addressed him with so direct a force, when illness and impoverishment became a matter of life and death, and life a veritable question of existence. What was at stake was how to live, and live meaningfully and with dignity, when dying was not an option. It was at this point exactly that Fou Lei reread and translated the following:

> Life is difficult. For those who do not resign themselves to the mediocrity of soul, it is an everyday combat, a sad combat most of the time, without grandeur, without pleasure, a combat carried in silence and in solitude. Oppressed by poverty, by tiresome domestic worry, by crippling and stupid tasks, through all of which strength uselessly goes to waste, without hope, without a gleam of joy, most of them are separated from one another; they do not even have the consolation of being able to give a hand to their brothers in misfortune, who do not know them, and whom they do not know. They must count only on themselves; there are times when the strongest of them crumple under their pain. They call for help, for a friend.[24]

Such are the words from Rolland's preface to his *Vie de Beethoven*, first published in 1903 and reprinted in 1927 at the centenary of the composer's death.[25]

---

23   Peculiarly, the absence of the other half of the correspondence, namely letters from Daniélou to Fou Lei that have not survived history, does not create in the reader a sense of want. Pre-occupied with matters of the heart, Fou Lei's letters to Daniélou between 1929 and 1931, all of which confessions in one form or another, read like condensed echoes of Werther's monologic letters to Wilhelm.

24   'La vie est dure. Elle est un combat de chaque jour pour ceux qui ne se résignent pas à la médiocrité de l'âme, un triste combat le plus souvent, sans grandeur, sans bonheur, livré dans la solitude et le silence. Oppressés par la pauvreté, par les âpres soucis domestiques, par les tâches écrasantes et stupides, où les forces se perdent inutilement, sans espoir, sans un rayon de joie, la plupart sont séparés les uns des autres, et n'ont même pas la consolation de pouvoir donner la main à leurs frères dans le malheur, qui les ignorent, et qu'ils ignorent. Ils ne doivent compter que sur eux-mêmes; et il y a des moments où les plus forts fléchissent sous leur peine. Ils appellent un secours, un ami.' Romain Rolland, original preface (1903) to *Vie de Beethoven*, viii.

25   The purpose of the above and following citations is three-fold: First, to demonstrate in the raw the intensity of Rolland's two short prefaces to a slim biography; second, to present the density with which Fou Lei wrote his translator's preface, its terse message now

The preface is a manifesto of Rollandian heroism. Seeing that 'Old Europe has become numb in a vitiated and heavy atmosphere. Petty materialism weighs on the mind; it hinders the action of governments and individuals. The world is dying of asphyxia in its chary and vile egoism. People gasp for air',[26] Rolland beseeched: 'Let us reopen the windows! Let us get some fresh air again! Let us breathe the breath of heroes.'[27] What Rolland called heroes were not those who triumphed by thoughts or by force, but those who had generous hearts, and the ones he chose to make subjects of his *Vies des hommes illustres* are those whose life was almost always a long martyrdom, and who were great as much by their vigour as through their misfortune.[28] And Beethoven, the 'strong and pure' Beethoven, is 'in the forefront of this heroic legion'[29] – 'the greatest and the best friend of those who suffer and who fight'.[30]

The romantic myth of the suffering artist continued, the creative genius is here marked by moral superiority in opposition to the banality of the society. What Taine had failed to tackle, or shunned tackling, namely 'the other, mysterious half'[31] of art, the inner force of the artist, is here treated with undivided attention. Here suffering assumes a positive value in this mysterious force,[32] justified transcendentally and by an ascetic ideal. In 1946, Fou Lei's translation of *Vie de Beethoven* was published.[33] With gravity he opened the translator's preface:

---

making sense in light of biographical details revealed in his letters to Daniélou; third, to observe parallels between the two.

26   'La vieille Europe s'engourdit dans une atmosphère pesante et viciée. Un matérialisme sans grandeur pèse sur la pensée; il entrave l'action des gouvernements et des individus. Le monde meurt d'asphyxie dans son égoisme prudent et vil. Le monde étouffe.' Romain Rolland, *Vie de Beethoven*, vii.

27   'Rouvrons les fenêtres! Faisons rentrer l'air libre! Respirons le souffle des héros.' Ibid., vii–viii.

28   Ibid., ix–x.

29   'En tête de cette légion héroïque, je donne la première place au fort et pur Beethoven.' Ibid., xi.

30   'Il est le plus grand et le meilleur ami de ceux qui souffrent et qui luttent.' Ibid., 91.

31   Fou Lei's formulation; see chapter 4, note 11.

32   'Je sais que la douleur est la noblesse unique' [I know that suffering is the sole nobility], as Baudelaire would say. See 'Bénédiction I' in *Les fleurs du mal* (1857).

33   Footnote to the translator's preface: '注：這部書的初譯稿，成於一九三二年，在存稿堆下埋藏了有幾十年之久——出版界堅持本書已有譯本，不願接受。但已出版的譯本絕版已久，我始終未曾見到。然而我深深地感謝這件在當時使我失望的事故，使我現在能全部重譯，把少年時代幼稚的翻譯習作一筆勾消。' [The original translation of this book was completed in 1932 and has been buried under shelved drafts for a decade – the publishers insisted that a translation already existed and

Only genuine suffering can drive out the suffering of romantic illusion; only by beholding heroic tragedies of surmounting ordeals can we endure cruel destiny; only by upholding the spirit of 'If I do not go to hell, who shall?' can a withered and selfish nation be saved: this was the lesson I learnt upon first reading this book fifteen years ago.[34]

We have, divided by two semicolons, three crescendo layers to unravel, and each of these interrelated notions to untangle: suffering, heroism, tragedy, and salvation. Berlin, in plain language, expressed the core inspiration of Beethoven in the Romantic age: 'But he has not sold out. He sits in his garret and he creates. He creates in accordance with the light which is within him, and that is all that a man should do; that is what makes a man a hero.'[35] Through negation Fou Lei summed up Beethovenian heroism:

To yield without having battled is false; to keep aloof without having gone through catastrophes and trials is frivolous; sagacity which escapes reality is low and cowardly; moderation, insouciance, petty wisdom, these are our fatal defects: such is my belief which has strengthened daily in the past fifteen years. And all this comes from the revelation of Beethoven.[36]

Witnessing Beethovenian robustness shook Fou Lei out of his despondency. Fortified, he resolved to look life squarely in the face. 'I dared not keep this revelation to myself,' said he, 'so I translated this book ten years ago.'[37] Writing to Romain Rolland on 3 March 1934,[38] Fou Lei recalled this revelation as almost

---

were unwilling to accept mine. But the existing version has long been out of print; I still have not seen it. Nevertheless, I am deeply grateful for this incident which disappointed me at the time, for now I am able to completely re-translate it, and write off the childish exercise of my youth.] *Complete Works*, vol. 11, 5.

34 '唯有真實的苦難，才能驅除浪漫底克的幻想的苦難；唯有看到克服苦難的壯烈的悲劇，才能幫助我們擔受殘酷的命運；唯有抱着"我不入地獄誰入地獄"的精神，才能挽救一個萎靡而自私的民族：這是我十五年前初次讀到本書時的教訓。' Fou Lei, 'Translator's Preface to Rolland's *Vie de Beethoven*' in ibid.

35 Isaiah Berlin, *Roots of Romanticism*, 13.

36 '不經過戰鬥的捨棄是虛偽的，不經劫難磨煉的超脫是輕佻的，逃避現實的明哲是卑怯的；中庸，苟且，小智小慧，是我們的致命傷：這是我十五年來與日俱增的信念。而這一切都由於貝多芬的啓示。' Fou Lei, 'Translator's Preface to Rolland's *Vie de Beethoven*' in *Complete Works*, vol. 11, 5.

37 '我不敢把這樣的啓示自秘，所以十年前就迻譯了本書。' Ibid.

38 Fou Lei had then translated all three of Rolland's *Vies des hommes illustres* – the other two being *Vie de Michel-Ange* and *Vie de Tolstoï* – and asked for the author's consent to their publication in China.

a religious experience: 'By chance I read your *Vie de Beethoven*. I cried like a baby. A divine light bathed me as I suddenly gained the strength for rebirth. From then on I exerted myself miraculously.'[39] 'Do not Books', said Carlyle, 'still accomplish *miracles*, as *Runes* were fabled to do? They persuade men... It is the strangest of things, yet nothing is truer.'[40] Rendering *Vie de Beethoven* into Chinese, far from being a mere act of translating, was for Fou Lei the temporal extension of a spiritual event, a lasting tribute taking physical shape.

A profound sense of indebtedness was hardly alien to Rolland. In 1927 he said: 'When I wrote – a quarter of a century ago – my little *Vie de Beethoven*, I did not think of producing a work of musicology. It was 1902.[41] I was going through a turbulent period rich in thunderstorms that both destroy and renew.'[42] Fleeing Paris, he went on a pilgrimage to Bonn, Beethoven's hometown. By the Rhine, 'kneeling down, I was helped up by his strong hand which baptised my little newborn baby Jean-Christophe;[43] blessed and comforted, I made my way back to Paris, having signed a new lease with life and singing a *Dankgesang*[44] [an act of thanksgiving] of a convalescent to the gods. – This *Dankgesang* was here, in these pages.'[45]

---

39   '偶讀尊作《貝多芬傳》，讀罷不禁嚎啕大哭，如受神光燭照，頓獲新生之力，自此奇蹟般突然振作。' Translated from the French by Luo Xinzhang in *Fou Lei's Letters to His Friends*, 5.

40   Thomas Carlyle, *Heroes and Hero-worship: extraits* (Paris: Hachette, 1925), 137.

41   Rolland's first marriage ended in 1901. Forty years later, he described the years 1901–02 as when '... se produisit une rupture dans ma vie sociale, qui dut totalement se réorganiser dans la pauvreté et l'isolement.' [... a rupture occurred in my social life, which had to totally reorganise itself in poverty and isolation.] Romain Rolland, *Mémoires* (Paris: Albin Michel, 1956), 309.

42   'Au temps où j'écrivais, – il y a un quart de siècle, – ma petite *Vie de Beethoven*, je ne songeais pas à faire oeuvre de musicologie. C'était en 1902. Je traversais une période toumentée, riche en orages qui détruisent et qui renouvellent.' Romain Rolland, *Vie de Beethoven*, i.

43   Rolland went on to write *Jean-Christophe* between 1904 and 1912. *Vie de Beethoven* was regarded by him and critics alike as a prelude to the ten-volume epic novel, its protagonist being an idealistic German musician. *Jean-Christophe* won Rolland the Nobel Prize in 1915; Fou Lei later translated the novel – twice – to perfection.

44   A reference to Beethoven's *Heiliger Dankgesang*, 'the song of holy thanks for recovering health', String Quartet op. 132 in A minor, movement III.

45   '[...] agenouillé, relevé par sa forte main, qui baptisa mon petit nouveau-né, l'enfant Jean-Christophe, sous le signe de sa bénédiction, je repris le chemin de Paris, réconforté, ayant signé un nouveau bail avec la vie, et chantant un *Dankgesang* [une action de grâces] du convalescent à la Divinité. – Ce *Dankgesang*, ce furent les pages que voici.' Romain Rolland, *Vie de Beethoven*, ii.

Religious vocabulary aside, the coupled theme of malady and remedy is once again present. So is the motif of gratitude. In his 1942 preface, after revealing several of his intentions as the translator, Fou Lei added:

> Besides, I have personal reasons. Healing my youthful *mal du siècle* was Beethoven; fostering my will to fight in life was Beethoven; impressing me immensely in my intellectual growth was Beethoven. Numerous have been the times when he braced me during my lapses; numerous have been the times when he solaced my woes – not to mention his collateral blessing of leading me into the kingdom of music.[46]

This is the language of love. 'I am an historian', wrote Rolland,

> But *Beethoven* was not written for science. It was a song for the wounded, suffocated heart who takes breath again, and who gets back up to thank his Saviour. I know well that I have transfigured this Saviour, but all acts of faith and love are like this. And my *Beethoven* was one such act.[47]

Reading these words – Fou Lei's and Rolland's – one hears a contrapuntal duet. And the *Dankgesang* goes on. Rolland was convinced that this experience, this sentiment, this power that Beethoven had over the human soul, were universal. 'When we are saddened by the suffering of the world, he comes to us, as if sitting at the piano next to a mother in mourning and, without saying a word, consoles her as she cries, with the song of his resigned protestation.'[48] Consoled by the song of grievance, Fou Lei was likewise convinced when he said, 'Other than passing on this blessing to the generation younger than I, I know

---

46   '此外，我還有個人的理由。療治我青年時世紀病的是貝多芬，扶植我在人生
       中的戰鬥意志的是貝多芬，在我靈智的成長中給我大影響的是貝多芬，多少次
       的顛撲曾由他攙扶，多少的創傷曾由他撫慰——且不說引我進音樂王國的這件
       次要的恩澤。' Fou Lei, 'Translator's Preface to Rolland's *Vie de Beethoven*' in *Complete
       Works*, vol. 11, 7.

47   'Je suis historien [...] Mais le *Beethoven* ne fut point écrit pour la science. Il fut un chant
       de l'âme blessée, de l'âme étouffée, qui reprend souffle, qui se relève et qui remercie son
       Sauveur. Je sais bien que ce Sauveur, je l'ai transfiguré. Mais il en est ainsi de tous les actes
       de foi et d'amour. Et mon *Beethoven* fut cet acte.' Romain Rolland, *Vie de Beethoven*, iii.

48   'Quand nous sommes attristés par les misères du monde, il est celui qui vient auprès de
       nous, comme il venait s'asseoir au piano d'une mère en deuil, et, sans une parole, conso-
       lait celle qui pleurait, au chant de sa plainte résignée.' Ibid., 91.

of no other way of repaying the debt that I owe to Beethoven and to his great biographer Romain Rolland. The best way to express gratitude, is to give.'[49]

It is an historically and conceptually valid, albeit somewhat disorienting, question to ask as to how Rolland's Beethovenian heroism became in Fou Lei's case a perceived and tested remedy for *mal du siècle*; was it romanticism corrected, continued, or mutated?[50] Were we to see remedy working as a chemical reaction, and the author's words as a prescription so to speak, more than often written as a therapeutic practice, we would need to examine the said author's own constitution as well as that of the reader. Leafing through Rolland's journal published with his own annotations in 1939, what one witnesses is a rich, tormented internal journey taken by the pacifist and moralist playwright, essayist, novelist, musicologist, and art historian in his student days.

Rolland began as a Hamlet incarné: 'Yes, the fatalist is a sick man. Hamlet is a sick man, and I am a sick man.'[51] Afflicted by a violence of feeling held back in his nature, his 'body and soul are on fire; all the exits are blocked. [...] Such an effort provoked a dangerous cerebral tension [...] (above all in 1888: I was twenty-two). – I was not the only one to suffer these attacks.'[52] He was not. Before him there was Taine. After him there was Fou Lei. At twenty-two, Rolland, too, withered. 'I lost my time and strength wanting to reconcile the irreconcilable', he recalled, 'and from these inner combats, these defeats, my health was critically weakened. Towards the end of 1899, I was a nervous wreck:

---

49   '除了把我所受的恩澤轉贈給比我年輕的一代之外，我不知還有什麼方法可以償
      還我對貝多芬，和對他偉大的傳記家羅曼羅蘭所負的債務。表示感激的最好的
      方式，是施予。' Fou Lei, 'Translator's Preface to Rolland's *Vie de Beethoven*' in *Complete
      Works*, vol. 11, 5.

50   Without revisiting the definition of Romanticism (see chapter 3), it is worth recalling An-
      dré Malraux's remark that Romain Rolland was 'le dernier des grands romantiques fran-
      çais' [the last of the great French Romantics] and investigating where Rollandian heroism
      stood in relation to Romanticism. See note 96 in this chapter.

51   'Oui, le fataliste est un malade. Hamlet est un malade, et je suis un malade', Romain Rol-
      land, *Mémoires*, 29. Rolland's own annotation reads: 'Mon ami et mon frère: – Hamlet. Je
      l'ai lu et relu, en ces années 1885–1886, comme mon propre bréviaire et je lui ai consacré
      un cahier entier de dialogues avec lui, de commentaires serrés, précis et passionnés.' [My
      friend and my brother: – Hamlet. I read and reread him, in the years 1885–1886, like my
      own breviary, and I dedicated to him an entire notebook of dialogues with him, and of
      close, precise and passionate commentaries.].

52   'Le corps et l'âme sont en feu; et toutes les issues sont bloquées. [...] Un tel travail provo-
      quait une dangereuse tension cérébrale, dont les crises, qui ne s'avouaient pas, mirent à
      l'épreuve ma santé, pendant les deuxième et troisième années d'École – (surtout pendant
      l'année 88: j'avais alors vingt-deux ans). – Je n'étais pas le seul à subir ces assauts.' Ibid., 54.

insomnia ate me away; my heart, head, intestines, my whole body hurt. I felt destroyed from all quarters. I wanted to be dead. I have sad notes from this time.'[53] Rereading his own journal entries between 1886 and 1889 – years he spent at École normale supérieure – Rolland, aged seventy-three, confessed: 'I look away, with irritated pity.'[54]

To what extent can internal crisis project itself onto external reality, in such a way that social salvation becomes an extension of personal salvation? During the Dreyfus affair (1894–1906), Rolland, like his divided country, was torn.[55] 'At that time, millions of individuals in France, a generation of oppressed idealists, waited anxiously for a liberating message. They found it in the music of Beethoven, and they came to implore him.'[56] Rollandian heroism, in the context of poignantly borne political uncertainties, served as a social critique,[57] as had Tainean historicism in a different context thirty years previously.[58] In 1942, from a Shanghai invaded and occupied by the Japanese, Fou Lei wrote: 'Haze has now covered the entire sky. More than at any other time we are in need of moral support; more than at any other time we are in need of heroism[59]

---

53   'Je perdais mon temps et mes forces à vouloir concilier l'inconciliable. Et de ces combats intérieurs, de ces défaites, ma santé fut gravement ébranlée. Vers la fin de 1899, ma résistance nerveuse fut à bout: les insomnies me rongeaient; le cœur, la tête, les intestins, le corps entier me faisaient souffrir. Je me sentais détruit, de toutes parts. J'aurais voulu être mort. J'ai de tristes notes, de ce temps.' (Ibid.) Cerebral exhaustion coupled with deteriorating physical health was likewise experienced by Fou Lei and Taine.

54   '[...] je m'en détourne, avec une pitié irritée.' Ibid., 53.

55   Rolland's family belonged to a typical state-serving bourgeois setting. His wife was Jewish. His father-in-law, a professor of philology at the Sorbonne and friends with Renan, wanted Rolland to take a stance; he did not. In his *Mémoires* Rolland recounted this period of acute conflicts.

56   Romain Rolland, *Vie de Beethoven*, iv.

57   Rolland's social and political concerns were manifested in the historical plays he wrote in the late 1890s and early 1900s.

58   Taine reacted to the aftermath of the Franco-Prussian War by commencing his *Origines de la France contemporaine*, which set out to question how his country had come to where it came to.

59   Fou Lei's formulation 大勇主義 (literally: 'great-courage-ism') is decidedly different from 英雄主義 (the usual translation of 'heroism'). It alludes to the proposition of 'great courage' 大勇 as opposed to 'petty courage' 小勇 in *Mencius* (孟子 梁惠王下; also D.C. Lau (tr.) *Mencius*, 62–63) and incorporates the translator's discussion with Rolland on Gandhi's nonviolent resistance in their 1934 correspondence, wherein Rolland stressed the spiritual, rather than physical, force of what true 'heroism' encompassed. The alluded *Mencius* passage happens to be that from which Fou Lei's courtesy name Nou-En originates.

that perseveres, contends, and dares challenge the gods.'[60] Fou Lei here coined 大勇主義[61] to mean the kind of heroism that resorts to moral, as opposed to physical, courage, whilst giving accent to the Confucian strand in his thinking by placing, on the first page of his published translation of *Vie de Beethoven*, a quote from *Mencius*: 'So it is that whenever Heaven invests a person with great responsibilities, it first tries his resolve, exhausts his muscles and bones, starves his body, leaves him destitute, and confounds his every endeavour. In this way his patience and endurance are developed, and his weakness are overcome.'[62]

Archaic moral principles were not the only bridge Fou Lei constructed between Rollandian heroism and his readers. Rolland spoke of faith and of Saviour; Fou Lei proposed 'If I do not go to hell, who shall?' – an allegedly sinicised self-sacrificing Buddhist doctrine – as the spirit needed for national salvation, one of the two missions of the May Fourth generation.[63] Both the author and the translator were resolute atheists. That Fou Lei felt free to employ, in a Chinese context, religious language in his own preface, demonstrates a facility for corresponding linguistically and spiritually to another writer in a different language. Such compatibility goes far beyond fidelity; it is quite literally re-creation and, shall we say, reincarnation. It also points to the murkiness that surrounds our notion of religion and its language, metaphorical by nature. At seventeen Rolland went through a spiritual crisis, and music took the place of Catholicism.[64] What he called 'faith' ever since had been a different faith. Having confessed to Daniélou that he 'lacked faith in religion, humanity and all that other people believe to be true and certain',[65] Fou Lei eventually found faith akin to that of a religious nature: his devotion to art. When this monstrously meticulous, impeccably precise translator rendered the words of Beethoven quoted in Rolland's biography – 'Sacrifice, always sacrifice the

---

60 '現在陰霾遮蔽了整個天空，我們比任何時都更需要精神的支持，比任何時都更需要堅忍、奮鬥、敢於向神明挑戰的大勇主義。' Fou Lei, 'Translator's Preface to Rolland's *Vie de Beethoven*' in *Complete Works*, vol. 11, 5.

61 See note 59 in this chapter.

62 Translation by David Hinton, *Mencius* (Berkeley: Counterpoint, 2015), 165. '……故天將降大任於斯人也，必先苦其心志，勞其筋骨，餓其體膚，空乏其身，行拂亂其所為，所以動心忍性，曾益其所不能。' *Mencius* 孟子 告子下.

63 啓蒙 [enlightenment] and 救國 [national salvation] being the proposed missions of the May Fourth intellectuals, it has often been argued that since, or even before the beginning of the Sino-Japanese War, 'enlightenment' had gradually given way to 'national salvation'.

64 'L'illumination musicale se fit en 1883. Elle fut étroitement mêlée à la crise religieuse.' Romain Rolland, *Mémoires*, 26.

65 Fou Lei's letter to Daniélou, 7 June 1930.

trivialities of life for your art! God above all!'[66] – he manipulated 'God above all!' into 'Art, that is the God above all!',[67] substituting God with Art.

In this mistaken manipulation, due principally to Rolland's ambiguous quoting in French and out of the translator's impulse to be exact, we witness, in effect, an altogether fitting accident revealing Fou Lei's own conviction.[68] For Fou Lei was an artist. His sensitivity, temperament, tastes, were all those of an artist. Having once referred to his writing as 'mon art',[69] throughout

---

66   'Sacrifie, sacrifie toujours les niaiseries de la vie à ton art! Dieu par-dessus tout! (O Gott über alles!)' Romain Rolland, *Vie de Beethoven*, 81.

67   '犧牲，永遠把一切人生的愚昧為你的藝術去犧牲！藝術，這是高於一切的上帝！' Fou Lei, 'Translator's Preface to Rolland's *Vie de Beethoven*' in *Complete Works*, vol. 11, 40.

68   Whereas the German original has 'O God above all!' as the second part of a sentence, following a comma, Rolland's French translation – 'Sacrifie, sacrifie toujours les niaiseries de la vie à ton art! Dieu par-dessus tout! (O Gott über alles!)' – replaces the comma with an exclamation mark and omits 'O' before 'God'. Exclamation marks in French do not necessarily break a sentence; here 'God above all' could well appear as a description of 'ton art'. The added German original of this phrase in parentheses, nevertheless, gives the impression that it is a separate clause. An independent sentence stating 'God above all' in Chinese would be both incomprehensible and hopelessly unfluent. The instinct of an adept translator would be to add something for it to make sense. Fou Lei had no way of investigating the original German quotation, for not only had Rolland not elucidated its historical context – which, as we recall, is not the trained historian's intention in this book – it is also abrupt, if not arbitrary. The quote was thrown in, undated and unreferenced, to end a chapter where he had just recounted Beethoven's illness in 1824–25 and the triumph of his Ninth Symphony in 1825. Musicologically speaking, one may not find this particular order of narration and use of quotation rigorous. It so happens that this sentence comes from Beethoven's diary dated 1818, at a time when he was writing his *Missa solemnis*. The full entry reads: 'Opfere noch einmal alle Kleinigkeiten des gesellschaftlichen Lebens deiner Kunst, o Gott über alles! denn die [dessen] ewige Vorsicht lenkt allwissend das Glück oder [und] Unglück sterblicher Menschen. [Sacrifice once and for all the trivialities of social life to your art, O God above all! For eternal Providence in its omniscience and wisdom directs the happiness and unhappiness of mortal men.]' – Quotation and translation in Maynard Solomon (ed.), *Beethoven's Tagebuch, 1812–1818* (Bonn: Beethoven-Haus, 2005), 284. The original German text makes it grammatically apparent that God here does not refer to art. The second sentence of this entry, a citation from *The Odyssey*, Book XX, lines 75–76, makes the assumed link with *Missa solemnis* still more convincing: Beethoven was doing his research. The pronounced religious framework of this entry is also confirmed by the previous entry in the diary, where Beethoven intended to go through all the Gregorian chants 'in order to write true church music'. Beethoven was of course thinking of his art, but the God he spoke of was quite God Himself as opposed to a metaphorical one that Fou Lei ended up suggesting.

69   See Fou Lei's letter to Daniélou, 7 June 1930.

his life Fou Lei placed ultimate importance on the proud and humbling word 工作 [work]. It meant, to him, being at the desk day after day, year after year, producing volume after volume with his pen. If one finds, in Fou Lei's shortened translation of *Vie de Beethoven* adapted for the newspaper in 1934, words at times too strong, expressions too pressing, and turns of phrases clumsy or stiff, he was not doing the author a grave injustice, for irregularity does every now and then feature in Rolland's otherwise fluid writing, and unselfconscious youthful outpouring was what dominated this little book to begin with. Yet, in his 1942 translation, one watches an enthusiastic rhapsody turn into pure elegance. Careful shifting of order can be observed within nearly every sentence. For instance:

> Mais ses intimes, seuls, connaissent l'exquise bonté qu'il cache sous cette gaucherie orgueilleuse.[70]
> [But his close friends alone know the exquisite goodness that he hides underneath this proud awkwardness.]
> 唯有和他親密的人，才能認識他在這種驕傲的愚拙之下，隱藏著無窮的仁慈。[71] (1934)
> [Only those who are close to him recognise that, underneath this proud awkwardness, hides infinite benevolence.]
> 但他藏在這驕傲的笨拙之下的慈悲，唯有幾個親密的朋友知道。[72] (1942)
> [But his compassion which is hidden underneath this proud awkwardness, only a few close friends know.]

It is but in comparison with the 1942 version that the 1934 rendition, perfectly accurate and polished, nearly resembles a translator's first draft. Chinese does not lend itself so readily to multiple clauses as does French. Making 'his compassion' the subject of the sentence and taking it forward enhances the overall limpidity. The number of clauses having thence been reduced from three to two, the adjectives are simplified too. After two '的's – 驕傲的 [proud] and 笨拙之下的 [underneath the awkwardness] – 'infinite benevolence' 無窮的仁慈 would have added another 的, giving the sentence too much of a mouthful to chew through. A noun, single, strong, and without adjective, is called upon to replace 'infinite benevolence': compassion 慈悲.

---

70   Romain Rolland, *Vie de Beethoven*, 15.

71   Fou Lei, *Complete Works*, vol. 11, 73.

72   Ibid., 19.

Wegeler dit qu'il ne connut jamais Beethoven sans une passion portée au paroxysme.[73]

[Wegeler says he never knew Beethoven without a passion taken to paroxysm.]

韋葛萊說他從沒看到貝多芬不把一種熱情推之極端的。[74] (1934)

[Wegeler says he never sees Beethoven not pushing a passion to its extreme.]

韋格勒說他從沒見過貝多芬不抱著一股劇烈的熱情。[75] (1942)

[Wegeler says he never sees Beethoven without acute passion.]

Literal translation of what is essentially a foreign expression, 'portée au paroxysme', gives way to an idiomatic choice of adjective, 'acute' 劇烈的. With fewer words describing what Beethoven does with his passion, the effect in Chinese is more direct, more intense.

C'est dans ces alternatives d'amour et de révolte orgueilleuse, qu'il faut chercher la source la plus féconde des inspirations de Beethoven.[76]

[It is in these alternatives between love and proud revolts that we must look for the source of Beethoven's most fertile inspirations.]

貝多芬靈感中最豐富的泉源便應當在這些愛的轉換和驕傲的反抗中探求。[77] (1934)

[The fountain of Beethoven's most overflowing inspiration need be sought amidst these shifts in love and proud revolts.]

貝多芬最豐滿的靈感，就當在這種時而熱愛、時而驕傲地反抗的輪迴中去探尋根源。[78] (1942)

[The root of Beethoven's most exuberant inspiration need be explored in the eternal return, now passionately loving, now proudly revolting.]

If, in 1934, Fou Lei did not quite grasp the structure of 'ces alternatives d'amour et de révolte orgueilleuse' [these alternatives between love and proud revolts] in his ambivalent 'shifts in love and proud revolts' 愛的轉換和驕傲的反抗, his 1942 arrangement 'the eternal return, now passionately loving, now proudly

---

73   Romain Rolland, *Vie de Beethoven*, 21.

74   Fou Lei, *Complete Works*, vol. 11, 75.

75   Ibid., 21.

76   Romain Rolland, *Vie de Beethoven*, 23.

77   Fou Lei, *Complete Works*, vol. 11, 75.

78   Ibid., 21.

revolting' 時而熱愛、時而驕傲地反抗的輪迴 is not only a grammatical amelioration, but an ingenious solution to a strenuous linguistic problem betraying a poetic urge. The added comma, moreover, introduces rhythm into his sentence, now architecturally balanced.

The differences between Fou Lei's 1934 and 1942 translations are considerable. The breathing has changed. The sharp edges are smoothed out. The flow from one sentence to the next is more even. The means are subtler, and the colours richer. Passion is all the more affecting with composure. Fou Lei effectively turned Rolland into a more classical writer, with tools utterly modern: what had changed was his own language.

> Il avait été frappé au coeur, et, jusqu'au jour de sa mort, il vécut sous l'impression de cette terrible scène.[79]
>
> [He was heart-stricken and, till the day of his death, he lived under the impression of this terrible scene.]
>
> 這個打擊使他心坎裏受了傷,直到他死的那天,他的生活中永遠充滿著這可怕的一幕的憧憬。[80] (1934)
>
> [This blow wounded his heart; until the day he died, his life was always filled with longings of this terrible scene.]
>
> 他心坎裏受了傷,至死不曾忘記這可怕的一幕的印象。[81] (1942)
>
> [His heart wounded, till death he never forgot the impression of this terrible scene.]

His sentence now half the length, Fou Lei chopped off all that was superfluous, grammatically and syntactically. Adding 'This blow' 這個打擊 and 'his life' 他的生活 in 1934 had been a clumsy attempt to make sense of the typically French expressions 'frapper au coeur' and 'vivre sous l'impression'; taking them out was the right decision, and the substituting constructions – 'heart wounded' and 'never forgot the impression' – are as becoming as they are accurate. Whilst 直到他死的那天 [until the day he died] is a transcription of 'jusqu'au jour de sa mort', 至死 [till death] is an indigenous Chinese locution, economical, classical.

Classicising devices grace Fou Lei's ferociously re-worked compositions:

---

79   Romain Rolland, *Vie de Beethoven*, 61.

80   Fou Lei, *Complete Works*, vol. 11, 79.

81   Ibid., 34.

Il se retrouva pauvre, malade, solitaire, – mais vainqueur: – vainqueur de
la médiocrité des hommes, vainqueur de son propre destin, vainqueur de
sa souffrance.[82]

[He found himself again poor, ill, alone, – but conqueror: – conqueror
of the mediocrity of men, conqueror of his own destiny, conqueror of his
pain.]

他仍舊是貧，病，孤獨——但是戰勝了……戰勝了人類的庸
俗，戰勝了他的命運，戰勝了他的痛苦。[83] (1934)

[He still was poor, ill, alone – but conquered… conquered the vulgarity
of humanity, conquered his destiny, conquered his pain.]

他貧病交迫，孤獨無依，可是戰勝了——戰勝了人類的平庸，
戰勝了他自己的命運，戰勝了他的痛苦。[84] (1942)

[He was oppressed at once by poverty and illness, alone with no one
to lean on, but conquered – conquered the mediocrity of humanity, conquered his own destiny, conquered his pain.]

When three adjectives 貧，病，孤獨 [poor, ill, alone] are turned into two
four-character idioms – 貧病交迫，孤獨無依 [oppressed at once by poverty
and illness, alone with no one to lean on] – both symmetry and cadence are
achieved. When the 'but' which precedes 'conquered' is adjusted from 但是 to
the interchangeable 可是， we understand to what extent Fou Lei was hyper-
conscious of intonation. With the 'àn' sound in the four '戰勝's (zhànshèng)
that immediately follow, the same 'àn' in 但是 (dànshì) is cumbrously bat-
tling to the ear. 可是 (kěshì), on the other hand, with its subdued accent, leads
agreeably on to the four vanquishing notes in repetition.

Il mourut pendant un orage, – une tempête de neige, – dans un éclat de
tonnerre.[85]

[He died during a storm, – a blizzard, – in a crack of thunder.]

他在一場大雷雨中，——在狂風大雪中，——在一聲暴雷中死
了。[86] (1934)

[In a rainstorm, – in great wind and heavy snow, – in a crack of violent
thunder, he died.]

---

82   Romain Rolland, *Vie de Beethoven*, 81.

83   Fou Lei, *Complete Works*, vol. 11, 81.

84   Ibid., 39.

85   Romain Rolland, *Vie de Beethoven*, 90.

86   Fou Lei, *Complete Works*, vol. 11, 81.

他在大風雨中，大風雪中，一聲響雷中，咽了最後一口氣。[87]
(1942)

[In the great wind and rain, great wind and snow, and a crack of deafening thunder, he breathed his last breath.]

In 1934, Fou Lei consciously implanted three '在's and three '中's: 在一場大雷雨中，——在狂風大雪中，——在一聲暴雷中. In 1942, taking out the unnecessary hypens inherited from Rolland's text, he gave a puristic construction led by a single 在 [in]: 在大風雨中，大風雪中，一聲響雷中. The refrain of 中 at the end of each clause is thus accentuated, and the anticipation built up by the iteration of 大風 [great wind] broken by 一聲響雷 [a crack of deafening thunder], and fittingly so. Every character is there for a just, rightful reason. Fou Lei orchestrated his words as a composer would his notes.

Vernacular Chinese under Fou Lei's pen was now in measured maturation, its vocabulary, phrasing, hues and tones his own invented devices, the fruits of daily experimentation. Work, in other words, is continued action. Serving a specific art in humble action was for Fou Lei the salvation out of darkness, nothingness and chaos. As the young Rolland, invigorated by Goethe and Voltaire, understood: 'To act, produce, create… I knew well then that this was the purpose, the law of life.'[88] Taine, after painfully reaching the bottom of scepticism, wrote at the age of twenty: 'To not act is to die.'[89]

'Youth, in its judgements, is almost always excessive',[90] said Rolland. 'I indulged in the excesses of an intellectual emotionalism which exerted itself in two opposite directions; their opposition was my self-defense: one of the excesses saved me from the other, and together they constituted the two ends of a pendulum which I carried on the tightrope that I walked, as does many a young man of twenty.'[91] Of the two, he named the more obsessive and dangerous end a 'cerebral mysticism by which I was poisoned. I cannot think of it without

---

87   Ibid., 43.
88   'Agir, produire, créer… Je savais bien que c'était le but, la loi de la vie.' Romain Rolland, *Mémoires*, 32.
89   'Depuis trois ans, il pense, il a détruit en lui-même la foi traditionnelle; il a touché douloureusement le fond du scepticisme, mais il sent que pour lui « ne pas agir, c'est mourir ». Il le dit dans une longue note écrite à vingt ans, en 1848, sorte de confession intellectuelle intitulée: *De la destinée humaine.*' André Chevrillon, 'Discours pour le centenaire d'Hippolyte Taine' (first version, conserved at Fonds Jacques Doucet).
90   'La jeunesse est, dans ses jugements, presque toujours excessive.' Romain Rolland, *Mémoires*, 52.
91   'J'étais livré aux excès d'une émotivité intellectuelle, qui s'exerçait en deux sens opposés; leur opposition m'était une autodéfense: l'un des excès me sauvait de l'autre, et tous les

repulsion. It bewitched me. All my efforts, day and night, for introducing order and clarity into it, only had me caught in its spider's web.'[92] Caught in quite a different spider's web, the intellectual pursuits of Fou Lei were dominated by a singularly incessant, and increasing, seeking of order and clarity; we recall, too, the exceedingly determined efforts of Taine with his *méthode* and *système* at a time when, he said, 'we have no hold on our feelings.'[93]

Whether such self-discipline and personal aspiration can be extended to social salvation is another question. Rolland, when old, read the diary of his *normale sup* days and diagnosed: 'I look back on this young dead person, and I feel detached from his illusions. [...] *Idéiste*[94] and mystic exaltation, to which this poor boy gave himself feverishly, appears to me to pertain to the maladies of a society.'[95] Youthful idealism as a cure for disillusionment can in turn become reason for further disillusionment. It is perhaps not incidental that *Jean-Christophe* (1904–12), conceived in Rolland's youth when he lived in Rome, fell quickly out of favour in a post-war Europe, whilst in a China steeped in its own wars, it commenced a sustained dialogue with its youth. If from the maladies of the society were born the young man's fever, *mal*, scepticism and idealism, such idealism was at once a revolt against and a product of the social illness; a self-defense, in Rolland's language; compensation, in another.[96]

---

deux formaient les deux extrémités du balancier, que je portais sur la corde raide, où je marchais, comme maint jeune homme de vingt ans.' Ibid., 53.

92   'Des deux, le plus obsédant et le plus périlleux était un mysticisme cérébral, dont j'étais empoisonné. Je ne puis y penser sans répulsion. Il m'envoûtait. Tous mes efforts, jour et nuit, pour y introduire l'ordre et la clarté, ne faisaient que m'engluer dans sa toile d'araignée.' Ibid.

93   See chapter 4, note 35.

94   *Idéiste*: a word invented in the nineteenth century, meaning 'to do with, and serving, ideas'.

95   '[...] je me remémore ce jeune mort, et je me sens détaché de ses illusions. [...] L'exaltation idéiste et mystique, à laquelle se livre fiévreusement ce pauvre garçon, me paraît appartenir aux maladies d'une société.' Romain Rolland, *Mémoires*, 53.

96   Awarded the Nobel Prize in Literature in 1915 for the 'lofty idealism' in his work, Rolland had consciously opposed 'false idealism' as the mortal enemy to idealism in 'Le poison idéaliste' (1900), dedicated to Péguy. Jacques Le Rider sees this 1900 essay as Rolland's Nietzschean statement, anti-Wagnerian, anti-décadent, and in Rolland's own words, 'heroic without romantic vainglory'. In light of Rolland's friendship with Malwida von Meysenbug (1816–1903) in the 1890s, and of von Meysenbug's own idealism and her friendship with Nietzsche, about whom she spoke often to Rolland, Le Rider's argument is convincing. See Jacques Le Rider, *Malwida von Meysenbug: Une Européenne du XIXe siècle* (Paris: Bartillat, 2005), 478–479; see also Malwida von Meysenbug, *Mémoires d'une idéaliste* (Paris: Fischbacher, 1900).

The curious fact is that, at the time he felt compelled to translate Taine and Rolland, Fou Lei would not have known much about the authors beyond their pages. In other words, the analogous components we have so far identified between the three men and their times were not theoretically conceived by the translator who, through reading, instinctively *felt* something – a sympathy, an affinity. Does there exist a psychic relation between the writer and the reader? Without knowing that they had, in fact, suffered the same *mal* at the same age, Fou Lei now embraced both the supposed scientific coldness of the Tainean remedy, and a Rollandian antidote unapologetically fervent, and poisonous all the same.

Years later, in 1965, Fou Lei wrote to his son Fou Ts'ong, exiled pianist in London:

> If, as an artist, you do not have a touch of a religionist's heart, you will be a purely technical or conceptual virtuoso, or one of those so-called abstractionist madmen; if, on the other hand, you do not have a bit of a philosopher in you, you will make yourself (and your companion) suffer, and never rise above it. [...] You say that you are an outcast wherever you are – that's it. Art too is a tyrant, for whoever is his slave is a willing one, hence this tyrant is a particularly dreadful one. Now that you have made art your master, all the bitterness and distress are your tribute to him; now that you believe in his religion, how can you not keep offering sacrifices? Each line has its humiliation and misery. To be able to resign is the only way to lessen pain. Have you ever thought about why, for the latter half of his life, Chopin voluntarily stayed in a foreign land? What was the price he had to pay for his work after Op. 25?[97]

It was Fou Ts'ong but also Fou Lei himself who had made art his master, and who had laboured, line after line, to pay his tribute. The duality of the religionist and the philosopher is a variation upon a theme: for Taine it is the poet and

---

97   '做一個藝術家，要不帶點兒宗教家的心腸，會變成追求純技術或純粹抽象觀念
      的virtuoso，或者像所謂抽象主義者一類的狂人；要不帶點兒哲學家的看法，
      又會自苦苦人了(苦了你身邊的伴侶)，永遠不能超脫。[…] 你自己說到處都是
      outcast，不就是這個意思嗎？藝術也是一個tyrant，因為做他奴隸的都心甘情
      願，所以這個tyrant尤其可怕。你既然認了藝術做主子，一切的辛酸苦楚便是
      你向他的納貢，你信了他的宗教，怎麼能不把少牢太牢去做犧牲呢？每一行
      有每一行的humiliation和misery，能夠resign就是少痛苦的不二法門。你可曾想
      過，蕭邦為什麼後半生自願流亡異國呢？他的Op. 25 以後的作品付的是甚麼代
      價呢？' Fou Lei's letter to Fou Ts'ong, 20 February 1965, in *Fou Lei's Family Letters*, 447.

the savant, for Rolland the emotional and the intellectual. For Fou Lei, heroism is for the heart what science is for the mind. If from *Philosophie de l'art* he learnt to love art as a scholar, after *Vie de Beethoven* he aspired to live life as an artist. Late in life he confided in Fou Ts'ong: 'Intellectually I am a pure Oriental; emotionally and instinctively I come extremely close to being an Occidental. In fact [the two poles are] also our inherent outlooks: one is the assumption that all is vain, the other the spirit to do the noble albeit impossible thing.'[98] The 'crise d'orient-occident' that Fou Lei had described to Daniélou in January 1931 was resolved by an overriding will of submission to art. Under a Faustian insistence on the *vita activa*, the perceived dichotomies within him between the Oriental and the Occidental, the sceptic and the idealist, were reconciled. Translation in particular, and action for a cause in general, became his self-salvation in effect and the first step towards national salvation in principle – Confucius would have us so believe.[99]

An admirer of Indian philosophy, Rolland came close to being Confucian in his appraisal of Jean-Christophe: Faith, not success, was his purpose.[100] Fou Lei, at the age of nineteen, envisioned his future as a defeated hero.[101] Is tragedy not a self-fulfilling prophecy, for those with the gift of Cassandra? Nietzsche said: 'It was during the years of my lowest vitality that I *ceased* to be a pessimist.'[102] Fou Lei never ceased to be a pessimist. When his pessimism reached a philosophical ground, there followed his resolution: life is what it is, and I do what I must do. Thus the inherent tragedy of life is worth the singing of the chorus. Nietzsche would have approved, not least since this was born from Beethoven's music.

---

98   '[...] intellectually 我是純粹東方人, emotionally and instinctively 又是極像西方人。其實也仍然是我們固有的兩種人生觀：一種是四大皆空的看法，一種是知其不可為而為之的精神。' Fou Lei's letter to Fou Ts'ong, 17 March 1963; ibid., 407. 四大皆空 [All is vain] is a sinicised Buddhist expression. 知其不可為而為之 [To do the noble albeit impossible thing] is a recorded saying of Confucius. See *Analects* 論語 憲問；D.C. Lau (tr.), *The Analects* (Hong Kong: Chinese University, 2000), 145.

99   The Confucian doctrine, in which Fou Lei invested unquestioning faith, of 修身 [cultivation of the person] *before* 治國 [governance of the State], is to be touched upon in the following chapter; see chapter 6, note 86.

100 'Pour le comprendre, il eût fallu qu'elle pût comprendre aussi que le succès n'était pas son but, que son but était sa foi. Il croyait dans l'art, il croyait dans *son* art, il croyait en soi, comme en des réalités supérieures non seulement à toute raison d'intérêts, mais à sa vie.' Romain Rolland, *Jean-Christophe* (Paris: Albin Michel, 1931, 2007), 414.

101 Fou Lei, 'In Mourning of Yiren' in *New North Weekly*, vol. 30 (19 March 1927). See chapter 1, notes 29 and 30.

102 Friedrich Nietzsche, *Ecce Homo* (London: Penguin, 1992), 10.

Light: A Willed Metamorphosis

In *I Ching* we read: 'The gentleman (*junzi*) changes like a leopard, his spots radiating with beauty.'[1] From a baby leopard he transforms into an animal of grandeur. Through continuous self-cultivation his *ingenium* shines. Fou Lei would have returned to China at the beginning of 1931 if not for staying on to help with Liu Haisu's summer exhibition in Paris.[2] He thus spent the spring in Italy – it was the highlight of his European sojourn.

Having made up his mind to leave, in January 1931 Fou Lei wrote, after a long silence, to Madame Berguerand: 'I am very sad thinking that I did not work well during these three years in France. I have just picked up a little language and caught a glimpse of the paths of my studies, and that's all.'[3] Self-critical as usual, he doubtless wished to learn and to see more. In the previous autumn he did not register at the Sorbonne. It has been assumed that Fou Lei studied there for the entirety of his stay in Paris; his registration card suggests otherwise (see *Fig.* 5). In a letter to Daniélou, which now confirms Fou Lei's absence in the academic year 1930–31, we learn that he had, by autumn 1930, moved to a suburban address (40 Grande rue, Nogent-Sur-Marne), and that the main reason for the discontinuation of his studies could well be financial. 'I would so much like to come to Laval to see you,' wrote he, 'if only I had the means. I often stay here for weeks without going to Paris, because I do not have the means.'[4]

One of Fou Lei's few extant personal documents gives us an idea of his preoccupation at the time: a passport issued by Légation de la République Chinoise in Paris on 17 March 1931, for 'Monsieur Fou-Nou-En, General Secretary of Chinese Artists in France and of Chinese Art Exhibition in Paris on a mission

---

1 '君子豹變，其文蔚也。' *I Ching* 易經 [The Book of Changes], Hexagram 49.

2 In a letter to Madame Berguerand on 18 January 1931, Fou Lei wrote : 'Si je ne suis pas obligé de rester pour m'occuper de l'exposition personnelle de Monsieur Liu, j'aurais pu rentrer maintenant. Mais je compte de rester en Europe jusqu'au mois de Juillet, tout au plus.' [Were I not obliged to stay in order to take care of Monsieur Liu's solo exhibition, I could have returned by now. But I count on staying in Europe until July at the latest.]

3 'Je suis bien triste en pensant que je n'avais pas bien travaillé pendant ces 3 ans de séjour en France. J'apprends juste un peu la langue et j'entrevois les chemins de mes études, et c'est tout.' Ibid.

4 'J'aurais tant voulu venir jusqu'à Laval, pour vous voir, si j'avais seulement le moyen. Je reste souvent des semaines sans aller à Paris, parce que je n'ai pas de moyen.' Fou Lei's letter to Daniélou, autumn 1930 (undated).

© KONINKLIJKE BRILL NV, LEIDEN, 2017 | DOI 10.1163/9789004343924_008

of artistic studies, who will travel to Switzerland and Italy and back.'[5] Having taken part in organising Chinese art exhibitions in Europe since 1929,[6] in 1931 Fou Lei joined Liu Haisu on a trip to Italy, for which the passport was issued. The knowledge we previously had of this trip has proved limited and inaccurate.[7] Fou Lei's lively account sent on 17 April 1931 to Daniélou gives a fuller picture.

---

5   'Monsieur Fou-Nou-En, Secrétaire Général des Artistes Chinois en France et de l'Exposition d'Art Chinois à Paris, en mission d'études artistiques qui se rend en Suisse, Italie et retour.' An image of this passport has been published in Claire Roberts, *Friendship in Art*.

6   In his letter to Daniélou on 24 August 1929, Fou Lei mentioned an exhibition planned by Liu Haisu that winter. 'Ce sera une exposition de dessin chinois et d'une partie des œuvres des étudiants chinois en France. Après cela, il y aura une exposition personnelle des œuvres de Monsieur Liu.' [It will be an exhibition of Chinese painting and some works of Chinese students in France. After this, there will be a solo exhibition of Monsieur Liu's work.] In summer 1930 Fou Lei travelled with Liu Haisu to Liège for the Exposition Internationale. It is noted in the published chronology of Fou Lei, edited by Fou Min and Luo Xinzhang, that he travelled to Belgium with Liu Kang in the spring (*Complete Works of Fou Lei*, vol. 20, 333). In his letter to Daniélou on 7 June 1930, Fou Lei wrote '[...] nous partirons probablement dans les premiers jours de juillet pour Liège, parce que M. Liu est invité par le Commissariat du Gouvernement Chinois de l'Exposition internationale de Liège, pour faire partie du Jury des œuvres d'art exposées.' [We will probably leave for Liège in the first days of July, for Monsieur Liu has been invited by the Chinese government's commission of the International Exhibition of Liège to sit on the jury.]

7   Fou Lei himself only wrote one sentence about it in his autobiography. The published chronology of Fou Lei notes the trip as having taken place in May and June 1931 (*Complete Works*, vol. 20, 333). According to Fou Lei's letter to Daniélou on 17 April 1931, it began at the end of March and was supposed to conclude in the middle of May. 'Je reste donc ici encore une dizaine de jours. J'étais parti pour Napoli et Sicile pendant 8 j. Je suis enthousiasmé de la visite de Pompéi. [...] Je partirai donc prochainement pour Florence, Venise, Milan et je rentrerai à Paris dans 3 ou 4 semaines.' [So I will stay [in Rome] for another ten days or so. I was in Napoli and Sicily for eight days. I am enthused over the visit to Pompeii. [...] I shall soon leave for Florence, Venice and Milan and return to Paris in three or four weeks.] In a letter to his then daughter-in-law, Zamira Menuhin, on 14 October 1963, Fou Lei mentioned this trip ('I did not manage to go to Florence or Venice') but remembered being in Rome in June to give two public speeches (*Fou Lei's Family Letters*, 418). Since Liu Haisu's solo exhibition in Paris was held between 1 and 15 June (dates shown on the catalogue sent to Madame Berguerand), it could have been a misrememberance on Fou Lei's part. He was likely to have left Italy in May as planned. There is, moreover, no evidence of Fou Lei's physical presence, in mid-March 1931, at the exhibition of Chinese art in Frankfurt, where Liu Haisu delivered a lecture on literati painting. Liu in his old age evoked Fou Lei's contribution to the writing of his Frankfurt lecture.

Both Izard and Daniélou had arranged for Fou Lei to meet their friends in Rome.[8] The result was altogether exciting. Jean de Menasce (1902–1973), Daniélou's friend and a distinguished theologian who knew fifteen languages,[9] took Fou Lei to see his parents,[10] who in turn introduced Fou Lei to 'beaucoup de personnalités importantes italiennes' [many important Italians]. These Italians, with 'an infinite sympathy for my country and having learnt that we are preparing a show of Chinese art in Paris', immediately put Fou Lei in contact with the 'aristocratic, artistic and literary world' with whom he conversed, and who envisaged with him an exhibition of Chinese art later in Rome.[11] This was how he became acquainted with the Countess Pasolini,[12] 'who took such an interest in me that she introduced me to the undersecretary of State for fine

---

8   On 6 April 1931, Daniélou received a postcard from Fou Lei, and wrote to his mother on the same day (the letter is now conserved at Archives jésuites de la Province de France): 'Je viens de recevoir une carte de Fou qui voyage en Italie et qui est bien installé à Rome grâce à Strapatti. Georges l'a très gentiment recommandé à un des ses amis de l'École de Rome.' [I have just received a card from Fou, who is travelling in Italy and comfortably settled in Rome thanks to Strapatti. Georges very kindly recommended him to one of his friends from l'École [française] de Rome.] It is probable that after receiving this card Daniélou wrote and recommended Jean de Menasce to Fou Lei, whose letter on 17 April reported their meeting.

9   About Jean de Menasce, Fou Lei said to Daniélou: 'Il est si charmant, si affectueux que je me figure de vous retrouver même dans sa personne. Chose curieuse, il se ressemble terriblement à vous, les manières, les gestes les plus insignifiants, sans parler la conversation qu'anime toute son âme.' [He is so charming, so affectionate that I imagine seeing you in his person. Funnily enough, he resembles you greatly, in manner and gesture, not to mention the conversation that animates all of his soul.] Fou Lei's letter to Daniélou, 17 April 1931, now conserved at Archives jésuites de la Province de France.

10   Jean de Menasce's father, the Baron Félix de Menasce, was a Jewish banker in Alexandria and had been ennobled by the Austrian emperor; his mother was French.

11   'Comme ils ont une sympathie infinie pour mon pays et ayant appris que nous sommes en train de préparer une manifestation artistique chinoise à Paris, ils me mettent tout de suit en rapport avec le monde aristocratique, artistique et littéraire pour que je puisse avoir une idée et un entretien avec eux qui me permettrait d'envisager plus tard une exposition d'art chinois à Rome.' Fou Lei's letter to Daniélou, 17 April 1931.

12   The Countess Maria Pasolini Ponti (1857–1938) was the mother-in-law of Princess Borghese. The American writer Edith Wharton (1862–1937) thus described her: '[...] my old friend the Countess Maria Pasolini of Rome and Ravenna, great lover of seventeenth and eighteenth century architecture, and an indefatigable guide in such a search as I was making.' See Edith Wharton, *A Backward Glance: An Autobiography* (New York: Scribner, 1998), 135. The Belgian politician and mayor of Brussels, Charles Buls (1837–1914), had the Countess and Luigi Luzzatti (1841–1927), Prime Minister of Italy in 1910–11, as his two great friends in Rome.

arts. Yesterday I dined at hers, and we had a long discussion.'[13] The Countess
decided that Fou Lei ought to give a speech on China at the Cercle Romain.[14]
So he did, and later at the invitation of the Società geologica italiana delivered
a lecture on 'The implications of the Northern Expedition of the Nationalist
army and of the wars amongst the Beiyang warlords' 國民軍北伐與北洋軍
閥鬥爭的意義.[15]

Another luminary that Jean de Menasce's mother presented to Fou Lei was
Enrico Caviglia (1862–1945), Marshal of Italy and titular military attaché in Beijing between c. 1905 and 1911, when China was still an empire. Fou Lei referred
to him as 'one of the greatest admirers of my country'[16] and, three years later,
was to recount this meeting in detail in a letter to Romain Rolland. Before reading Rolland's *Vie de Tolstoï*, Fou Lei held the belief that the only way to put an
end to the civil wars in China would be to abolish both taxes and the army, and
that when all soldiers became workers, the wars would end and the economy
would recover. According to Caviglia, Tolstoy once wrote to Gu Hongming expressing similar views.[17] Caviglia himself, having observed the Chinese as 'the
most diligent, moderate, and peaceful people',[18] believed that China need not
emulate the West, which had itself run into grave misfortune. In his view, the
Chinese could not and should not have organisations, for 'having no organisation is superior to having any organisation'.[19]

To Rolland Fou Lei confessed that Caviglia had regarded him as the archetype of the new Chinese generation who had imprudently dismissed their own
tradition, and added: 'I well reflected upon his critical words, just as I do today after translating your *Vie de Tolstoï*.'[20] This meeting with Caviglia had a
far-reaching effect on Fou Lei; already his reflections were making their way

---

13   '[…] qui s'intéresse tellement à moi qu'elle m'a recommandé au sous-secrétaire d'État aux
      Beaux-Arts. J'ai dîné hier soir chez elle, et nous avons eu un long entretien.' Fou Lei's letter
      to Daniélou, 17 April 1931.

14   The *Cercle Romain*, the *Cercle populaire national*, and the *Casino artistico* were the three
      major political societies in the Italian capital at the time.

15   'Fou Lei on Himself' in *Complete Works*, vol. 17, 5.

16   '[…] un des plus grands admirateurs de mon pays', Fou Lei's letter to Daniélou, 17 April
      1931.

17   This would be Tolstoy's 'Letter to a Chinese' (1905).

18   '元帥追憶一九〇八年遠東之行，認為中國人乃最勤勞、最淡泊、最平和之民
      族。' Fou Lei's letter to Romain Rolland, 3 March 1934; translation from the French by
      Luo Xinzhang in *Fou Lei's Letters to His Friends*, 6.

19   '"無組織"更勝於"有組織"。' Ibid., 7.

20   Ibid. For Tolstoy's longstanding Sinophilia, see Derk Bodde, *Tolstoy and China* (Princeton:
      Princeton University, 1950).

into his discussion with Jean de Menasce and into his Rome letter to Daniélou: 'I spoke at length with Jean de Menasce about the moral disquietude of youth and about the sentiment of religion.'[21] This disquietude, as we have seen, was a concern for Fou Lei before, during, and after his years in Europe. That he now attributed a moral nature to this disquietude, as he had previously done to his Orient-Occident conflict,[22] was arguably the outcome of his dialogue with Caviglia, who like Tolstoy had praised Chinese people in moralistic terms, and for whom (as it was for Tolstoy) Chinese wisdom, as they called it, was the counterpoison for Christian ills.[23]

Fou Lei's mention of his discussion of the 'sentiment of religion' in April 1931 is worthy of our attention and, indeed, of an attempted reconstruction.[24] The timing is important. What followed his rereading of Romain Rolland's *Vie de Beethoven* in spring 1931 can be justly described, in Sino-Buddhist terms, as a Sudden Enlightenment 頓悟.[25] Rolland himself experienced something similar after reading Spinoza, a revelation that he called *éclair*. After reading Freud's *The Future of an Illusion* (1927), in which religion was treated as a false belief, Rolland wrote to his Viennese friend and drew the latter's attention to 'the spontaneous religious sentiment' which he coined 'oceanic feeling', and proposed an analysis of this feeling as the origin of all religious beliefs.[26] The psychoanalyst's response was *Civilisation and Its Discontents* (1930),[27] in which

---

21   'J'ai longuement discuté avec Jean-de-Menasce sur l'inquiétude morale de jeunesse et le sentiment de religion.' Fou Lei's letter to Daniélou, 17 April 1931.

22   Fou Lei's letter to Daniélou, 8 January 1931; see chapter 5, note 10.

23   Tolstoy's 'Chinese Wisdom: Thoughts of Chinese Thinkers', composed around 1884 and published in 1907, makes a fascinating case of cultural translation.

24   One may assume, though not necessarily, Fou Lei's awareness at the time of Rolland's mysticism. In a much later letter (7 February 1953) to the translator and literary critic Stephen Soong 宋淇 (1919–1996), Fou Lei, speaking of 中外思想方式基本的不同問題 [the fundamental difference between Chinese and foreign ways of thinking], compared the mysticism of the beginning of Rolland's *Jean-Christophe* to that of the first chapter of *Dream of the Red Chamber* 紅樓夢 (1791). See *Fou Lei's Letters to His Friends*, 138–139.

25   See chapter 5, note 39 for Fou Lei's own account of this experience in his letter to Romain Rolland, 3 March 1934.

26   'Mais j'aurais aimé à vous voir faire l'analyse du sentiment religieux spontané ou, plus exactement, de la sensation religieuse qui est [...] le fait simple et direct de la sensation de l'éternel (qui peut très bien n'être pas éternel, mais simplement sans bornes perceptibles, et comme océanique).' See Rolland's letter to Freud, 5 December 1927, in *Un beau visage à tous sens: choix de lettres de Romain Rolland (1866–1944)* (Paris: Albin Michel, 1967), 264–266.

27   At the beginning of *Civilisation and Its Discontents*, Freud acknowledged: 'One of these outstanding men corresponds with me and in his letters calls himself my friend. [...] he

he argued that this feeling, which he himself did not have,[28] arose from 'the helplessness of the child and a longing for its father',[29] reiterating his view in the previous book.

In *The Varieties of Religious Experience* (1902), William James had discerned: '... the moment we are willing to treat the term "religious sentiment" as a collective name for the many sentiments which religious objects may arouse in alternation, we see that it probably contains nothing whatever of a psychologically specific nature.'[30] Rollandian 'religious sentiment', when assumed universal, would potentially bridge different religions as well as break down boundaries between the so-called believers and non-believers. 'Religion' would then take on as large and as indiscriminating a meaning as possible, provided that the 'oceanic feeling' be present.

The barrier that Fou Lei perceived between him and Daniélou, which he ascribed to religion, had long saddened him.[31] In a letter from June 1930 to his friend, he declared that he had nothing mystical in his soul,[32] and expressed this regret before explaining his atheism. Later in the autumn, he began a letter with an unprecedented demonstration of affection: 'My very dear Jean, tonight my heart is full of love, and constantly I think of you, for I often confound friendship with love. I love my friends with the same devotion and tenderness. Izard told me that you were happy there [in Laval]; I am so pleased. You are

---

said that he wholly agreed with my view of religion, but regretted that I had failed to appreciate the real source of religiosity. This was a particular feeling of which he himself was never free, which he had found confirmed by many others and which he assumed was shared by millions, a feeling that he was inclined to call a sense of "eternity", a feeling of something limitless, unbounded – as it were "oceanic".' Sigmund Freud, *Civilization and Its Discontents* (London: Penguin, 2002), 1–2.

28   In 1936, however, Freud told Rolland that he had 'experienced a sense of uncanniness akin to the oceanic feeling'. See Henri Vermorel, 'The Presence of Spinoza in the Exchanges between Sigmund Freud and Romain Rolland' in *International Journal of Psychoanalysis*, vol. 90, no. 6 (2009), 1247.

29   See Sigmund Freud, *Civilization and Its Discontents*, 11.

30   William James, *The Varieties of Religious Experience* (Cambridge, MA and London: Harvard University, 1985), 27. James went on to argue: '... there is no ground for assuming a simple abstract "religious emotion" to exist as a distinct elementary mental affection by itself, present in every religious experience without exception' (ibid., 28). Aware of each other's work, James and Freud met once in the United States in 1909.

31   See chapter 3, note 8. Daniélou disliked systematic minds ('Je ne suis pas à l'aise, moi, avec les esprits systématiques.' Daniélou, *Et qui est mon prochain?*, 72); Fou Lei was attracted to them. The 'barrier' could well have been more temperamental than religious. But we can only speculate.

32   'Je n'ai rien de mystique dans mon âme.' Fou Lei's letter to Daniélou, 7 June 1930.

truly made for that healthy and virtuous life! Bless you, my dear friend.'[33] His dispirited letter of 8 January 1931, however, ended on an apologetic note: 'I am so grateful to you for praying for me, for consoling me with divine words. But ... I dare not hurt you by telling you that your spiritual efforts could do nothing for me. Forgive me, my dear friend, this is nevertheless the truth, which makes me feel unforgivable, ungrateful vis-à-vis your kindness, your infinite goodwill for me.'[34]

It would have been neat if this 'barrier' were all; even with Daniélou's side of the correspondence missing, what is equally obvious, though less evident to make sense of, is their closeness. Around this time Daniélou believed that he could 'faire Chinois avec les Chinois',[35] and Fou Lei, writing with the child-like confidence unseen in his other, equally trusting correspondence, said to Daniélou: 'You are a moral support for me. Despite my unbelief, I always feel a power in your soul that comforts me, warms me! Oh, if only I could come to see you one day, to be reproved by you – as your sister Mrs Izard said – I would cry with joy!'[36] Did not Freud, an 'atheist Jew', make the confession to

---

33   'Mon Bien Cher Jean, Ce soir, mon cœur est plein d'amour, et incessamment je pense à vous car, je confonds souvent l'amitié avec l'amour. J'aime mes amis avec le même dévoue-ment, la même tendresse. Izard m'a dit que vous êtes heureux là-bas, j'en suis si content. Vous êtes vraiment fait pour cette vie saine et sainte! Sois [sic: Soyez] béni, mon cher ami.' Letter to Daniélou, autumn 1930 (undated). This was the first time Fou Lei addressed Daniélou by his first name. It is probable that Daniélou, after receiving Fou Lei's previ-ous long and condensed letter (dated 7 June 1930), in which many sentences are now underlined by pencil (likely by Daniélou), addressed Fou Lei by his first name in a warm response. Judging from correspondence between Daniélou and his close friends of this period, where *tu* was freely used, we know that he and Fou Lei, who addressed each other as *vous*, kept that little distance. It is, of course, also conceivable, though less likely, that Daniélou used *tu* with Fou Lei and that the latter, expressing elegant respect, insisted on *vous*. That Fou Lei, in this letter, wrote *sois* instead of *soyez*, causing grammatical incon-sistency, can be seen as a happy Freudian slip.

34   'Je vous suis si reconnaissant de prier pour moi, de me consoler avec des paroles divines. Mais... je n'ose pas vous blesser en vous disant que vos efforts spirituels ne pourraient rien pour moi. Pardonnez-moi, mon cher ami, c'est pourtant la vérité, c'est ce qui me fais sentir impardonnable, ingrat, vis-à-vis votre bonté, votre amitié infinie pour moi.' Fou Lei's letter to Daniélou, 8 January 1931.

35   Jean Daniélou, 'Election sur la Chine', conserved at Archives jésuites de la Province de France. See chapter 2, note 90.

36   'Vous êtes pour moi un soutien moral. Malgré mon incroyance, je me sens toujours une sorte de puissance dans votre âme, qui me réconforte, qui me réchauffe! Ô, si seulement je pouvais venir vous voir un jour, d'être grondé par vous, comme l'a dit votre sœur, Madame Izard, je pleurerais de joie!' Fou Lei's letter to Daniélou, autumn 1930 (undated).

Romain Rolland, a 'Christian without a church', in May 1931, seven years after their meeting in Vienna which lasted an hour, that 'I can tell you that I have almost never felt this mysterious attraction of one being for another except with you'?[37] Was not Charles Péguy, Catholic intellectual and spiritual mentor of Daniélou's circle, Romain Rolland's best friend who published the then little-known author's *Jean-Christophe* in his own *Cahiers*, and on whom Rolland wrote his last book *Péguy*?[38] Freud kept away from Rolland's mysticism. Rolland told Péguy, 'I am far from sharing your Catholicism.'[39] To Daniélou, who considered himself 'by nature a pagan', Fou Lei explained why he did not believe in God. It would appear, to put it crudely, that when it comes to spiritual attraction, 'religious barriers' articulate little; they are *made*. The question is who makes them, and why.

When from Rome he wrote to Daniélou, 'Despite the education that I have received in Europe and the devout Catholic friends such as yourself to whom I have been close, I am making a definitive return to our own philosophical sentiment',[40] with his restated atheism sounding more affirmed than ever, Fou Lei seemed almost relieved. The unusual choice of phrase 'sentiment philosophique', a linguistic rapprochement to 'sentiment religieux', could have been Fou Lei's way of establishing a common ground for the perceived polarity between the two mentalities, i.e., Christian and Chinese, before further reducing them to a contrasted pair of the religious and the philosophical. With this dichotomy Fou Lei was to settle from then on and, with little alteration, for the rest of his life.

In 'La crise de l'art chinois moderne' (1931) written for *L'Art Vivant*, Fou Lei took the initiative of analysing 'the profound reason why Oriental and

---

37 See Henri Vermorel, 'The Presence of Spinoza in the Exchanges between Sigmund Freud and Romain Rolland' in *International Journal of Psychoanalysis*, vol. 90, no. 6 (2009), 1241.

38 In 1912, Rolland noted in his journal: 'Je ne puis plus rien lire après Péguy. Tout le reste est littérature. Comme les plus grands d'aujourd'hui sonnent creux auprès de lui! Il est la force la plus géniale de la littérature européenne.' In 1943, nearly thirty years after Péguy's death, and a year before his own, Rolland wrote: 'Je pense encore de même aujourd'hui.' See *Pour l'honneur de l'esprit: correspondance entre Charles Péguy et Romain Rolland, 1898–1914* (Paris: Albin Michel, 1973), 8.

39 See letters between Rolland and Péguy (29 July 1912, 2 August 1912, and 14 July 1913 in ibid., 316, 317, 340) for mutual expressions of affinity despite their difference in faith.

40 'Malgré les instructions que j'ai reçues en Europe et les amis fervents catholiques, tels que vous, que j'ai fréquentés intimement, je fais un retour définitif à notre propre sentiment philosophique.' Fou Lei's letter to Daniélou, 17 April 1931.

Occidental concepts of art run afoul of each other'.[41] He judged the reason to be aesthetic, and explained that in China, 'art has exactly the same role as poetry and morality, which all come down to philosophy or metaphysics'[42] and that this runs counter both to Christian art which 'consists of evoking the love of God, the mystic passion' – because 'Chinese philosophy and metaphysics have never personified the divine to turn it into God, and exclude any human passion in order to achieve the Absolute Serenity' – and to Greek art – because Chinese art 'detests fugitive beauty and sensual pagan pleasure'.[43] In this readiness to generalise, this swiftness to define cultures as types, we encounter an impulse likewise palpable when we read Taine.

Compartmentalising discording ideas into a set of opposing poles – and freezing them there – is certainly one way of dealing with perceived conflicts; and perceived dichotomies of an external nature are often projections of internal duality. It is perhaps a simplification, but no exaggeration, to say that Fou Lei's intellectual efforts for the remainder of his life were driven by an incessant need to reconcile the conflicts he already beheld at the age of twenty-three, and to thereby construct, by way of language, a world of unity within the framework of sharp antipodes.

Thirty years later, in a long letter to Fou Ts'ong, Fou Lei wrote:

> The Chinese are largely moderate, peaceful, placid, simple and honest, more easily satisfied than the Westerners. [...] The wisdom of Buddhism is the exact opposite of the faith of Christianity. [...] Our people have always advocated wisdom. The Chinese ideal is to search for wisdom, not for faith. We only see our ancients mention Complete Enlightenment 徹悟; they never took firmness of belief as the joy in life (which is precisely what happiness means to the Westerners). You think more highly of Handel than of Bach, saying that the former is the crystallisation of

---

41   'Disons maintenant la raison profonde qui met aux prises les conceptions orientales et occidentales de l'art.' See Fou Nou-En, 'La crise de l'art chinois moderne' in *L'Art Vivant* (September 1931), 468.

42   'L'art a exactement le même rôle que la poésie, la morale, qui aboutissent toutes à la philosophie ou à la métaphysique.' Ibid.

43   'Il est donc différent de l'art chrétien qui consiste à évoquer l'amour de Dieu, la passion mystique, puisque la philosophie et la métaphysique chinoises n'ont jamais personnifié le divin pour le transformer en Dieu et excluent toute passion humaine afin d'atteindre à la Sérénité Absolue. Il est non moins different de l'art grec, ayant détesté la beauté fugitive et la volupté païenne.' Ibid.

wisdom and the latter that of faith: the root of this thinking also reflects the character of our nation.[44]

Self-idealisation aside, what presents itself here is multi-directional mirroring in motion: Fou Ts'ong expressed his view of Handel and Bach compared; Fou Lei concurred that the difference between the composers was one between wisdom and faith, and pushed this difference further, first as one between a pagan-inspired and a religious spirit,[45] and second as one analogous to the perceived contrast between Oriental wisdom and Christian faith; he then ascribed 'the character of our nation' to Fou Ts'ong's higher opinion of Handel, of which he thus made sense.[46]

What intrigues is this pertinacity of making abstract sense through rigid rationalisation rather than the validity of such rationalisation itself, where conceptual gaps can be spotted, and where semantics get in the way after all. For example, if we stop taking commonplace oppositions for granted, why could there not be faith in wisdom, and wisdom in faith? Behind this apparent obsession with polarities and with attributing everything to cultural distinctions, we wonder if, speaking of the Westerners who 'took firmness of belief as the joy in life' as though they were the only kind of Westerners that existed, Fou Lei did not have his 'devout Catholic friends' from thirty years ago still in mind, and whether the 'moderate, peaceful, placid, simple and honest people' that he evoked might not have had more to do with his, General Caviglia's, and Tolstoy's theoretical image of the civilisation than with the physical reality of the country, specifically the one in which he was living in 1961. It would appear that, after three years in Europe and unmoved by Catholicism, Fou Lei turned, in part through contact with some of his European friends, into a Sinophile.

---

44 '中華民族多數是性情中正和平、淡泊、樸實，比西方人容易滿足。[…] 佛教的智慧正好與基督教的信仰成為鮮明的對比。[…] 我們的民族本來提倡智慧。中國人的理想是追求智慧而不是追求信仰。我們只看見古人提到徹悟，從未以信仰堅定為人生樂事(這恰恰是西方人心目中的幸福)。你認為韓德爾比巴赫為高，你說前者是智慧的結晶，後者是信仰的結晶：這個思想根源也反映出我們的民族性。' Fou Lei's letter to Fou Ts'ong, 7 February 1961, in *Fou Lei's Family Letters*, 283.

45 We may conjecture that they were discussing Handel's *Semele*, for mention of this opera based on Greek myth appeared in their correspondence four months later. See also chapter 8, notes 77 and 78.

46 Instead of sending him to school, Fou Lei gave his son a carefully designed education at home; for years he was himself Fou Ts'ong's teacher of classical Chinese art and literature. Determined to expose him as much to 中國古典精神 [classical Chinese spirit] as possible, Fou Lei appeared to have consciously 'corrected' his own romantic tendencies as a youth in Fou Ts'ong's early formation. Pleased to see what he called healthy, balanced taste in his son, he considered it the fruition of his gardening.

What intrigues once more is the almost willful manner in which this resolution asserted itself. In summer 1931, during his voyage back to Shanghai Fou Lei wrote to Daniélou: 'One thing of which I am rather proud is not to have forgotten our own tradition. On the contrary, never have I loved so much as now, after three years in Europe, our culture and our ethics. I understand much better than four years ago that Chinese morality, cursed by young people, is infinitely superior to that which we want to transport from overseas.'[47] In this Ciceronian spirit,[48] Fou Lei's metaphysical return took place simultaneously with the physical one. The decision *not* to blame China's moral doctrine was in fact as radical as the anti-Confucian revolts – widespread since the beginning of the century, escalated during the New Culture Movement, and propagandised throughout the 1920s – for it would have been seen as conservative, against the post-revolutionary *Zeitgeist*, and reactionary. The conviction that the future of a civilisation depends on its past – or more precisely, one's understanding of it – and that one has the ability, and duty, to shape one's culture in the present, is, for want of a better word, humanistic.

The nature of Fou Lei's definitive position, I propose, was as psychological as it was conceptual. Let us note that his was a recapitulation of General Caviglia's criticism towards the young Chinese, of which Fou Lei was taken as the archetype. As the archetype neared home, he wrote to Daniélou: 'Approaching our country, I am profoundly saddened by the catastrophes caused by the floods and the perpetual civil war. I am spoiled by my three years' stay in Europe. I enjoyed too much tranquillity and became quite indifferent to all that is happening at home.'[49] His infantile guilt resurfaced,[50] coupled with compensational

---

47   'Une chose dont je suis assez fier, c'est de ne pas avoir oublié notre propre tradition. Au contraire, jamais je n'ai tant aimé qu'aujourd'hui, après 3 ans en Europe, notre culture et notre morale. Je comprends beaucoup mieux qu'il y a 4 ans que la morale chinoise, maudite par des jeunes gens, est infiniment supérieure à celle qu'on veut transporter d'outremer.' Fou Lei's letter to Daniélou, 17 September 1931; conserved at Archives jésuites de la Province de France.

48   'nescire autem quid ante quam natus sis acciderit, id est semper esse puerum; quid enim est aetas hominis, nisi memoria rerum veterum cum superiorum aetate contexitur?' [Not to know what happened before you were born is to remain always a child. For what is the time of a man, except it be interwoven with that memory of ancient things of a superior age?] *M. Tullius Ciceronis Orator Ad. M. Brutum*, chapter XXXIV, section 120.

49   'En approchant de notre pays, je suis profondément attristé par des catastrophes causées par des inondations et de la guerre civile perpétuelle. Je suis gâté pendant 3 ans de mon séjour en France. Je me suis jouis trop de tranquillité pour que je sois assez indifférent de tout ce qu'il se passe chez nous.' Fou Lei's letter to Daniélou, 17 September 1931. Grammatically shaky, Fou Lei's French deteriorated after a month at sea.

50   See chapter 1, note 39.

devotion to his country. This complex à la Hamlet was curiously underscored by the Chinese son's impulse of filial piety.[51] Only that, fatherless, Fou Lei had to create an abstract father for himself, not least to authenticate his own identity. That father was China's newly constructed cultural and moral tradition, the very phantom against which the May Fourth generation had rebelled and which they had half-knowingly and half-unknowingly strangled.

'To be rooted is perhaps the most important and least recognised need of the human soul',[52] wrote Simone Weil. Our anxious orphan worried as much about being uprooted as about the root itself being lost.[53] In 1931, before setting foot again on his native soil, Fou Lei estimated: 'I think it extremely dangerous to abandon our own culture and civilisation, wanting to borrow everything from the West. And what I fear the most is that before we have a material civilisation – let us admit that this is necessary for living in the twentieth century – we will have already lost our own spiritual civilisation. Then that would be real barbarism.'[54] The clichéd divide between a material West and a spiritual East aside, in this clairvoyance we hear Jacob Burckhardt (1818–1897), the 'prophet of doom', speaking in a nineteenth-century voice almost word for word,[55] warning against a civilised (i.e., materially advanced) barbarism in Europe with a want of interest in its own cultural past, and predicting the totalitarian direction that history could take.[56] The affinity between Fou Lei's historical and political thinking and that of Taine and Burckhardt – two great conservatives, or in Nietszche's eyes, nihilists – is astonishing. That Fou Lei's reawakening took off in Italy, Rolland's preferred country and the very

---

51   I base this analogy loosely on Ernest Jones' (1879–1958) interpretation of Hamlet's Oedipus Complex. According to Jones, Hamlet's devotion to his dead father was a compensation for the latent wish to kill him.

52   Simone Weil, *The Need for Roots: Prelude to a Declaration of Duties towards Mankind* (London: Routledge and Kegan Paul, 1952), 41.

53   Fou Lei was not alone in this condition. A good number of Chinese avant-garde artists, notably Lin Fengmian 林風眠 (1900–1991) and Pang Xunqing 龐薰琹 (1906–1995), studied in France in the 1920s and turned enthusiastically, whilst in Paris, to China's artistic past, according to their autobiographical accounts.

54   '[...] j'estime qu'il est excessivement dangereux d'abandonner notre propre civilisation et culture en voulant tout emprunter à l'occident. Et, ce que je crains le plus c'est qu'avant que nous ayons une civilisation matérielle – admettons qu'elle est nécessaire pour vivre au xxᵉ siècle – nous aurons déjà perdu notre civilisation spirituelle. Alors, ce serait le vrai barbarisme.' Fou Lei's letter to Daniélou, 17 September 1931.

55   See Jacob Burckhardt, *Judgments on History and Historians* (Indianapolis: Liberty Fund, 1999), particularly 'The Limits of Civilization and Barbarism'.

56   See Jacob Burckhardt, *Reflections on History* (Indianapolis: Liberty Classics, 1979).

site where Taine's and Burckhardt's historical imagination took wing, is also uncanny.[57] Might Fou Lei have been reading Taine's *Voyage en Italie* (1866) and Burckhardt's *Die Kultur der Renaissance in Italien* (1860) that summer?

Nearing home, Fou Lei, writing to Daniélou, analysed his mental return to China, starting with a Tainean botanical analogy: 'For each people has its special character that we cannot alter. It is impossible that, sowed into foreign soil, the sprout of a plant should grow as well as it does in its native land. For a hundred years, we think only about copying one system or another, none of which suits this old country. The revolutionaries are culpable for not studying China itself. They no longer know how to appreciate its glorious antiquity in the least.'[58] Echoing Taine's bitter blame of the Revolution for France's social ills, Fou Lei reinforced his point, several lines down: 'You French, you had Rousseau, Voltaire, Montesquieu, and all the encyclopedic minds who worked towards the French Revolution, and yet you suffered from it for an entire century. Whereas China has never had this thinking of the precursors, and we want to transform the monarchy into a republic in a few months; it would be too good to be true. It is only fair that we are severely punished today with these terrible disorders.'[59] His judgement informed by historical reflections, and his political

---

57   Incidentally, Taine and Burckhardt were the two thinkers whom Nietzsche held in the highest esteem. For Nietzsche's avid reading of Burckhardt, his colleague from Basel, at the home of Malwida von Meysenbug, see Jacques Le Rider, *Malwida von Meysenbug*, 374–375. A German author living mostly in Italy and friends with Schopenhauer and Wagner, not only had Malwida von Meysenbug corresponded with Taine, she was one of Romain Rolland's closest friends, exerting considerable influence on the idealistic young man during his stay in Rome between 1890 and 1893. See Malwida von Meysenbug, *Mémoires d'une idéaliste*; see also Romain Rolland, *Choix de lettres à Malwida von Meysenbug* (Paris: Albin Michel, 1948).

58   'Car, chaque peuple a son caractère spécial qu'on ne pourra pas modifier. Il est impossible qu'un germe d'une plante, semé sur un sol étranger, pousse aussi bien que sur son sol originel. Depuis 100 ans, on ne pense qu'à copier un système ou l'autre qui ne convient nullement à ce vieux pays. Les révolutionnaires sont bien coupables de ne pas étudier la Chine propre. Ils ne savent plus apprécier la moindre chose de son antiquité glorieuse.' Fou Lei's letter to Daniélou, 17 September 1931.

59   Note the emphatic use of *vous* and *nous* in Fou Lei's wording. 'Vous français, vous avez eu les Rousseau, les Voltaire, les Montesquieu, et tous les esprits encyclopédiques qui avaient travaillé la révolution française, et pourtant, vous en avez souffert pendant tout un siècle. Tandis que la Chine n'ayant jamais eu cette pensée des précurseurs, et nous voulons transformer la monarchie en république pendant quelque mois, ce serait trop beau si nous l'avions réussi. Il est trop juste que nous soyons sévèrement puni aujourd'hui avec ces désordres terribles.'

commentaries published in 1932 foreshadowed in these ruminations,[60] Fou Lei's critical stand recalled that of Taine, whose treatise on the fine arts he had briefly translated. Even his phrasing bears resemblance to that of the nineteenth-century thinker.[61] Unsurprisingly, it was Taine's work on the French Revolution that Burckhardt quoted when discussing 'the innermost core of the Revolution' in his *Judgements on History and Historians*.

It is of relevance that whilst 'studying Western painting in the Louvre', Fou Lei 'fell in love with Chinese painting',[62] and that having visited Pompeii and Rome, his thoughts were now on China's 'glorious antiquity'. In this appetite for finding cultural counterparts, and in this facility for juxtaposing aesthetic entities to generate contrapuntal understanding, we see the inclinations of a natural translator. What he then decided to do, in the face of the 'terrible disorders' in his country, is all the more telling. 'So here is what I think on my way back to China. I want to make an in-depth study (*une étude approfondie*) of the antique Orient as well as of the modern and historical Occident.'[63] By *approfondie* Fou Lei may have had in mind a comprehensive study of the fine arts and music,[64] and wished to undertake precisely that which he believed to be lacking in China's modern history, namely 'the thinking of the precursors', in the spirit of the encyclopedic minds. This linear thinking becomes less problematic if we look, once more, at how one's thinking manifests itself in one's action – or not. These aspirations, at which some of his contemporaries could well have arrived, were in Fou Lei's case anything but haphazard or fleeting. Verily, he seemed seldom to opine in fits and starts, and his opinions almost always bore consequences in his deeds. It is nothing short of striking to see, at this point, that the young man's cultural contemplation was to sculpt

---

60   See Fou Lei, 'Our Work' in *L'Art*, vol. 1, no. 8 (November 1932); see also chapter 2, note 52 and chapter 3, note 20.

61   See chapter 3, note 21.

62   See chapter 2, note 84.

63   'Voilà ce que je pense au retour en Chine, je veux faire une étude approfondie sur l'Orient antique aussi bien que l'Occident moderne et historique.' Fou Lei's letter to Daniélou, 17 September 1931.

64   Fou Lei wrote this letter on his way back to Shanghai. Onboard was the sinologist and musicologist Louis Laloy, who was on a government mission to investigate ancient Chinese music. Fou Lei and Liu Haisu were to help Laloy get to the Confucian temples to hear the music of rituals (mentioned in the same letter). Corresponding in the early 1960s with Liu Thai-Ker, eldest son of Liu Kang and distinguished architect then studying at the University of New South Wales, Fou Lei discussed the differences between classical Chinese and Japanese architecture. 'He was full of insight', recalled Liu Thai-Ker, 'I should still have his letter at the back of my cupboard.' (Interview with author, September 2008.)

not only his subsequent self-education – now that his formal education had ended – but the education of his children.[65] Twenty-five years later, discussing Fou Ts'ong's intellectual trajectory, Fou Lei wrote to the playwright and China's then Deputy Minister of Culture, Xia Yan 夏衍 (1900–1995): 'Ever since he was little, I have taken care to nurture his national soul, for I loathe artists who are neither Chinese nor Western, neither this nor that, and who take no roots in their own soil.'[66]

In spring 1931, conscious that his days in Europe were numbered, Fou Lei appeared to have had an overwhelming need to surmount this tormented sojourn and to bring it to a closure. 'I believe that right now, I enter a new phase of state of mind which is much more concrete',[67] he said to Daniélou. 'After the exaltation of a kind of unhealthy romanticism that is the fruit of this long social and moral disorder in China, I begin to calm down and to look for peace

---

65   See notes 58 and 46 in this chapter. Fou Lei closely observed Fou Ts'ong and Fou Min when they were children. Convinced of the gift of the former but not of that of the latter, he pulled Fou Ts'ong out of school, handpicked and handwrote texts of classical Chinese literature, philosophy and history, and tutored his son himself; mathematics, English and other subjects were taught by private teachers, some of them his friends. Fou Min, on the other hand, was left to school education, receiving less attention at home.

66   '從他小時起，我一向注意培養他的民族靈魂，因為我痛恨不中不西，不三不四，在自己的泥土中不生根的藝術家。' Fou Lei's letter to Xia Yan, 21 August 1956, in *Fou Lei's Letters to His Friends*, 198. The simultaneously nurturing and restricting effects of Fou Lei's care for Fou Ts'ong aside, his guiding rationale here expressed also illustrates, sadly, why he denied a teenage Fou Min the wish to train as a professional violinist. Determined not to see Fou Min become 'neither this nor that', with brutal honesty he told his son that holding an ordinary job was far more honourable than being a mediocre artist. Fou Min, Fou Lei discerned, would be a good teacher. In 1962, as a twenty-five-year-old Fou Min was about to take up his first teaching post in Beijing, Zhu Meifu wrote to Fou Ts'ong in London: '他資質差，就是經爸爸點撥，接受的能力有限，也就不夠深入。前兩個月他曾翻了兩篇短文章寄來，爸爸替他仔細校閱，糾正錯誤，還逐條加以說明，白天沒工夫，晚上加班加點。爸爸說，他非盡力幫助不可；為了兒子，做父親的任何代價都不惜的。你是深知爸爸的那股勁兒，我常常為之感動得流淚。爸爸常說：〝阿敏我教得太少，心裡不免內疚，現在得迎頭趕上。〞' [Untalented, and limited in his receptiveness, even with your father's tutoring he [Min] is unable to go deep. A couple of months ago he sent us two articles that he had translated. Your father carefully proofread and corrected them before adding annotation to each point. Busy during the day, on this he worked through the nights. He said he must do all he could to help; that any price was worth paying for his son. You know that zeal of his, which often moves me to tears. He said: 'Having taught Ah Min so little, I cannot help feeling guilty. Now is the time to catch up.'] Zhu Meifu's letter to Fou Ts'ong, 22 January 1962, in *Fou Lei's Family Letters*, 365.

67   'Je crois que maintenant, j'entre dans une nouvelle phase d'état d'âme qui est beaucoup plus concrète.' Fou Lei's letter to Daniélou, 17 April 1931.

in a spiritual escapism (*évasion d'âme*) that is purely impersonal, rather than in the Christian faith.'[68] In every beginning there is a conclusion. 'It is our mentality. Izard was right when he said that, after all, I remain profoundly Chinese.'[69] And the individual was again made tantamount to the collective when he continued: 'Chinese civilisation resists with an incomparable tenacity the endeavour of all the West. The disorder which has gone on for a hundred years and which still goes on is the proof.'[70]

Whether the 'endeavour of all the West' is to be taken as imperialism cultural or political, an agonised Fou Lei appeared not to – or was too proud to – blame this 'endeavour'; instead he held responsible the resilience of Chinese civilisation for the country's disorder. Since the mid-nineteenth century, China's cultural and political élite made – not without apprehension, caution or dissension, nor without fascination, persuasion or dedication – considerable efforts to 'learn from the West', wholesale Westernisation being out of the question. Resisting the 'endeavour of all the West' would mean, in this context, failure to learn. No nationalist in a narrow sense, Fou Lei seemed to have found Westernisation not inappropriate per se, but simply impossible, or at any rate too late, when he made a comparison with Japan: 'If we Chinese, we could adapt to all aspects of modernism as did Japan fifty years ago (of course, Japan also retains its essential character, but it quickly found a formula without a furious struggle between tradition and Western civilisation), we would have long had peace. But our culture is too deep and too strong for us to find a moral equilibrium in a short time when meeting the great current of Western spirit.'[71]

The exact relation between 'modernism' and 'Western civilisation' in Fou Lei's reasoning being unclear, a resemblance if not equivalence between the two was assumed, with both presupposed as necessarily at odds with tradition, and both deemed necessary nonetheless. Interlaced assumptions which

---

68   'Après l'exaltation d'une sorte de romantisme maladif qui est le fruit de ce long désordre social et moral en Chine, je commence à m'apaiser et à chercher une paix plutôt dans l'évasion d'âme qui est purement impersonnelle que dans la foi chrétienne.' Ibid.

69   'C'est notre mentalité, Izard a bien dit que malgré tout, je reste profondément chinois.' Ibid.

70   'La civilisation chinoise résiste avec une ténacité incomparable à la tentative de tout occident. Le désordre qui a duré depuis 100 ans et qui dure encore en est la preuve.' Ibid.

71   'Si, nous les chinois, nous pouvions nous adapter à tout modernisme comme le fit le Japon il y a 50 ans (bien entendu, le Japon garde aussi son caractère essentiel, mais il a vite trouvé une formule sans que la lutte s'engage furieusement entre la tradition et la civilisation occidentale.) nous aurions depuis longtemps la paix. Mais notre culture est trop profonde et trop solide pour que nous puissions trouver dans peu de temps un équilibre moral à la rencontre du grand courant d'esprit occidental.' Ibid.

lead only to a logical dead end, aside, Fou Lei went on to suggest that 'Chinese civilisation' was not so much incapable of adaptation as dependent on the context, for when an adaptation did take place, it so did as a matter of adoption, of which he gave an example: 'Through its philosophy, Buddhism came closer than any other civilisation to our mentality, so it was quickly adopted by our people. However, beware that our suppleness does not stretch all the way to completely adapting to any dogma.'[72] At stake were, albeit not in so many words, historically differing power relations between 'civilisations'. Resilience or suppleness? Apparently both, or neither. Having confessed in the same letter that he had renounced once and for all looking for peace in the Christian faith, Fou Lei may have here set Catholicism, with its imperialistic associations in early twentieth-century China, as his implicit target.[73] Daniélou may not have relinquished the idea of going to China as a missionary for no reason – in any case we may consider him sufficiently warned.

There is, let it be noted, nothing original in what Fou Lei said. Ten years previously, Russell wrote, and it well reflected his extensive dialogues with the Chinese élite, that 'China is much less a political entity than a civilisation [...] There have been foreign influences – first Buddhism, and now Western science. But Buddhism did not turn the Chinese into Indians, and Western science will not turn them into Europeans.'[74] Fou Lei's deduction was similar: 'Buddhism in China is an entirely different thing from the original. Hence ancient and pure China lives on and will always live on. In accordance with my own intellectual experiences, China will have, sooner or later, a third civilisation that is based on tradition, whilst absorbing all the new Western minds.'[75] Essentialising the 'ancient and pure China', a myth at best, Fou Lei, as he watched himself entering a new state of mind, envisaged China to eventually do the same and to do so in a manner as free and as dignified as it once did to 'adopt' Buddhism.

---

72   'Le Boudhisme, par sa philosophie, s'approche bien plus intimement que toutes autres civilisations à notre mentalité, il fut donc vite adopté par notre peuple. Cependant, il faut savoir que notre souplesse ne va pas jusque nous adapter complètement à un dogme quoi que ce soit.' Ibid.

73   How seriously Fou Lei had, till this point, looked for peace in the Christian faith is another question. Exisiting evidence betrays no sign of willing or sustained attempts. See also chapter 2, note 93.

74   Bertrand Russell, *The Problem of China*, 208.

75   'Le Boudhisme en Chine est toute autre chose que celui d'origine. Par conséquent la Chine ancienne et propre survit et survivra toujours. Selon mes propres expériences intellectuelles, la Chine connaîtra, tôt ou tard, une troisième civilisation qui sera basée sur la tradition, en s'alimentant de tous nouveaux esprits d'occident.' Fou Lei's letter to Daniélou, 17 April 1931.

This vision of a third civilisation was to dictate many of Fou Lei's choices. Whilst a teenage Fou Lei was studying in Shanghai, Russell returned from Beijing to England and wrote: 'The Chinese who have had a European or American education realise that a new element is needed to vitalise native traditions, and they look to our civilisation to supply it. But they do not wish to construct a civilisation just like ours; and it is precisely in this that the best hope lies. If they are not goaded into militarism, they may produce a genuinely new civilisation, better than any that we in the West have been able to create.'[76] If in ten years the optimism had waned, the wish remained. Translation, in this context, was the first step in an envisioned large-scale adoption. In 1932 Fou Lei wrote, after returning from Paris to Shanghai: 'Our work is to research and to introduce.'[77] What he later called great-courage-ism 大勇主義 inspired by Beethovenian heroism was not only what led him out of a personal crisis; it was what bridged the two supposed civilisations as he experienced them, whilst pointing to an alternative. In the 1930s at least, it was arguably the idealism of Rolland, whom Jean-Richard Bloch described as 'himself, in his person, a religious fact',[78] that provided Fou Lei with a mental exit from a predominantly Catholic compartment of the so-called West, with which the young sceptic was in touch and in which he was not entirely at ease – and he needed entirety.

In historical retrospect, it may be conjectured that Fou Lei was fleetingly, indeed unwittingly, caught between a specific branch of the Catholic revival and one of rationalism in interwar Europe. We have no way of knowing the content of the long discussion between Fou Lei and Jean de Menasce in spring 1931, but the latter, who converted to Catholicism in 1926, happened to know Russell well. Friends with the philosopher during his Oxford years, de Menasce had translated Russell's *Mysticism and Logic* (1918) into French in 1922. It is probable that he was acquainted with *The Problem of China*, likewise published in 1922, or with its author's views. Effectively, the unstated presence of Russell in Fou Lei's letter to Daniélou, after this Rome meeting with de Menasce, might not have been a coincidence. In 1942, somewhat weary of Rollandian idealism, which he now named the New Romanticism

---

76   Bertrand Russell, *The Problem of China*, 208.

77   '我們的工作，是研究、介紹。' Fou Lei, 'Our Work' in *L'Art*, vol. 1, no. 8 (November 1932).

78   Quoted in Henri Vermorel, 'The Presence of Spinoza in the Exchanges between Sigmund Freud and Romain Rolland' in *International Journal of Psychoanalysis*, vol. 90, no. 6 (2009), 1242.

新浪漫氣息 after having translated the ten-volume *Jean-Christophe*,[79] Fou Lei published his translation of Russell's *The Conquest of Happiness* (1930). The translator's preface read: 'In recent decades, efforts made in psychoanalysis have driven out many phantoms of the inner world; it is difficult however for this specialised scientific intellectualisation to be popular, and even more so for it to be applied.[80] Moreover, the art of life encompasses biology, ethics, sociology, history, economics, numerous other kinds of intelligence, big and small, and – especially – wisdom.'[81] In search of a book of wisdom both

---

79   Discussing the problematics of translation with Stephen Soong on 9 November 1953, Fou Lei wrote: '我越來越覺得中國人的審美觀念與西洋人的出入很大，無論讀哪個時代的西洋作品，總有一部分內容格格不入。[…] 至於羅曼羅蘭那一套新浪漫氣息，我早已頭疼。此次重譯，大半是為了吃飯，不是為了愛好。流弊當然很大，一般青年動輒以大而無當的詞藻宣說人生觀等等，便是受這種影響。我自己的文字風格，也曾大大的中毒，直到辦《新語》才給廓清。' [More and more I am aware of the difference in aesthetic outlooks between the Chinese and the Westerners. Whichever era of Western literature we read, there is always an aspect that does not fit or sink in. [...] The New Romanticism of Romain Rolland has long given me a headache. I re-translated [*Jean-Christophe*] this time chiefly to make a living, not out of love. Its side effects are of course immense. Many young people routinely advocate their worldview with pomposity, and that is the influence [of *Jean-Christophe*]. My own writing style too was heavily poisoned. It was not until I worked on *New Account* [a fortnightly review that Fou Lei co-founded and co-edited in 1945] that I had it all cleared out of my system.] *Fou Lei's Letters to His Friends*, 141.

80   It would be worth exploring the extent to which the translator was aware of contemporary studies in psychology. Certain turns of phrases at the end of his preface to Russell's *The Conquest of Happiness* (1930) curiously recall Freud's *Civilisation and Its Discontents* (1930), published in the same year. At the end of his book Freud wrote: 'I therefore dare not set myself up as a prophet *vis-à-vis* my fellow men, and I plead guilty to the reproach that I cannot bring them any consolation, which is fundamentally what they all demand, the wildest revolutionaries no less passionately than the most well-behaved and pious believers.' (Sigmund Freud, *Civilization and Its Discontents*, 106.) In what seems to be an echo to the paired 'revolutionaries' and 'pious believers', Fou Lei wrote: 'Since we can neither encourage everyone to become a revolutionary, nor suppress everyone's instinct of seeking life and happiness, is not the question of struggling for a free and sound mind under the existing burden, in order to taste the fruit of life, the most pressing one?' (*Fou Lei Discusses Literature*, 235; see chapter 3, note 27.)

81   '精神分析學近數十年來的努力，已驅除了不少內心的幽靈；但這種專門的科學智識既難於普遍，更難於運用。而且人生藝術所涉及的還有生物學，倫理學，社會學，歷史，經濟，以及無數或大或小的智識和——尤其是——智慧。' Fou Lei, 'Translator's Preface to Russell's *The Conquest of Happiness*' in *Fou Lei Discusses Literature*, 235.

comprehensive and accessible, Fou Lei deemed the oeuvre of Russell worthy of introduction.[82] Such an introduction, like others made by the translator, is highly *réfléchi* and purposeful.

It is in this light that we see Fou Lei, not only as a child of the New Culture Movement, but as a father to his own generation. The 'spiritual escapism (*évasion d'âme*) that is purely impersonal' to which he turned became the anchor in his life, the niche from where he was to cultivate his art and to send composed messages to the literate class. In these messages, a strong, robust public persona, at once passionate, stoic, candid and discreet, was asserted.[83] Calling it escapism revealed Fou Lei's humility, and a reasoned restraint from siding with what he considered underprepared, irresponsible meddling in the country's longstanding chaos. In effect, his disposition corresponded seamlessly – though perhaps unknowingly – with Burckhardt's 'taking a longer view of the immediate crisis'[84] and with the latter's aestheticised approach to a *wahre Bildung* [true cultivation] of the individual.[85] A conscious importation of *Bildung* had been effectuated in a post-revolutionary China by Cai Yuanpei, who had Karl Lamprecht (1856–1915) as his professor of history at Leipzig, and who championed 'aesthetic education' as a substitute of religion in a Young China that wished to keep Confucianism at bay. *Bildung*, however, was far from a foreign concept. A congenial counterpart, one may argue, had long existed. 修身 [cultivation of the person], 'the root of everything besides' and the obligatory step towards fulfilling one's social responsibilities, stands firm in the Confucian doctrine.[86]

---

82 '能綜合以上的許多觀點而可為我們南針的，在近人著作中，羅素的《幸福之路》似乎是值得介紹的一部。' Ibid.

83 The 'impersonal' aspect of this chosen escapism manifests itself also in the fact that in his published writing from autumn 1929 onwards, Fou Lei stopped talking about himself altogether. This is a complete break from his pre-Paris, juvenile publications, where the subject was always 'I'.

84 See Richard F. Sigurdson, 'Jacob Burckhardt: The Cultural Historian as Political Thinker' in *The Review of Politics*, vol. 52, no. 3 (Summer 1990), 420.

85 Ibid., 437.

86 '古之欲明明德於天下者，先治其國。欲治其國者，先齊其家。欲齊其家者，先修其身。欲修其身者，先正其心。欲正其心者，先誠其意。欲誠其意者，先致其知。致知在格物，物格而後知至。知至而後意誠。意誠而後心正。心正而後身修。身修而後家齊。家齊而後國治。國治而後天下平。自天子以至於庶人，壹是皆以修身為本。其本亂而末治者，否矣。' [The ancients who wished to illustrate illustrious virtue throughout the world, first ordered well their own States. Wishing to order well their States, they first regulated their families. Wishing to regulate their families, they first cultivated their persons. Wishing to cultivate their persons, they first rectified their hearts. Wishing to rectify their hearts, they first sought to be sincere in their

Rather than revolution, Fou Lei trusted cultivation. Instead of a hasty solution, he cared for preparation. It is in relation to this acquired and affirmed position, where liberalism, scepticism, and political conservatism cohered, that we come to grasp Fou Lei's *évasion d'âme*. Anticipating the Schopenhaurian prescription of aesthetic contemplation, *évasion d'âme* typically implied, for a *wenren*, private pursuits in art and literature. Often a self-propaganda of the literati, this escapist ideal had never been truly apolitical. In reality, Fou Lei embraced, in these two domains, public commitments of a thoroughly modern nature – journal contribution, literary publication, artistic exhibition – in lieu of direct involvement in politics.

At twenty-three Fou Lei was, intellectually and emotionally, the man he was at his death. He needed revelation and resolution. He willed his metamorphosis. Such precocity, obstinacy, and fortitude of mind remind us of none other than Taine. Like Taine, Fou Lei consciously eschewed political parties, his consciousness being all the while astutely political, albeit tastefully unpoliticised. The 'purely impersonal' nature of Fou Lei's personal maturation was self-defined against a constantly redefined dialogue with the society at large, from which he sought to remain ideologically independent, and with which he engaged critically through words, translated and written.

A decade earlier, Russell had observed: 'I have no doubt that if the Chinese could get a stable government and sufficient funds, they would, within the next thirty years, begin to produce remarkable work in science. It is quite likely

---

thoughts. Wishing to be sincere in their thoughts, they first extended to the utmost of their knowledge. Such extension of knowledge lay in the investigation of things. Things being investigated, knowledge became complete. Their knowledge being complete, their thoughts were sincere. Their thoughts being sincere, their hearts were then rectified. Their hearts being rectified, their persons were cultivated. Their persons being cultivated, their families were regulated. Their families being regulated, their States were rightly governed. Their States being rightly governed, the entire world was at peace. From the Son of Heaven down to the mass of the people, all must consider the cultivation of the person the root of everything besides. It cannot be, when the root is neglected, that what should spring from it will be well ordered] in *The Great Learning* 大學; see James Legge (tr.), *The Chinese Classics* (Taipei: SMC, 1994), vol. 1, 357–59. Sun Yat-sen, in his 'Three Principles of the People' 《三民主義》民族主義之第六講題 (1905), stressed the importance of 修身 [cultivation of the self] as the first step towards a well-governed, well-respected nation. In his *L'Art Vivant* article, Doctor Scié-Ton-Fa named Sun Yat-sen the creator of 'the religion of the Chinese Motherland' (chapter 2, note 68).

that they might outstrip us, because they come with fresh zest and with all the ardour of a renaissance. In fact, the enthusiasm for learning in Young China reminds one constantly of the renaissance spirit in fifteenth-century Italy.'[87] If this view of 1922 sounds lamentably naïve, it is possibly because we look upon it with hindsight. The key to Russell's speculation is the condition *if* – '*if* the Chinese could get a stable government and sufficient funds', which they did not. In a post-May Fourth China, a 'renaissance' quickly became sloganeered, but to what degree this presumed cultural potential was presumable remains to be investigated. Apprehending three generations' relentlessly individualist repositioning vis-à-vis a ceaselessly volatile socio-political status quo, scholars have questioned where China's intellectuals now stood vis-à-vis the cultural projects of their own making. Gaps between intention and repercussion aside, detectable throughout these decades is a commitment to cultural cosmopolitanism that did not flinch. Politics may be devastating and disillusionment a daily discovery, and yet these literati-turned-intelligentsia, reacting in varying ways, stayed attached to their propositions. In 1933, sixteen years after suggesting, from Columbia University, a language reform which initiated a literary revolution at home, Hu Shih, an incurable optimist whom Russell admired, delivered a series of lectures entitled 'The Chinese Renaissance' at the University of Chicago. With Nietzschean confidence he professed: 'Contact with strange civilisations brings new standards of value with which the native culture is re-examined and re-evaluated, and conscious reformation and regeneration are the natural outcome of such transvaluation of values. Without the benefit of an intimate contact with the civilisation of the West, there could not be the Chinese Renaissance.'[88] To which one may add: there could not be a renaissance without the renaissance person. In 'M.H. Taine, Artiste', Zola painted a portrait: 'Monsieur Taine is not a man of his times or of his body. Had I not known him, I would like to picture him square shouldered, splendidly dressed, somewhat dragging a sword, living in full renaissance.'[89] In truth Taine was thin and frail. So was Fou Lei, and Rolland too.

---

87   Bertrand Russell, *The Problem of China*, 193.

88   Hu Shih, *The Chinese Renaissance: The Haskell Lectures 1933* (Chicago: University of Chicago, 1934), 47.

89   'M. Taine n'est pas l'homme de son temps ni de son corps. Si je ne le connaissais, j'aimerais à me le représenter carré des épaules, vêtu d'étoffes larges et splendides, traînant quelque peu l'épée, vivant en pleine Renaissance.' Zola, 'M.H. Taine, Artiste' in *Mes Haines* (Paris: Flammarion, 2012), 220.

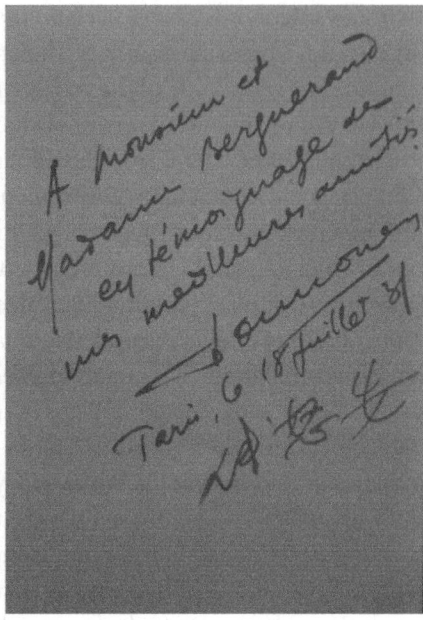

FIGURES 29 AND 30   *Fou Lei in Paris, 1931; his inscription on the reverse.*
THE BERGUERAND FAMILY ARCHIVE.

Arriving in Paris in 1928, Fou Lei had the wish that his visage would be still the same when he saw his family and friends again. In 1931, before leaving Paris, he had a photograph taken.[90] Sitting by the window, book in hand, gazing afar – this was no longer his visage of the past; this was the visage of his future. The young man had gone through a tremendous fight to make sense of his torn condition and to stay above his sorrow. The *Bildungsroman* that he could not write himself, he was to translate later.[91] 'I passed my youth and my

---

90   Fou Lei sent this photograph, now well published, to Madame Berguerand before leaving France in August 1931. His inscription on the reverse is dated 18 July 1931 (*Figs.* 29 and 30).

91   The remarks Fou Lei left in his translator's preface (1940) to the fourth and fifth volumes of Romain Rolland's *Jean-Christophe* (1904–12) can now be read, after we have witnessed his odyssey, as an allusion to his own youth: '在全書十卷中間，本冊所包括的兩卷恐怕是最混沌最不容易了解的一部了。因為克利斯朵夫在青年成長的途中，而青年成長的途程就是一段混沌、曖昧、矛盾、騷亂的歷史。' [Amongst the ten volumes of this book, perhaps these two are the most tumultuous and unfathomable. Because Jean-Christophe is on his way to maturing as a young man, and the journey of a young man's maturation is altogether a history of chaos, ambiguity, contradiction, and turmoil.] (*Complete Works*, vol. 8, 3); and the translator identified his own resolution with

adolescence in France',[92] he wrote to Madame Berguerand. The René that he was, weeping in front of a tombstone, he was not to forget. The Werther that he was, ready to kill himself with a pistol, he was not to forget. 'I did not study much', he said.[93] What he did, was live. Having lived, he now returned with his *idées fixes* and his heart firm. He was to marry his fiancée and to name her Marguerite – Marguerite of Faust.[94]

On 17 September 1931, his last day at sea, Fou Lei ended his long letter to Daniélou, 'mon meilleur ami en Europe', and signed: 'Croyez, très fidèlement votre'. For his loyalty he was to pay dearly. 'Not to cleave to a fatherland', cautioned the equally fatherless Nietzsche, 'though it be the most suffering and in need of help.'[95] As the Paquebôt Chenonceaux approached Shanghai, reality became frighteningly real.

---

that of Jean-Christophe: '一個人唯有在這場艱苦的鬥爭中得勝，才能打破青年期的難關而踏上成人的大道。' [Only by winning this grueling battle can one break through the crisis of youth and come of age.] (Ibid.)

92 '[...] j'ai passé ma jeunesse et mon adolescence en France', Fou Lei's letter to Madame Berguerand, 18 January 1931; the Berguerand family archive.

93 '讀書並不用功'. 'Fou Lei on Himself' in *Complete Works*, vol. 17, 5.

94 In *Vie de Beethoven* Romain Rolland left a footnote: as the young Félix Mendelssohn passed through Weimar in 1830, he observed that in the depth of Goethe's agitated and passionate soul, a mighty intelligence governs: '[...] (*Leidenschaftlicher Sturm und Verworrenheit*, comme Goethe disait lui-même), qu'une intelligence puissante maîtrisait.' (*Vie de Beethoven*, 48–49.) In 1930, Rolland's *Beethoven et Goethe* was published. In the same year, Charles Gounod's *Faust*, conducted by Heri Busser, played at Opéra de Paris.

95 Friedrich Nietzsche, *Beyond Good and Evil* (London: Penguin, 2003), 70.

PART 3

Shanghai in Turmoil: A Land of Chimera

∵

Moralising in Times of War: A Critic was Born

By the time Fou Lei left Paris, a critic was clamouring in him; the writing he published almost without delay in Shanghai was arguably a delayed delivery of his reflections in Europe. According to recollections of friends, on the back of his visiting card in the 1940s was a line in French: Critique d'Art.[1] His posthumous reputation being predominantly that of a translator and of a letter writer, Fou Lei's preferred identity, self-consciously generated and pronounced to the exclusion of others, is less acknowledged or discussed.

18 September 1931, the very day Fou Lei arrived in Shanghai, saw the Mukden Incident,[2] a staged railway explosion which served as Japan's pretext for invading Manchuria. The China to which he returned was no longer intact. It was to remain at war for the next eighteen years. Despite yet another course of social and political upheaval that ensued, and despite the halt it placed on everyday life, Fou Lei's immediate professional activities accorded with the plans he had made before reaching home. In winter 1931 he started teaching art history and French at Liu Haisu's Shanghai Art Academy 上海美專. In August 1932 he joined Liu in founding the Muse 摩社, a society of which artists such as Pan Yuliang 潘玉良 (1895–1977) were part. In September he joined the Paris-trained Pang Xunqin 龐薰琹 (1906–1995) and the Tokyo-trained Ni Yide 倪貽德 (1901–1970) in founding, after a long gestation and suspension, the Storm Society 決瀾社.[3] At exactly the same time, with Ni Yide he launched and co-edited *L'Art* 藝術旬刊, an ambitious thrice-monthly journal, in close

---

1   '從前在上海的時候，我們曾經陪傅雷招待一位法國朋友，鍾書注意到傅雷名片背面的一行法文：Critique d'Art (美術批評家)。他對美術批評始終很有興趣。' [Back then, living in Shanghai, we once accompanied Fou Lei in receiving a French friend. Zhongshu noticed a line in French on the back of Fou Lei's visiting card: Critique d'Art. He was always interested in art criticism.] Yang Jiang 楊絳, 'In Lieu of a Preface' 代序 to *Five Biographies Translated by Fou Lei* 傅譯傳記五種 (Beijing: Sanlian, 1983). Yang Jiang and her husband Qian Zhongshu were amongst Fou Lei's closest friends.

2   Known also as the 'September 18 Incident' 九一八事變, it enraged the Chinese public and was named the Day of National Humiliation 國恥日 by the Nationalist government. It is still commemorated nationally in China today.

3   See Ralph Crozier, 'Post-Impressionists in Pre-War Shanghai: The *Juelanshe* (Storm Society) and the Fate of Modernism in Republican China' in John Clark (ed.) *Modernity in Asian Art* (Sydney: Wild Pony, 1993), 136–154; see also Jo-Anne Birnie Danzker, Ken Lum and Zheng Shengtian (eds.), *Shanghai Modern 1919–1945* (Munich: Hatje Cantz, 2004), 234–253.

© KONINKLIJKE BRILL NV, LEIDEN, 2017 | DOI 10.1163/9789004343924_009

collaboration with members of the Muse and the Storm Society and with staff of the Shanghai Art Academy, publisher of the journal. As editor, Fou Lei wrote substantial articles alongside like-minded artists and theorists. Meanwhile, his literary and artistic commentary and his translations of French and English articles of the same genre appeared in the newspapers. The intensity and diversity of Fou Lei's activities during this short period of time, and the obstinacy and maturity with which he carried out all of them, are considerable.

Before leaving Paris, in his 1931 *L'Art Vivant* article Fou Lei gave an overview of contemporary Chinese art by singling out four exhibitions held between 1930 and 1931 in Japan, Belgium, Germany and France: the exhibition of teachers and students of the Hangzhou Art Academy in Tokyo (1930), Xu Beihong's solo exhibition in Brussels (April–May 1931), a contemporary *guohua* exhibition in Frankfurt (April 1931), and Liu Haisu's one-man show in Paris (June 1931). His narrative resorting to historiographical models of school attribution, Fou Lei saw these exhibitions as manifestations of three different schools at work, namely those of Lin Fengmian, Xu Beihong and Liu Haisu,[4] which together 'draw a reasonably accurate picture of the current state of modern art in China'.[5] In 'I Will Say It Again: Where Are We Headed?... To the Depths!' (*L'Art*, January 1933), Fou Lei was on a different track. Armed with a cyclical view of history, and assuming art in China to have entered an era of decline as did late Byzantine art, French academic painting of the eighteenth century and Italian post-Renaissance art, he now dismissed categories made through media: 'In reality, neither the self-confined *guohua* painters, nor those practising in oil who think themselves avant-garde or modern, are free from imitating; the difference is only in the object of their imitation, one being the ancients and the other, foreigners.'[6] For Fou Lei it all came down to a question of being genuine:

> The tradition that the *guohua* painters worship is no longer the original one, since tranquillity of sentiment, metaphysical hedonism and *évasion*

---

4 Fou Lei left *guohua* painters out of the equation, possibly because there was not a branded *guohua* school as such, and because Lin Fengmian, Xu Beihong and Liu Haisu all practised ink painting to one degree or another.

5 'Quatre expositions de trois groupes différents d'artistes eurent lieu, de 1930 à 1931, au Japon, en Belgique, en Allemagne et en France. Elles nous montrèrent un aspect assez exact de l'actualité artistique moderne en Chine.' See Fou Nou-En, 'La crise de l'art chinois moderne' in *L'Art Vivant* (September 1931), 468.

6 '現代的中國藝術界亦正是這樣：幽閉在因襲的樊籠中的國畫家或自命為前鋒，為現代化的洋畫家，實際上都脫不了模仿，不過模仿的對象有前人和外人的差別罷了。' Fou Lei, 'I Will Say It Again: Where Are We Headed?... To the Depths!' in *L'Art*, vol. 2, no. 1 (January 1933).

d'âme, having long ceased to exist in the modern materialistic world, are not felt by painters. Having transplanted schools and techniques from the West, those who practise in oil have not assimilated them in their minds and souls: other than enjoying the ready-made products of modern civilisation, have they really been affected in their hearts by the so-called time, so-called speed, so-called exoticism, and so-called modern style? If I may say something offensive, when Chinese oil painters make their work today, they have more or less lost sight of themselves.[7]

A severe character by nature, Fou Lei was not impressed by the general art scene and did not pretend to be. More upset still was he by the so-called 'proletarian art', asking: 'Isn't this turning art into propaganda? Isn't this an opportunist tool made for the silly shameless lot?'[8] Always the sceptic, and indifferent to the modernising fervour – in line with Benda and Péguy, he voiced misgivings as anti-modern as could be – and to the obsession with the *Zeitgeist*, Fou Lei stated: 'Express our time, yes. Not only do we need to express it, we need to presage it. But this expression is not photography. This presage is not politicised slogans; we must not forget that what the artist should express is art extracted from their heart.'[9] Already he smelled danger, and felt the need to exhort. Already he wrote, in 'Our Work' published in 1932: '[…] we need to observe and to discuss without arrogance. Looking for Truth is not easy. All doctrines are equal in our eyes. We cannot say the wind from the East has triumphed over the wind from the West, for that would be blind. Despotism in thinking is the biggest enemy of Truth.'[10] – Pause for a moment, and one realises that this chant of Eatern over Western wind, which enjoyed currency in early-1930s China, was

---

7　'現代的國畫家所奉為圭臬的傳統，已不復是傳統的本來面目：那種超人的寧靜恬淡的情操，和形而上的享樂與神遊（évasion d'âme）在現代的物的世界中早已不存在，而畫家們也感不到。洋畫家們在西方搬過來的學派和技法，也還沒有在它們的心魂中融化：他們除了在物質上享受到現代文明的現成的產物之外，所謂時間，所謂速度，所謂外來情調，所謂現代風格，究竟曾否在他們的內心上引起若干反響？如果我說一句冒瀆的話，現代的中國洋畫家在製作的時候，多少是忘掉了自我。' Ibid.

8　'這豈不是把藝術變了宣傳主義的廣告？這豈不是為一般無恥而無聊的人造成一種投機的工具？' Ibid.

9　'表現時代，是的。不獨要表現時代，而且還得預言時代。但這表現決非是照相。這預言決非是政綱式的口號；我們不能忘記藝術家應該表現的，是經過他心靈提鍊出來的藝術品。' Ibid.

10　'[…] 我們要虛心地觀察，探討。要找真理並非是怎麼容易的事。各種學說在我們的眼里一視同仁，我們不能把東風壓了西風，因為這是盲目的。思想上的專制是真理的最大敵人。' Fou Lei, 'Our Work' in *L'Art*, vol. 1, no. 8 (November 1932).

to be re-asserted by Mao on his visit to the Soviet Union in November 1957. Equally immune to iconoclastic and nationalistic ideologies, Fou Lei's 1932 call for equality and equity paralleled Taine's opening speech in *Philosophie de l'art*, originally delivered at École des beaux-arts in 1864. His scorn of sloganeering optimism likewise corresponded to Taine's pedantic circumspection: 'We dare not chant the high-pitched chant of synthesising Eastern and Western art and of prospering national culture, for we understand our own force [or the lack thereof].'[11] The didacticism of tone can hardly escape our attention. Again and again Fou Lei asked his country's artists, as he did its politicians, to slow down and to reflect. Upholding the same position as in politics, two months later he wrote: 'Under these circumstances, in art as in other domains, we need calm and patience. Amidst all kinds of slogans and calls to arms, we need to recognise: (1) It should be possible that the fundamental difference between Eastern and Western art be reconciled or left to fight; (2) The individual should hone his skills, edify his thoughts, and carry out long-term research.'[12]

Writing, the *exigeant* critic was at one with the audience he was addressing. Unconditionally he took his readers into his confidence. Advising the artists that 'it is absolutely not too late to decide whether to go left or right after a profound acquaintance with the theories of both Eastern and Western art'[13] – this is what he meant by going 'to the depths', an alternative to both left and right – he was not short of extending to others the demands he made on himself. He had, on his way back to Shanghai, wanted to 'make an in-depth study (*une étude approfondie*) of the antique Orient as well as of the modern and historical Occident'.[14] What he demanded of himself he saw no alternative but to fulfill, hence the conviction in his exhortation, which might otherwise have fallen short of reason. Despite, if not because of, the didactic vigour in Fou Lei's writing, its effect is one of intense persuasiveness, for he himself lived intensely his thoughts.

One thing distinguished Fou Lei from many of his European-educated contemporaries: believing in learning for its own sake, he *continued* his formation

<hr>

11   '我們不敢唱融合東西藝術，發揚民族文化那種高調，因為我們明白自己的力量。' Ibid.

12   '在這種情勢下，在藝術上和在其他的領域中一樣，我們需要鎮靜與忍耐。在各種口號和吶喊聲中，要認清：(一) 東方藝術和西方藝術的根本不同點，是應該是可以調和抑爭鬥；(二) 培養個人的技巧，磨鍊思想，做長時期的研究。' Fou Lei, 'I Will Say It Again: Where Are We Headed?... To the Depths!' in *L'Art*, vol. 2, no. 1 (January 1933).

13   '現代的中國藝術家 […] 把東西兩種藝術的理論有一番深切的認識之後，再來說往左或往右去，決不太遲。' Ibid.

14   See chapter 6, note 63.

after returning to his country.[15] Teaching, he wrote his lectures as one would a book. He also translated books, not articles, as supplementary reading material for his students. All this was carried out in the spirit of his envisioned *étude approfondie*, his long-term research. The books translated to complement his teaching were carefully chosen. In Rodin's *L'art: entretiens réunis par Paul Gsell* (1911), itself a sustained conversation between a master and his disciple about art and artists,[16] one finds traces of Fou Lei's lifelong creeds, and in his fatherly advice to Fou Ts'ong, 'Be a moral person first, then an artist; being a pianist comes last', one hears Rodin's words to Gsell: 'The important thing is to be moved, to love, to hope, to shiver, to live. Be a man before being an artist!'[17]

In 1932, Fou Lei published in *L'Art* some of his lectures, originally delivered at the Shanghai Art Academy. Beginning with Giotto, they are surveys of artists in Europe. In 1934, the recently resigned lecturer recopied these essays in elegant calligraphy, bound them with an astounding preface composed in classical Chinese, wrote on the frontispiece *Twenty Lectures on Masterpieces of World Art* 世界美術名作二十講, and shelved them. Published posthumously in 1985 and seen as Fou Lei's own writing, they are in fact, broadly speaking, a liberal translation of *Vingt leçons d'histoire de l'art* by L. Bordes.[18] Printed in 1927 to accompany the formal introduction of art history into France's secondary-school

---

15   In a touching note Sun Fuxi sent to Madame Berguerand in 1937 at the beginning of the Sino-Japanese War, with a photograph of him and his wife and daughter attached, Sun's French, once fluid, was gone. He could barely string a sentence together. As was the case with so many others, as soon as Sun went back to China, politics called upon him, as did bureaucratic, mundane, and existential obligations. (Sun Fuxi's note and photograph are in the Berguerand family archive.) See Qian Zhongshu's satirical novel *Fortress Besieged* for a superb sketch of the lives of his own generation of European-educated Chinese after they returned home.

16   For a contemporaneous response, see the review by S.S. in *Art and Progress*, vol. 2, no. 11 (September 1911), 334, which ended on the note: 'It is to be regretted that no English translation has yet appeared. A book so valuable in suggestion, so worthy to become a classic, should be available to the people.' In the bookshop of musée Rodin today, one finds Fou Lei's Chinese translation, which he finished in 1931–32 without intending to have it published; a dozen of so copies were made for circulation amongst his students. Its posthumous publication appeared in 1990.

17   'Le grand point est d'être ému, d'aimer, d'espérer, de frémir, de vivre. Être homme avant d'être artiste!' in Auguste Rodin, *L'art: entretiens réunis par Paul Gsell* (Paris: Grasset, 1986), 250.

18   At the end of the preface, Fou Lei acknowledged that he had consulted the work of living historians such as Bordes and Berenson. To my knowledge, no comparison between Fou Lei's *Twenty Lectures* and the two said historians has been made, and this posthumously published book goes unchallenged as Fou Lei's own. Unlike Berenson, Bordes is unknown.

curriculum,[19] *Vingt leçons* was judged by a contemporary Anglophone reviewer to be 'for teachers, not for pupils'.[20] In a manner recalling Elie Faure, Bordes' accomplished literary style was conceivably what appealed to Fou Lei. *Twenty Lectures* was, in effect, a lyrical translation of the lyrical *Vingt leçons*.

Speaking about art in an extravagantly descriptive and minutely analytical manner in early 1930s Shanghai was not something to be taken for granted. It was first and foremost a question of language. As much as thinking dictates language, language dictates thinking. Intellectual discourse within a specific discipline is groundless without an established vocabulary. The highly stylised use of classical Chinese – extravagant and minute in its own right – in discussions of the élite arts of painting and calligraphy, did not automatically translate, in post-New Culture Movement linguistic milieux, into a descriptive and analytical mode of discussing, say, Leonardo da Vinci. After conscious reforms of the 1910s and 1920s, vernacular Chinese, though used for centuries with finesse in literary creation, particularly and increasingly in the form of fiction, became conspicuously 'loose' compared to the decided terseness of classical Chinese. Japanese neologism and newly translated Western literature animated the written language, in terms of vocabulary but also of grammar, now wittingly open for manipulation.

The degree of flexibility and density in the use of the vernacular varied from writer to writer. In Fou Lei's case, translating was a visible stimulus for thinking, and thinking partly an auto-translation. The maturation of his style, with references at once to classical Chinese and French – and to a lesser extent, English – took place in a trilingual, at times quadrilingual, context. Examining *Twenty Lectures* vis-à-vis *Vingt leçons*, we notice that, because it was not meant as translation, Fou Lei's 'writing' was soaringly free, assured of its own expression. There were those who wrote well, such as Feng Zikai and Teng Gu, on art, but none with the clear sense of the role of language in tackling, as accurately as is feasible, something visual, or the highly conscious projection of a settled, sophisticated style. The young teacher of art history, versed in French when it came to his subject, equipped himself with equal eloquence in his mother tongue. Effectively making a new language as he went along, his was a veritable process of structuralist, colouristic, and musical creation. Experimentation was in the air, and liberation.

Released by the Catholic publishing house Gigord, *Vingt leçons d'histoire de l'art* came out in 1927, shortly before Fou Lei arrived in France.

19   See T.C., 'Review of *Vingt leçons d'histoire de l'art* par Bordes' in *Studies: An Irish Quarterly Review*, vol. 17, no. 65 (March 1928), 152.

20   Ibid., 153.

At twenty-four, Fou Lei was one of Shanghai's most authoritative critics and cosmopolites. Yet his academic career was short-lived. Through the Shanghai Incident (staged in January 1932), Japan provoked China into a brief war.[21] Fou Lei opposed the idea of students abandoning class to protest on the street. Still the Art Academy closed for half a year, during which time he worked as a translator at Agence France-Presse, and continued writing course material as well as preparing for the launch of *L'Art*. In autumn 1932, the Art Academy re-opened; Fou Lei resumed teaching on the condition that his resignation from the administrative position as Head of Office be accepted – already he found it difficult to operate in a bureaucratic system. In September 1933, upon his mother's death, Fou Lei resigned from the Academy altogether. In fact, he re-signed, almost always briskly and in a rage, from every post he had ever accept-ed, and almost for the entirety of his working life, Fou Lei was self-employed.

Fou Lei's relationship with Liu Haisu will now be considered, for it throws light not only on the choices made by the young critic between 1929 and 1936, but on the artistic climate in Shanghai in the 1930s. In his *L'Art Vivant* article, Fou Lei had showered praise upon Liu Haisu, and implicitly criticised Liu's en-emy Xu Beihong 徐悲鴻 (1895–1953) who had studied in Paris between 1919 and 1927.[22] Following Liu Haisu's solo exhibition in Shanghai in October 1932, a battle between Liu and Xu took the form of vehement letters the two publicly addressed to each other in the *Shanghai News* 申報. Fou Lei's 1931 article in Paris forecasted this feud.[23] His dedication to Liu Haisu and to what he took

---

21   Following the occupation of Manchuria, 一二八事變 (the January 28 Incident) became the climax of a series of ostensibly anti-Japanese incidents orchestrated by the Japanese in Shanghai as the pretext for further military advance in China.

22   Fou Lei introduced Liu Haisu as a genius who founded the Shanghai Art Academy at the age of sixteen, 'the same year of the proclamation of the Republic of China', to teach young artists how to paint in oil, and who gained the scandalous title 'Artist Rebel' for being the first to use nude models in life-drawing classes in China (1918). See Fou Nou-En, 'La crise de l'art chinois moderne' in *L'Art Vivant* (September 1931), 468. Fou Lei's account reflected more Liu's self-made myth.

23   Fou Lei alluded to 'former students of the Shanghai Art Academy' who, having studied in Europe, 'returned to China imposing their Ingres, their David and even their Parisian professors', when Liu's Academy 'endeavoured to assimilate Van Gogh, Cézanne and even Matisse' in their teaching (ibid.). Fou Lei was himself an admirer of Cézanne, having pub-lished his first piece of art criticism in Chinese on the artist in January 1930. Xu Beihong and Liu Haisu, who had a personal contempt as well as professional disrespect for each other, quarreled over this divergence of artistic orientation in their public letters of 1932. For a bigger picture of the dispute between Xu and Liu, see Éric Janicot, 'Les matières de la modernité: la diffusion de la peinture à l'huile en Chine républicaine' in *Revue d'histoire moderne et contemporaine* (1954–), vol. 49e, no. 3 (July–September 2002), 168–175; 'Les

to be their common cause at the time was total. Reading Fou Lei's admiring words, 'The Artist Rebel's return to tradition, after having traversed in a few years the entire history of European art, testifies to the profound intelligence and originality of M. Liu Haisu, who emerged out of his influences and awoke with his national soul',[24] one wonders if Fou Lei cared more about what Liu represented than what Liu painted. In his 1932 article entitled 'Liu Haisu' for *L'Art,* Fou Lei was to say: 'Right now, for the sake of argument, I ask not if China wants an artist like Liu Haisu. I ask only if China wants a person like him.'[25] It was Fou Lei who wanted a person like Liu Haisu, and it was Liu Haisu the person he needed.[26]

---

naissances de l'art moderne chinois (De la chute des Qing à la République populaire, 1911–1949)' in ibid., vol. 34e, no. 2 (April–June 1987), 231–256, of the same author; and Wen C. Fong, 'The Modern Chinese Art Debate' in *Artibus Asiae,* vol. 53, no. 1/2 (1993), 290–305.

24   'Le retour à la tradition de 'l'Artiste Rebelle' qui avait parcouru, en peu d'années, toute l'histoire de l'art européen, témoignait de la profonde intelligence et de l'originalité de M. Liu Hai-Sou qui se dégageait des influences et se réveillait avec son âme nationale.' Fou Nou-En, 'La crise de l'art chinois moderne' in *L'Art Vivant* (September 1931), 468.

25   '在現在，我且不問中國要不要劉海粟這樣一個藝術家，我只問中國要不要海粟這樣一個人。' Fou Lei, 'Liu Haisu' 劉海粟 in *L'Art,* vol. 1, no. 3 (26 November 1931).

26   Fou Lei was not the first young man to have been loyal to a big personality who, nevertheless, did not deserve his loyalty. René Étiemble's (1909–2002) relationship with Jean Paulhan (1884–1969) bears resemblance, to a degree, to that between Fou Lei and Liu Haisu. Interviewed in 1988 for the literary television series 'Apostrophes' by Bernard Pivot, and asked why he succumbed to the manipulative tyranny of Paulhan – 'Je n'arrive pas à comprendre comment vous, qui avez toujours l'esprit critique, avec votre intelligence, avec votre force de caractère, comment vous avez pu accepter pendant des années, des années de vivre une sorte d'esclavage chez Jean Paulhan.' [I cannot understand how come you, you who always have a critical spirit, with your intelligence and your force of character, could accept, for years and years, to live in a kind of enslavement to Paulhan.] – Étiemble, aged seventy-nine, answered: 'C'est très simple. Je n'ai jamais eu de père. Mon père est mort, j'avais deux ans et demi. Je m'en suis jamais remis. Ma mère n'a jamais voulu se remarier pour que je n'aie pas de beau-père, et je me suis trouvé dans ce vide sans imago paternel. Et je me suis cherché toujours un imago paternel. Et en Paulhan, j'ai trouvé le père dont j'avais besoin, et j'ai cru en lui comme en mon père.' [It's very simple. I never had a father. My father died when I was two and a half. I never got over it. My mother never wanted to remarry so that I wouldn't have a stepfather, and I found myself in this void without a paternal imago. I was always looking for a paternal imago, and in Paulhan I found the father I needed, and I had faith in him as I would in my father.] In *Lignes d'une vie: Naissance à la littérature ou le meurtre du père* (Paris: Arléa, 1988), Étiemble, in his post-bereavement for Paulhan, examined this difficult relationship. See also Jeannine Kohn-Étiemble, *226 lettres inédites de Jean Paulhan* (Paris: Klincksieck, 1975).

But this person quickly let him down, above all morally. In the first place, Fou Lei was disappointed with Liu as an educator. About his resignation from the Shanghai Art Academy, Fou Lei wrote in 1957: 'Because (1) Young and un-learned, I thought myself unqualified to teach. When my mother was alive, already disappointed that I did not obtain a degree overseas, she would have been heartbroken had I not worked. Also, at the time I was financially inde-pendent with only a small monthly subsidy from her, and had to earn my own living. (2) Liu Haisu treated me extremely well, but was mean to others. He ran the Academy like a businessman, to my great dismay. Therefore as soon as my mother died, I resigned.'[27]

It was likely, or at least in part, because of his estrangement from Liu Haisu that Fou Lei did not return to Europe in 1933, 'first to Rome, then to Paris and Berlin where we will hold three ancient and modern Chinese art exhibitions'[28] as he once planned. Whilst Liu Haisu and his new family (he had divorced and re-married) stayed at the chalet Berguerand after holding the 1934 Ber-lin exhibition,[29] Fou Lei stayed with his wife Zhu Meifu (they had married in January 1932) and their newborn son, Fou Ts'ong, in Shanghai. From there he wrote to Madame Berguerand; this was prompted by a letter he had received from Liu Haisu's eldest teenage son, who reported that Madame never stopped asking after him and his family.[30] In his letter Fou Lei was full of envy that Liu

---

27 '因（一）年少不學，自認為無資格教書，母親在日，以我在國外未得學位，再不
  工作她更傷心；且彼時經濟獨立，母親只月貼數十元，不能不自己謀生；（二）
  某某某待我個人極好，但待別人刻薄，辦學純是商店作風，我非常看不慣，故
  母親一死即辭職。' 'Fou Lei on Himself' in *Complete Works*, vol. 17, 6.

28 In his letter to Madame Berguerand in July 1931, Fou Lei wrote: '[J'espère] de pouvoir revenir en Europe en 1933, d'abord à Rome, ensuite à Paris et à Berlin où nous allons faire
  trois expositions d'art Chinois ancien et moderne. Je reviendrai sûrement passer quelque
  temps chez vous, avec ma femme, car, je vais épouser ma petite cousine en rentrant.'
  [I hope to be able to return to Europe in 1933, first to Rome, then to Paris and Berlin
  where we will hold three exhibitions of ancient and modern Chinese art. I will certainly
  come to spend some time at yours with my wife, for I shall marry my little cousin when
  I go back.] Without Fou Lei, whose mother had just died and whose wife was expecting,
  Liu Haisu returned to Europe at the end of 1933. The years 1934 and 1935 saw a string of
  Chinese art exhibitions in Europe, supported equally by the Chinese government and put
  up separately by Liu Haisu and his rival Xu Beihong. Back in China, Lu Xun wrote and
  mocked them both.

29 In 2013 Monique Werlen discovered, in her grandparents' stamp collection, envelopes of
  letters addressing Liu Haisu from Nanjing, Paris, and Berlin in 1934.

30 'Mon jeune ami, Liu Foh-Tchen, vient de m'écrire une lettre française en me disant que
  vous n'avez pas cessé de lui demander des nouvelles de nous. Je ne saurais m'excuser auprès de vous ni m'expliquer ce long silence.' [My young friend, Liu Foh-Tchen, wrote me

Haisu had the means to return to Europe and to stay in the 'pretty chalet facing the world's number one lake'.[31] Then came his reproach of Liu Haisu as a man. 'Madame Liu has changed, utterly changed, hasn't she? Little Foh-Tchen wrote to me: "The village is the same, and the chalet too. For me only the bedrooms have changed and also, my mother." Reading this, I could not stop my tears flowing. What do you think of this, dear Madame, you who are so tender and so kind? I nearly fell out with Monsieur Liu because I cannot watch my friend make such a big mistake. The "new" Madame Liu is Monsieur Liu's student, and mine too: poor studies, charming and sensual person, here is the grade I give to my former student.'[32]

Fou Lei did fall out with Liu Haisu two years later. In 1936, their common friend from Paris years, the artist Zhang Xian, died of a sudden relapse of liver disease coupled with a momentary loss of lucidity; he was thirty-five. Grief-stricken, Fou Lei was convinced that Zhang died, firstly, of general poor health because for years he was underpaid at the Art Academy by Liu Haisu, with whom Fou Lei had already argued about this matter and, secondly, of accumulated resentment towards the injustice of it all.[33] Fou Lei's reaction to Zhang's

---

a letter in French telling me that you never stopped asking after us. I do not know how to ask you for forgiveness or to explain this long silence.] Fou Lei's letter to Madame Berguerand, 6 September 1934; the Berguerand family archive.

31   'La famille Liu a des chances de pouvoir retourner chez vous, habiter dans ce joli chalet devant ce premier lac du monde. Oh! combien je voudrais être aussi chez vous, être votre hôte, manger à la même table avec vous comme autrefois.' [The Lius are fortunate to be able to return to your home, staying in this pretty chalet facing the world's number one lake. Oh, how I would like to be there with you as your guest, to eat at the same table with you like in the old days.] Ibid.

32   'Madame Liu est changée, tout à fait changé, n'est-ce-pas? Le petit Foh-Tchen m'écrit: « Le village est le même, le chalet aussi, pour moi seules les chambres à coucher sont changées et aussi... la mère ». En lisant cela, je ne peux empêcher mes larmes couler. Qu'en pensez-vous, chère Madame, vous qui êtes si tendre et si bonne? Je suis presque brouillé avec Monsieur Liu, rien parce que je ne peux pas voir mon ami commettre une faute aussi grande. La « nouvelle » Madame Liu est l'élève de Monsieur Liu, aussi l'élève de moi: mauvaises études, charmante et sensuelle personne, voici ma note sur mon ancienne élève.' (Ibid.) The new Madame Liu, Cheng Jiahe (1913–?) 成家和, was to betray and divorce Liu Haisu in 1943, whilst retaining a lifelong friendship with Fou Lei's family. Her sister Cheng Jialiu 成家榴 had a passionate relation with Fou Lei towards the end of the 1930s and the beginning of the 1940s.

33   Four months after Zhang Xian's death, on 6 December 1936, Fou Lei wrote to Liu Kang. Noting the salary of an ordinary college teacher whom he knew, which greatly exceeded that of either Zhang Xian or Liu Kang, Fou Lei commented: '張弦的氣死，越想越應該，像他那樣剛烈的人怎能不氣呢？' [The more I think about it, the more I see

death paralleled his interpretation of that of his own father, who developed tuberculosis in prison and died thereof three months after release. In Fou Lei's own account, the disease was omitted and the cause of death was given as anguish: 抑鬱而死.[34] In the same text, his portrayal of Zhang Xian's end was identical: 抑鬱而死.[35] Upon receiving news of Zhang's death from Liu Kang, Fou Lei, then on vacation, sent a cheque right away to fund the funeral, and asked if Liu Haisu, Zhang Xian's employer, was to do anything to take care of Zhang's family.[36] Upon returning to Shanghai, Fou Lei initiated and organised an exhibition of the dead artist's work to raise money for his widow and child. At the preparatory meeting for the exhibition, he rowed with Liu Haisu, stormed off, and stuck to the rupture for nearly twenty years.[37]

Fou Lei mourned long over this loss. Zhang Xian, in his eyes, was the ideal artist, pure, honest, and committed, all of which qualities that he increasingly found lacking in Liu Haisu, for whom he once had uncritical admiration and whose work he had persuaded the French government to purchase before leaving Paris.[38] His depreciation of the way Liu ran the Art Academy, his objection to Liu's divorce and re-marriage, and his indignation over Zhang Xian's death (which led to the rupture with Liu) were all based on moral grounds. Similarly we find a double judgement – moral *and* artistic – in Fou Lei's more sober opinion of Liu Haisu's painting, never voiced publicly for he never forgot that Liu had been good to him, but expressed openly to close friends. In 1961, after a twenty-five-year interruption of correspondence, Fou Lei heard from Liu Kang, who had moved at the outbreak of the Sino-Japanese war to Malaysia and then Singapore. In a very long letter, Fou Lei examined painting in China in the past

---

why Zhang Xian died of rage, for how could he not, him being someone so straight and unyielding?] *Fou Lei's Letters to His Friends*, 19.

34 ‘出獄後以含冤未得昭雪，抑鬱而死。’ [After release from prison but without exoneration, he died of anguish.] ‘Fou Lei on Himself’ in *Complete Works*, vol. 17, 5.

35 In the same statement, Fou Lei thus described Zhang Xian's death: ‘受美專剝削，抑鬱而死。’ [Exploited by the Art Academy, he died of anguish.] Ibid., 10.

36 See Fou Lei's letters to Liu Kang, 20 August 1936; 28 August 1936. *Fou Lei's Letters to His Friends*, 12–13.

37 ‘Fou Lei on Himself’ in *Complete Works*, vol. 17, 10–11.

38 ‘為其向法國教育部美術司活動，由法政府購劉之作品一件。’ [For him I contacted la direction des beaux-arts of Ministère de l'Éducation nationale, and the French government bought one of his works.] (Ibid., 6.) This was Liu Haisu's *Paysage de neige* 盧森堡之雪， oil on canvas executed in jardin du Luxembourg in 1931, now in the collection of musée du Jeu de Paume. The tableau was shown at the exhibition ‘Artistes chinois à Paris 1920–1958: de Lin Fengmian à Zao Wou-ki’ at musée Cernuschi, September–December 2011.

few decades – next to his *artiste préféré* Huang Binhong,[39] the one he appreciated the most was Lin Fengmian[40] – and stated his ultimate criticism of Liu Haisu, namely, that he never lost sleep over his art, that he was complacent.[41] Coincidentally, in a 1928 letter to Daniélou, *entre amis*, Georges Izard doubted the sincerity of Alain, Daniélou's brother, who 'never had the slightest *true, great* artistic concern'.[42] This parallel suggests the extent to which Fou Lei was in accord with his Parisian friends, in ways perhaps beyond his own knowledge.

---

39   The artist-critic relationship between Huang Binhong 黃賓虹 (1865–1955) and Fou Lei, who in twelve years exchanged more than two hundred letters before the artist's death, has been of interest to publishers and writers in recent years. In light of Fou Lei's vision of 'a third civilisation based on China's tradition' in 1931 (letter to Daniélou, 17 September 1931), we see how Huang Binhong, a master of ink painting, an erudite theorist when it came to art in China, and a cognoscente of art in Europe, was for Fou Lei the embodiment of such a civilisation. Huang Binhong, forty-three years Fou Lei's senior, likewise considered his young friend the one person who understood his art. Both Fou Lei and Huang Binhong eventually perceived little to no difference between so-called Chinese and Western painting. For a scholarly examination of this mutual appreciation, see Claire Roberts, *Friendship in Art*. Pierre Ryckmans (dit Simon Leys), one of the first scholars to study Huang Binhong, discussed in the 1970s Huang's painting with Étiemble, who had been given two Huang Binhong scrolls by Fou Lei in 1957. At one point, Ryckmans asked to read photocopies of letters that Fou Lei had sent Étiemble concerning the painter. Correspondence between Ryckmans and Étiemble is conserved at Bibliothèque nationale de France.

40   Fou Lei and Lin Fengmian quietly formed a deep empathy and esteem for each other, little discussed in existing literature. For Fou Ts'ong's wedding in London in 1960, Fou Lei sent the couple a painting by Lin Fengmian. In a remarkably short autobiography of two hundred and thirty-eight words, Lin Fengmian, having been imprisoned and released, and having lived to old age, humbly recounted: '記得很久以前，傅雷先生對我說藝術的追求有如當年我祖父雕刻石頭的精神。現在，我已活到我祖父的年歲了，雖不敢說是像他一樣的勤勞，但也從未無故放下畫筆。' [A long time ago, I remember, Mr Fou Lei said that I pursued art in the same spirit that my grandfather, a mason, carved stone. Having lived to my grandfather's age, I dare not say that I have been as diligent as he, but I have never put down my brush for no good reason.]

41   '他與我相交數十年，從無一字一句提到他創作方面的苦悶或是什麼理想的境界。你想他自高自大到多麼可怕的地步。' [In the decades that I have known him, never once has he mentioned any creative disquietude or ideal. So you get the frightening extent of his conceit.] Fou Lei's letter to Liu Kang, 7 May 1961, in *Fou Lei's Letters to His Friends*, 29.

42   In a letter dated 4 December 1928 to Daniélou (conserved at Archives jésuites de la Province de France), Georges Izard spoke of Alain Daniélou, who was then keen about dance: 'Il parle de vocation artistique. Je me demande où est son art, s'il a jamais eu le moindre *vrai, grand* souci artistique.' [He talks about artistic vocation. I wonder where his art is, if he has never had the slightest *true, great* artistic concern.]

If Liu Haisu had promised a father figure for Fou Lei, it would have been at best that of *un faux père*. Fou Lei, once matured, removed this disappointment from his life. In 1954, having recently run into Liu Haisu, Fou Lei wrote to Fou Ts'ong, then studying in Poland:

> In the morning I went to the museum to look at ancient painting and bronzes of the Shang, Zhou, and Warring State period, amongst other things; in the afternoon I went to the Culture Club to see the preview of works selected from the Eastern regions for the national art exhibition. Even Min kept shaking his head and complained it was insupportable. Mostly the genre of calendar painting, only cruder than decent advertisement design. Not to mention the amateurish woodblock caricature. A few older painters, eager to keep up with fashion, splashed glossy large-scale coloured postcards, some metres long. Seen from a distance, they resembled painted stage backdrops, and upon close examination no brushwork was to be detected. Lunlun's father was dreadfully affectionate with me when he saw me at Huang Binhong's exhibition.[43] In this preview I saw two of his oils and two inks. His *guohua* is still fraudulent, with all the pretence and no inner spirit, totally opportunistic and fooling the eyes of the ignorant. His Yellow Mountain cliffs are made up of tens of thousands of inept lines, all short and all broken, pieced together with no life of which to speak. [...] When I saw his work the other day, I knew his art would be hopeless for the remainder of his life. It had been decades, I had hoped that he had made *some* progress; what a surprise, things are just the same. What's more, his oils are even worse than before. No *touche*, and the colours are outrageously vulgar, almost unexpectedly so. In conclusion, whoever makes art must be true and loyal. All his life he lacks these two qualities. He boasts dazzlingly but is never modest at heart, and never does any hard work or research.[44]

---

43 That was Liu Haisu. Lunlun, i.e. Liu Yinglun 劉英倫 (1935–), is his daughter with Cheng Jiahe. The occasion would have been 黃賓虹先生作品觀摩會, an exhibition of Huang Binhong's work held in Shanghai in September 1954.

44 '上午到博物館去看古畫，看商周戰國的銅器等等；下午到文化俱樂部參觀華東參加全國美展的作品預展。結果看得連阿敏都頻頻搖頭，連喊吃不消。大半是月份牌式，其幼稚還不如好的廣告畫。漫畫木刻之幼稚，不在話下。其余的幾個老輩畫家，也是軋時髦，塗抹一些光光滑滑的，大幅的着色明信片，長至丈余，遠看也像舞台佈景，近看毫無筆墨。倫倫的爸爸在黃賓虹畫展中見到我，大為親熱。這次在華東出品全國的展覽中，有二張油畫，二張國畫。國畫仍是野狐禪，徒有其貌，毫無精神，一味取巧，騙人眼目；畫的黃山峭壁，千千萬萬的線條，不過二三寸長的，也是敗筆，而且是瑣瑣碎碎連接起來的，毫無生

Fou Lei was, without question, a moralist, for whom intellectual, ethical, and artistic integrity were one and the same. In 'The Lion Has Roared' 獅子吼了, a short piece for the *Shanghai News* critiquing a solo exhibition (1932) of Liu Shi 劉獅 (1910–1997), Liu Haisu's nephew, Fou Lei, himself a young man, wrote:

> Liu Shi is an extremely clever and smart young man. I often advise him to be clever but not smart; an artist especially needs to have a touch of daftness in him, and that is of course a long way from mere smartness. Liu Shi is easily influenced, because he is smart. It is unavoidable for an artist who has not yet attained success to be influenced. But influence is different from imitation, and the result of being smart is the confounding of the two, to the point where one's individuality vanishes. Liu Shi appears to have understood this. His efforts in the past year have been to free himself of the disquietude of being at a loss, and to search steadfastly for his own path. He gradually abandoned formal resemblance, flimsiness, colourfulness, and all those artificial, flashy techniques, and made unified, untainted, synthetic, composed experiments.[45]

His tone dogmatic, and his idea of an *artiste* – a *mélange* of the Confucian aspiration of the superior man and the romantic image of the artist as an ideal type – fixed, Fou Lei applied his criteria indistinguishably to art and literature.[46] In 'Thoughts After Reading Plays' 讀劇隨感 (November 1943), published under the pseudonym Woebegone 疾首 in *Ten Thousand Things* 萬象,

---

命可言。[…] 那天看了他的作品，我就斷定他這一輩子的藝術前途完全沒有希望了。我幾十年不見他的作品，原希望他多少有些進步，不料仍是老調。而且他的油畫比以前還退步，筆觸談不到，色彩也俗不可耐，而且俗到出乎意外。可見一個人弄藝術非真實、忠誠不可。他一生就缺少這兩點，可以嘴里說得天花亂墜，實際上從無虛懷若谷的謙德，更不肯下苦功研究。' Fou Lei's letter to Fou Ts'ong, 19 October 1954, in *Fou Lei's Family Letters*, 55.

45 '劉獅是一個十二分聰明伶俐的青年，我常勸他做人要聰明而不伶俐，做藝術家尤其要有三分戇氣，這當然離伶俐很遠。劉獅最易受人影響，因為他伶俐。一個未成功的作家當然免不了受人影響，但影響與摹仿有異，而伶俐的結果，往往會埋沒自己的個性，而把影響與摹仿相混。劉獅似乎已懂得這一點，一年來的努力都在想解脫他那徬徨歧途苦悶，深信不疑地尋覓他自己的途徑。他慢慢地丟棄肖似、纖巧、艷麗，那些膚淺的、眩人眼目的技巧，而作着統一、蘊純、綜合、沉着的試驗。' Fou Lei, 'The Lion Has Roared' 獅子吼了 in *Shanghai News* 申報 (14 September 1932). The critiqued artist's given name, shi 獅, means lion. I am grateful to Fou Min for sending me, in 2012, the transcription of this newly discovered publication.

46 From the 1910s onwards, art and literature were customarily grouped under a unified category 文藝 [literature and art].

Fou Lei asked: 'What is it really, art and literature?'[47] and was ready to define the author of a good work as '(s)he who enlarges, elevates, and purifies our spirit, and who inspires us to leave our lives behind to love everyone!'[48] It was through this lens, tinged with what one might call Rollandian longing – after all, he had not long finished translating *Jean-Christophe* – that Fou Lei published, also in *Ten Thousand Things*,[49] his most substantial and lasting piece of literary criticism, 'On the Novels of Eileen Chang' 論張愛玲的小說 (May 1944), under the pseudonym Rapid Rain 迅雨.

In 1943–44, a Japanese-occupied Shanghai saw the phenomenal rise to fame of a twenty-three-year-old writer. Unable to stay indifferent, Fou Lei commenced his appraisal echoing Rolland and Taine combined: 'At a time when the air is heavy, and in a place where the soil is sterile, no one has the illusion or expectation that, in the garden of art and literature, a rare flower should burgeon out.'[50] Having affirmed Eileen Chang's emergence as such a miracle, Fou Lei ecstatically deemed *The Golden Cangue* 金鎖記 (1943), her novella, 'one of the most beautiful harvests of our literary circle'.[51] As would do Taine, author of *History of English Literature* (1863), who advised his nephew André Chevrillon, a scholar of English literature, to 'citer, citer beaucoup'[52] [quote, quote a lot], Fou Lei lavishly cited Chang's sensational paragraphs in admiration, considering each line so appreciatively as to repaint Chang's cinematic scenes with his own pen. Without reservation he praised the structure, rhythm, and use of colour in *The Golden Cangue*, and highlighted three outstanding qualities: first, the novelist's psychoanalysis which 'connects action, speech, and psychology through suggestion rather than through long monologues or dull minute

---

47 　'那麼，文藝到底是什麼東西呢？' Fou Lei, 'Thoughts After Reading Plays' 讀劇隨感 in *Ten Thousand Things* 萬象 (November 1943).

48 　'是他，使我們的胸襟擴大，澄清，想拋棄了生命去愛所有的人！……' Ibid.

49 　This literary magazine was also where many of Eileen Chang's iconic works first appeared in 1943–44. Its editor-in-chief, Ke Ling 柯靈 (1909–2000), was a friend to both Fou Lei and Eileen Chang.

50 　'在一個低氣壓的時代，水土特別不相宜的地方，誰也不存在什麼幻想，期待文藝園地里有奇花異卉探出頭來。' Fou Lei, 'On the Novels of Eileen Chang' 論張愛玲的小說 in *Ten Thousand Things* (May 1944).

51 　'至少也該列為我們文壇最美的收穫之一。' (Ibid.) Fou Lei's view was echoed by C.T. Hsia, who wrote in 1961: '*The Golden Cangue*, a long story of over 28,000 words, is in my opinion the greatest novelette in the history of Chinese literature.' C.T. Hsia, *A History of Modern Chinese Fiction* (Bloomington, IN: Indiana University, 1999), 398.

52 　André Chevrillon, 'Discours pour le centenaire d'Hippolyte Taine' (first version, conserved at Fonds Jacques Doucet).

dissection'[53] (was it a coincidence that Taine had defined a novelist as 'a psychologist...[who] loves to picture feelings, to perceive their connections'?[54]); second, her use of *raccourci* as a narrative technique; third, style, namely her stunning language, parallelling Taine's appraisal of George Sand.[55] 'Without *The Golden Cangue*,' Fou Lei claimed, 'the author of this article would not have criticised *The Chain of Referents* so harshly later on; indeed, nor would he have written this article at all.'[56]

Before embarking, with an axe, on to *The Chain of Referents* 連環套, Chang's first novel then being serialised in *Ten Thousand Things*, Fou Lei cut with a knife through Chang's other short stories and novellas piece by piece, building up a case that the ruinous flaws of *The Chain of Referents* were always latent, and that the young writer was already going downhill. Spoiled by *The Golden Cangue*, Fou Lei found all of Chang's other works lacking in one way or another. Thus went his verdict on *Love in a Fallen City* 傾城之戀 (1943):

> [It is] without the seriousness, sublimity, and fatality of a tragedy; neither is the contrast between light and shade strong. Because it is a romance, passion does not play a theatrical rôle. The flirtation, which takes up two-thirds of the novella, is but flippant hedonism and a spiritual game: be it smart, elegant, witty, it is after all the product of a shrewd, almost morbid, society. [...] The impression that *Love in a Fallen City* gives is one of a delicately carved jade pagoda, not that of the spire of a Gothic cathedral. [...] Impoverished, bored, nonchalant, canny and petty people are not suited for the rôles of a tragedy.[57]

---

53 '並不採用冗長的獨白，或枯索繁瑣的解剖，她利用暗示，把動作、言語、心理三者打成一片。' Fou Lei, 'On the Novels of Eileen Chang' in *Ten Thousand Things* (May 1944).

54 See Martha Wolfenstein, 'The Social Background of Taine's Philosophy of Art' in *Journal of the History of Ideas*, vol. 5, no. 3 (June 1944), 343.

55 In 'George Sand', Taine wrote: 'Mais, avant tout, ce qui la met hors de pair, c'est le style.' See Hippolyte Taine, *Derniers essais de critique et d'histoire* (Paris: Hachette, 1896), 127.

56 '沒有《金鎖記》，本文作者決不在下文把《連環套》批評得那麼嚴厲，而且根本也不會寫這篇文字。' Fou Lei, 'On the Novels of Eileen Chang' in *Ten Thousand Things* (May 1944).

57 '沒有悲劇的嚴肅、崇高，和宿命性；光暗的對照也不強烈。因為是傳奇，情慾沒有驚心動魄的表現。幾乎占到二分之一篇幅的調情，盡是些玩世不恭的享樂主義者的精神遊戲：盡管那麼機巧，文雅，風趣，終究是精練到近乎病態的社會的產物。[…]《傾城之戀》給人家的印象，彷彿是一座雕刻精工的翡翠寶塔，而非哥特式大寺的一角。[…] 貧乏，厭倦，苟且，渾身小智小慧的人，擔當不了悲劇的角色。' Ibid.

Well, only if the story were meant to be a tragedy, or indeed, a certain type of tragedy. The novelist defended her purpose as quite something else later on. Fou Lei, with his resolved worldview, the one he had fought so hard to acquire and to uphold, sneered at the 'surrender without a fight'[58] of the sickly girl in *Glazed Tiles* 琉璃瓦: 'Knowing that there is no use in struggling, she does not struggle. Since resolution is to no avail, she gives up. This is oriental spirit through and through.'[59] Even the fictional figure did not escape the scrutiny of the moralist, who appeared not to have realised that *that*, too, was precisely tragic. Likewise, he reproached *Love in a Fallen City* for not being deep enough, and for having protagonists who did not talk straight or act thoroughly. He himself was transparent; he needed others to be the same. He himself was never frivolous; he could not stand flippancy. Not able to be glib, he tolerated no cliché. 'The defect of the two characters is by extension that of the work itself'[60] was his last word on *Love in a Fallen City*.

The defect of this reasoning is evident: one cannot make the characters morally defectless for the work to be artistically valid, whatever that means. Fou Lei, like Rolland, was decidedly interested in types and ideals. Eileen Chang, sharing a literary affinity with Somerset Maugham, was decidedly interested in people and their lives. 'The author of *The Golden Cangue* has no excuse for going backwards',[61] declared the critic. Curious logic. Eileen Chang's intricacy, ambiguity, playfulness and irony were lost on Fou Lei, whose heartfelt applause earlier might not have been all that pertinent either: the author of *The Golden Cangue* might not have had profound sympathy for her protagonist as he had presumed.[62] The young writer's pessimism, disdain for sentimentalism, and naturally cold distance from her stories, were alien to her Rollandian critic then embarking onto translating Balzac,[63] who now took it into his own hands to lecture the storyteller to 'forget about herself, make herself one of the characters in the story, accompany them in their physical and spiritual exploration,

---

58   '不經戰鬥的投降', ibid.

59   '明知掙扎無益，便不掙扎了。執著也是徒然，便捨棄了。這是道地的東方精神。' Ibid.

60   '兩個主角的缺陷，也就是作品本身的缺陷。' Ibid.

61   '《金鎖記》的作者沒有理由往後退。' Ibid.

62   '[…] 我們便有理由恨她嗎？作者不這麼想。在上面所引的幾段里，顯然有作者深切的憐憫，喚引着讀者的憐憫。' [Does that then give us reason to hate her? The novelist does not think so. In the aforecited paragraphs, the novelist's profound pity is apparent, which evokes pity in the reader.] Ibid.

63   Fou Lei had started translating Balzac's *Albert Savarus* in February 1944. Qiqiao, the héroïne of *The Golden Cangue*, is a thoroughly Balzacian figure. Fou Lei might have expected, at the time, all of Chang's fictional figures to have a touch of Balzac in them.

He gives a score.

laugh with them, and cry with them, in order to obtain the experience that she had not herself experienced'.[64] Convinced, Fou Lei added: 'All great artists do it like this, working whilst learning. Ms Chang has no doubt heard all these commonplaces';[65] he was nevertheless concerned that 'perhaps other, more agreeable voices have topped these dull ones'.[66]

It is rather unfortunate that when the critic, at once adoring, protective and condescending, begins to sound like a tactless friend, a stern parent or a frank coach, his insights appear at best those of a doctrinaire. 'Talent most likes to betray you',[67] he admonished. 'Write a lot, publish little, this in particular is the loyal attitude with which to serve art.'[68] Alas. Here was a genius. Fou Lei's reaction was almost anxious: What to do with it? This anxiety, self-inhibiting in effect, may well have contributed to Fou Lei's own perceived inability to write imaginative literature. The same anxiousness we see him exhibiting when his own son's musical ability was growing. Having identified Eileen Chang's gift, instead of laisser faire en attendant, Fou Lei decided: 'The growth of art and literature is in urgent need of criticism from the society rather than of cautious or frosty silence.'[69] At once delighted and thrown off balance, in practice he projected his own creative anxiety onto the burgeoning talent. Whilst this piece of Rapid Rain is generally seen as Fou Lei's venerable advice *to* an immature novelist, it is, to my mind, anticipation *from* an immature critic, himself now more than ever a would-be novelist.

Seven months later, Eileen Chang published 'My Own Writing' 自己的文章,[70] an essay responding fully, if not exclusively, to Rapid Rain's 'On the Novels

---

64   '現實世界所有的不過是片段的材料，片段的暗示經小說家用心理學家的眼光，
      科學家的耐心，宗教家的熱誠，依照嚴密的邏輯推索下去，忘記了自我，化
      身為故事中的角色(還要走多少回頭路，白花多少心力)，陪着他們作身心的探
      險，陪他們笑，陪他們哭，才能獲得作者實際未曾經歷的經歷。' Fou Lei, 'On
      the Novels of Eileen Chang' in *Ten Thousand Things* (May 1944).

65   '一切的大藝術家就是這樣一面工作一面學習的。這些平凡的老話，張女士當然
      知道。' Ibid.

66   '不過作家所遇到的誘惑特別多，也許旁的更悅耳的聲音，在她耳畔蓋住了老
      生常談的單調的聲音。' (Ibid.) Fou Lei was possibly referring to the overtly flatter-
      ing appraisals published by pro-Japanese writers in pro-Japanese magazines at the time,
      amongst whom the most notable being Hu Lancheng 胡蘭成 (1906–1981), a 'traitor' poli-
      tician serving Wang Jingwei's 汪精衛 (1883–1944) government in collaboration with the
      Japanese. Hu in August 1944 became Chang's first husband.

67   '才華最愛出賣人。' Ibid.

68   '多寫，少發表，尤其是服侍藝術最忠實的態度。' Ibid.

69   '文藝的長成，急需社會的批評，而非謹慮的或冷淡的緘默。' Ibid.

70   The title of Eileen Chang's article, 自己的文章, alludes to the saying '老婆是別人的
      好，文章是自己的好' [The better wife is someone else's; the better writing is one's

of Eileen Chang'. Beginning with the remark that, writing, she had not thought much of the theories of writing, which have, do, and will always, follow rather than predominate writing itself, and that she thought critiquing at best on equal footing with creating and not in a dictatorial position, she then, in a tone detached, defiant, elegant and earnest, engaged with every point Rapid Rain had raised. With regard to the supposed lack of contrast between light and shade in some of her themes, she said that she preferred to mix and to juxtapose, like matching scallion green with peach pink. With regard to the lack of tragedy in some of her stories, she said that she liked tragic but liked desolate more, that not every character could be a thorough one, and that ordinary people, not heroes, reflected our time. With regard to the semi-vernacular language, typical of classical Chinese novels and here employed in the foreigners' dialogues in *The Chain of Referents*, which Rapid Rain had criticised most of all, she confessed her original linguistic intention and admitted that something could be done to improve it. There was pride, and there was modesty: '[...] still I adhere to my own way, only that I regret not being quite skilled enough. And I am but an apprentice in literature.'[71] Despite their divergent views and tastes, the same combination of pride and modesty characterised Fou Lei's own attitude towards his work. And stubbornness. These are two of Shanghai's most remarkable writers in the 1940s, whose temperaments were as different as their participation in a discourse was articulate and genuine.

Some critics, such as T'ang Wen-piao 唐文標 (1936–1985) and Ke Ling 柯靈 (1909–2000), either stated or hinted that Eileen Chang's fulgent creativity faded after Fou Lei's warning criticism appeared, and that the latter foresaw her eventual downfall.[72] This oft-repeated speculation is unfounded. Fictional habits aside, patriarchal history-making has also something to do with it. If one simply looks at Chang's list of publications after May 1944, one sees that she continued to produce, at a brisk pace, substantial stories and essays of fine quality. The idea of a genius' 'downfall', particularly one which is predicted, seems to excite people; in reality, Chang's later undergoing different creative phases had more to do with the breakdown of her first marriage in 1946–47 and with the brutal changes in Shanghai's political and literary climate towards the

---

own.] 'My Own Writing' appeared in a periodical edited by Chang's then husband Hu Lancheng: *Bitter Bamboo* 苦竹, vol. 2 (December 1944).

71   '我還是保持我的作風，只是自己慚愧寫得不到家。而我也不過是一個文學的習
      作者。' Ibid.

72   See T'ang Wen-piao, *Studies on Eileen Chang* 張愛玲研究 (Taipei: Lianjing, 1984) and Ke Ling, 'To Eileen Chang, from Afar' 遙寄張愛玲 in *Anthology of Writings by Eileen Chang* 張愛玲文集 (Hefei: Anhui wenyi, 1991), vol. 4, 420–428.

end of the 1940s.[73] The reception of her work in mainland China after 1949 could not but suffer a 'decline'; in every sense politically incorrect, she was far from being the only one to be marginalised if not demolished. Moreover, reception is one thing, production another; Eileen Chang never stopped writing, later away from China. From what I can see, it could have been Eileen Chang's essay that had a concrete impact on Fou Lei, and it was certainly one of her short stories that changed his life.

Reading Eileen Chang's firm but courteous self-defense in 'My Own Writing', Fou Lei, the critiqued critic, a repressed artist, could not but realise precisely why *he* could not write a novel. Let us read Eileen Chang between the lines: 'Fighting is touching, because it is strong, but it is, at the same time, bitter too. Fighters have lost the harmony in life and look for new ones. Fighting for the sake of fighting is lacking in aftertaste, and made into a literary work, it may not be so good.'[74] Eileen Chang effectively deemed Fou Lei's newly finished and highly regarded translation of *Jean-Christophe* in 1941, with fighting as its supreme theme, inferior at best. In 1952 Fou Lei re-translated *Jean-Christophe*, 'to make a living, not out of love'.[75] In 1953 he confessed to Stephen Soong his efforts to clean Rollandian language out of his system, which he had only succeeded in doing in autumn 1945.[76] From the mid-late 1940s onwards, there was an increase in Fou Lei's re-working of his old translations and in his tormenting dissatisfaction with his own language, which he repetitively judged too angular, too solid.[77] One can hardly see this violent nature of his stylistic concern as in proportion with that of a mere translator. It is, indeed, what Izard called '*vrai, grand* souci artistique'. The more fluid language of the precocious Eileen Chang, of his revered friends, the devilishly gifted Qian Zhongshu 錢鐘書 (1910–1998) and Yang Jiang 楊絳 (1911–2016), and of his preferred novelist Lao She 老舍 (1899–1966), whom he read and reread to study, all painfully mirrored the rigidity of his own.

---

73 See Eileen Chang's autobiographical novel *Little Reunion* 小團圓, published posthumously in 2009 against her will, to understand the traumatic effect of breaking with Hu Lancheng; of this she had otherwise never written or spoken. Both T'ang Wen-piao and Ke Ling did however demonstrate understanding of the political constraints imposed on Eileen Chang's literary creation and on its contemporary reception.

74 '鬥爭是動人的，因為它是強大的，而同時是酸楚的。鬥爭者失去了人生的和諧，尋求着新的和諧。倘使為鬥爭而鬥爭，便缺少回味，寫了出來也不能成為好的作品。' Eileen Chang, 'My Own Writing' in *Bitter Bamboo*, vol. 2 (December 1944).

75 Fou Lei's letter to Stephen Soong, 9 November 1953. See chapter 6, note 79.

76 Ibid.

77 This was a recurring theme in Fou Lei's letters to Fou Ts'ong from 1954 onwards and to his friends such as Stephen Soong in the 1950s and to Étiemble in the 1960s.

Meanwhile, in 1964, Eileen Chang published, in the United States, her translation of a selection of Ralph Waldo Emerson's essays – an interesting choice for someone unimpressed by heroism. The austerity of her translator's preface brings to mind none other than the angularity and solidity of Fou Lei. In 1976, prefacing the republication of a selection of her old works, Eileen Chang criticised *The Chain of Referents* far more harshly than Fou Lei had done. 'Having not seen it in thirty years, although I had known it to be bad, I did not expect it to be *this* bad. It was baloney through and through, and I could not help but chuckle in horror. Reading, I could not stop grimacing in pain, making faces, frowning, gritting the teeth whilst laughing, and through teeth making a prolonged sound "Eeeeee!" (*yi* would be mistaken for a sigh, and *yi* would resemble a surprise; neither is right), and when even the teeth were shivering, I tasted the feeling of having "cold teeth" – being despised.'[78]

It is thought that Eileen Chang did not know who Rapid Rain was until the 1950s.[79] She plainly did. In 'My Own Writing' of December 1944, not only did she display a subtle understanding of the starting point of Rapid Rain as a Rollandian disciple, she also implicitly picked at specific points in Fou Lei's 'Thoughts After Reading Plays', published in 1943 under the pseudonym Woebegone. Furthermore, she had, in November 1944, published a short story based on Fou Lei's love affair with a beautiful soprano, the sister of Liu Haisu's wife Cheng Jiahe and who had briefly attended the same college as the now famed young author.[80] Eileen Chang, in effect, betrayed the confidence of her fellow collegian, and turned the latter's confession into a satire. At one point

---

78 '三十年不見，盡管自以為壞，也沒想到這樣惡劣，通篇胡扯，不禁駭笑。一路
    看下去，不由得一直齜牙咧嘴做鬼臉，皺着眉咬着牙笑，從齒縫里迸出一聲拖
    長的"Eeeeee!" (用"噫"會被誤認為歎息，"咦"又像驚訝，都不對) 連牙齦都寒颼颼
    起來，這才嘗到"齒冷"的滋味。' Eileen Chang, 'Preface to *Chang's View*' 《張看》 自
    序 in *Anthology of Writings by Eileen Chang*, vol. 4, 337.

79 See Stephen Soong, 'Speaking in Confidence of Eileen Chang' 私語張愛玲 in *Mingpao
    Monthly* 明報月刊 (March 1976). After moving to Hong Kong in 1952, Eileen Chang be-
    came close to Stephen Soong and his wife Mae Fong Soong. Friends with Fou Lei, Soong
    revealed Rapid Rain's identity to Chang. '她聽後的反應是驚訝，但也沒有當做一回
    大事。' [Her reaction was one of surprise, but she did not fuss over it.]

80 In a letter (disclosed in 2009) to her trusted friend Stephen Soong on 4 December 1982,
    with regard to the republication of her old writing, Eileen Chang expressed the wish not
    to include this short story: '《殷寶灩送花樓會》實在太壞，不改。是寫傅雷的。他
    的女朋友當真聽了我的話到內地去，嫁了個空軍，很快就離婚，我聽見了非常
    懊悔。' [*Yin Baoyan's Visit with a Bouquet* is, in all honesty, too bad. I will not change it. It
    was about Fou Lei. His girlfriend really followed my advice, went to inland and married a
    pilot, only to quickly divorce. Upon hearing about it I was full of remorse.]

she had the hero of the story, a professor of literature, lament: 'In this atmosphere where the air is heavy...'[81] Mimicking the opening line of Fou Lei's 'On the Novels of Eileen Chang', the allusion could not be more clear. At the end, 'I', the author named Eileen, asked her conflicted friend:

> 'Why can't he divorce?'
>
> She fidgeted with her sleeves, looking down at the jade-coloured lining: 'He has three children. Children are innocent. I cannot have them sacrifice their happiness, can I?'
>
> [...]
>
> 'But Baoyan, I am myself a child of divorced parents. I can tell you that I was not particularly unhappy compared to other children. [...] Anyway, now you are in pain, he is in pain, and that is the truth.'
>
> She contemplated for a good while. 'But you don't know, even if he is divorced, a neurotic like him, how can I marry him?'
>
> I too thought this an irrevocable tragedy.[82]

After the publication of the story, Baoyan, whose real name was Cheng Jialiu, left Fou Lei, left Shanghai, quickly married and divorced. In 1983, for the republication of *Yin Baoyan's Visit with a Bouquet*, Eileen Chang added a long note. After thirty-nine years, she regretted the consequences of her satire, which ended their romance. 'It is my fault', she wrote.[83] In this candidness she was oddly not dissimilar from Fou Lei who, like her, was a sensitive soul living in a time of turmoil. What they both foresaw, in 1940s Shanghai, was destructive forces at play and an impending catastrophe. In September 1944, for the second edition of her *Romances* 傳奇 – she refused to wait a day to publish, republish, nor to be famous, more famous – Eileen Chang wrote: 'Our epoch is in haste, it is in destruction, and an even bigger destruction is on its way. One day, our civilisation, be it in sublimation or in vain, will be a thing of the past.

---

81   '在這樣低氣壓的空氣里', see Eileen Chang, *Yin Baoyan's Visit with a Bouquet* 殷寶灩送
      花樓會 in *Magazine* 雜誌, vol. 14, no. 2 (November 1944).

82   '我又說：'他為什麼不能夠離婚呢？'她扯着袖子，低頭看着青綢里子。'他有
      三個小孩。小孩是無辜的。我不能讓他們犧牲了一生的幸福罷？'[…]'可是寶
      灩，我自己就是離婚的人的小孩子，我可以告訴你，我小時候並不比別的小孩
      特別地不快樂。[…]無論如何，現在你痛苦，他痛苦，這倒是真的。'她想了半
      天。'不過你不知道，他就是離了婚，他那樣有神經病的人，怎麼能同他結婚
      呢？'我也覺得這是無可挽回的悲劇了。' Ibid.

83   '是我错'，像那出流行的申曲剧名。' ['It is my fault', as goes the title of a popular
      Shanghai Opera.] – Eileen Chang's added note of 1983. Cheng Jialiu, who later moved to
      Hong Kong, remained for the rest of her life a close friend to Fou Lei and his family.

If the word I use the most is "desolate", it is for this vague threat that broods at the back of all my thinking.'[84]

In a Japanese-occupied Shanghai, Fou Lei shut himself away in his house to avoid having to bow to Japanese soldiers.[85] In winter 1944, in extreme anguish he organised a fortnightly salon at home, where a dozen or so friends – writers, scholars, scientists, politicians, doctors, architects and musicians – gathered to give talks on their respective areas of expertise and exchanged views on politics.[86] In September 1945, as soon as the Sino-Japanese War ended and the Civil War resumed, Fou Lei, with the Edinburgh-educated Zhou Xuliang 周煦良 (1905–1984), one of his fortnightly salon attendees, founded the fortnightly *New Account* 新語.[87]

This was Fou Lei's third attempt in the press business. Two years after *L'Art* 藝術旬刊 (1932) and shortly before co-founding and co-editing the newspaper *Current Affairs* 時事匯報 (1934) with his school friend Ye Changqing 葉常青, Fou Lei wrote to Madame Berguerand: 'Everything is going from bad to worse: Japan, our dangerous neighbour, having crossed off our three large provinces, the size of which is even larger than that of France and Switzerland put together, is not yet satisfied; it would like to have the entire north of China. The Russian-Japanese relation is very tense at the moment, and a war is to be feared. In other regions of China, no satisfactory order exists either: the brigands, the communists, and the agricultural crisis cover almost the entire country.' Sharply aware of the disproportionate nature of the exigency at stake and of the dislocation between his notionally élite class and the population at large, Fou Lei continued: 'What can we do, we young self-proclaimed intellectuals and leaders of an ignorant people? We pretend to have the power to do this and that, but our work is not worth the labour of farmers.'[88] Political

---

84 '時代是倉促的，已經在破壞中，還有更大的破壞要來。有一天我們的文明，不論是升華還是浮華，都要成為過去。如果我最常用的字是"荒涼"，那是因為思想背景里有這惘惘的威脅。' Eileen Chang, 'Preface to the Second Edition of *Romances*' 《傳奇》再版序 (September 1944); see *Anthology of Writings by Eileen Chang*, vol. 4, 135.

85 '抗戰期間閉門不出，東不至黃浦江，北不至白渡橋，避免向憲兵行禮，亦是鴕鳥辦法。' 'Fou Lei on Himself' in *Complete Works*, vol. 17, 7.

86 '一九四四年冬至一九四五年春，以淪陷時期精神苦悶，曾組織十余友人每半個月集會一次。' Ibid., 11.

87 The journal's title may have derived from *A New Account of Tales of the World* 世說新語, written collectively by literati in the fifth century. Fou Lei, like Lu Xun, was hugely fond of this book.

88 'Tout va de pire en pire: Le Japon, notre redoutable voisin, n'est pas encore satisfait de nous avoir radié trois grandes provinces dont la surface couvre toute la France, la Suisse,

concern underlined Fou Lei's initiative to engage media. *Current Affairs* ran into deficit after three months and closed down. Fou Lei sold some of his family land to cover the loss. Effectively, it was selling land piece by piece over fifteen years that supported his profession as a freelance translator and as an occasional journalist.

Eleven years on, the 'young self-proclaimed intellectuals and leaders of an ignorant people', now older, extended their discussions once more into print. A predominantly political review, *New Account* (1945) had for its contributors Fou Lei's circle of friends: Qian Zhongshu, Yang Jiang, Xia Mianzun 夏丏尊 (1886–1946), Ma Xulun 馬敘倫 (1885–1970)[89] and Lei Yuan 雷垣 (1912–2002).[90] Imbued with immediacy and oratorical force, Fou Lei's language recalled the journalistic style 社論體 in the tradition of Liang Qichao, the pioneering scholar, editor, commentator, and journalist who championed, half a century previously, learned elucidation, social engagement, and intellectual autonomy. After eight years of war with the Japanese – what they called 'the Tempest' 暴風雨 in the opening manifesto – these intellectuals' burning concern was with establishing domestic political order. In rapid succession and under different pseudonyms, Fou Lei published in his *New Account* some eighteen articles in four months,[91] his first call in its first issue being for a review of school education in China since 1911. Two months later, in 'The Citizens' Will Above All Else' 國民的意志高於一切 (November 1945), Fou Lei drew

----

et même plus; il voudrait encore la partie du nord de la Chine. Les rapports Russo-Japonais sont très tendus en ce moment, la guerre est à craindre. Dans d'autres régions de la Chine, l'ordre n'est pas satisfaisant non plus: des brigands, des communistes et la crise agricole couvre presque tout le pays. Que pouvons-nous faire, nous jeunes soi-disant intellectuels et dirigeant du peuple ignorant? Nous prétendons tous de pouvoir faire telle ou telle chose, mais notre travail ne vaut pas le labour des paysans.' Fou Lei's letter to Madame Berguerand, 6 September 1934; the Berguerand family archive.

89   With Ma Xulun, Zhou Jianren 周建人 (1888–1984) (Lu Xun's brother), Xu Guangping 许廣平 (1898–1968) (Lu Xun's widow), Zheng Zhenduo, Ke Ling et al., Fou Lei was to found, on 12 December 1945, the China Association for Promoting Democracy 中國民主促進會. He withdrew from the Association in 1950.

90   Lei Yuan, who obtained a doctorate in mathematics from the University of Michigan (1939), was Fou Lei's friend from Datong High School. The teenage Fou Lei learnt about Lei Yuan's orphanage and, without knowing him, went to introduce himself to his fellow sufferer. They became inseparable. Lei Yuan was Fou Ts'ong's first piano teacher in the early 1940s.

91   For an overview of the articles published in *New Account*, see chapter 1 of Han Han's excellent study, *Accountable Modernity: Periodical Material, Mass Media and China's Modern Literary System, 1919–1949* 可敘述的現代性：期刊史料、大眾傳播與中國現代文學體制 (1919–1949) (Taipei: Xiuwei zixun, 2011).

a distinction between 'the interests of parties' 黨的利益 and 'the interests of the country and the nation' 國家民族的利益. Suggesting sacrificing the former for the latter when necessary, he proposed a nationwide referendum before calling out in desperation:

> [...] because we [...] need to eliminate the civil war once and for all. Only street fights resort to blaming each other for being the first to strike [...]. The Republic of China, which has taken nearly a hundred years and tremendous efforts to establish, is now facing at once its only chance of a renaissance and a possible crisis beyond redemption: this is a moment of life and death, and all parties must obey the citizens' supreme judgement. In history, what come and go are dynasties and political parties; what does not die is the nation. And the will of the entire nation is this and this only: Do not fight![92]

At once rational and emotional, Fou Lei's impassioned intransigence bears striking resemblance to the pacifist cries of Rolland, who saw all European wars as civil wars, and who pled against wars, all wars, with his pen.[93] Protesting the

---

92   '[…] 因為我們並不需要追究啓釁的責任，而要根本消弭內戰。只有街頭的打架才以誰先動手來互相推諉 […] 以近百年的時間，千辛萬苦好容易締造起來的中華民國，遭逢了千載一時的復興機會，也臨到了萬劫不復的危機：在此生死關頭，一切的黨派都該服從國民的最高裁判。歷史上興亡起複的是朝代和黨派，不死的是民族；而全民族的意志只有一個：不許打！' Fou Lei (under the pseudonym Thunder 雷), 'The Citizens' Will Above All Else' 國民的意志高於一切 in *New Account* 新語, vol. 4 (November 1945).

93   Rolland's voice, once a beacon during the First World War, was considerably more subdued during the Second World War. Having supported the Soviet Union for nearly a decade, an increasingly critical Rolland, after the signing of the Nazi-Soviet Pact on 23 August 1939, came to total disillusionment, and wrote in his journal that, were he not married, had he not had a stepson who lived in Moscow, or were he still living in Switzerland, he would certainly have condemned *all* – the Soviet Union, Nazi Germany, Britain and France alike – more vehemently than he had done during the First World War, for their shared betrayal and destruction of democracy. 'Si je n'étais pas marié (et je le dis à ma femme), – surtout si je n'avais pas un beau-fils, que j'aime, otage à Moscou, – et si j'étais domicilié en Suisse, comme j'y serais resté, sans mon mariage, – j'eusse écrit certainment un nouveau *Au-dessus de la Mêlée*, beaucoup plus vigoureux et vangeur que le premier, et qui eût soulevé contre moi un ouragan de haines plus furieuses encore, – *des deux côtés*. – J'aurais tout dit, tout dénoncé; l'abominable trahison du gouvernement soviétique et son cynisme déshonorant et inhumain, – mais aussi, la perfidie des gouvernements ploutocratiques de Grande-Bretagne et de son satellite la France, qui a joué, depuis des années, un louche jeu avec les fascismes et les nazismes, comptant s'en servir

rule of the Kuomintang, in December 1945 Fou Lei demanded the abolition of censorship: 'In a country where there is no freedom of the press, the will of the people can never be exerted, and the politics can never be on track. In a country where books cannot be freely published, there is no culture whatsoever of which to speak.'[94] Three more issues, and the review was held in the post before release. This was the end of *New Account*. Censorship ruled.

The Civil War years witnessed the explosive marks Fou Lei left as a compelling political commentator, frequently read in influential newspapers such as *Democracy* 民主, *Zhou Bao* 周報, *Wenhui Bao* 文匯報 and *Observation* 觀察.[95] After publishing in *Wenhui Bao* (April 1947), along with a long preface, his translation of a series of articles by Edgar Snow – 'Why We Don't Understand Russia' (15 February 1947), 'How It Looks to Ivan Ivanovich' (22 February 1947) and 'Stalin Must Have Peace' (1 March 1947) – which originally appeared in the *Saturday Evening Post*, Fou Lei was maliciously attacked by left-leaners, notably Zhou Jianren, for his so-called 'anti-Soviet and pro-Imperialist' 反蘇 親帝 tendencies. In Zhou's crooked logic, Fou Lei's call for critically examining the Soviet Union's political agenda was synonymous with being 'anti-Soviet', and his suggestion that Russia was not an impeccable antithesis of the United States was tantamount to being 'pro-Imperialist'. In Zhou's accusation, Fou Lei's intention, characteristically stated with little obscurity, of fostering a nuanced

---

contre le bolchevisme, ou finalement de celui-ci contre les autres, en les ruinant les uns par l'autre et réciproquement, – jusqu'à provoquer la catastrophe d'aujourd'hui, où ils se retournent tous unis contre les démocraties.' Romain Rolland, *Journal de Vézelay, 1938–1944* (Paris: Bartillat, 2012), 274; entry of 29 September 1939. In 1934, Rolland married Maria Koudacheva who was Russian. In 1935 they visited Moscow and were received by Stalin. In 1938 they left Switzerland to live in Vézelay, France.

94   '沒有新聞自由的國家,民意決不能發揮,政治決不能上軌道。沒有圖書出版自由的國家,根本談不上文化。' Fou Lei (under the pseudonym Swift Wind 疾風), 'Abolition of Publication Censorship' 廢止出版檢查制度 in *New Account*, vol. 5 (December 1945).

95   Fou Lei's journalistic activities during the Civil War years (1945–49), in the context of the fantastically complex press culture at the time, merit an in-depth study on its own. What also calls for examination is the psychological states of several generations of Chinese *wenren* in this particular period, when each was in a position to take a position – their varied, inconsistent, or ambivalent political outlooks, as well as social networks and often overlapping relations which affected individual choices. Some attention has been given to this topic in recent years, but much remains to be done; most would indeed be factual groundwork, not least because of the large-scale distortion and omission of information that we inherit in a post-communist reality. Close studies of textual and material evidence are in need as ever; consciously interdisciplinary approaches, for precisely the aforementioned reasons, need be utilised in unpacking this muddled history.

rather than a propagandist position through Snow's firsthand observation, was turned upside down. In defense, Fou Lei published 'So-called "Anti-Imperialist and Pro-Soviet" 所謂反帝親蘇 in the liberal weekly *Observation*, whose editor Chu Anping 儲安平 (1909–1966?) had predicted on 8 March 1947: 'In all honesty, the "freedom" for which we fight under the rule of the Nationalists is a question of "much" or "little"; if the Communists come into power, this "freedom" will become a question of "yes" or "no".[96] –

> Arbitrariness is due often not to malice but to naïveté. It is through naïveté that religious fervour, blindness, and narrow-mindedness arise. [...] Modern thinking considers itself free of religion, but in reality it has created a new religion, just as charming and as frightening as all religions. [...] At a time when our general situation deteriorates daily and when the Nationalists and the Communists fight a deadly fight, it is to be expected that individuals get labelled, be it black or white, without justification. Those who dare speak the truth and call a spade a spade have always been the public enemy.[97]

And, calling a spade a spade, here is what Fou Lei thought about his China:

> The civil war will not last forever. Sooner or later the current situation will change. Undertakings far more vital and onerous than destruction will follow. China cannot afford facing the future with the attitude of the likes of Mr Zhou. Be it left or right, loyalists to doctrines or to dogmas, intolerance will never bring peace, nor will it benefit the people. When a nation comes to the point where thinking is united and heresies are extinct, it is also time when its civilisation withers to death, or when humans are sent as things into the world to bring big disasters.[98]

---

96 '老實說，我們現在爭取自由，在國民黨統治下，這個 "自由" 還是一個 "多" "少" 的問題。假如共產黨執政了，這個 "自由" 就變成了一個 "有" "無" 的問題了。' Chu Anping, 'The Political Situation in China' 中國的政局 in *Observation* 觀察, vol. 2, no. 2 (8 March 1947).

97 '武斷往往並非由於惡意，而由於天真。惟其天真，才會有宗教熱情，才會盲目，才會褊狹。[…] 近代思想界自以為擺脫了宗教，卻另創了一個新宗教。其迷人處與可怕處正與一切宗教無異。[…] 當此大局日趨惡化，國共兩黨作殊死戰之際，個人被戴帽子，不論為赤為白，都是意料中事。敢於道破真相，call a spade a spade 的人，一向是國民公敵。' Fou Lei, 'So-called "Anti-Imperialist and Pro-Soviet" 所謂反帝親蘇 in *Observation*, vol. 2, no. 24 (22 July 1947).

98 '話又得說回來，內戰決不會永久打下去，現狀遲早要改變。比破壞更重要更艱辛的事業還在後面，以周先生這種作風對付未來的局面，中國是付不起代價

In a conversation with Fou Ts'ong, I expressed stupefaction at the terrifying precision with which Fou Lei anticipated the imminent calamity in his wartime writing. To this Fou Ts'ong responded: 'Before 1949, intellectuals like my father were in total despair. There was the dilemma: they saw through the leftist ideology, but were instinctively reluctant to bail out.'[99]

In 1948 Fou Lei and his family left Shanghai. In June 1949, from Kunming they went to Hong Kong, where many intellectuals, sceptical of the communist regime, fled to and remained. In December, Fou Lei, against his better political judgement, made the decision to return to the mainland. They sailed to Tianjin, and stayed for a week in Beijing with Qian Zhongshu and Yang Jiang. The historian Wu Han 吳晗 (1909–1969) invited Fou Lei to teach French at Tsinghua University. Fou Lei said no; he only had interest in teaching art history. He and his family made their way back, once again, to Shanghai.

A number of reasons could be listed for Fou Lei's return, but none as important, or eloquent, as one simple fact: he returned with poison.

的。左派也罷，右派也罷，死抱住正統也罷，死抱住主義與教條也罷，不容忍決不會帶來和平，天下蒼生也不見得會沾光。一個民族到了思想統一，異端邪說誅盡滅絕的時候，即是它的文化枯萎以死的時候，或者是把人當做物，叫他到世界上去闖大禍的時候。' Ibid.

99　Interview with Fou Ts'ong, February 2012, London.

Translating, or the Search for a Brother

I hereby draw the reader's attention to Fou Lei's self-image, for he had a friend who recorded a detail of no little significance, and who knew exactly what to make of it: 'Some people thought Fou Lei lonely and proud like a crane in the clouds; speaking to Zhongshu and me, Fou Lei more than once considered himself a little mouse living in a hole in the wall – could it have been because Maurois called Voltaire a hare hiding in its form?'[1] Affirming Fou Lei's singular personality, Yang Jiang said that he was 'wholly sincere and loyal to all his friends', and that in the face of some of these friends' betrayal:

> ... he felt himself so honest as to be pitiable, so alone as to be vulnerable. Full of spikes he too often provoked people; with his short temper he could not help offending people. He knew himself to be no good at getting along with tact and delicacy, and that the only 'hole' where he would be safe was his study; like a mouse, he hardly ventured out of his hole to peep at the big outside world. Unlike a crane in the sky, who looks beyond the clouds and disregards earthly mud and slough, Fou Lei cared incessantly about his country and his people. Nevertheless, maybe he abode by the lesson of *Candide*, ducking into the study to do his work of translating?[2]

By 'the lesson of *Candide*' Yang Jiang would have been referring to 'we must cultivate our garden'. Retreating to his study was an overriding theme running

---

1 '有人說傅雷"孤傲如雲間鶴";傅雷卻不止一次在鍾書和我面前自比為"牆洞里的小老鼠"——是否因為莫羅阿曾把服爾德比作"一頭躲在窟中的野兔" 呢？' Yang Jiang, 'In Lieu of a Preface' to *Five Biographies Translated by Fou Lei*. Fou Lei translated Maurois' biography of Voltaire, the republication of which in 1983 was reason for Yang Jiang to preface the book with her recollections of the translator. To the mouse (*lao shu*) analogy she added that, behind Fou Lei's back, she and Qian Zhongshu thought of him, with his fiery temper, rather like a tiger (*lao hu*) at home – which is what 'Lao Fu' [Old Fou] sounded like in Shanghainese as Zhu Meifu addressed him.

2 '[…] 覺得自己老實得可憐，孤弱得無以自衛。他滿頭棱角，動不動會觸犯人；又加脾氣急躁，止不住要衝撞人。他知道自己不善在世途上圓轉周旋，他可以安身的"洞穴"，只有自己的書齋；他也像老鼠那樣，只在洞口窺望外面的大世界。他並不像天上的鶴，翹首雲外，不屑顧視地下的泥淖。傅雷對國計民生念念不忘，可是他也許遵循《剛第特》的教訓吧？只潛身書齋，做他的翻譯工作。' Ibid.

through Fou Lei's adult life. The mouse had a pal. Taine described himself as 'a kind of intellectual beaver of the île Saint-Louis, used and constrained to a solitary and sedentary life'.[3] Like this French beaver, our Chinese mouse was not identified with any school or party. He guarded his autonomy. Being a full-time translator guaranteed it, even though it meant, at times, social isolation.

On 20 December 1949, Fou Lei and his family returned to Shanghai and settled at 5 Passage 284, Kiangsu Road, a property rented from the family of Stephen Soong, with whom they had originally planned the immigration, and who now stayed put in Hong Kong. In 1950–51, Fou Lei combatted a severe relapse of tuberculosis. In 1952–53, having translated two more Balzacs (*La cousine Bette* and *Le cousin Pons*) and having re-translated *Le père Goriot*, he re-translated the ten-volume *Jean-Christophe*, fifteen years after the publication of his first translation of its first volume. The first major undertaking and serious success Fou Lei had as a translator, its appearance in 1937 coincided with the eruption of the Sino-Japanese War. Rolland's 'stupendous and earnest'[4] roman-fleuve, dedicated 'to the free souls of all nations who suffer, who struggle, and who shall vanquish',[5] was particularly resonant during the First World War in a European context.[6] This resonance, through Fou Lei's translation, took on a new life during the Second World War in China. If Jean-Christophe the idealistic German musician gave heart to the defeated, post-1870 nation that was France, he gave no less courage to a post-1919, or shall we say, post-1840 China in its existential struggle. Rolland's conviction in universal values

---

3   'In a letter recently published he wrote: Je suis un reclus; une espèce de castor intellectuel de l'île Saint-Louis, habitué et contraint à la vie solitaire et sédentaire. [Cf. le Figaro, 21 avril 1928, Quelques Lettres Retrouvées. This particular letter has as a matter of fact already been published by Loliée in La Païve, Paris, 1920.]' in Horatio Smith, 'The Taine Centennial: Comment and Bibliography' in *Modern Language Notes*, vol. 44, no. 7 (November 1929), 442.

4   William A. Drake, 'Romain Rolland: Son but n'était pas le succes; son but était la foi' in *The Sewanee Review*, vol. 32, no. 4 (October 1924), 404.

5   'Aux âmes libres de toutes les nations qui souffrent, qui luttent, et qui vaincront.' Romain Rolland's dedication following the title page of *Jean-Christophe*.

6   The novel was originally serialised in Péguy's *Cahiers de la Quinzaine* between 1904 and 1912. For its 'lofty idealism' Rolland was awarded the Nobel Prize in 1915. The reception of Rolland's work in China took place as early as June 1926, when Jing Yinyu 敬隱漁 (1901–1930) translated and published, in the *Short Story Monthly* vol. 17, no. 16, part of *Jean-Christophe*. Jing later studied in Lyon and visited Rolland. In May and June 1926, Jing's translation of Lu Xun's *The True Story of Ah Q* into French appeared in *Europe*, a literary magazine founded by Rolland. See Paul B. Foster, *Ah Q Archaeology: Lu Xun, Ah Q, Ah Q Progeny and the National Character Discourse in Twentieth Century China* (Oxford: Lexington, 2006), 253–268. The poet and translator Liang Zongdai 梁宗岱 (1903–1983), friends with Fou Lei in Paris, reportedly visited and corresponded with Rolland as early as 1929.

transcending nations was as elevating as his evocation of the brotherhood of human souls was consoling.

In 1912, after reading the end of the novel, the philosopher Alain wrote: 'Jean-Christophe is dead. [...] more than one unknown friend will mourn this moving death [...].'[7] Jean-Christophe himself thus acted after the death of his friend Olivier:

> He was in the middle of a deserted countryside, – meadows, broken up here and there with clumps of fir trees, the vanguard of a forest. He strode into it. Barely had he taken a few steps when he flung himself on the earth and cried out:
> – Olivier!
> He laid across the path and wept.[8]

In John Dos Passos' 1925 novel *Manhattan Transfer* we read:

> Jimmy Herf sat reading on a green couch under a bulb that lit up a corner of a wide bare room. He had come to the death of Olivier in Jean Christophe and read with tightening gullet. In his memory lingered the sound of the Rhine swirling, restlessly gnawing the foot of the garden of the house where Jean Christophe was born. Europe was a green park in his mind full of music and red flags and mobs marching. Occasionally the sound of a steamboat whistle from the river settled breathless snowysoft into the room. From the street came a rattle of taxis and the whining sound of streetcars.
>
> There was a knock at the door. Jimmy got up, his eyes blurred and hot from reading.[9]

---

7   'Jean-Christophe est mort. [...] plus d'un ami inconnu pleurera sur cette mort aussi émouvante que cette première enfance, que je croyais trop belle pour pouvoir jamais être égalée.' Alain, 'Propos d'un normand' in *La Dépêche de Rouen et de Normandie* (23 November 1912). Alain is the nom de plume of Émile Chartier (1868–1951). See Alain and Romain Rolland, *Salut et fraternité* (Paris: Albin Michel, 1969), 66–67. Alain had, in June 1908, dedicated his *Les cent un propos d'Alain* (1908) 'A Monsieur Romain Rolland, un admirateur et un ami de Jean-Christophe'. (Ibid., 62.)

8   'Il se trouva au milieu de la campagne déserte, – des prairies, coupées çà et là de bouquets de sapins, avant-garde d'une forêt. Il s'y enfonça. À peine y eut-il fait quelques pas qu'il se jeta par terre, et cria:
   – Olivier !
   Il se coucha en travers de la route, et sanglota.' Romain Rolland, *Jean-Christophe*, 1242.

9   John Dos Passos, *Manhattan Transfer* (London: Penguin, 2000), 178.

That there was a deeply personal dimension to Fou Lei's translating *Jean-Christophe* after 1936 is beyond question. The question is how to understand it. In 1933, their first child died as Zhu Meifu gave birth. In his letter to Madame Berguerand in September 1934, Fou Lei described Fou Ts'ong's birth in March 1934 as 'the same angel coming back to us'.[10] In September 1933 his mother died. In August 1936 Zhang Xian died; shortly afterwards he fell out with Liu Haisu. The principal living links to Fou Lei's youth were gone, as was his hope of returning to Europe. Eight years had passed since he travelled to Abbaye de Saint-André, where in the Père Dom Édouard Neut he found 'a friend, an elder brother, a father, a ...' Perhaps Fou Lei had always been in search of a brother. Perhaps, in translating *Jean-Christophe*, he gave birth, in his own language, to his chosen kin.

Essentially, all his life Fou Lei was working with biographies or biographies in guises. If we line up the characters he translated – Beethoven, Michelangelo, Tolstoy, Voltaire, Chaplin, Jean-Christophe, numerous Balzacian characters, Carmen, Candide, Ingénu, Mozart, Chopin, even the masters in his *Twenty Lectures* – we see him allying himself with one after another figure, real or fictional, in his 'hole in the wall'.[11] In varying historiographical and literary traditions, be they Greek, Roman, or Chinese, this interest in biography is central. Taine, though observed by Zola as being embarrassed to discuss personality in his writing,[12] was convinced that 'les petits faits significatifs' with which he built his scholarship were the facts of psychology, and that the only history was that of the human soul.[13] At twenty he understood: '... before knowing the destiny of man, one had to know the man himself.'[14] Romain Rolland, whilst a

---

10   'Ma femme a mis au monde ce printemps un gros fils, c'est déjà le second bébé depuis notre mariage. Le premier est perdu au moment d'accouchement, il paraît que c'est le même ange qui nous revient, parce que les deux se ressemblent extraordinairement.' Fou Lei's letter to Madame Berguerand, 6 September 1934; the Berguerand family archive.

11   We know that Fou Lei also had plans to translate a biography of Balzac and to author one of Lin Fengmian.

12   See chapter 4, note 11. Edward Hyams, translator of Taine's *Notes sur l'Angleterre* into English, understood the Frenchman as 'yet, strikingly, an Eminent Victorian'. Edward Hyams, 'Introduction' to *Notes on England* (London: Thames and Hudson, 1957), xxv.

13   'Tout de suite il a compris que ces faits élémentaires sont ceux de la psychologie, qu'il n'y a d'histoire que de l'âme humaine.' André Chevrillon, 'La jeunesse de Taine'; conserved at Fonds Jacques Doucet.

14   'Je compris qu'avant de connaître la destinée de l'homme, il fallait connaître l'homme lui-même.' Hippolyte Taine, *De la destinée humaine* (March 1848), quoted in Pascale Seys, *Hippolyte Taine et l'avènement du naturalisme: un intellectuel sous le Second Empire* (Paris and Montréal: l'Harmattan, 1999), 14.

History student at École normale supérieure in 'the Paris of letters in the last days of Taine and Renan',[15] wanted to write 'a psychological and realist history – a history of souls – but in their flesh.'[16] Twenty years later, authoring 'Beethoven in His Thirtieth Year', the trained historian reaffirmed: 'History in the hands of conscientious savants who go to the archives for the life of a man but forget to look for it in the man himself is a form of treason.'[17]

Jean-Christophe, for Fou Lei, was the ultimate artist, a moral genius not a million miles away from the ideal man in the Confucian sense; a truthful mirror, a valiant guide, a friend. As Rolland himself identified with his protagonist – he confessed many a time 'I was a young Jean-Christophe'[18] – this *Bildungsroman* of his double was also an autobiography. In Fou Lei we witness Jean-Christophe's rage, Jean-Christophe's compassion. And in Jean-Christophe's combat in Paris, we see Fou Lei's own.

Christophe was turning over a new leaf. Christophe was turning over a new soul. And, seeing the weary and withered soul of his childhood fall, he had no idea that growing in him was a new one, younger and stronger. As one's body changes in life, one's soul changes too; and the metamorphosis does not always take place slowly, with the passing of each day: there are hours of crisis, when everything is renewed at once. The old skin drops. In these hours of anguish, a person thinks everything is

---

15   'Le Paris des lettres, aux derniers temps de Taine et de Renan' – Rolland's description in his *Mémoires,* 189.

16   'Je veux écrire une histoire psychologique et réaliste, – une histoire des âmes, – mais en leur chair.' Romain Rolland, *Mémoires,* 57.

17   Romain Rolland, 'Beethoven in His Thirtieth Year' in *Romain Rolland's Essays on Music* (New York: Allen, Towne and Heath, 1948), 282. 'These man', Rolland reproached, '[...] have no psychology.'

18   'Je vous ai dit que j'étais un jeune Jean-Christophe, intolérant, injuste, mal embouché [...] Quand on se mêle d'être Jean-Christophe, il faut du moins ne pas l'être à moitié. Je perdais mon temps et mes forces à vouloir concilier l'inconciliable. [...] Mais l'excès du mal est, pour une âme vigoureuse, un principe de renouvellement. Si la machine du corps n'est pas brisée dans la crise, on en ressort beaucoup plus fort.' [I have told you that I was a young Jean-Christophe, intolerant, unjust, foul-mouthed [...] When one gets involved with being Jean-Christophe, one should at least not do it half-heartedly. I lost my time and strength wanting to reconcile the irreconcilable. [...] But the excess of the malady is, for a vigorous soul, a principle of renewal. If the machine of one's body is not broken in the crisis, one comes out of it much stronger.] (Romain Rolland, *Mémoires,* 307–308.) In trying to 'reconcile the irreconcilable' and in referring to his own 'machine of the body', Rolland, without knowing it, echoed the young Taine.

finished. And everything is about to begin. A life dies. Another has already been born.[19]

'We can only really translate well the books we wish we had written',[20] disclosed Simon Leys. Translating was for Fou Lei writing in disguise. What began as identification and as a desire for appropriation was carried through as an artistic construction of its own order. Not only did translation provide a framework within which creative energy was channeled, it was the surest way of allaying anxiety and of recoiling from the tormenting uncertainty of raw creation. That Fou Lei spent his entire adult life translating a language he had little chance to speak suggests a state of intoxicated solitude. With austerity he adhered to his profession. His was a romantic enthusiasm sustained by discipline.

For reasons social and temperamental, Fou Lei took to translating like a fish to water. To read his translation is to observe, veiled under seeming effortlessness, a frantic course of satisfying two ends to the extreme. The paired demands of fidelity and artistry appear redundant, a given: in Fou Lei's world, to be truthful *is* to be artistic, as to be beautiful *is* to be loyal. On the one hand, his métier appeased his exigent personality; on the other, it accommodated his manifold faculties. Translating, he was entering and reconciling the supposedly irreconcilable through reason and through instinct. That is to say, his emotion and intellect were simultaneously present, alert, keen.

Emulating, especially in the 1940s and early 1950s, Lao She's Pekinese and Northern dialects in his writing and translation, Fou Lei spoke mandarin with Shanghainese intonation. The stylistic unfolding of his language deserves separate study. Precision he always had. Refinement was acquired. His late style – from the 1950s onwards, that is – is at once passionate and restrained, exuberant and stoic. The plasticity, tactility, and monosyllabic crunchiness, unusually

---

19   'Christophe faisait peau neuve. Christophe faisait âme neuve. Et, voyant tomber l'âme usée et flétrie de son enfance, il ne se doutait pas qu'il lui en poussait une nouvelle, plus jeune et plus puissante. Comme on change de corps au courant de la vie, on change d'âme aussi; et la métamorphose ne s'accomplit pas toujours lentement, au fil des jours: il est des heures de crise, où tout se renouvelle d'un coup. L'ancienne dépouille tombe. Dans ces heures d'angoisse, l'être croit tout fini. Et tout va commencer. Une vie meurt. Une autre est déjà née.' Romain Rolland, *Jean-Christophe*, 261–262.

20   'On ne peut vraiment bien traduire que les livres dont on aurait souhaité être soi-même l'auteur.' Simon Leys, *L'ange et le cachalot* (Paris: Seuil, 1998), 145. In 'L'expérience de la traduction littéraire' in the same book, Leys, himself a translator and a novelist, gives a penetrating analysis of the psychology of the translator and of translation as sublimation for creation.

and unsubtly pronounced in his early writing, became nuanced and cadenced. More painterly, and more musical. And, as if by chance, his commentary on the plastic arts often evokes sounds, and that on music frequently summons imagery. Wherefore with Taine and Rolland, two writers whose styles differ radically, Fou Lei was equally adept and naturally at ease: both Taine and Rolland studied and taught art history; both were accomplished pianists. When turning French or English into vernacular Chinese, finding equivalents or choosing, or creating, the fitting vocabulary is the least challenging task. The more intricate, and less noticed, is phrasing, which affects how the reader breathes, senses and reasons. Nietzsche knew: 'that which translates worst from one language into another is the tempo of its style, which has its origin in the character of the race, or expressed more physiologically, in the average tempo of its "metabolism".'[21] Given the flexibility of Chinese syntax, sentences can be structured according to one's own logical judgement and, indeed, taste in the tempo, the latter being seldom realised or analysed. Translating, akin to a musician's interpretation, thus demands musical intuition as well as grammatical calculation. Interpreting Rolland's *Jean-Christophe*, the language of which, in the author's own words, is like the Rhine, Fou Lei was not only setting a new verse to a song, but singing a new song altogether, one which departs from, invokes, and returns to, the thoughts and emotions of the original composer.

'See deep enough, and you see musically',[22] wrote Carlyle, whose violent style Taine appraised with violent excitement.[23] Fou Ts'ong, whose musical understanding is imbued with a love for poetry and painting, confirmed his father's taste in music to be exquisite.[24] In a letter sent to his son on 28 July 1954, Fou Lei examined *Pipa Xing* 琵琶行, a poem by Bai Juyi 白居易 (772–846), in purely musical terms – staccato, pause, attack – and noted that, whenever depicting melancholy, Bai would, without exception, employ oblique tones 仄聲韻.[25] This hypersensitive understanding of sound and emotion is rare. Blessed with this gift, Rolland wrote as a musician, and Fou Lei translated as

---

21   Friedrich Nietzsche, *Beyond Good and Evil*, 59.

22   Thomas Carlyle, *Heroes and Hero-worship*, 78.

23   See Hippolyte Taine, *L'idéalisme anglais: étude sur Carlyle* (Paris: G. Baillière, 1864), a passionate musical read.

24   The author's interview with Fou Ts'ong, June 2009, London.

25   '白居易對音節與情緒的關係悟得很深。凡是轉到傷感的地方，必定改用仄聲韻。《琵琶行》中 "大弦嘈嘈" "小弦切切"一段，好比 staccato (音與音之間互相斷開)，像琵琶的聲音極切；而 "此時無聲勝有聲" 的幾句，等於一個長的 pause; "銀瓶……水漿迸" 兩句，又是突然的 attack, 聲勢雄壯。' Fou Lei's letter to Fou Ts'ong, 28 July 1954, in *Fou Lei's Family Letters*, 33.

one. As it often takes a fine musician to understand another, Fou Lei's translation of Rolland's *vers libre* was the inspired reaction of a *zhiyin* 知音 – one who
understands another's music – turned into his own composition.

Of Fou Lei's published oeuvre, his family letters have attracted the most popular as well as scholarly attention.[26] Over three hundred letters from him and
Zhu Meifu to Fou Ts'ong survive. The correspondence began in January 1954,
when Fou Ts'ong left Shanghai, first for Beijing, then for Warsaw, to prepare
for the International Chopin Piano Competition, in which he was to win the
Third as well as the special Mazurka Prize in 1955. The ensemble of their letters
spans over a decade and can be read as an epic poem from beginning to end.
Sent almost immediately after Fou Ts'ong's departure, the first letter strikes a
dramatic overture. Out poured Fou Lei's newly awakened paternal love as he
repented the injustice he had done his son: 'What I felt, last night, on the plat-
form, I had not felt in years. Pain in the chest, the stomach turning – I had
only experienced this before when lovelorn.'[27] In his childhood, Fou Ts'ong was
subject to the quick temper of his father, who now reproached himself with all
his might: 'My child, I mistreated you. I am forever sorry. I can never atone for
my sin! [...] Truly, Balzac said it well: some sins can be atoned but not covered
up!'[28] ... Afflicted, he continued: 'Poor child, how come your childhood so resembled mine?'[29] Writing this, Fou Lei was forty-five, exactly the age at which
his mother died – could this have been on his mind? 'I have never loved you
so profoundly as I do now, and it happens to be now, now that my love is at its
most profound, that comes parting!'[30] Strong-willed, Fou Ts'ong was not easily

---

26   For a critical reading of these letters, see Nicolai Volland, 'A Close Reading of Fou Lei's
      Family Letters: Cultural Context, State Sovereignty, and the Dilemma of Translators' 細
      讀傅雷家書：文化脈絡，國家領導權，與譯者的困境 in Peng Hsiao-yen (ed.),
      Textual Translation and Cultural Context: China, Japan, and the West since the late Ming
      文化翻譯與文本脈絡：晚明以降的中國、日本與西方 (Taipei: Zhongyang yanjiu
      yuan, Zhongguo wenzhe yanjiusuo, 2013), 129–162. See also Nicolai Volland, 'Fou Lei's
      Family Letters: Kulturaustausch in der Volksrepublik China und die Strategien eines Mit-
      tlers zwischen zwei Welten' in Antje Richter and Helmolt Vittinghoff (eds.), *China und die
      Wahrnehmung der Welt* (Wiesbaden: Harrassowitz, 2007), 221–244.

27   '昨夜月台上的滋味，多少年來沒嘗到了，胸口抽痛，胃里難過，只有從前失戀
      的時候有過這經驗。' Fou Lei's letter to Fou Ts'ong, 18 January 1954, in *Fou Lei's Family
      Letters*, 3.

28   '孩子，我瘧待了你，我永遠對不起你，我永遠補贖不了這種罪過！[...] 巴爾扎
      克說得好：有些罪過只能補贖，不能洗刷！' Ibid.

29   '可憐的孩子，怎麼你的童年會跟我的那麼相似呢？' Ibid.

30   '我從來沒愛你像現在這樣愛得深切，而正在這愛的最深切的關頭，偏偏來了離
      別！' Ibid.

destroyed. Fou Lei refused to forgive himself: 'End result is one thing, facts in the past another. I have buried my past but never my faults. My child, my child, my child, how should I embrace you to express my regret and my love!'[31]

It is characteristic of Fou Lei that, once a realisation was articulated, what took place was his action in exact accordance with what he then decided, unambiguously, to do. In the following three hundred letters, he exerted in the only way he could, and that is through written words, his love. As his twenty-year-old son went abroad to study, which he himself had done twenty-six years previously, Fou Lei was attentive and anticipative to every need, intellectual and emotional, Fou Ts'ong might have.[32] Already in July 1954, Fou Lei wrote: 'Alone and away, if you have any spiritual disquietude, do not hide it, and do not fear being chided.'[33] In October 1954 he wrote:

> Such episodes of low-spiritedness will recur. I have been there myself; in no way am I startled by it. Neither should you agonise over it, or keep it bottled up without telling us. If your heart's gloom is not vented in letters to your family, where does it go? A man lives his entire life traversing ups and downs. Only the life of the mediocre stays like still water. Or else one need be extremely cultivated to be truly detached. [...] All the pains described in your last letter, I understand; I sympathise greatly, and I would do all I can to comfort you, encourage you. Didn't Christophe

---

31 '可是結果是一回事，當年的事實又是另一回事：盡管我埋葬了自己的過去，卻始終埋葬不了自己的錯誤。孩子，孩子，孩子，我要怎樣的擁抱你才能表示我的悔與熱愛呢！' Ibid.

32 In *Pianos and Politics in China: Middle-class Ambitions and the Struggle over Western Music* (New York and Oxford: Oxford University, 1989), Richard Curt Kraus' take on Fou Lei's letters to Fou Ts'ong appears cynical. Writing in 1989, Kraus dutifully acknowledged the source of much of his information as being Hong Kong gossip. It is respectable to note this, but irresponsible to pass gossip as history, particularly when textual evidence is available for examination, which need not be at odds with reading texts as constructions of personae. The presumed gossip with which the estimable political scientist was supplied, and which he supplied in turn, is puzzling. Whilst it is, on the one hand, conceivable that the first edition of *Fou Lei's Family Letters* (1981), selected for their literary value and devoid of triviality, gave the impression of severe stoicism à la Seneca, thus leading to frankly bizarre speculations in Kraus' book – that Fou Lei was jealous of his son for staying away from China, or that Fou Ts'ong was overjoyed to escape his father by fleeing to England – it is, on the other hand, unsettling, for interpretations such as these fail to take into consideration precisely the political conditions which Kraus took to be the subject of his study. See note 53 in this chapter.

33 '在外倘有任何精神苦悶，也切勿隱瞞，別怕受埋怨。' Fou Lei's letter to Fou Ts'ong, 27 July 1954, in *Fou Lei's Family Letters*, 33.

go through this many times? Isn't he the epitome of all artists? Gradually you will develop a different disposition towards the past, and think about it without being acutely stirred. [...] I wrote to you before about the ruin of emotions, for I would like you to regard it as the ashes of your soul, so that when you look at it, you do so without tormenting yourself, but with the sentiment one has when standing, in awe, in front of an ancient battlefield.[34]

Jean-Christophe was here summoned to speak to Fou Ts'ong as a kindred spirit. The metaphor of antique ruins mirrored that in Rolland's epic novel, where Jean-Christophe 'stayed devastated amidst these ruins. [...] His heart was in mourning.'[35] 'I have been there myself', Fou Lei said. At work was empathy between father and son, as it was between the translator and the translated.

Another man who had been there was Taine. He, too, went all out to help when his nephew was in a similar state. At the end of September 1887, Chevrillon, aged twenty-three, wrote from Brest, where he was teaching English at École Navale: '[...] what frightens me most of all is not ennui, but the feeling of isolation, the absence of friendly people and the perpetual contact with indifferent strangers. I felt this violently two years ago in London, and I could not stand it. I spent the day in a sort of dreary prostration; at night I could not sleep or I had nightmares. Touching a book would have been impossible. I had to leave before the set date. If this happens now I will leave Brest at all costs.'[36] Taine replied, on 2 October 1887, beginning with a calm diagnosis:

---

34 '這種精神消沉的情形，以後還是會有的。我是過來人，決不至於大驚小怪。你也不必為此擔心，更不必硬壓在肚里不告訴我們。心中的苦悶不在家信中發泄，又哪裡去發呢？人一輩子都在高潮—低潮中浮沉，唯有庸碌的人，生活才如死水一般；或者要有極高的修養，方能廓然無累，真正的解脫。[…]這次來信所說的痛苦，我都理會得；我很同情，我願意盡量安慰你、鼓勵你。克利斯朵夫不是經過多少回這種情形嗎？他不是一切藝術家的縮影與結晶嗎？慢慢的你會養成另外一種心情對付過去的事：就是能夠想到而不再驚心動魄，[…]我以前在信中和你提過感情的 ruin，就是要你把這些事當作心靈的灰燼看，看的時候當然不免感觸萬端，但不要刻骨銘心的傷害自己，而要像對着古戰場一般的存着憑吊的心懷。' Fou Lei's letter to Fou Ts'ong, 2 October 1954; ibid., 51–52.

35 'Après, il restait abattu, au milieu de ces ruines. Il eût mieux aimé perdre un bras que ses saintes illusions. Son coeur était en deuil.' Romain Rolland, *Jean-Christophe*, 379.

36 '[...] ce qui m'effraye par-dessus tout, ce n'est pas l'ennui, mais le sentiment de l'isolement, l'absence de figures amies, le contact perpétuel d'indifférents et d'étrangers. J'ai senti cela très violemment il y a deux ans à Londres et je n'ai pas pu le supporter; je passais la journée dans une sorte de prostration morne; la nuit je ne dormais pas ou j'avais des cauchemars. Toucher un livre m'eut été impossible. J'ai dû quitter avant la date fixée. Si cela vient je quitterai Brest coûte que coûte.' André Chevrillon's letter to Taine, received at the end of September 1887; conserved at Fonds Jacques Doucet.

'Your melancholy and pessimistic anticipations come from your highly-strung state.'[37] After giving practical counsel, he told Chevrillon: 'I have high hopes for you, and end by saying these words upon which I have well reflected: if you work a lot, if you study composition and style diligently, if you write five or six pages every eight days as a way of trying your hands at it, if you apply your sensitivity and imagination to the art of writing to become a master of it in detail and in depth, I think there are in you the makings of a writer.'[38] Whilst his pedantic uncle's word *bien pesé* was on its way, Chevrillon sent another letter at the beginning of October in desperation: 'It is wrong of me to bother you like this, twice with the same subject, but today, I feel that I break down utterly.'[39] His uncle replied on 4 October: 'My dear child, I am pained by your sadness and despondency; write to me, as much as you want and can, at least to pour your feelings out and also to chat about your thesis. [...] To be specific, your first task must be to *translate* into French, by yourself and in as precise and as literary a fashion as you can, *Peter Plymley's Letters* [...]. Look at my *La Fontaine*, [...] I was in Nevers, without books; I finished the rest in Paris: around this original core, all the rest came together easily.'[40] *La Fontaine et ses fables* was Taine's doctoral work in Literature, completed in isolation and desolation after his agrégation in Philosophy was rejected by the jury for the radicalism of his thesis. Making this an analogous example for his nephew's thesis on Sydney Smith (1771–1845),[41] Taine prescribed the act of not

---

37 '[...] ta mélancolie et tes prévisions pessimistes viennent de ton état nerveux.' Taine's letter to Chevrillon, 2 October 1887; conserved at Fonds Jacques Doucet.

38 'Moi, j'ai de grandes espérances pour toi, et te dis en finissant un mot que j'ai bien pesé: si tu travailles beaucoup, si tu étudies assidument la composition et le style, si tu écris cinq ou six pages tous les huit jours de manière à t'exercer et à te faire la main, si tu appliques ta sensibilité et ton imagination à l'art d'écrire pour t'en rendre maître en détail et à fond, je pense qu'il y a en toi l'étoffe d'un écrivain.' Ibid.

39 'J'ai tort de vous ennuyer ainsi deux fois du même sujet, mais aujourd'hui, je sens que je break down utterly.' Chevrillon's letter to Taine, sent from Hôtel des Voyageurs in Brest and received at the beginning of October 1887; conserved at Fonds Jacques Doucet.

40 'Mon cher enfant, Je suis bien affligé de ta tristesse et de ton découragement; écris-moi, tant que tu voudras et pourras, au moins pour t'épancher, et aussi pour causer de ta thèse. [...] Pour préciser, ton premier travail doit être de *traduire* toi-même en français, d'une façon aussi serrée et aussi littéraire que possible, Peter Plymley's Letters, [...] Regarde mon La Fontaine; [...] j'étais à Nevers, sans livres; j'ai complété le reste à Paris: autour de ce noyau primitif, tout le reste est venu se grouper sans peine.' Taine's letter to Chevrillon, 4 October 1887; conserved at Fonds Jacques Doucet.

41 Seven years later, in 1894, Chevrillon's doctoral thesis on the author of *Peter Plymley's Letters* was published under the title *Sydney Smith et la renaissance des idées libérales en Angleterre au XIXe siècle*.

reading, not writing, but *translating* the English author's work into French at a time when Chevrillon was breaking down.

To some scholars, Taine appears unsympathetic and unlovable.[42] Rigid and reserved he may have been, but if this judgement, too, derives from the stoically selected posthumous publication of his letters, *Hippolyte Taine: sa vie et sa correspondance* (1902–1907), we cannot but admit how little we know men and yet how readily we judge.[43] At the end of this letter Taine wrote: 'Being separated from one's family and friends and entering into life is always hard; I felt it. Nevers was a much worse hole than Brest. [...] Tell me what you think of my moral, literary and physical advice, and keep me informed of your life as your best friend.'[44] In the same vein Fou Lei wrote to Fou Ts'ong: 'And do not be afraid of disquieting me. If father does not care for his child, for whom does he care? If father does not help the child, who does? If the son in agony does not turn to his father for rescue, to whom does he turn?'[45] We recall that Fou Lei never had a father to turn to. Neither did Taine.[46]

Before leaving for Poland, in 1953 Fou Ts'ong spent a month and a half at home, discussing art and music with Fou Lei every day (see *Fig.* 31). 'It was the happiest time in our life. [...] I am happy that I have one more friend; my son has become my friend, what happiness is comparable to this!'[47] Fou Lei, indeed, was remarkably happy in the early 1950s. Under the Communist regime, he

---

42   See Hilda Laura Norman, 'The Personality of Hippolyte Taine' in *PMLA*, vol. 36, no. 4 (December 1921), 550.

43   See note 32 in this chapter. The view that Taine had very little humour is perhaps also unjustified. His sense of humour, quite a dry one, manifests itself in letters such as one sent in 1886 to Chevrillon, then in England: 'Ne sois pas trop shy, ou plutôt surmonte ta shyness' [Don't be too shy, or rather overcome your shyness]; 'ne crains pas de mettre ton habit noir et ta cravate blanche; tâche d'entrer comme auditeur dans un debating-club.' [Don't be afraid of putting on your black dress-coat and your white necktie; try to get into a debating-club as a member of the audience.] Taine's letter to Chevrillon, 4 June 1886; conserved at Fonds Jacques Doucet.

44   'Être séparé de sa famille et de ses amis, entrer dans la vie est toujours dur; je l'ai senti; Nevers était un trou bien pire que Brest, [...] Dis-moi ce que tu penses de mes conseils moraux, littéraires et physiques et tiens-moi au courant de ta vie, comme ton meilleur ami.' Taine's letter to Chevrillon, 4 October 1887; conserved at Fonds Jacques Doucet.

45   '也別怕引起我心煩，爸爸不為兒子煩心，為誰煩心？爸爸不幫助孩子，誰幫助孩子？兒子苦悶不向爸爸求救，向誰求救？' Fou Lei's letter to Fou Ts'ong, 11 December 1955, in *Fou Lei's Family Letters*, 136.

46   Taine's father, who had taught his boy Latin, died when Taine was thirteen. Taine's uncle, who had taught his nephew English, sent him to the best school in France.

47   '[...]是我們一生最愉快的時期；[...]我高興的是我又多了一個朋友；兒子變了朋友，世界上有什麼事可以和這種幸福相比的！' Fou Lei's letter to Fou Ts'ong, 30 January 1954, in *Fou Lei's Family Letters*, 5.

had gradually taken on the rôle of an independent public intellectual engaged in helping the party rebuild the nation.[48] This commitment can be similarly observed in, for example, Lao She, who happened also to be early fatherless and who took still less of a critical distance. *All* Chinese intellectuals who stayed in or returned to China after 1949 changed, in one way or another. Some resisted the 'Marxist-Leninist thinking' more, some less. Some believed in the new government more, some less. By and large, we discern an overwhelming sense of relief at their country being undivided and at peace, for the first time in over a hundred years.

FIGURE 31   *Fou Lei, Fou Ts'ong and Zhu Meifu in the study, 1953.*
              THE FOU FAMILY TRUST.

---

48   Confined as he had been for two decades at home to do his translation, Fou Lei now had to decline, sometimes without success, invitations to attend meetings, give talks, and inspect faraway provinces to gauge a 'scientific' picture of the achievements of the Socialist State and to publish his responses.

This trust was not reciprocated, and this relief not to last. In 1956 began the Hundred Flowers Campaign. In 1957, the lightness, joy, hope, excitement, and humour in the letters from Fou Lei and Zhu Meifu to Fou Ts'ong since 1954 came to a standstill. The Anti-Rightist Campaign had begun.[49] With mass 'labelling' as its authorised exterminator, this mass purge, which saw over half a million labelled, was as preposterous as it was ruthless. Chains of conceptual falsehood stuffed with linguistic confusion effected the ideological engineering of one after another brutal campaign in the 1950s and 1960s. In what sense were the accused 'capitalists' capitalist in an already socialist society? By what reasoning could the implicated 'bourgeois', barely bourgeois in the social denotation as Marx used it, be denounced as enemies of the people in point of fact? 'Left' and 'Right' continually took on arbitrary meanings and non-meanings. Words lost their integrity. A language systematically gone mad is a violation of logic and a collective abandonment of reason. Having dutifully 'spoken out' since 1956, exactly as Mao had decoyed intellectuals into doing, Fou Lei published, in exasperation, political commentaries in *Wenhui Bao* (June and July 1957) which read as scarcely more than pitiful announcements for the blatant purpose of self-protection, and which necessarily took on the form of allegation. We are now looking at a condition where virtually everyone was betrayed and where everyone was forced to betray. Nothing was safe, and no one could afford to be good. Conspiracy was the norm. Paranoia poisoned all. All were ensnared in a mechanism designed to deny human beings dignity and to turn inhumanity into normality. From Poland Fou Ts'ong was called back that summer for 'self-criticism' before returning to continue his studies. After ten meetings of 'denouncement' and three forced self-criticisms, and after fiercely refusing to confess or concede, Fou Lei was eventually labelled a rightist in April 1958. And the proof? His 'So-called "Anti-Imperialist and Pro-Soviet"' (1947) in *Wenhui Bao*.[50]

Sceptical of all ideologies, critical equally of left and right, conservative by intellect and radical by temperament, Fou Lei, in his political views, was

---

49   See Frank Dikötter, *The Tragedy of Liberation: A History of the Communist Revolution 1945–1957* (London: Bloomsbury, 2013).

50   See chapter 7, notes 97 and 98. See also Fang Fei, "'I Did Not Kill Boren; Boren Died Because of Me" – Fu Lei's Relation with a Newspaper' '我雖不殺伯仁，伯仁因我而死' ──傅雷與一份報紙的因緣 in *Shu Cheng* 書城 (20 November 2006) for a brief countdown of Fou Lei's contribution to *Wenhui Bao* between 1947 and 1957; these publications were used against him in 1957 and 1958.

effectively not to be classified. His point of reference being nearly always moral rather than political, that was of course in itself 'incorrect'. Discussions of
whether it was *just* to label him this and that are, to my mind, absurd. Labelling
was wrong to begin with. With the starting points all wrong, how could there
be anything but injustice from that point on?

Now the 'rightist' translator, incriminated, disgraced, cast out, who had lived
on every word he published, was banished from publishing. Still he continued
to work. He was, of course, bereft of income. After 1950, Fou Lei was one of the
two acclaimed authors in the country who did not take a state salary.[51] Publishers now suggested that he opt for a pseudonym. He refused. 'Publish under
my name, or not at all.'[52] His health deteriorated. Fou Ts'ong, knowing that if
he returned from Poland, he and his father would both be forced to condemn
each other and, because they both would not do so, would both perish, fled to
London at the end of 1958.[53] As the plane landed in Heathrow, Fou Ts'ong was
branded a traitor in his own country. In January 1959 he sent a long letter to his
parents. In October 1959 they resumed correspondence.

Between June 1958 and May 1959, Fou Lei translated, in seclusion and with
no certainty of its publication, Taine's *Philosophie de l'art*. Twenty-nine years
earlier, he had first fallen for this book.[54] If translating Balzac up to this point

---

51   The other was Ba Jin 巴金 (1904–2005).

52   See 'Fou Lei Chronology' in *Complete Works*, vol. 20, 342.

53   In a 2010 publication of the *Family Letters*, we see subtle warnings of menacing political
      conditions at home (often taking the form of irony, no doubt since their correspondence
      could have been intercepted) from Fou Lei and Zhu Meifu to Fou Ts'ong, then in Warsaw,
      in 1957.

54   Fou Lei's translator's preface, now with twenty-nine years' distance, echoed contem-
      porary critical voices from 1928 at Taine's centenary. See, for example, A. Lombard's 'Le
      Centenaire de Taine' in *Nouvelle Semaine Artistique et Littéraire* (Neuchâtel, Switzerland,
      7 April 1928) – 'Son influence est partout. Nous la retrouvons... dans nos méthodes de
      travail, dans nos idées générales, mais aussi dans nos imaginations.' – and M. Lévy-Bruhl's
      article in *Le Temps* (25 May 1928) – 'Son œuvre a pu être dépassée; mais l'impulsion qu'il
      a donné se fait encore sentir, la voie qu'il a indiquée était la bonne.' – for parallel judge-
      ments by Fou Lei: '[...] 他在歐洲學術界的影響至今還沒有完全消失，多數的批評
      家即使不明白標榜種族，環境，時代三大原則，實際上還是多多少少應用這個
      理論的。' [In European academia, his influence has not disappeared completely. Most
      critics do not ostentatiously propose the principle of 'race, milieu, moment'; in reality
      they still more or less apply this theory.] Fou Lei, 'Translator's Preface to Taine's *Philoso-
      phie de l'art*' 丹納《藝術哲學》譯者序 (1959) in *Fou Lei Discusses Art*, 153.

had been in part for its political safety – Balzac was Engels' favourite writer –
the return to Taine was a pure act of love, *évasion d'âme* in its complete form.[55]
An escape, indeed, at once linguistic, aesthetic, and historical.

Let us behold, for an instant, Taine's description of the Netherlands:

> ... ce ciel blafard, pluvieux, sans cesse rayé d'averses, et même dans les
> beaux jours, violé comme d'une gaze délicate par les vapeurs légères qui
> s'envolent du sol moite et forment un dôme diaphane, un tissu aérien
> de minces flocons neigeux au-dessus de la grande corbeille verdoyante
> ouverte à perte de vue et arrondie jusqu'à l'horizon.[56]

and Fou Lei's rendition:

> 灰白的天空經常有暴雨掠過，便是晴天也像籠着輕紗一般，因
> 為濕漉漉的泥地上飄起一陣陣稀薄的水汽，織成一個透明的天
> 幕，一匹雪花般的絕細的紗羅，罩在一望無際，滿眼青綠的大
> 地上。[57]

Taine painted a landscape. Fou Lei painted another. With nuanced hues he
crafted his canvas. 'Un vert *funèbre*'[58] is 慘綠 [59] [miserable green]; les 'événements *funèbres*'[60] are 不祥之事 [61] [inauspicious events]. 'Des contemporains
mélancoliques'[62] are 愁眉不展的人 [63] [people whose distressed eyebrows
are never unfurrowed]; 'les idées qu'il a reçues [...] sont *mélancoliques*',[64]
感受的觀念都令人悲傷 [65] [perceived concepts all make one mournful].
Taking the indication of 'caprice' in 'Leur coeur a des caprices, des violences,

---

55   That said, Fou Lei's letters to publishers in April 1959 made the case that '迄今為止，我
      國尚無一部比較詳盡的西洋美術史。' [Till this day, there does not exist in our coun-
      try a relatively comprehensive history of Western art.] (*Fou Lei's Letters to His Friends*,
      178–181) and that Taine's *Philosophie de l'art*, serving such an educational purpose, was
      politically correct and publishable.

56   Hippolyte Taine, *Philosophie de l'art* (Paris: Hachette, 1918), vol. 1, 35.

57   Fou Lei, *Complete Works*, vol. 17, 45.

58   Taine, *Philosophie de l'art*, vol. 1, 53.

59   Fou Lei, *Complete Works*, vol. 17, 52.

60   Taine, *Philosophie de l'art*, vol. 1, 58.

61   Fou Lei, *Complete Works*, vol. 17, 54.

62   Taine, *Philosophie de l'art*, vol. 1, 58.

63   Fou Lei, *Complete Works*, vol. 17, 54.

64   Taine, *Philosophie de l'art*, vol. 1, 58.

65   Fou Lei, *Complete Works*, vol. 17, 54.

des abattements',[66] he transformed violence and despondency into paired adjectives with the capricious construction 忽而激烈，忽而頹喪[67] [now violent, now despondent]. Where Taine employed a Christian term 'une vallée de larmes'[68] [valley of tears; *valle lacrimarum*], Fou Lei matched it with 苦海[69] [sea of bitterness], a Buddhist term likewise symbolising earthly life. Whilst 'le public'[70] he translated as 群眾,[71] a politically charged, class-conscious term, in 'invasion d'une province'[72] he delivered 'province' as 郡縣,[73] a thoroughly classical turn of phrase.

It would be worth examining how much of Fou Lei's post-1949 'politicised' language was voluntary, how much of it a compromise, and how much a natural mutation.[74] In the 1950s and 1960s, his translation was censored linguistically before publication. An ideological control, the policy resembling the Orwellian Newspeak sometimes denounced Fou Lei's language as 'obsolete'.[75] That in 1963, Fou Lei considered himself 'un des rares puristes de nos jours' [one of the rare purists today],[76] suggests a highly conscious resistance to linguistic deracination in his daily practice.

---

66   Taine, *Philosophie de l'art*, vol. 1, 79.

67   Fou Lei, *Complete Works*, vol. 17, 65.

68   Taine, *Philosophie de l'art*, vol. 1, 80.

69   Fou Lei, *Complete Works*, vol. 17, 65.

70   Taine, *Philosophie de l'art*, vol. 1, 58.

71   Fou Lei, *Complete Works*, vol. 17, 54.

72   Taine, *Philosophie de l'art*, vol. 1, 58.

73   Fou Lei, *Complete Works*, vol. 17, 54.

74   See Nicolai Volland, 'A Linguistic Enclave: Translation and Language Policies in the Early People's Republic of China' in *Modern China*, vol. 35, no. 5 (September 2009), 467–494, where Fou Lei's three versions of *Père Goriot* from 1946, 1951 and 1963 are exemplarily compared. See also Serena S.H. Jin, 'The Art of Translation in Fou Lei's Translation of *Le Père Goriot*' in Chan Sin-wai, *A Topical Bibliography of Translation and Interpretation: Chinese-English · English-Chinese* (Hong Kong: The Chinese University of Hong Kong, 1995) and Nicolai Volland, 'Translating the Socialist State: Cultural Exchange, National Identity, and the Socialist World in the Early PRC' in *Twentieth-Century China*, vol. 33, no. 2 (April 2008), 51–72.

75   See letters exchanged between Fou Lei and various publishers between 1956 and 1965 (*Fou Lei's Letters to His Friends*, 169–193), which reveal the translator's painstaking negotiations to retain the integrity of his language.

76   In a letter (now conserved at Bibliothèque nationale de France) to Étiemble on 24 February 1963, Fou Lei wrote: 'Enfin, mes travaux pendant les dernières cinq années commencent à être publiées un à un: la Rabouilleuse de Balzac et la Philosophie de l'Art de Taine ont déjà paru, je compte de vous en envoyer un exemplaire en pensant que peut-être ces traductions sont-elles utiles à aider vos étudiants à apprendre le chinois parlé et

By now Fou Lei was prematurely an old man. Severely ill and in no condition to read or write, he spent over a month copying, in small elegant calligraphy, the chapter on Greek sculpture from his unpublished translation of *Philosophie de l'art*. In the form of an annotated manuscript, this Herculean act of love reached London (*Figs.* 32 and 33). 'After reading that', wrote Fou Ts'ong, 'I found my conviction that Handel's music, specially his oratorio is the nearest to the Greek spirit in music, strengthened. His optimism, his radiant poetry, which is as simple as one can imagine but never vulgar, his directness and frankness, his pride, his majesty and his almost physical ecstasy.'[77] Back and forth, a special dialogue divided by the oceans took place in this dreamland called ancient Greece. 'I had expected your excitement', wrote Fou Lei, 'Such an era, once gone, will never come back, like the lovely phase of a child growing to be an adolescent. It is also like our pre-Qin (221 B.C.) and Wei-Jin (220–589). I have been reading *A New Account of the Tales of the World* 世說新語 lately (I am in search of a copy, not too heavy, to send you), and consider the ethos at the time a touch like that of ancient Greece, and a touch like that of Renaissance Italy; but its loftiness, tranquillity, and simplicity are unlike any period in the cultural history of the West.'[78]

Never forgetting 'our China' – be it in 1928 or in 1961 – in his real *and* imaginary journeys to the West, Fou Lei identified distant native counterparts to his preferred European epochs. It was likewise his country of the past that Fou Ts'ong could not forget: 'In this decadent world, after having spent so many

---

le style moderne dont je suis considéré comme un des rare puristes de nos jours.' [Finally, my work of the past five years begins to be published one by one: Balzac's *La Rabouilleuse* and Taine's *Philosophie de l'art* have already been released; I intend to send you a copy, as these translations are perhaps useful in helping your students learn spoken Chinese and the modern style [of writing], of which I am considered one of the rare purists today.] Étiemble, versed in fifteen languages and author of *Parlez-vous franglais?* (1964), was likewise a purist in French.

77   Fou Ts'ong's letter to Fou Lei, summer 1961. This paragraph was written in English. Fou Lei, in his letter of 1 August 1961, quoted it back with his translation of it in Chinese, to check if he had understood his son *precisely* and to help the latter stay close to his mother tongue. He added apologetically, '像這樣不打草稿隨手翻譯，在我還是破題兒第一遭。' [This is the first time in my life that I translate something without having first made a separate draft.] See *Fou Lei's Family Letters*, 335.

78   '我早料到你讀了《論希臘雕塑》以後的興奮。那樣的時代是一去不復返的了，正如一個人從童年到少年那個天真可愛的階段一樣。也如同我們的先秦時代、兩晉六朝一樣。近來常翻閱《世說新語》(正在尋一部鉛印而篇幅不太笨重的預備寄你)，覺得那時的風流文采既有點兒近古希臘，也有點像文藝復興時期的意大利；但那種高遠、恬淡、素雅的意味仍然不同於西方文化史上的任何一個時期。' Fou Lei's letter to Fou Ts'ong, 26 June 1961, in *Fou Lei's Family Letters*, 318.

years in the West, I have met many people whom I admire and love, from whom I learn, but none has taken me to a place at once passionate and serene, profound and simple, affectionate and proud, subtle and straightforward as you do. [...] Time after time you remind me of a place idealistic, generous, devoted, loyal, kind, and selfless, which I find in my memories.'[79]

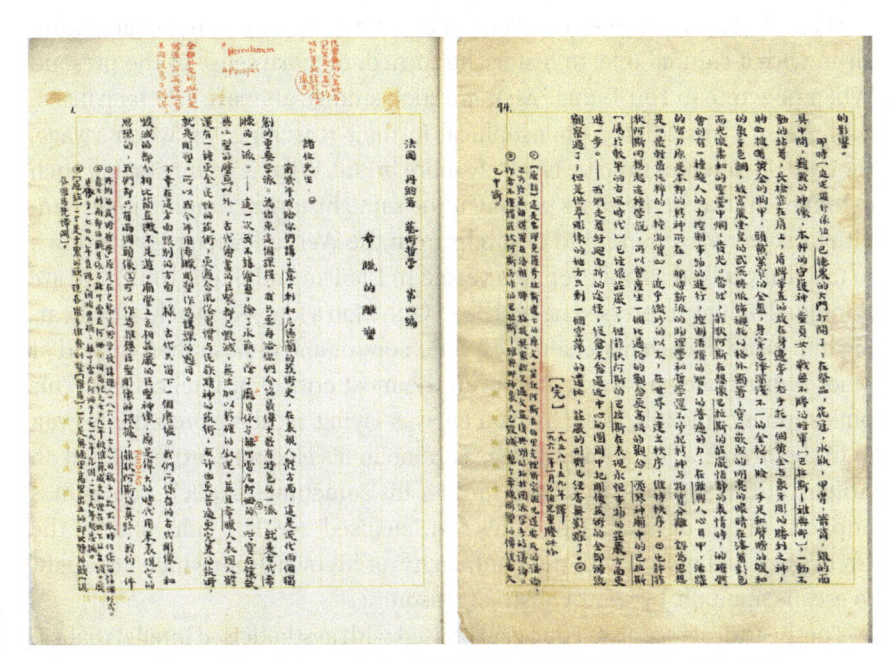

FIGURES 32 AND 33   *Fou Lei's translation of 'Greek Sculpture' from* Philosophie de l'art *by Hippolyte Taine. Manuscript sent to Fou Ts'ong, 1961.*
THE FOU FAMILY TRUST.

Two artists, both now outcasts, met in a *pays des chimères*. Let it be recalled that Taine's ancient Greece, more a romantic fantasy tinged with a Hegelian vision of classicism to begin with, had little to do with historical truth. Smitten by Taine's manner of historicising, Fou Lei, like the poet-logician, was perhaps too strong a temperament to be an historian. If, in 1929, Fou Lei's initial excitement upon reading *Philosophie de l'art* was inseparable from the generational search for a cultural alternative, his identification now with a Tainean Greece was far more complex. Disillusioned by one's own country, own time, own reality, one's yearning launches into the faraway, the bygone, the illusory. And from ancient Greece the crane flew on: 'Do you like pictures of stone carving

---

79   Fou Ts'ong's letter to Fou Lei, 18 June 1961.

石刻畫? Can you feel that, unlike Dunhuang frescoes and Yungang carvings which married with foreign elements, this is the true art of the Han? Simply gazing at the ample robes, large sleeves, strong succinct lines, unified, organic silhouettes, plain archaic houses and chariots, and robust, majestic horses, makes my heart throb and leap into the land of two thousand years ago (the effect is even better when the picture is framed).'[80]

With 'the true art of the Han', Fou Lei could now substitute political nationalism with a cultural one; to history he turned, to make sense of the present. When he wrote to Fou Ts'ong, 'Men are such strange animals. When civilised, they are so civilised, and philosophical in their reasoning; yet when savage, they are no different from beasts, only more brutal. What is strange is that such extremes appear in the same people of the same historical time. So many ambitious schemers, tyrants and oligarchs from the Wei-Jin, when they sat down to talk, they talked as philosophers versed in Daoism and Buddhism!',[81] we are reminded of how impressed he had been with Mao a few years back, after hearing him give a speech in person. 'Top-notch orator and philosopher', he said of Mao, whose charisma worked on even the most critical of intellectuals. This philosopher could kill, was what Fou Lei was saying, recalling precedents even in his beloved era.[82] Page after page, as Taine in his eloquent prose painted an Athens of the Sophists, it is hard to miss his sometimes explicit, sometimes implicit critique of the malady of his own 'civilised' age. The 'simplicity' of the Greeks was juxtaposed with the 'complexity' of his own, from which he sought to escape mentally by way of abstract reasoning.

This historical escapism Fou Lei exercised with aestheticised intellectualisation in parallel. To evoke the flamboyant yet serene eccentrics of the Wei-Jin,

---

80   '石刻畫你喜歡嗎？是否感覺到那是真正漢族的藝術品，不像敦煌壁畫雲岡石刻
      有外來因素。我覺得光是那種寬袍大袖、簡潔有力的線條、渾合的輪廓、古樸
      的屋宇車輛、強勁雄壯的馬匹，已使我看了怦然心動，神遊於兩千年以前的天
      地中去了 (裝了框子看更有效果)。' Fou Lei's Letter to Fou Ts'ong, 26 June 1961, in *Fou
      Lei's Family Letters*, 318.

81   '人真是奇怪的動物，文明的時候會那麼文明，談玄說理會那麼雋永，野蠻的時
      候又同野獸毫無分別，甚至更殘酷。奇怪的是這兩個極端就表現在同一批人同
      一時代的人身上。兩晉六朝多少野心家，想奪天下、稱孤道寡的人，坐下來清
      談竟是深通老莊與佛教哲學的哲人！' Ibid.

82   Taine had similarly discussed the 'beaux monstres' with amazement. *Philosophie de l'art*
      was quoted in Fou Lei's letters, written in French, to Yehudi Menuhin. Political commentary on the current situation may be read between the lines in some of Fou Lei's historical and philosophical musings. See, for example, chapter 5, note 97: 'Art *too* is a tyrant. [...]
      Have you ever thought about why, for the latter half of his life, Chopin voluntarily stayed in a foreign land?'

he used words such as 天真 and 可愛, mirroring Taine's *naturel, plus homme* and *adorablement idéaliste* for the Greeks. The idea of individualism being at the same time universal is an obvious point for comparison between the two departed ages; a pantheistic worldview possibly another: after all, Taine, like Rolland, was a disciple of Spinoza. It so happens that we might also redraw Fou Lei's analogous thinking in motion. As Taine wrote of ancient Greece, 'Here, philosophy is a conversation; it is born in the gymasium, under the arcades, along the tree-lined paths; the master speaks whilst taking a walk, followed by others',[83] Fou Lei annotated: 'Such were the practices during our Wei-Jin!'[84] In effect, Wei-Jin gentlemen held what they called 'pure conversation' 清談, discussing metaphysics as a way of life. It would here appear that, when a linguistic equivalent was readily available, a conceptual link was fast established, and cultural analogy made, an impulse hard to resist. To what extent was Fou Lei's cultural identification and appropriation a linguistic operation?

Reading Fou Lei's lines of intellectual delight, one would not have thought that he was hardly in the physical condition to sit at his desk. In his letters he barely spoke of himself; other than recurring expressions of discontentment with his work, rarely a word of complaint. No doubt at their son's request, from time to time Zhu Meifu wrote, telling Fou Ts'ong about his father's suffering – a chronic back pain, cerebral exhaustion, failing eyesight, insomnia, constant worry, acute daily headaches sometimes lasting more than ten hours. Neither did she speak of her own health – she had a heart condition, and revealed only in 1961 that she weighed but ninety-five pounds, and Fou Lei a hundred.[85] The years in which Fou Lei was denied the right to publish coincided with the Great Famine (1959–61). A consequence of the failed Great Leap Forward (1958), it was the largest famine of the twentieth century, taking the lives of tens of millions. Malnutritioned and impoverished, Fou Lei could not bring himself to mention it, let alone ask for help. Learning of the critical situation in general, Liu Kang sent food and medicine from Singapore, as did Fou Ts'ong and his then father-in-law, Yehudi Menuhin (1916–1999), from London.

---

83 'Ici, la philosophie est une conversation; elle naît dans les gymnases, sous les portiques, sous des allées de platanes; le maître parle en se promenant, et on le suit.' Taine, *Philosophie de l'art*, vol. 2, 125. '在希臘哲學是一種清談，在練身場上，在廊廡之下，在楓楊樹間的走道上產生的；哲學家一邊散步一邊談話，眾人跟在後面。' Fou Lei, *Complete Works*, vol. 16, 235–236.

84 '此是我們兩晉六朝的風氣。' Fou Lei, *Complete Works*, vol. 16, 236.

85 '爸爸雖然身體瘦，過去一直維持在一百二十磅上下，如今掉到一百磅，[…] 我自己九十五磅，也掉了十五磅。' Zhu Meifu's letter to Fou Ts'ong, 9 February 1961, in *Fou Lei's Family Letters*, 287.

In May 1961, Fou Lei described in a letter the paintings by Lin Fengmian that he was about to send as a present to Fou Ts'ong: 'This time [...] there is one similar to the genre of a dreamlike immortal world (the Yellow Mountain) that I once sent you, and one resembling the kind of rich, vibrant, almost Berliozian orchestration that I once sent your father-in-law. There is also a light, luminous scene of the West Lake (green, black and white tones); one of a fisherman – fishing birds – bateau and bulrush in ink; one of a few boats with interlacing sails in black and brown hues; one of strongly contrasted (brown, blue, black and white), audaciously outlined opera figures...'[86] Born under suffocating circumstances, Fou Lei's romantic reverie took himself and Fou Ts'ong into a world not of their reality, but of their aspiration. Marcel Proust, shaken by the vision of the 'pays mystérieux' of Gustave Moreau, wrote: 'The land, of which works of art are thereby fragmentary apparitions, is the poet's soul, his true soul, the very deepest of all his souls; it is his true country, but one in which he lives only for rare moments.'[87] For these rare moments Fou Lei lived. Like strange birds looking for strange lands, through the power of their minds, the physically weak mouse and beaver could fly.

On Taine the 'intellectual beaver of the île Saint-Louis', Irving Babbitt in 1913 contemplated: 'Life was never so hideous, he says of one period of the Renaissance, and this hideousness is the truth. Thus Taine's head finds its truth and reality in an order that is abhorrent to his heart. The instinct of the heart is to escape from such a reality into a *pays des chimères*. This is what he calls creating for yourself an alibi.'[88] To the despondent Fou Ts'ong, Fou Lei wrote: 'The heart of a newborn child knows not loneliness. Lonely, he will create a world, and create many of his heart's friends!'[89] To the suffering Chevrillon, Taine advised: 'On no account should you give up on Sydney this year; he will be your

---

86   '此次有我選定暫存家中的，有像送你一類富於夢境的神仙世界(黃山)，也有像送你岳父那樣非常富麗、明快，近於柏遼茲的orchestration的(以上各一)。又有比較清淡的西湖風景(綠、黑、白三個色調)；一幅是水墨的漁翁——捕魚鳥——小艇和蘆葦；一幅是幾條船，帆檣交錯，色調是黑與棕色；一幅是對比強烈(棕色、藍、黑、白)，線條潑辣的戲劇人物 […]' Fou Lei's letter to Fou Ts'ong, 25 May 1961; ibid., 312–313.

87   'Le pays, dont les œuvres d'art sont ainsi des apparitions fragmentaires, est l'âme du poète, son âme véritable, celle de toutes ses âmes qui est le plus au fond, sa patrie véritable, mais où il ne vit que de rares moments.' Marcel Proust, *Trois notes sur le « pays mystérieux » de Gustave Moreau* (La Rochelle: Rumeur des âges, 2008), 16.

88   Irving Babbitt, *The Masters of Modern French Criticism*, 234.

89   '赤子便是不知道孤獨的。赤子孤獨了，會創造一個世界，創造許多心靈的朋友！' Fou Lei's letter to Fou Ts'ong, 26 January 1955, in *Fou Lei's Family Letters*, 88–89.

alibi, your intellectual excitement in Brest.'[90] 'One such alibi', continued Babbitt, '[...] is to lose yourself in aesthetic contemplation of the forms of outer nature. Another way of creating an alibi is to study history. [...] A third way of creating an alibi is by music. *Jouez du Beethoven*.'[91] As Beethoven said to one friend, 'My kingdom is in the air',[92] and to another, 'Poor Beethoven, there is no happiness for you in this world. Only in the region of the ideal can you find friends',[93] Taine cried out: 'I crave to be with my books which do not lie.'[94]

We now come to the coupled theme of moral isolation and spiritual alliance, whereupon loom the constructs of universality. At a young age Romain Rolland wrote: 'I drink the blood of the great dead.'[95] During and after the First World War, he lived for the most part a reclusive life in Switzerland,[96] where like-minded figures such as Gandhi visited.[97] In the same year that Fou Lei's translation of *Jean-Christophe* was completed, his seven-year-old son began playing the piano. Obtaining a classical, indeed élite, education conceived by Fou Lei,[98] Fou Ts'ong grew up reading the French-speaking German musician to whom his father had given a Chinese voice. As the American screenwriter

---

90 '[...] A aucun prix, il ne faut renoncer à Sydney cette année; il sera ton alibi, ton excitation intellectuelle à Brest; [...]' Taine's letter to Chevrillon, 12 October 1887, in *H. Taine: sa vie et sa correspondance* (Paris: Hachette, 1902–1927), IV, 251.

91 Irving Babbitt, *The Masters of Modern French Criticism*, 234.

92 '« Mon empire est dans l'air, » [...] (*Mein Reich ist in der Luft*)', Romain Rolland, *Vie de Beethoven*, 53.

93 ' « Pauvre Beethoven, [...] il n'est point de bonheur pour toi dans ce monde. Dans les régions de l'idéal seulement, tu trouveras des amis. »' Beethoven's letter to A. Gleichenstein; see Romain Rolland, *Vie de Beethoven*, 43.

94 'J'ai besoin d'être avec mes livres qui ne mentent pas.' Taine's letter to his wife, 9 June 1878, in *H. Taine: sa vie et sa correspondance*, IV, 66.

95 'Je bois le sang des grands morts.' Romain Rolland, *Mémoires*, 32.

96 Rolland, too, had lived for a time in Saint-Gingolphe – the French rather than the Swiss side of the village where Fou Lei stayed in summer 1929 – before moving to the nearby village Vevey in 1921. Haute-Savoie happens to be Taine's favourite region, where he had a house and spent summers writing books. See François Vermale and Émile Gaillard, *Taine en Savoie* (Chambéry: Dardel, 1930).

97 Rolland wrote about Gandhi in 1924 and corresponded with him. They met in 1931 in Villeneuve. In the correspondence between Fou Lei and Rolland in 1934, Gandhi was spoken of. Upon learning the assassination of Gandhi in 1948, Fou Lei shut himself away in his study and for three days could not eat.

98 Fou Lei's connoisseurship of Huang Binhong's art, too, exerted considerable influence on Fou Ts'ong. Incidentally, Hermann Hesse, in his 1960 article, remarked that in Fou Ts'ong's piano playing he saw an ancient Chinese master painting with a brush.

William A. Drake (1899–1965) judged in 1924, 'Jean-Christophe is such a cosmopolite. Indeed, a temperament like his cannot be confined within the limits of any specific nationality',[99] when the German poet Hermann Hesse (1877–1962), who in 1918 had appraised, 'A novel such as *Jean-Christophe* is not only art. It does not only express the conduct of a character, it is also the attempt of a mind to judge intellectually, and to a certain extent with a sense of collective justice, the structure of an epoch, a culture, a section of humanity',[100] heard in 1960 an unknown pianist on the radio, he was transfixed. Overnight he wrote an article, in which he deemed it a miracle that this 'only true interpreter of Chopin' captured the melancholy and scepticism peculiar to nineteenth-century Warsaw and Paris.[101] How could he have understood and incarnated the heart of Europe? Hesse wondered.[102] It was Fou Ts'ong that he heard, of whom he knew nothing, and yet he imagined this Oriental to be stepping right out of *Zhuangzi*.

---

99   William A. Drake, 'Romain Rolland: Son but n'était pas le succes; son but était la foi' in *The Sewanee Review*, vol. 32, no. 4 (October 1924), 387.

100   'Un roman tel que le *Jean-Christophe* n'est pas seulement de l'art, n'exprime pas seulement le comportement d'une âme, il est aussi la tentative d'un esprit de juger intellectuelle-ment at à un certain point avec un sens de justice collective la structure d'une époque, d'une culture, d'une partie de l'humanité.' Hermann Hesse, '*Jean-Christophe*' in *Vossische Zeitung* (Berlin, May 1918); see Hermann Hesse and Romain Rolland, *D'une rive à l'autre: correspondance et fragments du journal* (Paris: Albin Michel, 1972), 50–51.

101   See Jin Shenghua's translation of Hesse's article into Chinese in Fou Min (ed.), *Fou Ts'ong: Going on Seventy!* 傅聰：望七了！ (Tianjin: Tianjin shehui kexue, 2004), 11–13.

102   On Jean-Christophe and Paris Hesse had written: 'Le musicien *Jean-Christophe* n'est point uniquement un personnage représentatif, une vision originale d'un créateur, il est en même temps une entité, porteuse de nombreuses significations, presque un mythe. Il est l'esprit de la musique, l'esprit du génie allemand, pesant et contraint, auquel Paris, gracieux, aimable, dépravé, puéril, fou et splendide, lui est miroir, stimulant, excitant, séduction paradisiaque, et lui devient indispensable: là est sa destinée.' [The musician Jean-Christophe is not only a representative figure, an original vision of a creator, he is at the same time an entity carrying numerous meanings, a myth almost. He is the spirit of music – that of the German genius, weighty and constrained, for which the gracious, pleasant, degenerate, puerile, crazy and splendid Paris is a mirror, stimulating, exciting, a paradisiacal seduction, and becomes essential to him: there is his destiny.] Hermann Hesse, '*Jean-Christophe*' in *Vossische Zeitung* (Berlin, May 1918). See Hermann Hesse and Romain Rolland, *D'une rive à l'autre*, 50–51.

Now, shall we ask, in the spirit of Zhuangzi, how could Hesse have understood the spirit of *Zhuangzi*?[103] After their first meeting in 1915,[104] Rolland recorded Hesse's passion in his diary: 'For some years, he has been increasingly
attracted to the intellect and the art of Asia, first by India, then by China. Like a
German élite of today, he is curiously marked by Laozi.'[105] Five years later, Rolland again noted: 'Hesse told me about the surprising attraction the thought
of Asia held for modern Germany.'[106] Another year, and Rolland was writing to
Hesse asking for bibliographical advice on *Laozi*.[107]

Seeing Europe as one, Hesse had published, after the outbreak of the First
World War, 'O Freunde, nicht diese Töne' in *Neue Zürcher Zeitung* (3 November 1914), warning German intellectuals against patriotism. He was subsequently attacked by the German press and alienated by friends. Having not
yet met Hesse, after reading the article Rolland remarked in his diary: 'This
man is one of the best of his race.'[108] For his impartial attitude during the War,
Rolland, with his anti-war article 'Au-dessus de la mêlée' in *Journal de Genève*
(15 September 1914), was considered a traitor in France. 'Hermann Hesse is in-
sulted by his compatriots, as I am by mine', reflected Rolland after they met.[109]
In 'Jean-Christophe à Paris' (*März*, 30 June 1917) Hesse claimed: 'Every Frenchman who is not overcome with belligerent hatred is infinitely valuable for us.

---

103   I here allude to a dialogue between Zhuangzi and Huizi recorded in *Zhuangzi* 莊子 (3rd
      century B.C.). On their stroll along a waterfall, Zhuangzi drew Huizi's attention to the
      happiness of fish. Huizi asked: 'You are not a fish. How do you know the happiness of
      fish?' 子非魚，安知魚之樂？ – to which Zhuangzi replied: 'You are not me. How do
      you know that I do not know the happiness of fish?' 子非我，安知我不知魚之樂？
104   They were both living in Switzerland at the time, Rolland in Vevey, Hesse in Bern.
105   'Il est, depuis des années, attiré de plus en plus par l'esprit et l'art d'Asie. D'abord par l'Inde,
      puis par la Chine. Comme une élite allemande d'aujourd'hui, il a curieusement subi
      l'empreinte de Lao-Tseu.' Hermann Hesse and Romain Rolland, *D'une rive à l'autre*, 29.
      Rolland went on to note: 'D'une façon générale, il adore la forme de pensée et d'expression
      chinoise, cet idéal harmonieux et calme qui ne sacrifie rien de la vie, qui sait jouir sereine-
      ment de la terre et du ciel à la fois, cette perfection de la vie aristocratique et bien or-
      donnée.' [Generally speaking, he loves the Chinese form of thought and expression, this
      harmonious and calm ideal which sacrifices nothing of life, and which knows how to
      serenely enjoy at once heaven and earth, this perfection of aristocratic and orderly life.]
106   'Hesse me dit l'étonnante attraction de la pensée d'Asie sur l'Allemagne moderne.' Romain
      Rolland's journal entry, September 1920; ibid., 69.
107   Rolland's letter to Hesse, 7 November 1921; ibid., 72–73.
108   'Celui-ci est un des meilleurs de sa race.' Rolland's journal entry in November 1914; ibid., 15.
109   'Hermann Hesse est injurié par ses compatriotes, comme moi par les miens.' Rolland's
      journal entry in December 1915; ibid., 36.

Amongst these rare few, the best and noblest is Romain Rolland.'[110] Six months into the War, Rolland had written to Hesse: 'If the war goes on, I reckon we must affirm this purely spiritual union between freethinkers of all nations.'[111] The War went on. Before it ended, Hesse confessed to Rolland: 'The attempt to apply love to matters political has failed.'[112]

This tension between nationalism and europeanism in a Franco-German context had long existed. After the Franco-Prussian War, Taine was deeply disturbed, his admiration for German culture, typical of his generation of intellectuals, shaken, and his critical view of his own country agravated.[113] Variously described as 'German' and 'Victorian' for his systematic spirit and Puritan impulse, the French savant had painted in *Idéalisme anglais: étude sur Carlyle* (1864) a near self-portrait: 'Carlyle is profoundly German'[114] [...] 'He is almost German for his force of imagination, his antiquarian's perspicacity and his broad general views.'[115] Six decades later, Rolland was considered 'not French'.[116] Echoing Stefan Zweig who named Rolland the élite who 'reconciles France and the world',[117] William A. Drake asserted: 'the genius of Romain Rolland, French by the accident of birth, belongs to the world.'[118] – a world, one might add, of yesterday.[119] As Rolland's *Vie de Tolstoï* (1921) induced

---

110 'Tout Français qui n'y est pas submergé par la haine guerrière est pour nous d'une valeur infinie et dans ce petit nombre le meilleur et le plus noble est Romain Rolland.' Ibid., 43.

111 'Si la guerre se prolonge, j'estime qu'il faudrait que nous affirmions cette union purement spirituelle entre les penseurs libres de toutes les nations.' Rolland's letter to Hesse, 26 February 1915; ibid., 18.

112 Hesse's letter to Rolland, 1917; see Ralph Freedman, *Hermann Hesse, Pilgrim of Crisis: A Biography* (New York: Pantheon, 1978), 117.

113 The result was *Les Origines de la France contemporaine*, published between 1875 and Taine's death in 1893.

114 'Carlyle est profondément Germain.' Hippolyte Taine, *L'idéalisme anglais*, 24.

115 'Il est presque Allemand par sa force d'imagination, par sa perspicacité d'antiquaire, par ses larges vues générales.' Ibid., 51.

116 'For certainly, the temperament of Romain Rolland is not French.' William A. Drake, 'Romain Rolland: Son but n'était pas le succes; son but était la foi' in *The Sewanee Review*, vol. 32, no. 4 (October 1924), 387.

117 '[...] cette élite réconcilie la France avec le monde.' Stefan Zweig, *Romain Rolland: sa vie, son oeuvre* (Paris: Belfond, 2000), 96.

118 William A. Drake, 'Romain Rolland: Son but n'était pas le succes; son but était la foi', 387.

119 See Stefan Zweig's *The World of Yesterday* to picture a 'Golden Age of Security' brought down by the First World War. Zweig observed, also, how printed words of intellectuals held immense significance during the First World War, but much less so during the Second.

wonderment in Hesse – 'It is a rare and extraordinary pleasure to read how this Frenchman has understood this Russian, how this man of culture, artist and connoisseur has understood the naïve and smashing accuser of art, how this European socialist mind has understood this mystic Oriental and done him justice.'[120] – we recall that for Tolstoy, art was 'an activity intended to convey from man to man the loftiest of intentions and the best of the human soul'.[121] When art is believed to be such an activity, it necessarily breaks down boundaries; the question becomes, then, not one of being French, German, English, Russian, or Chinese, but one of aspirations chosen and values shared, for 'one feels that', as Jean-Christophe said to Grazia, 'whoever loves art and suffers for it is one's brother.'[122]

And so the Chinese translator of Rolland's *Vie de Tolstoï* wrote to his son in Poland: 'What is of utmost importance to an artist, apart from intellect, is love! What I call the heart of a newborn child is not only one that is pure, innocent and guileless, but one that loves! There is a French expression, *grande âme*, and that means "love"!'[123] 'The heart of a newborn child'[124] 赤子之心 would have been another Mencian allusion: 'The great man is he who does not lose the heart of a newborn.'[125] More than two millennia after Mencius uttered these words, resounded Carlyle: 'I know not in the world an affection equal to that of Dante. It is a tenderness, a trembling, longing, pitying love: like the wail of Æolian harps, soft, soft; like a child's young heart; – and then that stern,

---

120 Hesse and Rolland, *D'une rive à l'autre*, 80. Rolland's *Vie de Tolstoï* (1921) was re-edited and re-released in 1928 at Tolstoy's centenary. Upon his arrival in France in 1928, Fou Lei could easily have been exposed to it – as he was to Taine's work, whose centenary was in the same year before eventually translating and writing to Rolland about it in 1934 (chapter 6, note 20). Fou Lei's letter to Daniélou on 7 June 1930, which refers to Beethoven, Goethe and Tolstoy as '*grandes âmes* who are tireless warriors', suggests he had encountered Rolland's biographies of *hommes illustres* by then.

121 'Tolstoï définit l'art comme « une activité ayant pour but de transmettre d'homme à homme les sentiments les plus hauts et les meilleurs de l'âme humaine ».' Arthur Levy, *L'idéalisme de Romain Rolland* (Paris: A.G. Nizet, 1946), 124.

122 'On se sent fraternel à tous ceux qui aiment l'art et qui souffrent pour lui.' Romain Rolland, *Jean-Christophe*, 1379.

123 '藝術家最需要的，除了理智以外，還有一個"愛"字！所謂赤子之心，不但指純潔無邪，指清新，而且還指愛！法文里有句話叫做"偉大的心"，意思就是"愛"。' Fou Lei's letter to Fou Ts'ong, 29 February 1956, in *Fou Lei's Family Letters*, 159.

124 See note 89 in this chapter for Fou Lei's previous letter to Fou Ts'ong, 26 January 1955.

125 '大人者，不失其赤子之心者也。' *Mencius* 孟子 离娄下; see also D.C. Lau (tr.), *Mencius*, 130.

sore-saddened heart!'[126] For Dante, exiled poet and child of no country, his home was beyond earthly bounds.

Hesse died long before Fou Ts'ong, during an odyssey to Poland in the 1970s, would ever read his article. 'The one who understands another's music' exists. Little did Hesse know that his dear friend Rolland had been, in spirit, this unknown musician's alibi.[127]

Let us return, for a moment, to *Jean-Christophe*:

> Then again this void, total and absolute. Christophe found himself all alone once more, more alone than ever, in this big city, foreign and hostile. He was no longer so affected by it. He began to believe that this was his destiny, and that he would thus remain, for life.
>
> He did not know that a *grande âme* is never alone, that even when fate deprives him of friends, he always ends up creating them, that he radiates around him the love that fills him, and that at this very moment, when he thought himself alone for ever, he was richer in love than the happiest men on earth.[128]

In 1957, René Étiemble (1909–2002), Chair of Comparative Literature at the Sorbonne, went on an official trip to China. His travel journals were published under the title *Tong Yeou-ki ou le nouveau singe pèlerin* in 1958. An entry (19 June) records:

> Here I am at No. 5, 284 Kiangsu Road, Shanghai, 27. The translator of Voltaire, Mérimée, Balzac, Maurois, some Duhamels, and the complete oeuvre of Romain Rolland, receives me in an immense house filled with Chinese and European books, and paintings that immediately compel one to look. A landscape of Lin Fengmian, one of the most beautiful I have seen, a perfect harmony between Chinese poetry and Western

---

126   Thomas Carlyle, *Heroes and Hero-worship*, 87.

127   Hermann Hesse dedicated his *Siddhartha* (1922) to Romain Rolland, 'my dear friend'.

128   'Et puis, ce fut le vide, de nouveau, complet, absolu. Christophe se retrouvait seul, une fois de plus, plus seul que jamais, dans la grande ville étrangère et hostile. Il ne s'en affectait plus. Il commençait à croire que c'était sa destinée, et qu'il resterait, toute sa vie, ainsi.

   Il ne savait pas qu'une grande âme n'est jamais seule, que si dénuée qu'elle soit d'amis par la fortune, elle finit toujours par les créer, qu'elle rayonne autour d'elle l'amour dont elle est pleine, et qu'à cette heure même, où il se croyait isolé pour toujours, il était plus riche d'amour que les plus heureux du monde.' Romain Rolland, *Jean-Christophe*, 739.

technique. Monsieur Fou Lei shows me a collection of drawings, wash drawings and paintings that his friend Huang Binhong has given him.[129]

[...] From painting to music, from *Les Lettres françaises* to *La Table Ronde*, from Romain Rolland to Sichuanese opera [...], from classical opera to the Ming and Qing literati who produced *kunqu* [...], from *Les Thibault* to Mauriac, whom Fou Lei also wishes would be translated into Chinese, from the works of Qian Zhongshu, scholar of comparative literature and equally fluent in English, German, Italian and French, to those of his wife Yang Jiang (perfectly written as they are, they have had little success since the Liberation because in them the author portrays the only milieu that she knew: the bourgeoisie), meeting with Fou Lei filled me with wonder: so much understanding and taste, so much culture and freshness, so much enthusiasm and moderation, all of which compose a veritable *junzi*, an accomplished man who combines traditional education with an experience of the world, and what sense, what love of beauty![130]

Fou Lei's knowledge of the war-time French Resistance magazine *Les Lettres françaises* (co-founded by Étiemble's mentor Jean Paulhan in 1941) and of the

---

129 'Me voici enfin au N° 5, passage 284, de Kiang-sou lou, Changhaï, 27. Le traducteur de Voltaire, de Mérimée, de Balzac, de Maurois, de certains Duhamels, des oeuvres complètes de Romain Rolland, me reçoit dans une vaste maison riche en livres chinois, européens, en tableaux qui d'emblée s'imposent au regard. Un paysage de Lin Feng-mien, l'un des plus beaux que j'aie vus, accord parfait de la poésie chinoise et de la technique occidentale. M. Fou Lai m'ouvre une collection de dessins, lavis et peintures que lui offrit son ami Wang Pin-hong.' René Étiemble, *Tong Yeou-ki ou le nouveau singe pèlerin* (Paris: Gallimard, 1958), 261. Étiemble spelled Fou Lei's given name 雷 as Lai, as did Fou himself. In French, this transliteration is phonetically perfect.

130 'De la peinture à la musique, des Lettres françaises à la Table Ronde, de Romain Rolland au théâtre du Sseu-tch'ouan – dont le choeur pourrait orienter vers de puissantes nouveautés l'art ancien de l'opéra – de l'opéra classique aux lettrés Ming et Ts'ing qui produisirent le K'ouen-K'iu (il faut que j'aille en voir à Pékin avant de partir; M. Tseng déjà me l'avait conseillé), des *Thibault* à Mauriac, que Fou Lai souhaite lui aussi qu'on traduise en chinois, des travaux de Ts'ien Tong-chou, le comparatiste, également à l'aise en anglais, allemand, italien et français aux oeuvres de sa femme Yang Kiang (parfaitement écrites celles-ci, elles n'ont guère de succès depuis la libération car l'auteur y peint le seul milieu qu'elle connût: la bourgeoisie), l'entretien de Fou Lai m'est un émerveillement: tant de savoir et de goût, tant de culture et de fraîcheur, tant d'enthousiasme et de modération composent un véritable *kiun tseu*, un homme accompli qui joint à la formation traditionnelle une expérience du monde entier, et quel sens, quel amour du beau!' Ibid., 261–262.

post-war publications of *La Table Ronde* (founded in 1944) – to both of these the Catholic Mauriac, Daniélou's close friend, was a regular contributor – demonstrates the extent to which the Chinese francophone was *au courant*. The discussion of *Les Thibault* (1922–28), Roger Martin du Gard's interwar roman-fleuve depicting the pre-war lives of a Catholic bourgeois family, would have transported Fou Lei back to his student days in Paris. As Fou Lei was reading French literature at the Sorbonne, Étiemble was learning Chinese at École des langues orientales; they were the same age. A communist with Maoist sympathies,[131] Étiemble had translated, in the early 1930s, left-wing authors from Chinese to French. Collaborating with him was Dai Wangshu 戴望舒 (1905–1950), who studied in France from 1932 to 1935. Thirty-eight years after Dai's death, in an interview Étiemble spoke of the Chinese poet as 'mon frère humain'.[132]

Rolland, who did not live to see the War end, in his *Mémoires* recollected at length his own student days:

> Christian Sénéchal, in his lucid survey of *Grands courants de la littérature française contemporaine*, accurately depicts 'the crisis of the civilisation' which reached its pinnacle in the decade 1880–1890. Masters of the time, Taine, Renan, confessed it without the slightest hope (one could have said without the slightest desire) to get through. Bourget,[133] in his *Essais de psychologie contemporaine*, published when I was studying philosophy in lycée, noted 'a fatal fatigue to live, a mournful perception of the vanity of all effort' in France's élite. And Barrès, in his *Taches d'encre*, denoted in Verlaine 'the extreme irritation of a worn-out race'. 'France is dying', wrote Renan,[134] 'Do not upset her death throes!'[135]

---

131   See Étiemble, *Quarante ans de mon maoïsme: 1934–1974* (Paris: Gallimard, 1976).

132   See Bernard Pivot's interview with Étiemble on 'Apostrophes' (1988).

133   Paul Bourget was one of 'Taine's sons between science and morals'; see Thomas Loué, 'Les Fils de Taine, entre science et morale. À propos du Disciple de P. Bourget' in *Cahiers d'Histoire, Revue d'histoire critique*, no. 65 (1996), 44–61. In *Le Disciple* (1889), published six years after his *Essais de psychologie contemporaine*, Bourget alluded to the positivism of Taine which, in this novel, led to a young man's imprisonment following his young lover's suicide. This grieved the aged philosopher, who commented in 1889: 'discrédit de la morale ou discrédit de la science: voilà les deux impressions totales que laisse ce livre' [discredit to morals or discredit to science: these are the two general impressions left by the book.]

134   In 1886, Rolland had written to Renan whilst a student at École normale supérieure.

135   'Christian Sénéchal a, dans son lucide panorama des *Grands courants de la littérature française contemporaine*, dépeint avec exactitude "la crise de la civilisation", qui eut son faîte,

Back we are in nineteenth-century France with which the May-Fourth China had identified, its leading intellectuals' voices of furious gloom finding lingering refrains. Forty years separate Taine and Rolland, as forty separate Rolland and Fou Lei. Four months after Taine's death and one year before the Dreyfus affair, Rolland anticipated: 'There are times which, at the bottom of all their thoughts and in the kernal of their heart, bear death. Ours is one such: it has no faith in its existence: it is right, it will perish. [...] Whoever believes in death, will die...'[136] Two years after Rolland's death and two before the Communists seized power, Fou Lei predicted: 'It is to be expected that individuals get labelled, be it black or white, without justification. [...] When a nation comes to the point where thinking is united and heresies are extinct, it is also time when its civilisation withers to death...'[137]

After Étiemble returned to France, Fou Lei was labelled a rightist. The sinologist effectively snatched his friend's portrait before all went wrong:

Fou Lei has not yet read the speech [in the newspaper] about which everyone is speaking (I disturbed him from 9:30), but he has a high opinion of Chairman Mao's classical learning and praises his liberal spirit. He is happy that the Hundred Flowers will soon blossom, but do not talk to him about getting rid of Chinese characters. On that matter he thinks like the Minister of National Education. When I left him after three hours that I found enriching, we had put in place a number of projects relating to Franco-Chinese cultural exchange, and I was carrying with me two original paintings by Master Huang.[138]

---

dans le décennal 1880–1890. Les maîtres de l'heure, Taine, Renan, la confessaient, sans le moindre espoir (on eût dit même, sans le moindre désir) d'en sortir. Bourget, dans ses *Essais de psychologie contemporaine*, parus quand j'étais sur les bancs de philosophie, au lycée, constatait dans l'élite de France "une mortelle fatigue de vivre, une morne perception de la vanité de tout effort". Et Barrès, dans ses *Taches d'encre*, dénotait en Verlaine "le dernier degré de l'enervement dans une race épuisée". – La France se meurt, écrivait Renan, ne troublez pas son agonie!' Romain Rolland, *Mémoires*, 198–199.

136 'Il est [...] des époques qui portent la mort au fond de toutes leurs pensées, dans le noyau de leur coeur. La nôtre est telle, elle n'a pas foi en sa vie: elle a raison, elle périra. [...] Qui croit à la mort, mourra...' Ibid., 210.

137 Fou Lei, 'So-called "Anti-Imperialist and Pro-Soviet"' in *Observation*, vol. 2, no. 24 (22 July 1947). See chapter 7, notes 97 and 98.

138 'Fou Lai n'a pas encore lu le discours dont tout le monde parle (je l'ai dérangé dès 9h.30), mais il fait grand cas de la culture classique du Président Mao, dont il loue l'esprit libéral. Il lui plaît de voir bientôt s'épanouir les *cent fleurs*; mais ne lui parlez pas de supprimer les caractères. Il pense là-dessus comme le ministre de l'Education nationale. Quand je

Three hours sealed their friendship. It was not until four years later, when Fou Lei's 'rightist' label was lifted, that they resumed correspondence.[139] Fou Lei's tone, by now, was restrained with melancholy and poignant with apology. 'Perhaps you already guessed the reason for my silence and have forgiven me', he wrote in the first letter of 1961, '[...] so many events, unforseen and terrible, happened that one has the impression of having lived through all the major periods of modern history.'[140] Assuring Fou Lei of his total understanding, Étiemble urged him to above all restore to health.[141] In 1962, Fou Lei reproached himself again of 'this involontary silence': '[...] you who have knowledge of ancient and modern China, you more than anyone understand the state of mind of certain of our intellectuals.'[142] Relating his life as 'rather withdrawn, in a manner simple and scheduled, entirely absorbed in work',[143] he admitted: 'The echo of grave events reaches all the way into *mon cabinet*, the one you know, and torments me.'[144] 'Yes, I think often of *votre cabinet de*

---

le quitte, après trois heures qui m'ont enrichi, nous avons mis au point un certain nombre de projets relatifs aux échanges culturels franco-chinois et j'emporte deux peintures originales de Maître Wang.' Étiemble, *Tong Yeou-ki*, 262. Here Étiemble misspelled Huang Binhong's surname. For this error he was to apologise for decades to come, in books published and interviews given.

139   Étiemble had then met Fou Ts'ong in London. Fou Lei's label was lifted on 30 September 1961. Four days later he wrote to Étiemble. Their correspondence, now conserved at Bibliothèque nationale de France, bears witness to an extraordinary set of historical and emotional occurances. I am grateful to Madame Étiemble for the authorisation to study and publish these letters.

140   'Probablement vous avez deviné la cause de mon silence et m'en avez pardonné. En effet, tant d'événements imprévus et terribles se sont succédés qu'on a l'impression d'avoir vécu toutes les grandes périodes dans l'histoire moderne.' Fou Lei's letter to Étiemble, 4 October 1961; conserved at Bibliothèque nationale de France.

141   'Ne vous excusez surtout pas d'un silence dont j'avais fort bien compris les raisons. Puissiez-vous du moins rétablir votre santé!' Étiemble's letter to Fou Lei, 2 November 1961; conserved at Bibliothèque nationale de France.

142   'Enfin, vous qui connaissez la Chine ancienne et moderne, vous saisirez mieux que tout autre l'état d'âme de certains intellectuels chez nous.' Fou Lei's letter to Étiemble, 2 December 1962; conserved at Bibliothèque nationale de France.

143   Fou Lei's working schedule was such that, for years, he rarely stepped out of his house save for visits to the barber. After 1958, he disappeared from public view. The barber visited him.

144   'Il est vrai que nous ne vivons pas dans une grande bousculade comme vous à Paris, je vis plutôt retiré, d'une façon bien simple et régulière, absorbé entièrement dans le travail, mais aujourd'hui on ne se détache pas du monde extérieur comme on veut, l'écho des grands événements parvient jusque dans mon cabinet que vous connaissez, et qui me

travail, Étiemble reminisced, 'and I hope circumstances allow me to return to see you before long';[145] one month later, he reiterated: '[...] stubborn, I guard the hope to see you again.'[146] Again Fou Lei lamented, in 1963: '[...] despite my reclusive life, the echo of grave events manages to affect me and to disturb my mind, often putting me in such a mood that it is impossible to write.'[147]

Of Fou Lei's *cabinet* Yang Jiang told in 1983: 'I envied Fou Lei's study, for its organisation provided all possible conveniences to his work. The books of which he had frequent use, he could reach without standing up. On a circular revolving table, various big dictionaries were spread out. Aligned along the wall were cabinets full of books for reference. On top of the bookshelf was a very beautiful photograph of Meifu in a frame. There was also a photograph of Fou Lei in his youth, which he, in the old days, gave to Meifu as a present.'[148] In 2013, Fou Lei's younger son, Fou Min, delineated from memory his father's *cabinet* at my request: 'The desk, he designed himself; the lamp too, and the table for big dictionaries. When you entered the study, on the bookshelf to your right were *The Twenty-Four Histories* 二十四史. Two entire shelves were filled with thread-bound books 線裝書.'[149]

---

tourmente beaucoup. Vous comprenez bien que, quand l'esprit se trouble d'une façon ou d'autre, on se contente de s'engourdir dans une vie presque végétale et n'a guère du courage à s'entretenir avec des amis lointains, tout en se reprochant bien souvent de ce silence involontaire.' Fou Lei's letter to Étiemble, 2 December 1962; conserved at Bibliothèque nationale de France.

145 'Oui, je pense souvent à votre cabinet de travail et je souhaite que les circonstances me permettent d'ici quelque temps de retourner vous revoir.' Étiemble's letter to Fou Lei, 23 December 1962; conserved at Bibliothèque nationale de France.

146 'Veuillez croire néanmoins que je pense souvent à notre rencontre et que je garde, obstiné, l'espoir de vous revoir.' Étiemble's letter to Fou Lei, 21 January 1963; conserved at Bibliothèque nationale de France.

147 '[...] malgré ma vie recluse, l'écho des grands événements arrive aussi à m'atteindre et troubler mon esprit, ce qui me met souvent dans une humeur impossible à écrire.' Fou Lei's letter to Étiemble, 1 September 1963; conserved at Bibliothèque nationale de France.

148 '我很羨慕傅雷的書齋，因為書齋的佈置，對他的工作具備一切方便。經常要用的工具書，伸手就夠得到，不用站起身。轉動的圓架上，攤著幾種大字典。沿牆的書櫥裏，排列著滿滿的書可供參考。書架頂上一個鏡框裏是一張很美的梅馥的照片。另有一張傅雷年輕時的照片，是他當年贈給梅馥的。' Yang Jiang, 'In Lieu of a Preface' to *Five Biographies Translated by Fou Lei*.

149 The author's interview with Fou Min, November 2013, Beijing.

FIGURE 34
Fou Lei and Zhu Meifu in the study, 1961.
THE FOU FAMILY TRUST.

Politics being hardly ever discussed,[150] hovering like a ghost in every letter, books became the thread binding Fou Lei's correspondence with Étiemble. 'As a translator', he confessed in October 1961, 'I never find dictionaries and reference books sufficient';[151] the language of Balzac, he added, was 'so wide and varied, its use of phrases so free – often with modifications that perplex foreigners, I waste a lot of time not being able to specify the meaning (or nuance)

---

150   There were two exceptions. On 15 February 1964 Fou Lei expressed hope after the re-establishment of the official relation between France and the PRC: 'Je suis personnellement ravi en pensant que j'aurai probablement le plaisir de vous revoir en Chine, – et bientôt!' Étiemble agreed on 12 November 1965, noting his own contribution: 'J'ai eu l'honneur d'assister au déjeuner offert par notre ministère des Affaires étrangères à votre délégation chargée de négocier les nouveaux accords culturels. Les négociations semblent avoir été très fructueuses et nous ne pouvons que nous en réjouir vous et moi.' In July – August 1965, André Malraux, with whom Étiemble had founded Les Amis du peuple chinois in 1934, visited Mao as France's Ministre de la culture; Mao reportedly showed little interest in France.

151   'Comme traducteur, je ne trouve jamais suffisants les dictionnaires et les livres de références.' Fou Lei's letter to Étiemble, 4 October 1961.

of certain passages'.[152] Thence, one linguistic purist asked another for advice on finding a dictionary of slangs with their evolution in history, or a work which specifically explained jargons used in the nineteenth century, expressing, moreover, the need for a 'very comprehensive and detailed' grammar book, since 'Larousse of the twentieth century hardly suffices'.[153] '[...] count on me', wrote Étiemble, '[...] I hope to be able to rapidly send you the working instruments that you need.'[154] In February 1962 he announced: 'During a trip abroad, I was able to find a dictionary of Parisian slang, an edition even more complete than mine, for it was published ten years later than mine. As the Flinker bookstore has not been able to find you one, I sent it to you yesterday by airmail. Given the uncertainty of communication, I would be happy to know that this book, to you indispensable, reaches you at last. We are, and we will be, taking care of finding you the Grammaire of Bruneau and Brunot.'[155]

In March 1962, Fou Lei mentioned that, with sadness he had learnt about the discontinuation of the periodical Horizons, regretting: 'Since we suffer a lot here from not having any intellectual contact with the outside world, our mind and outlook become increasingly narrow and our thoughts go rancid. We know absolutely nothing about what is happening outside, be it in the domain of politics or in that of literature or art. I, in particular, feel provincial in all branches of knowledge that are essential for a modern man.'[156] From

---

152 'Comme vous savez, le vocabulaire de Balzac est tellement étendu et varié, son usage des locutions est tellement libre – souvent avec des modifications qui déroutent les étrangers, que je perds beaucoup de temps sans pouvoir préciser la signification (ou la nuance) de certains passages.' Ibid.

153 'Du reste, je me demande s'il existe un dictionnaire d'argot avec son évolution historique, ou existe-t-il un ouvrage qui explique particulièrement les argots employés le siècle dernier? Je vous serais infiniment reconnaissant si vous vouliez m'indiquer une liste des livres de références (avec les noms d'auteurs et d'éditeurs) utiles à mon travail. J'ai aussi besoin d'une grammaire très compréhensive et détaillée, – la Grammaire Larousse du XXᵉ siècle ne me suffit guère.' Ibid.

154 'Quant à vos traductions, comptez sur moi. [...] J'espère [...] pouvoir vous envoyer rapidement les instruments de travail dont vous avez besoin.' Étiemble's letter to Fou Lei, 2 November 1961.

155 'Au cours d'un séjour à l'étranger, j'ai pu trouver une édition du Dictionnaire de l'argot parisien, plus complète même que la mienne, car elle est de dix ans plus tardive. La librairie Flinker n'ayant pas encore pu vous en dénicher une, j'ai envoyé celle-ci par avion dès hier. Etant donné l'incertitude des communications, je serais heureux d'apprendre que cet ouvrage, pour vous indispensable, vous est enfin parvenu. On s'occupe et l'on s'occupera autant qu'il le faudra de vous trouver la Grammaire de Bruneau et Brunot.' Étiemble's letter to Fou Lei, 25 February 1962; conserved at Bibliothèque nationale de France.

156 'Comme on souffre beaucoup chez nous de ne pas avoir de contacts intellectuels avec le monde extérieur, notre esprit et vue devient de plus en plus étroits et nos pensées rancies.

then on, Étiemble took out a subscription to the journal *Critique* for Fou Lei as a present.[157] Conscientious, Fou Lei again and again insisted on knowing the cost of everything, anxious to instantly pay back.[158] Again and again Étiemble responded 'Do not worry at all about money',[159] asking Fou Lei to trust that for him it was a pleasure to take part, however little, in his work.[160] In letters to his son, Fou Lei spoke repeatedly of his indebtedness to the sinologist – 'he has been very earnest with me';[161] 'he is too good to me'.[162] Fou Ts'ong, since 1963, continuously sent cheques to Étiemble from London. Following these transactions attentively, Fou Lei made sure that his friend was promptly reimbursed, or that a sufficient sum had been in place in advance.[163]

On ne connait absolument rien de ce qui se passe en dehors, ni dans le domaine politique, ni dans le domaine littéraire ou artistique. Moi, je me sens particulièrement provincial dans toutes les branches de la connaissance qui sont indispensables pour un homme
moderne.' Fou Lei's letter to Étiemble, 12 March 1962; conserved at Bibliothèque nationale
de France.

157 See Étiemble's letter to Fou Lei, 11 June 1962; conserved at Bibliothèque nationale de
France.

158 'Mais, Cher Monsieur, il faut absolument me dire combien vous avez dépensé, le livre
épuisé coûte cher, et la poste aérienne est aussi bien coûteuse: c'est déjà beaucoup de vous
occuper de mes recherches de livres, je ne supporterai pas d'abuser de votre amitié davantage.' (Fou Lei's letter to Étiemble, 12 March 1962.) 'Merci beaucoup pour l'abonnement
de « CRITIQUE », cela vous coûte cher, je vais tâcher de vous rembourser de l'argent par
Ts'ong.' (Handwritten in the margin of Fou Lei's letter to Étiemble, 2 December 1962.)

159 '[...] je vous prie très sincèrement de considérer que vous n'avez jamais à redouter de
m'importuner en me demandant de vous faire parvenir des livres.' (Étiemble's letter to
Fou Lei, 7 November 1963.) 'Nous allons nous occuper maintenant de votre troisième liste.
Ne vous souciez nullement pour l'argent.' (Étiemble's letter to Fou Lei, 7 March 1964.) 'Ne
vous souciez pas des questions d'argent, je vous en prie une fois encore.' (Étiemble's letter
to Fou Lei, 15 January 1965.)

160 'Veuillez être assuré, en effet, que c'est un plaisir pour moi de collaborer, si peu que ce
soit, à vos travaux balzaciens.' Étiemble's letter to Fou Lei, 14 March 1965; conserved at
Bibliothèque nationale de France.

161 '又巴黎大學教授，《東遊記》作者Étiemble與我見過面，在英也同你們夫婦吃
過飯。他去年到現在替我買了好幾本書，不肯收錢；又定了一份文學雜誌送
我，很不好意思。想等你經濟稍寬裕時寄一些款子存在他那裏，以後買書等等
可不必再由你零星匯去，你說行不行？[…] 他幾年來對我非常誠懇。' Fou Lei's
letter to Fou Ts'ong, 2 December 1962, in *Fou Lei's Family Letters*, 401.

162 '三月十五日後的法國演出，到底肯定了沒有？務望詳告！巴黎大學的Monsieur
Étiemble一定要送票！他待我太好了，多年來為我費了多少心思搜求書籍。'
Fou Lei's letter to Fou Ts'ong, 17 February 1966; ibid., 477.

163 'Le Michel-Ange de Romain Rolland m'est bien parvenu, mais je suis confus de recevoir
tant de livres de vous sans connaître le prix et partant impossible de vous rembourser.

This having been arranged, Fou Lei was now relaxed enough to send a list of books to be obtained in Paris. Four lists between October 1963 and September 1964 give an indication of the research, ferocious to say the least, carried out by the translator of Balzac.[164] Equally eager was he to send books in Chinese to Paris.[165] Huang Binhong's painting could no longer leave the country, having been classified as 'national treasure';[166] Fou Lei mounted and sent a scroll, presumably a landscape, by an artist of his own age to Étiemble: 'It is surely not a work on a par with our old master Huang Binhong, but it will remind you a little of our country.'[167]

The more one scrutinises Fou Lei's life and work, the more one conceives, with admiration and sometimes irritation, the intimidating coherence of his punctiliousness. Since the 1940s, he translated one after another Balzac; between 1957 and 1961, he did *not* stop. In September 1961, when the 'rightist' label was lifted, his reaction was one of indifference.[168] In November 1961 he told

---

Je résolus donc de ne plus vous troubler par les commandes de livres dont j'ai besoin sans vous faire envoyer une somme quelconque par mon fils préalablement.' (Fou Lei's letter to Étiemble, 1 September 1963); 'Dites-moi, je vous en prie, si vous avez enfin reçu le second envoi de l'argent de Londres? Pour achat des livres à Paris, je vais vous faire parvenir continuellement de l'argent nécessaire; mais comme mon garçon est presque constamment en voyage (il m'est difficile de l'attraper en temps voulu), veuillez m'excuser s'il vous arrive à être obligé d'avancer quelque somme pour moi.' (Fou Lei's letter to Étiemble, 15 February 1964.)

164   Fou Lei's first list of 14 October 1963, for ten books; his second list of 8 December 1963, for seven books; his third list of 15 February 1964, for thirty books; and his fourth list of September 1964, for eight books (in short, a total of fifty-five titles, all related to Balzac, in eleven months) are conserved at Bibliothèque nationale de France.

165   'Je vous ai envoyé une Histoire de la Littérature Chinoise en 3 volumes (le 10 novembre), vous trouverez ci inclus un compte rendu sur le livre, peut-être vous intéressera-t-il aussi bien que le livre.' (Fou Lei's letter to Étiemble, 2 December 1962.) 'Avez-vous reçu "Les statues en poterie" que je vous ai expédié le 4 janvier? et "Les contes des T'ang"? Si vous vous intéressez à quelque publication chinoise, dites-le moi, je vous en procurerai.' (Fou Lei's letter to Étiemble, 15 February 1964.)

166   Fou Lei's letter to Étiemble, 4 October 1961.

167   'Je suis en train de faire monter une peinture chinoise (par un artiste contemporain qui est de mon âge) que je vais vous envoyer. Ce n'est certainement pas une oeuvre du niveau de notre vieux maître Houang Pin-Hong, mais elle vous rappelerera un peu de notre pays.' Fou Lei's letter to Étiemble, 24 February 1963; conserved at Bibliothèque nationale de France.

168   The first thing Fou Lei did, as a 'rightist' could not have done, was write to the Minister of Culture and urge that the Beijing Library preserve the manuscripts of the composer Tan Xiaolin 譚小麟 (1912–1948). Considered by Fou Lei to be where the hope of modern Chinese music lay, Tan had studied in the United States from 1939 to 1946, and died a mere

Étiemble: 'The preparatory study of the *Illusions Perdues* is completed (it took about six months). I am beginning the first draft of the translation which will be finalised after four revisions. [...] A list of questions, several pages long, has been sent to my old *camarade* and friend, the abbot Jean Daniélou, who will task his former students with elucidating them for me.'[169] One month later, he enquired about the typical salary of a young lycée teacher in the Paris of 1961, so as to compensate such a teacher recommended by Daniélou 'in a way more

---

two years after his return; he was thirty-six. Outraged, as he held the Chinese familial and social systems responsible for this death, Fou Lei wrote to Tan's professor Paul Hindemith (1895–1963) at the Yale University School of Music. Learning, after sending his letter, that Hindemith was on sabbatical, Fou Lei then wrote to Bruce Simons (1896–1989), principal of the Yale University School of Music; see *Fou Lei's Letters to His Friends*, 124–125. Hindemith replied to Fou Lei immediately after his return. See Chen Zishan, 'Tan Xiaolin, Hindemith and Fu Lei' 譚小麟，欣德米特和傅雷 in *Wenhui Bao* (20 March 2002). Informing Hindemith of the loss, Fou Lei asked if he had kept decipherable versions of his student's compositions, and if he could preface a collection of Tan's music to be published. All of this materialised. Thirteen years later, Fou Lei pushed for Tan's work to be conserved. He succeeded.

169 'L'étude préparatoire des Illusions Perdues est terminée (qui m'avait coûté 6 mois environs), je commence de faire le premier brouillon de traduction qui ne sera mise au point qu'après 4 rédactions. [...] Une liste de plusieurs pages de questions a été envoyée à mon ancien camarade et ami, l'Abbé Jean Daniélou qui chargera ses anciens élèves de m'éclaircir.' (Fou Lei's letter to Étiemble, 19 November 1961; conserved at Bibliothèque nationale de France.) In Archives jésuites de la Province de France, Fou Lei's youthful letters (1929–31) to Daniélou are kept alongside a typewritten letter dated 4 June 1953 from Shanghai. No other letter from him to Daniélou has been located by this author, in the said archive or in that of Institut Catholique de Paris, where Daniélou taught since 1944. Correspondence between them may have been sporadic over the years. At the beginning of the 1953 letter, Fou Lei asked if Daniélou had received 'les trois petites peintures chinoises' [the three small Chinese paintings] sent on 6 February 1952. Having just finished re-translating *Jean-Christophe*, Fou Lei was now to 'reprendre Balzac' [take up Balzac again], because 'pour vivre, il me faut continuellement faire la traduction, et Balzac est un des auteurs français qu'on ne condamne pas chez nous' [to make a living, I have to continuously translate, and Balzac is one of the French authors not condemned here]. To this letter Fou Lei attached a list of questions on *Le Colonel Chabert – Honorine – L'interdiction* (Balzac), having arranged for his friend Stephen Soong to send Daniélou a cheque from Hong Kong; to Stephen Soong Fou Lei also provided bibliographical services over the years. In the letter Fou Lei asked Daniélou, with desperation, to find him 'une bonne édition complète de Balzac' [a good complete edition of Balzac] published by Conard and revised and annotated by Marcel Bouteron and Henri Longnon – a task which none of the friends and acquaintances in France to whom Fou Lei had written in the past three years was able to perform.

useful than sending small presents'.[170] We may consider this act in juxtaposition with his indignation over the death of Zhang Xian, poorly paid thirty years previously at the Shanghai Art Academy.[171]

In a letter of October 1960, after explaining to Fou Ts'ong his father's acute suffering, Zhu Meifu had written: '[...] you needn't worry. I'll let him slowly calm down. As long as he can work, he will be calm.'[172] Work became once again Fou Lei's salvation. Surmounting his physical reality, he launched a race with the fanatic worker that was Balzac in the *Illusions Perdues*. In letters to Étiemble, the countdown of his progress in translating the magnum opus came to resemble the calculation of a broken machine, determined to function.[173]

'Count on me', said Étiemble. With equal punctiliousness he kept his promise. On 16 November 1963, he told Fou Lei: 'Three books are on their way towards you [...]. All the rest, for the moment, are out of print or being reprinted. *Balzac* by Billy will probably be available by the end of the year and will be sent to you as soon as it is reprinted. As for the other titles [on your list], I am trying to find the ones that are available at second hand. At any rate, I will write to

170 'Comme mon ami Jean Daniélou a donné mes questions sur Illusions Perdues à quelque jeune professeur pour m'éclaircir, je voudrais les récompenser d'une manière plus utile que de leur envoyer des petits cadeaux. Mais avant de faire cela, il faut d'abord connaître un peu la vie parisienne; pouvez-vous, Cher Monsieur, me dire combien touche comme honoraire un jeune professeur dans les lycées, par exemple, de troisième classe?' Fou Lei's letter to Étiemble, end of 1961; conserved at Bibliothèque nationale de France.

171 See chapter 7, notes 33 and 35; see also note 168 in this chapter.

172 '爸爸的病，主要是長期的失眠，不斷的顧慮，使他的神經脆弱到極點，容易緊張、失眠，一些刺激都不能受，於是引起各種神經性毛病，非常痛苦。這不是藥力能達到的。你向來知道爸爸的為人與性格。對一個極度神經質的人這種現象都在意料之中，所以你不要擔憂，我會讓他慢慢安靜下來，只要他能工作，就會冷靜。' Zhu Meifu letter to Fou Ts'ong, 7 October 1960, in *Fou Lei's Family Letters*, 257.

173 In July 1962 he confided in Étiemble: 'Malgré ma santé précaire, je n'interrompts point ma traduction des Illusions Perdues, mais j'avance très lentement. [...] Et j'aurais mis deux ou trois fois plus de temps dans la traduction que l'auteur n'y eut mis pendant sa création: quelle pitié!' [Despite my precarious health, I have not interrupted my translation of the *Illusions Perdues*, but I make very slow progress. [...] And I will have spent two or three times longer on the translation than the author had done during its creation: it is such a pity!]; and again in September 1963: 'Ma traduction d' "Illusions Perdues" s'achève bien lentement: le premier brouillon est fini, les 2 premières parties sont déjà corrigées, il me reste la troisième à retoucher (et aussi les deux premières à reviser), tout ne finira pas avant l'été prochain.' [My translation of the *Illusions Perdues* is coming very slowly to an end: the first draft is finished; the first two parts are already corrected; there remains the third to improve (and also the first two to revise). The whole thing will not be finished until next summer.]

Bernard Guyon to ask if he might have a copy of his *Pensée politique et sociale* which he could send you.'[174] On the same day Étiemble wrote to Guyon: 'For a Chinese friend, translator of Balzac and *un grand lettré libéral*, I search in vain your *Pensée politique et sociale* which, I was told, is out of print. Is it being reprinted? If not, do you have at your disposal some copies of which you could let me have one, so that I may send it urgently to Monsieur Fou Lei. As time is running out, I cannot wait till next month.'[175] In October 1964 Étiemble updated Fou Lei: 'Since I am hardly leaving France this year, I can keep a close watch on the search for the books you still need. Count absolutely on my goodwill.'[176]

In May 1965 Fou Lei requested: 'For packaging, it would be better to use strong paper, as parcels take much longer than letters by air.'[177] A week later Étiemble replied: '[...] having just left on their way towards you, solidly wrapped up in a cardboard box, are finally two of the books that I have long looked for in second-hand bookshops: *Les comptes dramatiques de Balzac* and *Balzac* by Emile Faguet.'[178] The receipt was acknowledged: 'A thousand thanks for the book package which I received this morning. Apart from *Les comptes*

---

174 'Trois ouvrages sont partis vers vous: Guyon, la Création littéraire chez Balzac; Donnard, les réalités économiques et sociales dans la Comédie humaine; enfin, le Balzac de Gaétan Picon qui fait un bilan récent des études qui vous intéressent. Tout le reste, pour le moment, est épuisé ou en réimpression. Le Balzac de Billy sera sans doute disponible d'ici la fin de l'année et vous sera envoyé aussitôt que reparu. Pour les autres titres, je fais rechercher d'occasion ceux qui seraient disponibles. Enfin, je vais écrire à Bernard Guyon pour lui demander s'il ne lui resterait pas un exemplaire de sa Pensée politique et sociale qu'il puisse vous envoyer.' Étiemble's letter to Fou Lei, 16 November 1963; conserved at Bibliothèque nationale de France.

175 'Pour un ami chinois, traducteur de Balzac et grand lettré libéral, je cherche en vain votre Pensée politique et sociale, qu'on me dit épuisée. Est-elle en réimpression? Sinon, disposez-vous de quelques exemplaires dont vous pourriez me céder l'un, afin que je l'envoie d'urgence à M. Fou Lai. Comme cela presse, je n'attends pas le mois prochain.' Étiemble's letter to Bernard Guyon, 16 November 1963; conserved at Bibliothèque nationale de France.

176 'Comme cette année je ne quitterai presque pas la France, je pourrai surveiller de plus près la recherche des titres qui vous manquent. Comptez absolument sur ma bonne volonté.' Étiemble's letter to Fou Lei, 19 October 1964; conserved at Bibliothèque nationale de France. When Étiemble travelled, his secretary at the Sorbonne acted on his behalf, searching for and sending books to Fou Lei.

177 'Pour l'emballage, il vaut mieux d'employer des papiers bien solides, parce que les colis voyagent beaucoup plus longuement que les correspondances par avion.' Fou Lei's letter to Étiemble, 14 May 1965; conserved at Bibliothèque nationale de France.

178 '[...] viennent de partir vers vous, solidement empaquetés dans une caissette de carton, deux des livres enfin que je faisais rechercher depuis longtemps chez les libraires d'occasion: Les Comptes dramatiques de Balzac et le BALZAC d'Emile Faguet.' Étiemble's letter to Fou Lei, 21 May 1965; conserved at Bibliothèque nationale de France.

dramatiques de Balzac, in it I found a book by Faguet, but alas, not on Balzac as I had wanted and as you had announced in your letter of 21 May, but on Flaubert! This is probably the bookseller's error. Do you want me to send it back? Because, as this is an 1899 edition, it must be also quite expensive.'[179] Étiemble contacted the Librairie A.G. Nizet: 'In the first parcel that you sent at the end of May to Monsieur Fou Lei, my friend from Shanghai, you included, by mistake, a book by Faguet on Flaubert instead of Balzac. Disappointment of the recipient. Can you urgently find for him the volume in question? At the same time, I would appreciate your letting me know if you were able to find some of the other books – all related to Balzac – of which I had made and given you a list? Thank you in advance.'[180] On the same day he wrote to his friend in Shanghai: 'Keep the *Flaubert*, please. We are looking for another *Balzac* for you, and the other books which you still need. [...] I will go and rummage through the library in my little mountain chalet, where I believe I have one or two out-of-print books. I will be delighted to offer them to you, if indeed I can find them there.'[181]

At the outset of this tenacious search for books, in March 1962 Fou Lei dedicated a poem in classical Chinese to Étiemble as a token of gratitude, his calligraphic style now rounded, archaic.[182] For signature, his pseudonym (hào) 怒庵 [fury monastery] was used in lieu of his courtesy name (zì) 怒安 [fury peace].

His translation of *Illusions Perdues* finalised in August 1964, and that of *La maison du chat-qui-pelote* settled in 1965 after four revisions, Fou Lei's machine broke down. His eyes gave out. In September 1965 he wrote to Étiemble: '[...] one is never happy when work does not go well. [...] I have not yet resigned myself to inaction, whilst mental frailty leaves me more and more in a desperate state.' And he apologised, once more, for 'the tone always a little morose in

---

179 'Mille remerciements pour le paquet de livres que j'ai reçu ce matin. J'y ai bien trouvé hors Les comptes Dramatiques de Balzac, un livre de Faguet, mais hélas, non sur Balzac comme j'ai désiré et que vous avez annoncé dans votre lettre du 21 Mai, mais sur Flaubert! C'est probablement dû à l'erreur du libraire. Voulez-vous que je vous le retourne? car, comme c'est une édition datée de 1899, elle doit coûter aussi assez cher.' Fou Lei's letter to Étiemble, 10 July 1965; conserved at Bibliothèque nationale de France.

180 Étiemble's letter to Librairie A.G. Nizet, 31 July 1965; conserved at Bibliothèque nationale de France.

181 'Gardez le Flaubert, je vous en prie. On vous cherche un autre Balzac, et les titres qui manquent encore. [...] J'irai fouiller la bibliothèque de mon petit chalet montagnard, où je crois bien avoir un ou deux des ouvrages épuisés. Je me ferai une joie de vous les offrir, s'ils s'y trouvent en effet.' Étiemble's letter to Fou Lei, 31 July 1965; conserved at Bibliothèque nationale de France.

182 The poem, handwritten with a brush, is conserved at Bibliothèque nationale de France.

my letters, rather dry and short'.[183] 'How would I not understand the tone of your letters', wrote Étiemble, 'I want to believe, nonetheless, that it is your severity towards yourself that incites you to judge that you do not work well.'[184]

FIGURE 35   *Fou Lei at his desk, 1962.*
THE FOU FAMILY TRUST.

In their correspondence, Étiemble used the word 'fidèle' fifteen times, and Fou Lei, fourteen. Eight letters ended with the autograph: 弟 傅雷 [Your brother Fou Lei].

'Christophe heard the rolling noise of cannons coming. They were to wreck this exhausted civilisation, this little dying Greece.'[185]

---

183   '… et l'on n'est jamais gai tant que le travail ne marche pas. Je ne me suis pas encore résigné à l'inaction tandis que la faiblesse mentale me laisse de plus en plus dans un état désespéré. Vous excusez donc, je l'espère, du ton toujours un peu morose dans mes lettres qui sont plutôt sèches et courtes.' Fou Lei's letter to Étiemble, 26 September 1965. 'The tone always a little morose' can be detected in Fou Lei's other correspondences throughout these years. In letters to Fou Ts'ong he made the most effort to conceal it. Both he and Zhu Meifu took great care not to anguish their son who, too, was suffering in exile, and who exercised similar restraint.

184   'Comment ne comprendrais-je pas le ton de vos lettres. Je veux croire toutefois que c'est votre sévérité pour vous-même qui vous incite à juger que vous travaillez mal.' Étiemble's letter to Fou Lei, 12 November 1965.

185   'Christophe entendait venir le roulement des canons, qui allaient broyer cette civilisation épuisée, cette petite Grèce expirante.' Romain Rolland, *Jean-Christophe*, 662.

Creatures of Prometheus, or Unresolved Grief

In 1801, Beethoven was sure that he was going deaf. In that year he composed *Creatures of Prometheus*.

Having asked Étiemble in 1964 for advice on a biography of Balzac,[1] in March 1965 Fou Lei rejoiced: 'A flyer from the bookshop informed me that *Prométhée ou la vie de Balzac* by André Maurois has just been published by Hachette. You will be very kind to get hold of a copy for me – paperback, 25 FR. Perhaps you already noticed this publication and thought of me.'[2]

In *Jean-Christophe*, the Beethovenian hero was warned many times by his friend Olivier:

> Be careful. You rely too much on your strength. [...] An artist must capture his genius; [...] Channel your force. Constrain yourself to habits, to a hygiene of everyday work at fixed hours. Habits are as necessary to the artist as those of military gestures and marches are to the soldier who must fight. There come times of crisis – and they always come – this iron armature prevents the soul from falling. I know it well! If I am not dead, it is because this saved me.[3]

Fou Min remembers his father's routine. 'Eight in the morning, out of bed. Physical exercise, which he designed himself. Breakfast, then work till half past twelve; lunch on the dot. A thirty-minute nap. Work till four, tea break; then

---

1 To which Étiemble replied: 'En ce qui concerne la biographie de Balzac, je suis embarrassé. Je demanderai conseil à Castex ou à M. Pommier.' Étiemble's letter to Fou Lei, 19 October 1964.

2 'Un circulaire de librairie m'a annoncé que le "Prométhée ou la Vie de Balzac" par André Maurois vient de paraître chez Hachette. Vous serez bien aimable de m'en faire procurer un exemplaire – broché, 25 FR. Peut-être avez-vous déjà remarqué la publication et pensé à moi.' Fou Lei's letter to Étiemble, 14 March 1965; conserved at Bibliothèque nationale de France.

3 '– Prends garde. Tu te fies trop à ta force. [...] Un artiste doit capter son génie; [...]. Canalise ta force. Contrains-toi à des habitudes, à une hygiène de travail quotidien, à heures fixes. Elles sont aussi nécessaires à l'artiste que l'habitude des gestes et des pas militaires à l'homme qui doit se battre. Viennent les moments de crise – (et il en vient toujours) – cette armature de fer empêche l'âme de tomber. Je le sais bien, moi! Si je ne suis pas mort, c'est qu'elle m'a sauvé.' Romain Rolland, *Jean-Christophe*, 1313.

© KONINKLIJKE BRILL NV, LEIDEN, 2017 | DOI 10.1163/9789004343924_011

again till half past six, dinner.'[4] Fou Ts'ong, who recalls 'If a visitor kept him from work one day in the week, he made up for it at the weekend',[5] practises the same till this day.

In October 1961, to Étiemble Fou Lei grumbled: 'But physical condition only allows me to seriously work three to four hours a day.'[6] In May 1965 he groaned: 'My days are filled, without giving me the slightest satisfaction for my work. I have the bitterness of being increasingly displeased with my translation and incapable of improving it.'[7] Étiemble understood: 'I see, in your discontent with yourself, the best evidence of the quality of what you do. Only the mediocre are proud of themselves.'[8] And the accomplished seem never complacent. An eighteen-year-old Romain Rolland fiercely declared 'It is immoral to stay voluntarily in mediocrity'[9] after having inscribed, in all his notebooks, a line from Goethe: 'A useless life is death in anticipation.'[10] Balzac, with his immense gift, bemoaned: 'All my anguish comes from the little talent that I know in me.'[11] Taine, in 1869, already the celebrated author of *Histoire de la littérature anglaise* (1864) and the revered scholar delivering *Philosophie de l'art* at École des beaux-arts (1864–69), confided in his mother: 'My only miseries are the difficulty of my work, the times of fatigue and of dryness',[12] 'days of

---

4   The author's interview with Fou Min, November 2013, Beijing. To my question 'What did he wear whilst working?', Fou Min replied: '夏天穿紡綢衫，冬天穿 smoking jacket.' [Silk shirt in the summer, smoking jacket in the winter.]

5   The author's interview with Fou Ts'ong, February 2012, London.

6   'Mais l'état physique ne me permet de travailler sérieusement que de 3 à 4 heures par jour.' Fou Lei's letter to Étiemble, 4 October 1961.

7   '[...] mes journées sont bien remplies sans me donner la moindre satisfaction pour mon travail, j'ai l'amertume d'être de plus en plus mécontent de ma traduction et incapable de l'améliorer.' Fou Lei's letter to Étiemble, 14 May 1965.

8   'Moi, de loin, j'admire que vous continuiez à si bien travailler et je vois, dans votre mécontentement de vous, la meilleure preuve de la qualité de ce que vous faite. Seuls les médiocres sont fiers de soi.' Étiemble's letter to Fou Lei, 21 May 1965.

9   Rolland's journal entry of 23 May 1884 reads: 'Il est immoral de rester, de plein gré, dans la médiocrité.' Romain Rolland, *Mémoires*, 28.

10   'Bien avant 1884, en tête de tous mes cahiers, je répète obstinément cette inscription de Goethe: – *Une vie inutile est une mort anticipée.*' Ibid.

11   'Tous mes chagrins viennent du peu de talent que je me reconnais.' Quoted in Stefan Zweig, *Balzac: le roman de sa vie* (Paris: Albin Michel, 1950), 45.

12   'Mes seules misères, c'est la difficulté de mon travail, les moments de fatigue et de sécheresse.' Taine's letter to his mother, 23 March 1869; quoted in Hilary Nias, *The Artificial Self: the Psychology of Hippolyte Taine* (Oxford: Legenda, 1999), 174.

half-success, of discouragement'.[13] In his student days, Taine was nicknamed 'le grand bûcheron' for his diligence. Once, recounted Chevrillon, on a promenade he said to Maupassant: 'Work all day long, and wash the instruments at night to recommence the next day.'[14] Maupassant approved.

Towards the end of June 1965, working at his desk, Fou Lei suddenly felt his brain on fire; his mind went blank. For the first time, he stopped.[15] In August he resumed work. In September, his vision was mostly gone. He again stopped. Stopping, or the doctor said he would go blind, he was tormented by not being able to read or write for more than one hour a day. In despair, he took up gardening. Typically conscientious, he took it as a science and as an art. With seeds sent from London, Paris and Hong Kong, he cultivated over fifty species of roses in his garden. When he could not see the branches well enough to do the grafting, Zhu Meifu helped him.

Fou Lei could not have had a more virtuous companion. In October 1961, concerned that Fou Ts'ong's temperament, not unlike his father's in its intensity, would hurt her then daughter-in-law, Zamira Menuhin, whom she had never met, Zhu Meifu wrote:

> You most love your mother, and should most understand her too. All the compromises and concessions that I make of your father's dispositions and temperament are principled, because I know him too well. There is reason for his consistent surliness and abhorrence for all evils – your grandfather, bullied and oppressed by local gentries, died of anguish aged only twenty-four. The widow and the orphan (your grandmother and your father) led a woeful, miserable life. Your father's cloistered childhood is unbearable to recollect. Upon entering adulthood, he fought alone, in love of truth and in hatred of all fallacious traditions and murderous feudal ethical codes. He is uncompromisingly honest, and wholly loyal to his work. I love him. I forgive him.[16]

---

13 'Des jours de demi-réussite, des jours de découragements; [...] quelle différence entre projeter et exécuter.' Taine's letter on the same subject to his mother, 3 June 1869; ibid., 175.

14 '[...] travailler toute la journée, et le soir nettoyer ses instruments pour recommencer le lendemain.' André Chevrillon, 'La jeunesse de Taine'; conserved at Fonds Jacques Doucet.

15 '今年六月底爸爸工作時頭腦發熱，空洞好似一張白紙，覺得再撐下去有危險了，自動停止。八月初恢復工作，到九月底忽然眼睛發花，每分鐘都有雲霧在眼前飄動，不得不又放下工作。' Zhu Meifu's letter to Fou Ts'ong, 26 November 1965, in Fou Lei's Family Letters, 472.

16 '你是最愛媽媽的，也應該是最理解媽媽的。我對你爸爸性情脾氣的委屈求全，逆來順受，都是有原則的，因為我太了解他，他一貫的秉性乖戾，嫉惡如仇，是有根源的——當時你祖父受土豪劣紳的欺侮壓迫，二十四歲上就鬱悶而

The mother's confession led to the humbling counsel: 'Your father has the gnawing regret that he influenced you too much with his bad temper, so we would like you to take precaution, and restrain yourself, thus bringing this tragic stigma of our family to an end. This end must begin with you, so that it will not be passed on to posterity.'[17] The doctrine on heredity and the expression 'cloistered childhood' take us to Balzac. In his biography of the novelist, whom Baudelaire deemed 'the most romantic of heroes', Stefan Zweig portrayed a 'child exiled in an ecclesiastical school under Spartan discipline'.[18] Balzac's wretched childhood would have resonated with Fou Lei, who had himself written a long letter in August 1960 after receiving news of Fou Ts'ong's engagement: 'Those without a happy childhood are particularly vulnerable (there are those who are trained to be exceptionally strong, but they are minorities), particularly sensitive. If you think about your own past, you will know how delicate and discreet you must be with your loved one.'[19]

'I love him whose soul is deep even in its ability to be wounded, and whom even a little thing can destroy.' Thus spoke Zarathustra.[20] In the hermit's life of Hermann Hesse, Romain Rolland smelled the yearning for self-protection – 'Mais il est faible au fond, ce faux loup...'[21] [But deep down he is vulnerable,

---

死，寡母孤兒(你祖母和你爸爸)悲慘淒涼的生活，修道院式的童年，真是不堪回首。到成年後，孤軍奮鬥，愛真理，恨一切不合理的舊傳統和殺人不見血的舊禮教，為人正直不苟，對事業衷心耿耿，我愛他，我原諒他。' Zhu Meifu's letter to Fou Ts'ong, 5 October 1961, in *Fou Lei's Family Letters*, 352.

17   '爸爸常常抱恨自己把許多壞脾氣影響了你，所以我們要你及早注意，克制自己，把我們家上代悲劇的烙印從此結束，而這個結束就要從你開始，才能不再遺留到後代身上去。' Ibid.

18   '[...] enfant relégué dans une école ecclésiastique sous une discipline spartiate', Stefan Zweig, *Balzac*, 17.

19   '凡是童年不快樂的人都特別脆弱 (也有訓練得格外堅強的，但只是少數)，特別敏感，你回想一下自己，就會知道對待你的愛人要如何 delicate, 如何 discreet 了。' Fou Lei's letter to Fou Ts'ong, 29 August 1960, in *Fou Lei's Family Letters*, 253. On the same night (5 October 1961) that Zhu Meifu wrote her long letter, Fou Lei wrote an equally long one: '天下父母的心總希望子女活得比自己更幸福；只要我一旦離開世界的時候，對你們倆的結合能有確定不移的信心，也是我一生極大的酬報了！' [All parents wish for their children a life happier than their own; if, when I leave this world, I leave with the unmovable confidence in the union of you two, it would be the great reward in this life of mine!] (*Fou Lei's Family Letters*, 355.) Fou Ts'ong and Zamira Menuhin divorced in 1969. He and fellow pianist Patsy Toh met in 1975 and were married in 1987.

20   Friedrich Nietzsche, *Thus Spoke Zarathustra*, 45.

21   Romain Rolland's letter to Paul Amann, 26 January 1928, after reading Hesse's novel *Steppenwolf* (named after the lonesome wolf of the steppes); see Hermann Hesse and Romain Rolland, *D'une rive à l'autre*, 121.

this false wolf...]. In *Louis Lambert* Balzac etched his double: 'Cet enfant, si faible et si fort...'[22] [This child, so fragile and so strong]. At twenty Fou Lei quoted *René* – 'A *grande âme* must contain more grief than a small one' – and mourned – 'I have it in abundance, grief, and yet I am so small!!';[23] at fifty he reassured Fou Ts'ong: 'My back is aching, and my eyes can hardly see. I cannot continue writing. I bless you. I love you. I want you to be strong, stronger, to always be a strong person, a strong person with a benevolent heart!'[24] Emerging concurrently now are seemingly contradictory attributes in these psyches.

Let us again consider childhood bereavement which marked the lives of Fou Lei, Taine, Rolland, Étiemble – to name only a few of the writers we have so far discussed. Shared experience of losing a sibling and of partaking in their mothers' grief was touched upon by Rolland and Freud in their respective writing after their only meeting.[25] 'Violent mourning walled my mother up in her agony', recollected Romain, 'She was in a state of perpetual war against death, which had taken from her a little girl, her treasure; and she locked me in with her in an armed fortress.'[26] At seventy, with indulgent sympathy Rolland looked back: '[...] the more the child was fragile, the more we must admire that he found the strength to rouse himself from nothingness.'[27] Little wonder that they all trusted books. Taine, who believed 'Je suis si petit' [I am so small], had since

22   Stefan Zweig, *Balzac*, 19.

23   'René a dit: « Une grande âme doit contenir plus de douleur qu'une petite »; j'en ai d'une abondance, la douleur, et cependant, je suis si petit!!' Fou Lei's letter to Daniélou, 10 June 1929; see chapter 3, note 6.

24   '我腰酸背疼，兩眼昏花，寫不下去了。我祝福你，我爱你，希望你強，更強，永遠做一個強者，有一顆慈悲的心的強者！' Fou Lei's letter to Fou Ts'ong, 18 March 1957, in *Fou Lei's Family Letters*, 206.

25   See Henri Vermorel, 'The Presence of Spinoza in the Exchanges between Sigmund Freud and Romain Rolland' in *International Journal of Psychoanalysis*, vol. 90, no. 6 (2009), 1235–1254. See also Romain Rolland, *Le voyage intérieur* (Paris: Albin Michel, 1942) and Sigmund Freud, 'Eine Erinnerungsstörung auf der Akropolis. Brief an Romain Rolland' (A disturbance of memory on the Acropolis), written in January 1936 for Rolland's seventieth birthday and first published in 1937; Freud, *Gesammelte Werke: chronologisch geordnet* (London: Imago, 1991), vol. 16, 250–257.

26   'Un deuil farouche murait ma mère dans sa douleur. Elle était en état de guerre perpétuel contre la mort, qui lui avait pris une petite fille, son trésor; et elle m'enfermait avec elle dans une enceinte armée.' Romain Rolland, *Mémoires*, 20.

27   'À présent, des lointains de mes soixante-dix ans, en relisant ces notes de jeunesse orgueilleuse qui flétrit, humiliée, son passé jouvenceau, il me semble que j'en jugerais avec plus d'indulgence et même de sympathie: car, plus l'enfant était faible, plus on doit admirer qu'il eût trouvé des forces pour s'arracher au néant.' Ibid., 22.

youth reconciled his intellectual superiority with a bookish seclusion.[28] If this trait in Taine and Rolland can be ascribed to their both being *normaliens*, in Balzac, one of Taine's two favourite novelists, it was an auto-defense. For Balzac the child, said Zweig, books are safety: 'They cancel out all the torments, all the humiliations in school. [...] Books constitute his true existence.'[29]

'In any period of my life', confessed Fou Lei, 'even when most passionately in love, I never let go of my loyalty to learning. Learning first, art first, truth first, love second – this is my principle, so far unwavered.'[30] Watchful of the compensatory nature of noble insistence, Nietzsche addressed the most serious: 'Take care, philosophers and friends of knowledge, and beware of martyrdom! Of suffering "for the sake of truth"!'[31] For the sake of truth Fou Lei told: 'All my life, in everything I do, there comes always first frankness, second frankness, and third, still frankness.'[32] Determined to 'chercher la vérité pour elle-même' [look for truth for its own sake], Taine was missed most of all for his 'royal honesty'.[33] Zweig named Rolland 'the greatest moral event of our epoch'.[34] And Étiemble, the self-proclaimed *emmerdeur*, the intransigent pain in the neck,

---

28   The young Taine once said that something had died in him, and that he never managed to recover. See Hilary Nias' analysis in *The Artificial Self*, 12.

29   'Ces livres sont [...] le salut. Ils annulent tous les tourments, toutes les humiliations de l'école. [...] Les livres constituent sa véritable existence.' Stefan Zweig, *Balzac*, 21.

30   '我一生任何時期，鬧戀愛最熱烈的時候，也沒有忘卻對學問的忠誠。學問第一，藝術第一，真理第一，愛情第二，這是我至此為止沒有變過的原則。' Fou Lei's Letter to Fou Ts'ong, 24 March 1966, in *Fou Lei's Family Letters*, 21.

31   Friedrich Nietzsche, *Beyond Good and Evil*, 55. Nietzsche lost his father at five and his younger brother at six.

32   '我一生做事，總是第一坦白，第二坦白，第三還是坦白。' Fou Lei's Letter to Fou Ts'ong, 11 May 1955, in *Fou Lei's Family Letters*, 123.

33   See Horatio Smith, 'The Taine Centennial: Comment and Bibliography' in *Modern Language Notes*, vol. 44, no. 7 (November 1929), 443.

34   'Ce livre n'a pas pour unique objet de décrire une œuvre européenne, mais avant tout de rendre témoignage à l'homme qui fut pour moi, et pour beaucoup d'autres, le plus grand évènement moral de notre époque.' Stefan Zweig, *Romain Rolland*, 7. Twenty-one years after publishing these words in his biography of Rolland, Zweig in exile recalled Rolland's letters: 'For much as I love his published works, I think it is possible that later his letters will be considered the finest and most humane utterances of his great heart and passionate intellect. Written to a friend on the other side of the frontier – and thus officially an enemy – in the deep distress of a compassionate mind, and with the full, bitter force of impotence, they represent perhaps the most powerful moral documents of a time when it was a massive achievement to understand what was going on, and keeping faith with your own convictions called in itself for great courage.' Stefan Zweig, *The World of Yesterday*, 265–266.

refused four times to enter the French Academy, for 'there are politically dirty hands, and there are literarily dirty hands. I don't like dirty hands. I wash my hands fairly often, and I don't like shaking dirty hands.'[35] We witness, in effect, a manifestation of the Nietzschean 'instinct for cleanliness'.[36]

What, indeed, is the relationship between grieving at a young age and solitary courage? Can it be understood as a repairing impulse to counter the loss of trust – for how could orphans take life for granted – with acquired strength and with excessive discipline? To the point that, looking at Balzac's life, Zweig concluded: 'death alone can set boundaries to his Promethean will.'[37]

In February 1965, Fou Lei wrote to Fou Ts'ong: 'Now that you have made art your master, all the bitterness and distress are your tribute to him; [...] Each line has its humiliation and misery.'[38] The worse the political situation, the more restrained his words. The worse his condition, the calmer his tone. One has to read between the lines to grasp that proud resignation exercised by what appears to be unfathomable will. Treading on his correspondence of the 1960s, one senses that, disillusioned, paralysed, crucified, and mortified by the hellish state his country had run into, Fou Lei was prepared both to work every day with undaunted zeal till the day he died, and to die any day without a moment's fuss.

On 24 March 1966, Fou Lei wrote to Étiemble, asking if he would be able to collect reviews in the French press after Fou Ts'ong's concert in Paris. There was a delay in Étiemble's receiving the letter, and as soon as he did, he wrote to publishers to commission this research for 'mon ami de Changaï'.[39] In July, he sent copies of these reviews from March, assuring his friend of 'the incontestable

---

35 'Il y a des mains politiquement sales, et il y a des mains littérairement sales. Je n'aime pas les mains sales. Je me lave les mains assez souvent, et je n'aime pas serrer des mains sales.' Étiemble's 1988 interview with Bernard Pivot on 'Apostrophes'.

36 'May I venture to indicate one last trait of my nature which creates for me no little difficulty in my relations with others? I possess a perfectly uncanny sensitivity of the instinct for cleanliness [...].' Friedrich Nietzsche, *Ecce Homo*, 18.

37 '[...] seule la mort peut poser des bornes à sa volonté prométhéenne.' Stefan Zweig, *Balzac*, 137.

38 Fou Lei's letter to Fou Ts'ong, 20 February 1965, in *Fou Lei's Family Letters*, 447. See chapter 5, note 97.

39 Étiemble's letter to Yves Dandelot, 28 June 1966; conserved at Bibliothèque nationale de France. In his first letter to Étiemble on 4 October 1961, Fou Lei had enquired about the reception of Fou Ts'ong's concert in Paris in March 1959. In his response on 2 November 1961, Étiemble wrote that the French public had yet to learn to appreciate 'le talent de votre fils' [your son's talent] as had done England.

"triumph" obtained at last in France by Fou Ts'ong'.[40] At the end he spoke, lovingly, of another few books on the cultivation of roses that he had sent – 'c'était un signe de ma fidèle pensée'.

In March 1966, Fou Ts'ong had written:

> Dear Mr Étiemble:
> I am sorry to hear that you are not well, and I am very touched that you still take so much trouble to write to me.
>
> My father has often told me about your kindness and generosity, and I know how much he is grateful to such devoted friendship from so far away, and I have been wanting to thank you since a long time.
>
> You have brought to my poor father in his desolate solitude a ray of sunshine, a sense of belonging to a universal world which unfortunately is cut off from him.
>
> [...] I have in the past sent roses to my father, and I am sure it will give him great pleasure if you send him some roses too. And I must thank you again for your kind thought.
>
> Yours most sincerely
Fou Ts'ong[41]

In summer 1966, the Cultural Revolution began. Flaunting two sacred words in its appellation, in reality it had little to do with revolution and still less with culture. On 12 August, two days before the second birthday of their grandson, Fou Lei dictated a letter which Zhu Meifu typed in English:[42]

> Everything about Lin Siao excites us greatly, especially Mamma, who since last July had never ceased counting the days. 'One month later, it will be Lin Siao's birthday; three weeks later it will be Lin Siao's birthday.' Last night she said: 'It remains now three days only.' Absolutely as though the baby is living with her.
>
> What delight for you to observe your child growing up from day to day! What a touching scene to imagine our grandson looking at our photos in your living-room and kitchen and knowing thus his remote grandparents!

---

40   Étiemble's letter to Fou Lei, 12 July 1966.

41   Fou Ts'ong's letter to Étiemble, 30 March 1966; conserved at Bibliothèque nationale de France.

42   Fou Lei sent letters in French to his Swiss-educated and French-speaking then daughter-in-law, Zamira Menuhin. To Fou Ts'ong he usually wrote in Chinese. When his letters addressed them both, Fou Lei wrote in English. Zhu Meifu, too, read and wrote in English.

Nevertheless, I see no hope at all to meet him one day, to embrace him, taking him in my arms. Mamma does believe in this possibility, but not I.

Don't thank us for the knittings. Mamma regrets always that she can do so little to express her great love for the baby and for you.

We are waiting for Lin Siao's pictures of his second birthday party. If we can have a copy of his photo in full face, we will be so happy!

...

Life is hard everywhere, we have to 'reform' ourselves constantly, struggling against every bit of traditional, capitalistic, non-Marxist thinking and sentiments and customs. We should repulse all our old philosophy of life, old social standards.

For a person who lived more than 40 years in the old society, imbued with 'reactionary western capitalistic democratic ideas', his (Mao's) 'self-reform' is of course a tremendously difficult task. We are trying our best to fulfill these requirements imposed by the present 'proletarian cultural revolution' with much strain and pain ...

I can only read for five minutes at one time. The long articles in newspapers are read to me by Mamma.

This letter is typewritten by her under my dictation ...

Much love to you all,

Papa, Mamma[43]

Spelling politics out with unreserved clarity, this was the last of Fou Lei's family letters. Before he and Zhu Meifu received Lin Siao's birthday photo in full face, on 30 August, a group of Red Guards raided their house. The assaults – interrogation, accusation, verbal abuse, beating, confiscating their belongings and uprooting all the roses in the garden in search of criminal evidence – lasted four days and three nights.

In the early morning of 3 September, Fou Lei and Zhu Meifu were found dead. They had hanged themselves.

Their will, written by Fou Lei in elegant calligraphy and signed by both, addressed Zhu Meifu's brother.

Renxiu:

Although the so-called anti-Party evidence (a small mirror and an old faded pictorial) was searched out in our household and not to be argued with, we would rather die than admit that they are ours (they were in a

---

43 The English original of this letter is published in Fou Min (ed.), *Commemoration of Fou Lei Centenary* 傅雷百年誕辰紀念 (Beijing: Beijing tushuguan, 2008), 234.

suitcase that someone had left with us). We may be accused of tens of thousands of crimes, but have never even dreamed of subversion. We do know that although such evidence is incontestable, the People's Republic of China under the direction of the Wise Communist Party and the Great Leader Chairman Mao would not give us a heavy sentence. But to be wronged and not to be able to defend one's honour is much more difficult to live with than imprisonment. Not to mention the Traitor Fou Ts'ong that we have educated, which alone suffices to condemn us to death in front of the People! Not to mention the Wasteful Nuisances that we are, coming from the Old Society and who should have retreated from the Stage of History long ago!

Because you are Meifu's brother, and because we do not have other close relatives, we can only entrust you to deal with the aftermath of our death. If you cannot accept for reasons of political position, please ask for instructions from your superiors before taking action.

Here are the things we ask you to do:

1. Pay, on our behalf, the rent for September, 55.29 yuan (cash enclosed).
2. Shen Zhongzhang from Room 606, Wukang Building (end of Huai-hai Road) left with us his Omega watch to be repaired. Please return it to him.
3. The money my dead mother left us. Renxiu, you may do what you like with it.
4. A used pocket watch (steel) and a used small woman's watch are gifts for our cleaning lady Zhou Judi.
5. A certificate of deposit of 600 yuan for Zhou Judi, as maintenance for the transitional period. She is from the working class and has lived a hard and lonely life. We do not want her to be unduly affected by us.
6. Aunt Fu Yi left a certificate of deposit of 600 yuan with us. Please return it to her.
7. Aunt Fu Yi also left with us a receipt from Lianyi Shanzhuang Cemetery. After the Red Guards' search, we looked everywhere but could not find it. We are very sorry.
8. The jewelries that Aunt Fu Yi left here have, together with our own, been confiscated by the Red Guards. We can only put in place three certificates of deposits (370 yuan in total) and three small savings as compensation.

9. The jewelries that Sister Zhu Chun left with us have also been confiscated. Please apologise to her on our behalf. Two suitcases of clothes that she left here (third floor) have been temporarily sealed; along with a wooden case of porcelain, please accept and take them back on her behalf the day the State unseals them. There are also a few pieces of furniture, about which you may enquire Zhou Judi.

10. An Omega watch that I used, and another used man's watch which we had wished to give to Min and his friend. But we fear this may implicate their political position, therefore they are at Renxiu's disposal.

11. Cash of 53.30 yuan, for our cremation.

12. The furniture that we borrowed from the Soong family upstairs, please let Chen Shutao take it back according to the list.

13. Our own furniture is at your disposal. Books, calligraphy and painting are at the State's disposal.

It disquiets us to involve you in this, but we have no one else to ask. Please forgive us, forgive us!

Fou Lei

Meifu

The night of 2 September 1966[44]

---

44 人秀：

　　儘管所謂反黨罪證 (一面小鏡子和一張褪色的舊畫報) 是在我們家裏搜出的，百口莫辯的，可是我們至死也不承認是我們自己的東西(實系寄存箱內理出之物)。我們縱有千萬罪行，卻從來不曾有過變天思想。我們也知道搜出的罪證雖然有口難辯，在英明的共產黨領導和偉大的毛主席領導之下的中華人民共和國，決不至凶之而判重刑。只是含冤不白，無法洗刷的日子比坐牢還要難過。何況光是教育出一個叛徒傅聰來，在人民面前已經死有余辜了！更何況像我們這種來自舊社會的渣滓早應該自動退出歷史舞台了！

　　因為你是梅馥的胞兄，因為我們別無至親骨肉，善後事只能委託你了。如你以立場關係不便接受，則請向上級或法院請示後再行處理。

　　委託數事如下：

一、代付九月份房租五十五點二九元 (附現款)。

二、武康大樓(淮海路底)606室沈仲章托代修歐米茄自動男手錶一只，請交還。

三、故老母余剩遺款，由人秀處理。

四、舊掛錶 (鋼) 一只，舊小女錶一只，贈保姆周菊娣。

五、六百元存單一紙給周菊娣，做過渡時期生活費。她是勞動人民，一生孤苦，我們不願她無故受累。

六、姑母傅儀寄存我們家存單一紙六百元，請交還。

'Life is what I want. Justice is also what I want. You cannot have both. Leave life, and take justice',[45] said Mencius. In the same logic deduced Marcus Aurelius: 'Are you reduced to indignity? Leave life with calm.'[46]

Fou Lei and Zhu Meifu died when it was better not to live.[47]

News of his parents' death reached Fou Ts'ong weeks later. On 21 October 1966, he wrote to Étiemble:

> Zamira has written to you about the tragic news. I have been expecting it for quite a while knowing as well as I do my own father and my own mother.
>
> Nevertheless it is too horrifying and too absurd to conceive, and I am quite numb to even feel outraged. It is not my parents who committed suicide, it is not thousands of the carriers of a great civilization who committed suicide. It is China itself committing suicide!
>
> I am so deeply moved by your devotion to my parents, your compassion for my country, my people. Compassion, which is the noblest of all human emotions and greatest quality of the universal intellectuals!

七、姑母傅儀寄存之聯義山莊墓地收據一紙，此次經過紅衛兵搜查後便覓不得，很抱歉。

八、姑母傅儀寄存我們家之飾物，與我們自有的同時被紅衛兵取去沒收，只能以存單三紙 (共三百七十元) 又小額儲蓄三張，作為賠償。

九、三姐朱純寄存我們家之飾物，亦被一並充公。請代道歉。她寄存衣箱貳隻 (三樓) 暫時被封，瓷器木箱壹隻，將來待公家啟封後由你代領。尚有家具數件，問周菊娣便知。

十、舊自用歐米茄自動男手錶一只，又舊男手錶一只，本擬給敏兒與某某，但恐妨礙他們的政治立場，故請人秀自由處理。

十一、現鈔五十三點三〇元，作為我們火葬費。

十二、樓上宋家借用之家具，由陳叔陶按單收回。

十三、自有家具，由你處理。圖書字畫聽候公家決定。

使你為我們受累，實在不安，但也別無他人可托，諒之諒之！

傅雷
梅馥
一九六六年九月二日夜

45   '生，亦我所欲也；義，亦我所欲也。二者不可得兼，舍生而取義者也。' *Mencius* 孟子告子上; see also D.C. Lau (tr.), *Mencius*, 166.

46   'Es-tu réduit à l'indignité? Sors de la vie avec calme...' Romi, *Suicides passionnés, historiques, bizarres, littéraires* (Paris: Serg, 1964), 13.

47   'Human virtue demands her champions and martyrs, and the trial of persecution always proceeds. It is but the other day that the brave Lovejoy gave his breast to the bullets of a mob, for the rights of free speech and opinion, and died when it was better not to live.' Ralph Waldo Emerson, *Character and Heroism* (New York and Boston: H.M. Caldwell, 1900), 80–81.

You are one of the very few men outside of China who really knew my father, who really knew what kind of man he was, what's more, you also knew he belongs to the few hundreds, perhaps few thousands that represent China at its best, and that he shares the fate with them all![48]

Grave resonances continued. Before Fou Ts'ong was born, Rolland had named the First World War the 'suicide of Europe'. During the Second World War, Zweig committed suicide with his wife in Brazil.

Around the time Fou Lei and Zhu Meifu took their own lives, Lao She drowned himself in the lake in Beijing. Chu Anping disappeared. Every day in Fou Lei's neighbourhood, people, known or unknown, killed themselves.[49]

Fou Ts'ong's younger brother Fou Min, English teacher in Beijing, attempted suicide several times during the Cultural Revolution.

Between 1957 and 1976, millions died at the hands of one another. Millions more had their lives crushed and broken.[50]

In 1979, Fou Lei was 'rehabilitated'.[51]

---

48 Fou Ts'ong's letter to Étiemble, 21 October 1966; conserved at Bibliothèque nationale de France.

49 Half a century on, thinking of his parents' death Fou Ts'ong said: 'It was not just my parents... Ten professors from Shanghai Conservatory of Music alone committed suicide in the same week. I think about my parents all the time... In those days, every day I wanted to die.' The author's interview with Fou Ts'ong, March 2016, London.

50 Discussing the contested death toll, in 1987 Anne F. Thurston wrote: 'Whatever the figures, the Cultural Revolution was a human tragedy of untold proportions, a catastrophe that brought China to the brink of collapse.' Anne F. Thurston, *Enemies of the People: The Ordeal of the Intellectuals in China's Great Cultural Revolution* (Cambridge, MA and London: Harvard University, 1987), xvi. In her petrifying work of oral history, Thurston presents the Cultural Revolution as 'a failure of morality' (xix).

51 In 1976, Étiemble, who had remained sober in a late 1960s Paris enthused by Mao's revolution, published *Quarante ans de mon maoïsme: 1934–1974*. At the end we read: 'Je me dis tout bas que je n'avais peut-être pas tout à fait tort, en 1966, de condamner la prétendue révo cul; et que j'ai peut-être raison de penser à tous ceux (comme Lao Che, ou mon cher Fou Lai) qui ne sont plus là-bas pour qu'on les promeuve, les décore, les honore enfin autant qu'ils le méritent. Désespérés de voir leur pays tomber si bas, ces deux-là se sont suicidés.' [I think that I was perhaps not altogether wrong, in 1966, to condemn the so-called cultural revolution, and that I may be right in thinking of all of those – like Lao She, or my dear Fou Lei – who are no longer there to be finally promoted, decorated and honoured as much as they deserve. Seeing their country ruined, in despair these two committed suicide.] Étiemble, *Quarante ans de mon maoïsme*, 440.

In a 1989 video footage of the Tiananmen Square in the days leading to the bloody massacre, I caught a glimpse of a banner held by students. On it were words from Fou Lei's 1942 preface to *Vie de Beethoven*: '唯有真實的苦難，才能驅除浪漫底克的幻想的苦難；唯有看到克服苦難的壯烈的悲劇，才能幫助我們擔受殘酷的命運；唯

In 1980, Fou Min visited his brother in England, from where he wrote to Étiemble. The latter replied:

Dear Sir,
Please forgive this typewritten (and poorly typewritten) letter. My health was bad, improved, but is getting worse: my right eye does not work well, a.s.o.

I was deeply moved to receive news from Fou Lei's younger son. I still deeply feel the ill-fate of your family and I hate those who were responsible for the tragic outcome.[52]

The search for books went on. In 1981, as Fou Min began organising his father's posthumous publications, Étiemble wrote to Librairie Gallimard:

Cher Monsieur,
From Beijing, one of the sons of one of the most illustrious victims of the 'Cultural Revolution', Fou Lei, with whom I had had the chance of a meeting which sealed our friendship, asks me if it would be possible to send him Maurois' *Voltaire* that Fou Lei translated from the Gallimard edition illustrated with 24 drawings, as well as Taine's *Philosophie de l'art* in the Hachette edition (Paris, 1928), the text from which Fou Lei began. Monsieur Fou Min, his son, is preparing a complete edition of his father's translations. These sources are missing, for his parents' house was plundered in September 1966 by the ostensible 'Red Guards'. Fou Lei and his wife committed suicide after this 'visit'.

有抱着"我不入地獄誰入地獄"的精神，才能挽救一個萎靡而自私的民族。' [Only genuine suffering can drive out the suffering of romantic illusion; only by beholding heroic tragedies of surmounting ordeals can we endure cruel destiny; only by upholding the spirit of 'If I do not go to hell, who shall?' can a withered and selfish nation be saved.] (See chapter 5, note 34.)

This detail, like the entire history to which it belongs, has been erased.

In 2011, following the Jasmine Revolution, the pro-democracy protests in China and the arrest of dissidents, notably Ai Weiwei, I was invited to a conference titled 'Fou Lei's Spirit' in Shanghai. My paper was censored before delivery. When I raised a scholarly question at the end and suggested a discussion, otherwise unscheduled, I was silenced.

The fear of recent horror hovers, unspoken. The dead are commemorated in a way the dead would have detested.

52   Étiemble's letter to Fou Min, 24 March 1980; conserved at Bibliothèque nationale de France.

If I could help Monsieur Fou Min in his project of filial piety and of the restoration of French culture in China, I would be doubly happy.[53]

Watching Étiemble in a 1988 interview curiously recalls Fou Lei's visage in his unlived old age. The interviewer said, at the end, that one word would summarise Étiemble, and that it was a word little used today: *un lettré*. Étiemble said, immediately: In the Confucian sense, yes – that is to say, someone who would give his life to tell the truth.[54]

---

53   'De Pékin, l'un des fils de l'une des plus illustres victimes de la « révolution culturelle » Fou Lai, avec qui j'avais eu la chance d'une rencontre qui scella notre amitié, me demande s'il m'est possible de lui faire parvenir le Voltaire de Maurois que Fou Lai avait traduit d'après l'édition Gallimard ornée de 24 dessins, ainsi que la Philosophie de l'art de Taine dans l'édition Hachette, Paris, 1928, texte dont partit Fou Lai. M. Fou Ming, son fils, prépare en effet là-bas une édition complète des traductions élaborées par son père. Il lui manque ces deux sources, car la maison de ses parents fut pillée en septembre 66 par les prétendus « gardes rouges ». Fou Lai et son épouse se suicidèrent après cette « visite »... Si je pouvais aider M. Fou Ming à mener à bien son œuvre de piété filiale et de restauration de la culture française en Chine, j'en serais doublement heureux.' Étiemble's letter to Monsieur Poulin at Librairie Gallimard, 22 October 1981; conserved at Bibliothèque nationale de France.

54   Étiemble's 1988 interview with Bernard Pivot on 'Apostrophes'. In his letter of 16 November 1963 to Bernard Guyon, Étiemble referred to Fou Lei as 'un grand lettré libéral'; see chapter 8, note 175.

Epilogue

In his laconic autobiography, Fou Lei mapped out his life in neat correlation with political events: his father was wronged and imprisoned in the year of the Xinhai Revolution (1911); his adolescence saw him participating in the May Thirtieth Movement (1925); from France he returned to his country on the day of the Mukden Incident (18 September 1931); his teaching was interrupted and suspended by the Shanghai Incident (28 January 1932); in fury he resigned from his research post in Luoyang after the Xi'an Incident (12 December 1936); he travelled to Fuzhou to teach the day after the Marco Polo Bridge Incident (7 July 1937); because of it he rushed back (4 August 1937) and, learning that the Kuomintang had decided to fight the Japanese, fled Shanghai (6 August 1937); stuck on his way to escape, he returned via Hong Kong three months later, just as the Kuomintang was retreating (November 1937); from Kunming he left for Hong Kong in June 1949, only to return in December. 'I have been in Shanghai ever since', he wrote in July 1957. What he did not write and what we can now add, is that in May 1957 he had attempted to travel to France on a self-proposed and officially rejected research trip, just before the Anti-Rightist Campaign began; and that at the outset of the Cultural Revolution, in 1966, he killed himself. His life was spent between two revolutions – one genuine, one feigned – in China's modern history, one marking the death of his father, the other his own.

From the cradle to the grave, not for a second did Fou Lei not think it his duty to care about, and to contribute to, his country's civic future. A resolute outsider, cautiously *engagé*, in neither lofty independence nor precarious endurance could he be left in peace. His childhood was an internal exile, as was his entire working life. He was perpetually on guard against politics; politics engulfed him. In justice he invested desperate faith; justice was denied him. Under expulsion he lived his last years; under expulsion he did not sell out. Expelling barbarity, he took his own life. The question of entwined identities of a Confucian literatus and a Foucauldian lettré is not so pressing as this: that a public intellectual was ultimately robbed of both public and private space; that this impossible position was far from unique in his times.

To Elias Canetti, it is a sign of human decency to be ashamed of having lived in the twentieth century. The atrocities that slaughtered and scarred hundreds of millions of innocents deride our oblivion in the darkness of night. Despotism takes on ever more elaborate guises. If reasoned arguments do not articulate against absurdity, step by step one knows not reason; one knows not absurdity. Today, I think of Fou Lei and his vigilance.

© KONINKLIJKE BRILL NV, LEIDEN, 2017 | DOI 10.1163/9789004343924_012

Bibliography

In English

Andrews, Julia F. and Shen Kuiyi. 'The Japanese Impact on the Republican Art World: the Construction of Chinese Art as a Modern Field' in *Twentieth-Century China*, vol. 32, no. 1 (November 2006), 4–35.

Arendt, Hannah. *Men in Dark Times*. London: Cape, 1970.

Arendt, Hannah. *On Revolution*. New York: Viking, 1963.

Arendt, Hannah. *The Origins of Totalitarianism*. 2nd edition. New York: World Publishing, Meridian Books, 1958.

Babbitt, Irving. *The Masters of Modern French Criticism*. Boston and New York: Houghton Mifflin, 1913.

Berlin, Isaiah. *Political Ideas in the Romantic Age: Their Roots and Influence on Modern Thought*. London: Pimlico, 2006.

Berlin, Isaiah. *The Roots of Romanticism*. London: Pimlico, 1999.

Bloom, Alfred. *The Linguistic Shaping of Thought: A Study in the Impact of Language on Thinking in China and the West*. Hillsdale, NJ: Lawrence Erlbaum, 1981.

Bodde, Derk. *Tolstoy and China*. Princeton: Princeton University, 1950.

Burckhardt, Jacob. *The Civilization of the Renaissance in Italy*. Oxford and London: Oxford University, 1945.

Burckhardt, Jacob. *Judgments on History and Historians*. Trans. Harry Zohn. Indianapolis: Liberty Fund, 1999.

Burckhardt, Jacob. *Reflections on History*. Ed. Gottfried Dietze. Indianapolis: Liberty Classics, 1979.

Carlyle, Thomas. *Heroes and Hero-worship: extraits*. Anno. L. Cazamian. Paris: Hachette, 1925.

Chan, Pedith. 'The Institutionalization and Legitimatization of Guohua: Art Societies in Republican Shanghai' in *Modern China*, vol. 39, no. 5 (September 2013), 541–570.

Chan Sin-wai. *A Topical Bibliography of Translation and Interpretation: Chinese-English, English-Chinese*. Hong Kong: The Chinese University of Hong Kong, 1995.

Chen, Joseph T. *The May Fourth Movement in Shanghai: The Making of a Social Movement in Modern China*. Leiden: Brill, 1971.

Clark, Priscilla P. and Terry N. Clark. 'Writers, Literature, and Student Movements in France' in *Sociology of Education*, 42, no. 4 (Autumn 1969), 293–314.

Clunas, Craig. 'Chinese Art and Chinese Artists in France (1924–1925)' in *Arts Asiatiques*, vol. 44 (1989), 100–106.

T.C. 'Review of *vingt leçons d'histoire de l'art* par Bordes' in *Studies: An Irish Quarterly Review*, vol. 17, no. 65 (March 1928), 152–153.

Crozier, Ralph. 'Post-Impressionists in Pre-War Shanghai: The *Juelanshe* (Storm Society) and the Fate of Modernism in Republican China' in *Modernity in Asian Art*. Ed. John Clark. Sydney: Wild Pony, 1993.

Danzker, Jo-Anne Birnie, Ken Lum and Zheng Shengtian, eds., *Shanghai Modern 1919–1945*. Munich: Hatje Cantz, 2004.

Davies, Katherine Jane. 'Three Voices of the Interwar French Catholic Revival: Jacques Maritain, Charles du Bos and Gabriel Marcel and the Tensions of Reconciliation with the World'. Ph.D. diss. University of Manchester, 2008.

Denton, Kirk, ed. *Modern Chinese Literary Thought: Writings on Literature 1893–1945*. Stanford: Stanford University, 1995.

Derrida, Jacques. 'Onto-theology of National Humanism' in *Oxford Literary Studies*, 14:1–2 (1992), 3–23.

Dikötter, Frank. *The Tragedy of Liberation: A History of the Communist Revolution 1945–1957*. London: Bloomsbury, 2013.

Doleželová-Velingerová, Milena, Oldřich Král and Graham Sanders, eds. *The Appropriation of Cultural Capital: China's May Fourth Project*. Cambridge, MA and London: Harvard University, 2001.

Dos Passos, John. *Manhattan Transfer*. London: Penguin, 2000.

Drake, William A. 'Romain Rolland: Son but n'était pas le succes; son but était la foi' in *The Sewanee Review*, vol. 32, no. 4 (October 1924), 386–404.

Duara, Prasenjit. 'De-Constructing the Chinese Nation' in *The Australian Journal of Chinese Affairs*, no. 30 (July 1993), 1–26.

Duara, Prasenjit. *Rescuing History from the Nation: Questioning Narratives of Modern China*. Chicago: University of Chicago, 1995.

Duara, Prasenjit. 'Response to Philip Huang's "Biculturality in Modern China and in Chinese Studies"' in *Modern China*, vol. 26, no. 1 (January 2000), 32–37.

Duara, Prasenjit. Viren Murthy and Andrew Sartori, eds. *A Companion to Global Historical Thought*. Chichester: Wiley Blackwell, 2014.

Eisenstadt, S.N. *Comparative Civilizations and Multiple Modernities*. Leiden: Brill, 2003.

Elman, Benjamin. *A Cultural History of Modern Science in China: New Histories of Science, Technology, and Medicine*. Cambridge, MA and London: Harvard University, 2006.

Elshakry, Marwa. 'When Science Became Western: Historiographical Reflections' in *Isis*, vol. 101, no. 1 (March 2010), 98–109.

Emerson, Ralph Waldo. *Character and Heroism*. New York and Boston: H.M. Caldwell, 1900.

Fan, Fa-ti. 'Redrawing the Map: Science in Twentieth-Century China' in *Isis*, vol. 98, no. 3 (September 2007), 524–538.

Fong, Wen C. 'The Modern Chinese Art Debate' in *Artibus Asiae*, vol. 53, no. 1/2 (1993), 290–305.

Foster, Paul B. *Ah Q Archaeology: Lu Xun, Ah Q, Ah Q Progeny and the National Character Discourse in Twentieth Century China*. Oxford: Lexington, 2006.

Freedman, Ralph. *Hermann Hesse, Pilgrim of Crisis: A Biography*. New York: Pantheon, 1978.

Freud, Sigmund. *Civilization and Its Discontents*. Trans. David McLintock. London: Penguin, 2002.

Freud, Sigmund. *The Future of an Illusion*. Trans. James Strachey. New York: W.W. Norton, 1961.

Freud, Sigmund. *On Murder, Mourning and Melancholia*. Trans. Shaun Whiteside. London: Penguin, 2005.

Fung, Edmund S.K. 'Were Chinese Liberals Liberal? Reflections on the Understanding of Liberalism in Modern China' in *Pacific Affairs*, vol. 81, no. 4 (Winter 2008/2009), 557–576.

Furst, Lilian R. 'Romanticism in Historical Perspective' in *Comparative Literature Studies*, vol. 5, no. 2 (June 1968), 115–143.

Gay, Peter. *Freud for Historians*. New York and Oxford: Oxford University, 1985.

Goetz, Thomas H. *Taine and the Fine Arts*. Madrid: Playor, 1973.

Hinton, David, trans. *Mencius*. Berkeley: Counterpoint, 2015.

Hockx, Michel. 'Is There a May Fourth Literature? A Reply to Wang Xiaoming' in *Modern Chinese Literature and Culture*, vol. 11, no. 2 (Fall 1999), 40–52.

Horney, Karen. *The Neurotic Personality of Our Time*. New York and London: Harper and Bros., 1937.

Hsia, C.T. *A History of Modern Chinese Fiction*. 3rd edition. Bloomington, IN: Indiana University, 1999.

Hsia, C.T. 'The Continuing Obsession with China: Three Contemporary Writers' in *Review of National Literatures*, vol. 6, no. 1 (Spring 1975), 76–99.

Hu Shih, *The Chinese Renaissance: The Haskell Lectures 1933*. Chicago: University of Chicago, 1934.

Isaacs, Harold R. *The Tragedy of the Chinese Revolution*. London: Secker and Warburg, 1938.

James, William. *The Varieties of Religious Experience*. Cambridge, MA and London: Harvard University, 1985.

Jordan, Donald A. *Northern Expedition: China's National Revolution of 1926–28*. Honolulu: University of Hawaii, 1976.

Kraus, Richard Curt. *Pianos and Politics in China: Middle-class Ambitions and the Struggle over Western Music*. New York and Oxford: Oxford University, 1989.

Kwok, David. *Scientism in Chinese Thought, 1900–1950*. New Haven and London: Yale University, 1965.

Lalande, André. 'Philosophy in France, 1919' in *The Philosophical Review*, vol. 29, no. 5 (September 1920), 413–436.

Lau, D.C., trans. *The Analects*. Hong Kong: Chinese University, 2000.

Lau, D.C., trans. *Mencius*. Harmondsworth: Penguin, 1984.

Legge, James, trans. *The Chinese Classics*. 3rd edition. 4 vols. Taipei: SMC, 1994.

Liu, Lydia. *Translingual Practice: Literature, National Culture, and Translated Modernity – China, 1900–1937*. Stanford: Stanford University, 1995.

Lucas, F.L. *The Decline and Fall of the Romantic Ideal*. Cambridge: Cambridge University, 1948.

Macpherson, James. *The Poems of Ossian*. 2 vols. London: W. Strahan and T. Cadell, 1784.

Marcus, Aurelius. *Meditations*. Trans. Maxwell Staniforth. London: Penguin, 1964.

Mazur, Mary G. 'Intellectual Activism in China during the 1940s: Wu Han in the United Front and the Democratic League' in *The China Quarterly*, no. 133 (March 1993), 27–55.

Nias, Hilary. *The Artificial Self: the Psychology of Hippolyte Taine*. Oxford: Legenda, 1999.

Nietzsche, Friedrich. *Beyond Good and Evil*. Trans. R.J. Hollingdale. London: Penguin, 2003.

Nietzsche, Friedrich. *Ecce Homo*. Trans. R.J. Hollingdale. London: Penguin, 1992.

Nietzsche, Friedrich. *Thus Spoke Zarathustra*. Trans. R.J. Hollingdale. London: Penguin, 2003.

Norman, Hilda Laura. 'The Personality of Hippolyte Taine' in *PMLA*, vol. 36, no. 4 (December 1921), 529–550.

Orwell, George. *Nineteen Eighty-Four*. London: Secker and Warburg, 1949.

Phillips, David P. 'The Influence of Suggestion on Suicide: Substantive and Theoretical Implications of the Werther Effect' in *American Sociological Review*, vol. 39, no. 3 (June 1974), 340–354.

Pitt, Alan. 'The Irrationalist Liberalism of Hippolyte Taine' in *The Historical Journal*, vol. 41, no. 4 (December 1998), 1035–1053.

Pitt, Alan. 'The Cultural Impact of Science in France: Ernest Renan and the Vie de Jesus' in *The Historical Journal*, vol. 43, no. 1 (March 2000), 79–101.

Roberts, Claire. *Friendship in Art: Fou Lei and Huang Binhong*. Hong Kong: Hong Kong University, 2010.

Roe, Glenn H. 'Contre Taine et Renan: Charles Péguy and the Metaphysics of Modern History' in *French Forum*, vol. 34, no. 2 (Spring 2009), 17–37.

Rolland, Romain. *Romain Rolland's Essays on Music*. Ed. David Ewen. New York: Allen, Towne and Heath, 1948.

Russell, Bertrand. *The Problem of China*. London: George Allen, 1922.

Russell, Bertrand. *The Conquest of Happiness*. London and New York: Routledge, 1993.

Said, Edward. *Orientalism*. New York: Pantheon, 1978.

Said, Edward. *Reflections on Exile and Other Literary and Cultural Essays*. London: Granta, 2001.

Schmitt, Hans A. *Charles Péguy: the Decline of an Idealist*. Baton Rouge: Louisiana State University, 1967.

Schneider, Axel. 'Between Dao and History: Two Chinese Historians in Search of a Modern Identity for China' in *History and Theory*, vol. 35, no. 4 (December 1996), 54–73.

Schwarcz, Vera. *The Chinese Enlightenment: Intellectuals and the Legacy of the May Fourth Movement of 1919*. Berkeley and London: University of California, 1986.

Schwartz, Benjamin I. *In Search of Wealth and Power: Yen Fu and the West*. Cambridge, MA: Harvard University, 1964.

Schwartz, Benjamin I. ed. *Reflections on the May Fourth Movement: A Symposium*. Cambridge, MA: Harvard University, 1972.

Shroder, Maurice Zorensky. *Icarus: the Image of the Artist in French Romanticism*. Cambridge, MA: Harvard University, 1961.

Sigurdson, Richard. *Jacob Burckhardt's Social and Political Thought*. Toronto: Toronto University, 2004.

Sigurdson, Richard. 'Jacob Burckhardt: The Cultural Historian as Political Thinker' in *The Review of Politics*, vol. 52, no. 3 (Summer 1990), 417–440.

Smith, Horatio. 'The Taine Centennial: Comment and Bibliography' in *Modern Language Notes* vol. 44, no. 7 (November 1929), 437–445.

Solomon, Maynard, ed. *Beethovens Tagebuch, 1812–1818*. 2nd edition. Bonn: Beethoven-Haus, 2005.

Starr, William Thomas. *Romain Rolland and a World at War*. Evanston, IL: Northwestern University, 1956.

S.S. 'Review of Auguste Rodin: *L'Art* by Paul Gsell' in *Art and Progress*, vol. 2, no. 11 (September 1911), 344.

Sullivan, Michael. *Art and Artists of Twentieth-century China*. Berkeley and London: University of California, 1996.

Taine, Hippolyte. *Notes on England*. Trans. Edward Hyams. London: Thames and Hudson, 1957.

Thurston, Anne F. *Enemies of the People: The Ordeal of the Intellectuals in China's Great Cultural Revolution*. Cambridge, MA and London: Harvard University, 1987.

Vermorel, Henri. 'The Presence of Spinoza in the Exchanges between Sigmund Freud and Romain Rolland' in *International Journal of Psychoanalysis*, vol. 90, no. 6 (2009), 1235–1254.

Volland, Nicolai. 'A Linguistic Enclave: Translation and Language Policies in the Early People's Republic of China' in *Modern China*, vol. 35, no. 5 (September 2009), 467–494.

Volland, Nicolai. 'Translating the Socialist State: Cultural Exchange, National Identity, and the Socialist World in the Early PRC' in *Twentieth-Century China*, vol. 33. no. 2 (April 2008), 51–72.

Wang, David Der-wei. *The Monster that is History*. Berkeley, CA and London: University of California, 2004.

Weil, Simone. *The Need for Roots: Prelude to a Declaration of Duties towards Mankind*. Trans. Arthur Wills. London: Routledge and Kegan Paul, 1952.

Wharton, Edith. *A Backward Glance: An Autobiography*. New York: Scribner, 1998.

Whitney, Susan B. *Mobilizing Youth: Communists and Catholics in Interwar France*. Durham and London: Duke University, 2009.

Wolfenstein, Martha. 'The Social Background of Taine's Philosophy of Art' in *Journal of the History of Ideas*, vol. 5, no. 3 (June 1944), 332–358.

Wong, Aida-Yuen. 'A New Life for Literati Painting in the Early Twentieth Century: Eastern Art and Modernity, a Transcultural Narrative?' in *Artibus Asiae*, vol. 60, no. 2 (2000), 297–326.

Zweig, Stefan. *The World of Yesterday*. London: Pushkin, 2009.

In French

Alain et Romain Rolland. *Salut et fraternité*. Paris: Albin Michel, 1969.

de Balzac, Honoré. *Œuvres complètes de M. de Balzac*. Ed. Jean A. Decourneau. 32 vols. Paris: Les Bibliophiles de l'Originale, 1965–1976.

Barlow, Michel. *Le socialisme d'Emmanuel Mounier*. Toulouse: Édouard Privat, 1971.

Baudelaire, Charles. *Le spleen de Paris: petits poèmes en prose*. Paris: Garnier Frères, 1962.

Baudelaire, Charles. *L'art romantique*. Paris: Garnier-Flammarion, 1968.

Baudelaire, Charles. *Les fleurs du mal*. Paris: Gallimard, 2009.

Baudouin, Charles, ed. *Hommage à Romain Rolland*. Genève: Mont-Blanc, 1945.

de Beauvoir, Simone. *Mémoire d'une jeune fille rangée*. Paris: Gallimard, 1958.

de Beauvoir, Simone. *La force de l'âge*. Paris: Gallimard, 1960.

Benda, Julien. *Trahison des clercs*. Paris: Grasset, 1927.

Bergson, Henri. *Oeuvres complètes d'Henri Bergson*. Genève: Albert Skira, 1945.

Bouteron, Marcel. *Le culte de Balzac*. Abbeville: F. Paillart, 1924.

de Boysson, Emmanuelle. *Le cardinal et l'hindouiste: le mystère des frères Daniélou*. Paris: Petite Renaissance, 2008.

de Boysson, Emmanuelle. *Georges Izard: avocat de la liberté*. Paris: Presses de la Renaissance, 2003.

de Chateaubriand, François-René. *Œuvres complètes de M. le Vicomte de Chateaubriand*. 10 vols. Paris: Gosellin, 1837–1839.

Chevrillon, André. *Sydney Smith et la renaissance des idées libérales en Angleterre au XIXe siècle*. Paris: Hachette et Cie., 1894.

Cointet, Jean-Paul. *Hippolyte Taine: un regard sur la France*. Paris: Perrin, 2012.

Crépon, Marc. 'L'art de la Renaissance selon Burckhardt et Taine (la question des appartenances)' in *Revue germanique internationale*, vol. 13 (2000), 131–139.

Daniélou, Jean. *Et qui est mon prochain?: Mémoires*. Paris: Stock, 1974.

Daniélou, Jean. *Le mystère du salut des nations*. Paris: Seuil, 1946.

Durkheim, Émile. *Le suicide: étude de sociologie*. Paris: Presses universitaires de France, 1960.

Étiemble, René. *Lignes d'une vie: Naissance à la littérature ou le meurtre du père*. Paris: Arléa, 1988.

Étiemble, René. *Parlez-vous franglais?* Paris: Gallimard, 1964.

Étiemble, René. *Propos d'un emmerdeur*. Paris: Arléa, 1994.

Étiemble, René. *Tong Yeou-ki ou le nouveau singe pèlerin*, 4th edition. Paris: Gallimard, 1958.

Étiemble, René. *Quarante ans de mon maoïsme: 1934–1974*. Paris: Gallimard, 1976.

Evans, Colin. *Taine: essai de biographie intérieure*. Paris: Nizet, 1975.

Giraud, Victor. *Essai sur Taine, son oeuvre et son influence*. Paris: Hachette et Cie., 1902.

von Goethe, Johann Wolfgang. *Les souffrances du jeune Werther / Die Leiden des jungen Werthers*. Paris: Montaigne, 1931.

de Goncourt, Edmond et Jules. *Journal: mémoires de la vie littéraire*. 4 vols. Paris: Fasquelle Flammarion, 1956.

Hesse, Hermann et Romain Rolland. *D'une rive à l'autre: correspondance et fragments du journal*. Paris: Albin Michel, 1972.

Horguelin, Paul. *Anthologie de la manière de traduire: Domaine français*. Montréal: Linguatech, 1981.

Janicot, Éric. 'Les matières de la modernité: la diffusion de la peinture à l'huile en Chine républicaine' in *Revue d'histoire moderne et contemporaine*, vol. 49e, no. 3 (July – September 2002), 168–175.

Janicot, Éric. 'Les naissances de l'art moderne chinois (De la chute des Qing à la République populaire, 1911–1949)' in *Revue d'histoire moderne et contemporaine*, vol. 34e, no. 2 (April – June 1987), 231–256.

Kohn-Étiemble, Jeannine. *226 lettres inédites de Jean Paulhan*. Paris: Klincksieck, 1975.

Leiner, Jacqueline. *Le destin littéraire de Paul Nizan et ses étapes successives: contribution à l'étude du mouvement littéraire en France de 1920 à 1940*. Paris: Klincksieck, 1970.

Levy, Arthur. *L'idéalisme de Romain Rolland*. Paris: A.G. Nizet, 1946.

Leys, Simon. *L'ange et le cachalot*. Paris: Seuil, 1998.

Leys, Simon. *Orwell ou l'horreur de la politique*. Paris: Hermann, 1984.

Leys, Simon. *Essais sur la Chine*. Paris: R. Laffont, 1998.

Leys, Simon. *Les habits neufs du président Mao*. Paris: Champ libré, 1971.

Loué, Thomas. 'Les Fils de Taine, entre science et morale. À propos du Disciple de P. Bourget' in *Cahiers d'Histoire, Revue d'histoire critique*, vol. 65 (1996), 44–61.

Maritain, Jacques. *Art et scolastique*. Paris: Louis Rouart et fils, 1927.

Maritain, Jacques. *Primauté du spiritual*. Paris: Plon, 1927.

Maritain, Jacques and Raïssa. *Œuvres completes*. 17 vols. Paris: Saint-Paul, 1982–1999.

Maritain, Raïssa. *Journal de Raïssa*. Paris: Desclée de Brouwer, 1964.

Mauriac, François. *Voltaire contre Pascal*. Paris: La Belle Page, 1929.

von Meysenbug, Malwida. *Mémoires d'une idéaliste*. Paris: Fischbacher, 1900.

Mouton, Jean. *Charles Du Bos: sa relation avec la vie et avec la mort*. Paris: Desclée de Brouwer, 1955.

de Musset, Alfred. *La confession d'un enfant du siècle*. Paris: Charpentier, 1859.

Nietzsche, Friedrich. *Le cas Wagner*. Trans. Jean-Claude Hémery. Paris: Gallimard, 1980.

Paul, A. 'À propos de Taine' in *Revue d'histoire moderne*, vol. 10, no. 16, nouv. ser. tome 4 (January – February 1935), 67–71.

Le Pavec, Michèle et el., *Taine au carrefour des cultures du XIXᵉ siècle*. Paris: Bibliothèque nationale de France, 1996.

Péguy, Charles. *Notre jeunesse*. 4th edition. Paris: P. Ollendorf, 1910.

Péguy, Charles. *Œuvres complètes de Charles Péguy, 1873–1914*. 20 vols. Paris: NRF, Gallimard, 1916–1955.

Péguy, Charles et Romain Rolland, *Pour l'honneur de l'esprit: correspondance entre Charles Péguy et Romain Rolland, 1898–1914*. Paris: Albin Michel, 1973.

Priest, Deborah, ed. *Debussy, Ravel et Stravinski: textes de Louis LaLoy (1874–1944)*. Paris: l'Harmattan, 2007.

Proust, Marcel. *Trois notes sur le « pays mystérieux » de Gustave Moreau*. La Rochelle: Rumeur des âges, 2008.

Renan, Ernest. *Vie de Jésus*. Paris: Michel Lévy Frères, 1863.

Renan, Ernest. *L'avenir de la science: pensées de 1848*. Paris: Calmann-Lévy, 1890.

Rider Le, Jacques. *Malwida von Meysenbug: Une Européenne du XIXᵉ siècle*. Paris: Bartillat, 2005.

Rodin, Auguste. *L'art: entretiens réunis par Paul Gsell*. Paris: Grasset, 1986.

Rolland, Romain. *Jean-Christophe*. Paris: Albin Michel, 1931, 2007.

Rolland, Romain. *Mémoires*. Paris: Albin Michel, 1956.

Rolland, Romain. *Un beau visage à tous sens; choix de lettres de Romain Rolland (1866–1944)*. Paris: Albin Michel, 1967.

Rolland, Romain. *Vie de Beethoven*. Paris: Hachette, 1927.

Rolland, Romain. *Vie de Tolstoï*. Paris: Hachette, 1921.

Rolland, Romain. *Le cloître de la rue d'Ulm*. Paris: Albin Michel, 1952.

Rolland, Romain. *Le voyage intérieur*. Paris: Albin Michel, 1942.

Rolland, Romain. *Péguy*. Paris: Albin Michel, 1948.

Rolland, Romain. *Choix de lettres à Malwida von Meysenbug*. Paris: Albin Michel, 1948.

Rolland, Romain. *L'esprit libre: au-dessus de la mêlée*. Paris: Albin Michel, 1953.

Rolland, Romain. *Journal de Vézelay 1938–1944*. Paris: Bartillat, 2012.

Romi [pseud. Robert Miquel]. *Suicides passionnés, historiques, bizarres, littéraires*. Paris: Serg, 1964.

Seys, Pascale. *Hippolyte Taine et l'avènement du naturalisme: un intellectuel sous le Second Empire*. Paris and Montréal: l'Harmattan, 1999.

Suarès, André. *Cette âme ardente...: choix de lettres de André Suarès à Romain Rolland*. Paris: Albin Michel, 1954.

Taine, Hippolyte. *Essais de critique et d'histoire*. Paris: Hachette, 1904.

Taine, Hippolyte. *Derniers essais de critique et d'histoire*. Paris: Hachette, 1896.

Taine, Hippolyte. *La Fontaine et ses fables*. Paris: Hachette et Cie., 1898.

Taine, Hippolyte. *L'idéalisme anglais: étude sur Carlyle*. Paris: G. Baillière, 1864.

Taine, Hippolyte. *Les origines de la France contemporaine*. Paris: R. Laffont et le Club Français du Livre, 1972.

Taine, Hippolyte. *Philosophie de l'art*. Paris: Hachette, 1918.

Taine, Hippolyte. *H. Taine: sa vie et sa correspondance*. Paris: Hachette, 1902–1907.

Taine, Hippolyte. *Voyage en Italie*. Paris: Hachette, 1905.

Van Tieghem, Paul. *Le romantisme dans la littérature européenne*. Paris: Albin Michel, 1948.

Van Tieghem, Paul. *Ossian en France*. Paris: F. Rieder, 1917.

Vermale, François et Émile Gaillard. *Taine en Savoie*. Chambéry: Dardel, 1930.

Voltaire. *Candide*. Paris: Gallimard, 1993.

Voltaire. *Traité sur la tolérance*. Paris: Flammarion, 1989.

Weil, Simone. *La source grecque.* Paris: Gallimard, 1953.

Weil, Simone. *Lettre à un religieux*. Paris: Gallimard, 1999.

Wharton, Edith. *Chez les heureux du monde*. Trans. Charles du Bos. Paris: Plon-Nourrit et Cie., 1908.

Zola, Émile. *Mes Haines*. Paris: Flammarion, 2012.

Zweig, Stefan. *Balzac: le roman de sa vie*. Paris: Albin Michel, 1950.

Zweig, Stefan. *Sigmund Freud: La guérison par l'esprit*. Paris: Belfond, 1999.

Zweig, Stefan. *Romain Rolland: sa vie, son oeuvre*. Paris: Belfond, 2000.

In Chinese

Chang Eileen [Zhang Ailing] 張愛玲. *Zhang Ailing Wenji* 張愛玲文集 [Anthology of Writings by Eileen Chang]. Eds. Jin Hongda 金宏達 and Yu Qing 于清. 4 vols. Hefei: Anhui wenyi, 1991.

Chang Eileen. *Xiao tuanyuan* 小團圓 [Little Reunion]. Beijing: Shiyue wenyi, 2009.

Chen Zishan 陳子善. 'Tan Xiaolin, Xindemite he Fu Lei' 譚小麟，欣德米特和傅雷 [Tan Xiaolin, Hindemith and Fu Lei] in *Wenhui Bao* 文匯報, 20 March 2002.

Di Ma 狄馬. 'Fu Lei zhi si' 傅雷之死 [The Death of Fu Lei] in *Hunan Wenshi* 湖南文史, vol. 5, 2003.

Fang Fei 芳菲. '"Wo sui bu sha Boren, Boren yin wo er si"—Fu Lei yu yifen baozhi de yinyuan' '我雖不殺伯仁，伯仁因我而死'——傅雷與一份報紙的因緣 ['I did not kill Boren, Boren died because of me' – Fu Lei's relationship with a newspaper] in *Shu Cheng* 書城, 20 November 2006.

Fou Lei 傅雷 [Fu Lei]. *Fu Lei quanji* 傅雷全集 [Complete Works of Fou Lei]. 20 vols. Shenyang: Liaoning jiaoyu, 2002.

Fou Lei. *Fu Lei tan wenxue* 傅雷談文學 [Fou Lei Discusses Literature]. Ed. Fou Min 傅敏. Nanjing: Jiangsu wenyi, 2010.

Fou Lei. *Fu Lei tan yishu* 傅雷談藝術 [Fou Lei Discusses Art]. Ed. Fou Min 傅敏. Nanjing: Jiangsu wenyi, 2010.

Fou Lei. *Fu Lei jiashu* 傅雷家書 [Fou Lei's Family Letters]. Ed. Fou Min 傅敏. Nanjing: Jiangsu wenyi, 2010.

Fou Lei. *Fu Lei zhi youren shuxin* 傅雷致友人書信 [Fou Lei's Letters to His Friends]. Ed. Fou Min 傅敏. Nanjing: Jiangsu wenyi, 2010.

Fou Min 傅敏. ed. *Fu yi zhuanji wuzhong* 傅譯傳記五種 [Five Biographies Translated by Fou Lei]. Beijing: Sanlian, 1983.

Fou Min. ed. *Fu Lei Bainian danchen jinian* 傅雷百年誕辰紀念 [Commemoration of Fou Lei Centenary]. Beijing: Beijing tushuguan, 2008.

Fou Min. ed. *Fu Cong: wang qi le!* 傅聰：望七了！ [Fou Ts'ong: Going on Seventy!]. Tianjin: Tianjin shehui kexue, 2004.

Han Han 韓晗. *Ke xushu de xiandaixing: qikan shiliao, dazhong chuanbo yu Zhongguo xiandai wenxue tizhi (1919–1949)* 可敘述的現代性：期刊史料、大眾傳播與中國現代文學體制 (1919–1949) [Accountable Modernity: Periodical Material, Mass Media and China's Modern Literary System, 1919–1949]. Taipei: Xiuwei zixun, 2011.

Huaxushe 華胥社, ed. *Huaxushe wenyi lunji* 華胥社文藝論集 [Huaxu Press Anthology of Essays on Art and Literature] Shanghai: Zhonghua shuju, 1931.

Jin Mei 金梅, ed. *Fu Lei zhuan* 傅雷傳 [Biography of Fou Lei]. Changsha: Hunan wenyi, 1993.

Jin Shenghua 金聖華, ed. *Fu Lei yu tade shijie* 傅雷與他的世界 [Fou Lei and His World]. Beijing: Sanlian, 1996.

Liu Haisu 劉海粟. *Liu Haisu sanwen* 劉海粟散文 [Essays of Liu Haisu]. Ed. Shen Hu 沈虎. Guangzhou: Huacheng, 1999.

Liu Haisu. *Ou you suibi* 歐遊隨筆 [Essays from Travels in Europe]. Beijing: Dongfang, 2006.

Mengzi 孟子 [Master Meng]. 3rd century B.C.

Peng Hsiao-yen 彭小妍, ed. *Wenhua fanyi yu wenben mailuo: wan Ming yi jiang de Zhongguo, Riben yu xifang* 文化翻譯與文本脈絡：晚明以降的中國、日本與西方 [Textual Translation and Cultural Context: China, Japan, and the West since the late Ming]. Taipei: Zhongyang yanjiu yuan, Zhongguo wenzhe yanjiusuo, 2013.

Qian Zhongshu 錢鐘書. *Weicheng* 圍城 [Fortress Besieged]. Shanghai: Chengguang, 1947.

Qiu Luohen 裘蘿痕 and Feng Zikai 豐子愷. *Zhongwen mingge wushi shou* 中文名歌五十首 [Fifty Songs in Chinese]. Shanghai: Kaiming, 1927.

Sun Fuxi 孫福熙. *Shanye zhuishi* 山野綴拾 [Reminiscences from the Wild]. Shanghai: Xinchao she, 1925.

T'ang Wen-piao 唐文標. *Zhang Ailing yanjiu* 張愛玲研究 [Studies on Eileen Chang]. Taipei: Lianjing, 1984.

Yang Jiang 楊絳. *Xizao* 洗澡 [Baptism]. Beijing: Renmin wenxue, 2004.

Yi jing [*I Ching*] 易經 [Book of Changes]. 7th century B.C.

Zhang Ruikuan 張瑞寬. *Zhongguo meishu de xiandaihua: meishu qikan yu meizhan huodong de fenxi (1911–1937)* 中國美術的現代化：美術期刊與美展活動的分析 (1911–1937) [The Modernisation of Chinese Art: An Analysis of Art Periodicals and Art Exhibitions, 1911–1937]. Beijing: Sanlian, 2008.

Zhuangzi 莊子 [Master Zhuang]. 3rd century B.C.

In German

Eckermann, Johann Peter. *Gespräche mit Goethe in den letzten Jahren seines Lebens.* Leipzig: Insel, 1981.

Freud, Sigmund. *Gesammelte Werke: Chronologisch geordnet.* 19 vols. London: Imago, 1991.

Volland, Nicolai. 'Fu Lei jiashu: Kulturaustausch in der Volksrepublik China und die Strategien eines Mittlers zwischen zwei Welten' in *China und die Wahrnehmung der Welt.* Eds. Antje Richter und Helmolt Vittinghoff. Wiesbaden: Harrassowitz, 2007.

In Latin

M. Tullius Ciceronis Orator Ad. M. Brutum. Cambridge: Cambridge University, 1885.

Newspapers and Journals

Saturday Evening Post
The Romanic Review

Critique
Journal de Genève
La Table Ronde
L'Art Vivant
L'Express
Le Figaro
Le Temps
Nouvelle Semaine Artistique et Littéraire
Revue des deux Mondes

März
Neue Zürcher Zeitung
Vossische Zeitung

Beixin zhoukan 北新週刊 [New North Weekly]
Chenbao 晨報 [Morning Paper]
Dongfang zazhi 東方雜誌 [Eastern Miscellany]
Gongxian 貢獻 [Contribution]
Guancha 觀察 [Observation]
Guoji yibao 國際譯報 [International Translation]
Jiefang ribao 解放日報 [Jiefang Daily]
Kuzhu 苦竹 [Bitter Bamboo]
Mingbao yuekan 明報月刊 [Mingpao Monthly]
Minzhu 民主 [Democracy]
Qingnian zazhi 青年雜誌 [La Jeunesse]
Shenbao 申報 [Shanghai News]
Shishi huibao 時事匯報 [Current Affairs]
Shishi xinbao 時事新報 [New Review of Current Affairs]
Wanxiang 萬象 [Ten Thousand Things]
Wenhui bao 文匯報 [Wenhui Bao]
Xiaoshuo shijie 小說世界 [The World of Fiction]
Xiaoshuo yuebao 小說月報 [Short Story Monthly]
Xin qingnian 新青年 [La Jeunesse]
Xinyu 新語 [New Account]
Xuesheng zazhi 學生雜誌 [The Students' Magazine]
Yishu xunkan 藝術旬刊 [L'Art]
Zazhi 雜誌 [Magazine]
Ziluolan 紫羅蘭 [Violet]

Index

Printed in the United States
By Bookmasters